John Anderson'

JOHN ANDERSON (1726-96). Professor of Natural Philosophy in the University of Glasgow and founder of Anderson's University (portrait possibly by William Cochrane *c.*1775).

JOHN BUTT

John Anderson's Legacy

The University of Strathclyde
and its antecedents
1796-1996

TUCKWELL PRESS
in association with
THE UNIVERSITY OF STRATHCLYDE

First published in 1996 by

Tuckwell Press Ltd
The Mill House
Phantassie
East Linton EH40 3DG
Scotland

Text Copyright © 1996 John Butt

Illustrations Copyright © 1996 University of Strathclyde
unless otherwise indicated

The cost of this publication has been met by the University, through its
Bicentenary Fund, but the author and the University gratefully
acknowledge the generous support of the Scottish Higher Education
Funding Council and the University's own Graduates' Association.

ISBN 1 898410 68 2 (paperback)

British Library Cataloguing-in-Publication Data:
A Catalogue record for this book is available
on request from the British Library

Designed by Combined Arts, Edinburgh
Printed and bound by Toppan Printing Co., Singapore

Contents

Preface

I FIRST BECAME INTERESTED IN THE HISTORY of the Royal College of Science and Technology shortly after I joined the staff in 1959. My choice of Ph.D. topic in 1960 – a business biography of James Young – led me to Anderson's University, Professor Thomas Graham, David Livingstone, Lyon Playfair and others who had been part of an earlier educational world. The history of the University of Strathclyde and its antecedents was, therefore, part of my intellectual progression through a more general career in Economic and Social History.

My debts are many. Professor I.F. Clarke encouraged my initial research efforts in this field, and I am most grateful for that early support. Professor S.G.E. Lythe persuaded the Court to commission this history and also passed on to me his papers relating to the merger with the Scottish College. The Carnegie Trust for Scotland made a small grant to support my initial work in archives outside Scotland, and I acknowledge gratefully that assistance. Three Principals, Sir Samuel Curran, Sir Graham Hills and Professor John Arbuthnott, encouraged its progress. The late Professor Sydney Checkland gave me useful advice during my time as a doctoral student and afterwards and Olive Checkland made available to me information about Japanese students in Glasgow in the late nineteenth century. Professor Emeritus Adam S.T. Thomson through the agency of Professor Emeritus John Paul made available papers about the Engineering Group and its development between 1946 and 1974. J. Malcolm Allan of the Andersonian Library Rare Books Department introduced me to the full range of John Anderson's papers.

The Archives of the University were inevitably a major source; these were first made available to me by the late George H. Thomson, Secretary/Treasurer of the Royal College, who also allowed me the use of his office in the early days of my research. Now organised more systematically under the direction of Dr. James McGrath, the Archives have been my main working territory, and I am most grateful for the help I have received from Roddy Mackenzie, Assistant Archivist, Pauline Gallagher, Archival Assistant, and Robin Dalgleish, Archival Assistant.

Many of the issues in Chapters Four and Five were first raised in fruitful discussions with Dr. Leslie L. Forrester, whose thesis is listed in the bibliography and should be read by specialists in the period 1870 to 1914. Professor Donald C. Pack read parts of Chapters Seven and Eight and made most useful comments upon them.

My principal debt over the years is to Charles Geoffrey Wood, Emeritus Librarian, with whom I first went to examine the private papers of James Young in 1960. Charles Wood has organised forty-two annual meetings of the 96 Group and been responsible more than anyone else for focussing attention on the history of the University and its antecedents. Many 96 Group papers figure in the references of this book, but I am particularly grateful for the generous way in which he has made available to me the fruits of his own researches on John Anderson about whom he is the best authority. Charles Wood commented extensively on Chapter One, and I hope that in consequence it is greatly improved.

Unless otherwise stated, all the illustrations in this book come from the University's own rich sources – the Archives and Audio-Visual Media Services. Eileen Heraghty of the Photographic Unit of Audio-Visual Media Services has been a great help to Dr. John Tuckwell and me, as we have made the final choice, and we are most grateful to her. I also gratefully acknowledge the financial help provided by the University of Strathclyde and by the Graduates' Association.

I also acknowledge the excellent support provided by Mrs. Jean Fraser, my secretary for fourteen years, and, now in 'retirement', my indefatigable aide in preparing the manuscript for the press. Dr. John Tuckwell, the publisher, has provided good humour, technical expertise and guidance in equal measure ever since he received the commission from the University.

Finally, I would like to thank my wife and family for their fortitude and patience during the long period of composition.

JOHN BUTT

ABBREVIATIONS

ABACUS	Architecture and Building Aids Computer Unit
ALRBD	Andersonian Library Rare Books Department
AUT	Association of University Teachers
BP	British Petroleum
BPP	British Parliamentary Papers
BUS	Bulletin of the University of Strathclyde
CAD	Computer Aided Design
CAE	Computer Aided Engineering
CAM	Computer Aided Manufacture
CASM	Centre for Advanced Structural Materials
CEPE	Centre for Electrical Power Engineering
DMEM	Department of Mechanical Engineering and Design, Manufacture and Engineering Management
DSIR	Department of Science and Industrial Research
EC	European Community
EPSRC	Engineering and Physical Science Research Council
ESPRIT	European Strategic Programme of Research and Development in Information Technology
GWSTC	Glasgow and West of Scotland Technical College
JBC	John Butt Collection
MASS	Maintenance Activities Subsea Surface
MIG	Merger Implementation Group
PRO	Public Record Office
RAE	Research Assessment Exercise
RCST	Royal College of Science and Technology
RTC	Royal Technical College
SASS	Newsletter of the Faculty of Arts and Social Studies
SHEFC	Scottish Higher Education Funding Council
SISTERS	Special Institutions of Scientific and Technological Education and Research
SQUIDS	Superconducting Quantum Interference Devices
SRO	Scottish Record Office
STEAC	Scottish Tertiary Education Advisory Council
SUA	Strathclyde University Archives
TQA	Teaching QualityAssessment
UFC	Universities Funding Council
UGC	University Grants Committee
UMG	University Management Group

CHAPTER ONE

John Anderson (1726-96) and His Will

'He boasts of a teacher of his own, one whom he familiarly calls Jolly Jack Phosphorus, who ... was in his day a great enemy of lucre-loving professors.'

The Glasgow Chronicle, 11 December, 1821

MANY DRAMATIC EVENTS TRANSFUSED the dull tedium of day-to-day existence for Glaswegians during the course of the eighteenth century: deep religious controversies, occupation by the Young Pretender, the shocks occasioned by the American Revolution and the failure to crush the colonists, and the rise of radicalism nurtured by the ideas of the Enlightenment and sustained by the early days of the French Revolution. Beneath these events rested the even more powerful forces of commercial and industrial development which were accompanied by the physical and demographic expansion of the city. The tribulations of individuals or institutions appear insignificant compared with these great underlying processes, and yet individuals shape and alter History.

Such an individual was John Anderson (1726-96)[1], son and grandson of the manse and raised on disputation. Both his father and grandfather were ministers of the Church of Scotland, the latter, the Reverend John Anderson (1680-1721), an eminent divine who had defended the true religion (i.e. Presbyterianism) in Dumbarton (1698-1717) against all comers. A noteworthy controversialist, who disputed with his Elders regarding the form of church service, he justified pugnaciously his right to use the Lord's Prayer which they attempted to deny him, although the General Assembly approved of his stance. Called to the Ramshorn Kirk in Glasgow in 1717, he was faced with another disputatious congregation but again showed his mettle, leaving his grandson a model of obduracy about principle and a pile of private papers and religious tracts as a record of a lifetime immersed in religious controversy.[2]

James Anderson followed his father into the Church of Scotland and accepted the charge of Roseneath. He married into a prominent Greenock family, the Turners, and he and his wife, Margaret, had a family of four sons and a daughter. Since the standard annual stipend was £44, the lot of the Scots minister's family in the early eighteenth century approached that of the proverbial church mouse. The eldest son, John Anderson, and his brother, William, were boarded out to give them a better chance in life; John was brought up in the family of his uncle, the Reverend Thomas Turner, Minister of the High Kirk in Stirling. Anderson retained fond memories of his youth spent in Stirling, and when, in his old age, he was asked to compose an inscription for a marble tablet to be placed at the entrance to the Trades House, he did so with pleasure. Reputedly, it was his aunt Turner who paid his fees at Glasgow University, from which he graduated in 1745 at the age of nineteen. Despite his relative youth, John Anderson was a volunteer officer in the corps which defended Stirling during the 'Forty-five and throughout his life retained a keen interest in the art of war. The twenty-year old Anderson produced two short satirical publications written in biblical style soon after the 'Forty-five and published in 1746, attacking the Jacobites and indicating his complete support for the Hanoverian succession – *The Book of the Chronicles of his Royal Highness William, Duke of Cumberland* (24 pages); *Dathan's second book of the chronicles of William the son of George II. With the book of the prophecy of John, the scribe; being a continuation of the progress of the present rebellion* (28 pages).

However, he was a born academic – a fine scholar versed in the Classics, interested in Science, and fascinated by the idea of teaching. Moreover, a Chair in a university offered much better prospects than the Church. But vacancies were few and highly prized. Like his grandfather, who had been Preceptor to John, second Duke of Argyll (1678-1743), Anderson decided to seek a tutorship in an aristocratic family. He first unsuccessfully sought a post in the service of Charles, second Duke of Richmond and Gordon (d.1750), explaining that he was the 'Son of a Gentleman', totally fluent in Latin and Greek and widely read in the classical authors. 'My Father is deceas'd and the Fortune He has left me is so small, that it cannot maintain me even in a moderate way.'[3] What he did not indicate – perhaps wisely – was that he was widely read in the standard works of the Enlightenment and clearly concerned about the development of civilised society, the nature of the economy, human behaviour and psychology, the role of the law and the rights and duties of citizens.

In February 1750 he was still in Glasgow, tutoring Latin students and active in the Considerable Club, a small discussion group with seventeen regular attenders, to which papers were read. John Anderson's friend, Gilbert Lang, later minister at Largs, had sent an 'Essay on Miracles' which had been read to the Club by Anderson and was well received. In thanking Lang for his paper, Anderson reveals both a sharp turn of phrase and a regard for material prosperity. His sister was being married on 14 February, 1750 to 'one Adams, a young lad in Falkirk, the only child of mean but very honest Parents who have left him in entire possession of £1,500, £1,000 in land and £500 in money'. Anderson's view of Adams was that despite a good education, 'He is Sheepish in Company – the greatest Blemish in his Character is that He is not so much engaged in Trade as one of his Stock might be'.[4]

Later that year, John Anderson obtained a post in the service of James, eighth Earl of Moray (1708-67), acting as tutor to his son, Francis, Lord Doune (1737-1810), later ninth Earl. Writing to Lang in December 1750 from London after a visit to Holland, Anderson explained that the Earl had just arrived in the city for the season, and that his annual salary for the first year was to be £40 with the prospect of an increase 'if my Behaviour gives Satisfaction after due trial'. Affairs at Glasgow College were never far from Anderson's mind; he had learned of Adam Smith's candidacy for the Chair of Logic where there was competition from George Muirhead, later Professor of Humanity (1754-73); he was delighted that there were such good candidates.[5]

Lord Doune was attending Harrow School, and Anderson boarded with his pupil in the household of the Master, Dr. Thomas Thackeray, and his wife. Apparently, he greatly enjoyed his three years at Harrow, attending Lord Doune on social occasions such as regular visits to the theatre; he dealt with general expenditure, allocated his lordship's pocket money at the rate of one guinea a week, and was responsible for keeping within the budget set by the Earl. This he occasionally found difficult: 'My Lord was almost every night at the play … or … at Whist and was often a loser … and I never found him willing to go to the Pit … '. Apart from tutoring his charge, Anderson arranged for special tuition as required – a native Italian speaker, for instance, to avoid the ' … danger of acquiring a bad Habit on the pronunciation from me … '. He also purchased textbooks for his lordship and supplemented them with subscriptions to a circulating library.[6]

Apparently, Anderson's efforts produced sufficient progress in his charge for the Earl to raise his salary to £50 after the first year.[7] His stay in London produced other benefits. He established contacts with the booksellers in the Strand with whom he corresponded long afterwards; in Soho he met the dealers in geological specimens and thereafter built up a significant collection of fossils. He became very friendly with William Lorimer, who in 1752 was tutor to Sir James Grant of Grant. When Lorimer died in 1768, he left Anderson his gold watch as a keepsake.[8] The fascination and opportunities for discovery which London life presented to Anderson always ever afterwards exerted an influence upon him. He became a more cosmopolitan, responsible and mature character.

Anderson's next post was as tutor-companion to the son of Sir James Campbell on a tour of France. Together they went via Dublin to Bordeaux in the summer of 1754 and spent the next six months in Gascony. Bordeaux Anderson found very impressive: 'that large city adorned with Spires, a beautiful River filled with Ships'. For a time they lived in Montauban, Anderson forming impressions of France and the *ancien régime*. He was critical of arbitrary imprisonment and the corruption and iniquities of some of the *intendants*, noting the buying and selling of legal offices. He did not believe the French to be as law-abiding as the British and noted high import duties and transport charges and the inequitable and oppressive taxes raised by the Farmers-General, the plethora of weights and measures, and the wide disparities in the prices of basic articles, such as corn and salt, affected by local taxes. Anderson also made notes about road construction and soldiers' pay and commented on the number of Huguenots in Bordeaux and district and the pressure on them to convert.[9] It was during this period that he became a great admirer of Montesquieu – who was born in Bordeaux – and his *L'Esprit des Lois*. Anderson ascribed four great qualities to the eminent *philosophe*: 'An Excellent Judgement, a fine Imagination, great Wit and vast Erudition'.[10]

In an exuberant and humorous letter written to Gilbert Lang from Toulouse in January 1755, John Anderson indicated that he was about to return to Glasgow. He had not written to Lang since his arrival in France: 'I will not try to alleviate my Fault with a French Apology. I will tell you the plain Truth even tho I have been for six Months in Gascony'. He goes on, 'Alma Mater, you know was so unfortunate as to lose a fine Scholar and a good Man soon after my Arrival in this Country; and from that time till Friday last I did not know whether I was to be Professor of Latin or of Hebrew'. The Principal and other senior members of the university had written to Archibald, third Duke of Argyll (1682-1761), a dominant patron in an age of deference, to seek his views on who was 'the properest Person to fill up the Vacancy' in Latin. The Duke had recommended Anderson; the Rector, the Principal and four professors had thought him the best candidate but Dr. William Cullen (1710-90), Professor of Medicine, and Adam Smith 'in a manner I need not relate jockied me out of it'.[11]

However, on 17 December 1754 Anderson learned that he had been elected Professor of Oriental Languages; this post was primarily concerned with teaching Hebrew to students of Divinity. There is little doubt that Anderson considered himself less qualified for this post than for the Chair in Latin: 'let me beg of you, my dear Gilbert, to pray fervently for me as a Teacher or rather as a Learner of the Sacred Tongue'. More jocularly, he went on, 'I am as grave, I assure you, as a Rabbi. I would not eat Pork yesterday to my Dinner, and my landlady asked me with a blushing leer, whether I intended to go thro *all* the Rites of the Jewish Religion'.

At this stage Anderson expected to be in Paris at the beginning of April 1755 and in London by June or July. Sir James Campbell intervened, however, because he wanted Anderson to remain with his son to the end of his French tour. Thus, the original starting date for the university appointment, October 1755, was deferred for a year with the agreement of the Faculty. Deterioration of Franco-British relations, however, made it politic for Anderson and his charge to return early and so he was back in Glasgow and began his appointment as Professor of Oriental Languages on 25 June 1755.[12]

In addition to Hebrew, no doubt to meet needs expressed by the merchant community, John Anderson taught French on four days a week and 'some things relating to the English language every Friday'.[13] A cultured man amid a galaxy of talent, he possessed the formidable obduracy of his grandfather who never wavered in stating what he believed to be right, an intellectual commitment to scientific rationalism, a belief in the force of law which he had imbibed from Locke, Montesquieu and his hero, George Buchanan, and a definite Whiggish sense that enlightenment should be accompanied by improvement, especially in the system of education.

Anderson was not long in his first Chair, however; when Robert Dick died, he was translated to the more congenial and more senior Chair of Natural Philosophy on 21 October, 1757. His election was not without controversy, for Anderson took part in the discussions about Dick's successor despite protests from some of his colleagues, including Adam Smith. Technically, Anderson was within his rights, but his stance was impolitic, since Smith, for one, indicated that he would have voted for him anyway.[14]

Having repaid a loan of £30 with interest to the Fund for the provision of widows and children of ministers, which he had received as Professor of Oriental Languages in 1755, Anderson took up his new responsibilities.[15] Initially, he changed very little, for Dick had a fine reputation as a scholar and teacher and had introduced a number of sound innovations. Dick's executors had submitted an inventory of the apparatus and instruments belonging to the College, and Anderson signed it as a correct record.[16] The later inventory of 1760, also signed by Anderson, showed a number of acquisitions but more importantly reveals the wide range of demonstrations given by Anderson to his Natural Philosophy students, covering Mechanics, Hydrostatics, Pneumatics and Optics in detail but also including a survey of Astronomy and Natural History.

Apparatus and instruments had been purchased on behalf of the University since 1658, but both Dick and Anderson added significantly to what they inherited. The 1760 list mentions a lodestone, 'old' and 'new' electrical apparatus bought in London, balances, models of a compound water engine, of a chain pump, of a mill with undershot and overshot wheels and with sails, and of a diving bell, a large double-barrelled air pump, a pendulum, two pyrometers, apparatus for experiments with light, microscopes, telescopes, three *camera obscura* and a magic lantern. At this relatively early stage Anderson had purchased items for his own use and intended to buy more; he therefore intended to keep a separate inventory of these, 'always lying in a particular place in the Experiment Room in order to prevent disputes at my Death'.[17]

Dick had taken a great interest in James Watt when he came to Glasgow in 1754, advised him to go to London to learn the art of mathematical instrument-making and employed him on his return in 1756 to work on the instruments for the new Macfarlane Observatory. Watt was a friend of Anderson's brother, Andrew, and a fellow scholar at Greenock Grammar School. A model Newcomen engine had been commissioned by Dick from Jonathon Sissons, a well-known London instrument-maker, but it was still in Sissons' hands in 1760. Anderson was authorised by the Faculty to spend up to £2 in retrieving this model in June 1760; this he did, but the Newcomen model never worked properly. Watt, who had worked in Sissons' London workshop, was later asked by Anderson to remedy the defects in this engine, and in 1764-5 Watt began his epoch-making work on improving the steam engine.

During this period Anderson and Watt must have met and talked regularly, especially in such a close community as Glasgow College. Later, in 1778 Watt made a micrometer which he presented to Anderson, a sure sign of his regard. In 1795 John Anderson sent Watt his *Essays on*

Field Artillery and a copy of the French translation. The latter was for James Watt junior; since he … 'understands French it will be a good French exercise for him in the Mechanical way to read the French Essays with the English'. He also added that when Watt revisited the College, 'he may see a working model of the Field Piece referred to … '[18] Clearly, Anderson and Watt stayed in touch, despite Watt's presence in Birmingham.

One of Dick's main commitments was to 'Experimental Philosophy', a popular evening class, explaining propositions and demonstrating practical proofs. The course was advertised in the local newspapers so that Glasgow citizens could attend.[19] This class was greatly developed by Anderson, and his style of teaching was so popular that his lecture room could not accommodate all those who wished to attend; it was, therefore, extended twice, first of all in 1769.[20] Anderson's interest in combustibles and controlled explosions led to the incorporation of ballistics into his courses and also to his nickname, 'Jolly Jack Phosphorus'. Clearly, he was a dramatic performer in the lecture theatre, although he made no major theoretical contribution to his subject. Students, however, gained from his practical interests which added an extra dimension to his teaching. So that they had a summary of his course, Anderson prepared for his full-time students, to whom he lectured for fourteen hours a week, a small volume, *A Compendium of Experimental Philosophy*, printed in 1760 by the celebrated Glasgow brothers, Robert and Andrew Foulis. This book was also read by his 'anti-toga' students who attended two evenings a week; this class included 'town's people of almost every rank, age and employment'.[21]

This first textbook naturally evolved into a more detailed exposition in his *The Institutes of Physics*, a major work of about 400 pages which appeared in 1786. *The Institutes* went through five editions by 1795 and by then consisted of 507 pages. It contained a complete account of his coursework, together with descriptions and results of appropriate experiments. In the book Anderson distinguished two courses in Physics, one called 'the Mathematical' and the other 'the Experimental'. Students were encouraged to be sceptical about theories and to assess the utility of experiments: 'theories without experiments have been the great bane of philosophy in every age and in every country'. Anderson believed, 'we must despise every theory that does not rest upon decisive experiments, or well established facts; we must remember that the Law by which a Cause acts may be investigated, though the cause itself be unknown'.[22]

The book had fifteen parts divided into sections. Some reveal very clearly the practical emphases within Anderson's teaching: there was an extensive section on Mechanics in Part VIII which included discussions of mass, gravity and other forces, friction, balance, weight and levers, the pendulum and oscillation, the science associated with handball, tennis, billiards and golf, wheels and pulleys. The section on Electricity discusses meteors, 'erecting thunder rods' and making buildings secure against lightning. Practical applications of science also included machines and instruments for agriculture, industry and architecture; carriages and other conveyances; and, central to Anderson's researches, military technology. Anderson's 'operator' – or laboratory assistant and demonstrator – Parsell later recalled his master's weariness when correcting the page proofs of the fifth edition: 'Thank God, this is finished … I am almost finished myself'. To ensure that Parsell and his predecessor, Robert Cross, had adequate guidance and that demonstrations were well conducted, Anderson provided a book of 'Directions to Operator'.[23]

Students naturally responded to Anderson's efforts to make his classes relevant and interesting. He began with 38 students in the 'Experimental' class and by the early 1790s was regularly teaching 150 to 200. A fragment of a list dating from the 1780s (after 1784) begins at student number 105 and proceeds to 162. Eleven were from New York and one each from Boston and 'Carolina'; there were a number from Ulster. William Millar from Boston paid his fee of one guinea and is described as 'the Friend of my Brother James'. John Falconer (No.132) was the son of the Episcopalian minister in Glasgow and gave Anderson a model of a still. John Fraser (No.154) 'is Minister of the Gaelic Chapel in Glasgow. With Difficulty I persuaded him to take back his Money'.[24]

There is much evidence of John Anderson's practical interest in industrial processes apart from his textbooks. He met skilled workmen and their masters in his 'anti-toga' class and in their workshops; to some, he gave free tickets for his lectures. Science, for him, was not an abstraction divorced from the real world but rather a major instrument for improving human life. In October 1784 he relates to Ilay Campbell, the Lord Advocate, that ... 'I have lately been inspecting the Lace Workers in Renfrew and Glasgow' on behalf of the Board of Trustees which gave premiums, bounties or prizes on his recommendation. This responsibility would not have been assigned to Anderson, if it was thought that he was not familiar with the best workshop practice.[25]

Anderson's research was concerned with practicalities, applications of science to the production of material objects; this may explain why some historians of Glasgow University and John Cable have denigrated his research achievements or denied their existence.[26] John Anderson's interest in weather and instruments for measuring wind, barometric pressure, temperature and rainfall led him to build a rain gauge which was fitted to the roof of his house. From 1760 he collected rainfall data and used them in his teaching. In 1780 he produced an *Essay on Rain Gauges* and presented a paper to the Royal Society in 1792 in which he discussed the design improvements he had made, including a vernier scale device to measure rainfall in inches, tenths, hundredths and thousandths. Thus, he was one of those who made it possible to measure accurately one fundamental in climatic behaviour.[27]

As the man who entertained Benjamin Franklin when he visited Glasgow, John Anderson naturally took an interest in 'thunder rods' or lightning conductors. Franklin and Anderson became friends and correspondents, Franklin telling Anderson that he approved very much of *The Institutes* and complaining of the gout and stone.[28] After Franklin's visit to Glasgow in 1771, Anderson installed a lightning conductor on top of the College tower in 1772. Electricity and magnetism were central parts of Anderson's curriculum; the correspondence with Franklin, including an exchange of books, and the practical example of the 'thunder rod' must have contributed to the modernity of his teaching.[29]

However, it was Anderson's interest in ballistics and mechanics which absorbed most of his research efforts. In the early 1780s he was the author of 'A cheap and speedy Plan for increasing the Power of Artillery; without making any change upon the Guns; and with a great Saving of Powder'.[30] Despite improvements, Anderson observed, 'the Gunner's Art is still very imperfect'. Cannon achieved widely differing distances when fired; irregularity in the structure of cannon balls did not help, and he also commented on wind resistance. He took this subject so seriously that he built a six-pounder to his own design and conducted experiments in long vacations at Dumbarton Castle, where he had quarters in the summer of 1782, examining the rock and antiquarian remains of covenanting times.

By 1782 he was ready to parade his ideas about cannon before a wider and more influential audience. Charles, third Duke of Richmond and Gordon (1735-1806), had become Master-General of the Ordnance in 1782, and Anderson approached the political master in Scotland, Henry Dundas, the Lord Advocate, to seek an *entrée* to the new armaments man. Dundas commended a letter written by Anderson to Richmond in which Anderson indicated that he had made successful experiments to increase the range of cannon and developed a better projectile than the standard cannonball. Moreover, he was willing to go to Woolwich Arsenal for trials.[31] In response, Richmond informed Dundas that pressure of the American War made it impossible for him to pay immediate attention to Anderson's invention but he would return to it when time permitted.[32]

Somewhat despondent because of this lack of interest but about to return to his lecturing duties in Glasgow, Anderson decided to end his experiments at Dumbarton,

in making which I met with great interruptions from the weather and from the Farmers near the Line of Fire. The first was uncommonly bad for the time of year; and the second wanted to get some of my money, having taken it for granted that I was paid by the Government for what I did, which is certainly not true.

More mercenary and seven years older and wiser, in 1789 he approached Richmond again about his new 'field piece', which he was prepared to demonstrate at Woolwich. Its main novelty compared with the 1782 model was the gun carriage: 'there will be no Permission given to examine the internal structure of the Carriage; nor will I answer any question concerning it, till I shall be sure of a proper Reward'. He was patriotic enough to offer his inventions for the sole use of the British Government but asked Richmond to reply within three months. Otherwise, he would regard himself as free to approach foreign powers, 'my own Country having despised it'.[33]

Years before, Anderson had corresponded with the Intendant at Woolwich, Major Bloomfield, and therefore he wrote to him again, telling him of the terms of his correspondence with Richmond. Anderson's gun had been built at Carron, and he told Bloomfield that army officers from Edinburgh and Perth might witness a firing trial in Scotland, but as 'it is College Time at present, I must have the choice of the day'. In 1788 Anderson's *Essays on Field Artillery* was published; this book may have encouraged military experts to take him more seriously.

Anderson's book consisted of four forthright essays, sparing neither friend nor foe. His criticisms of the carronade – Carron Company's principal source of government revenue – drew a naturally hostile response from Joseph Stainton,[34] the manager, particularly since he had given Anderson certificates signed by nine skilled artificers verifying the performance of his gun.[35] John Anderson attempted to smooth Stainton's ruffled feathers, denied that he had intended to damage Carron's reputation and indicated that he was willing to inform Bloomfield and Richmond about the quality and merits of Carron products. However, he still displayed a certain truculence by telling Stainton that he had deliberately sought Carron certification for his gun but could have obtained it from Clyde Ironworks.[36]

Although he did not normally 'entertain non-military men', Richmond was sufficiently impressed by the Carron certification to order Captain Shand and Captain Thompson of the Royal Artillery to watch firing trials of Anderson's gun.[37] He offered to act on their report and to provide a 'reasonable Reward' for information about the construction of the gun carriage. Anderson's failure to maintain good relations with Stainton was critical, for he was refused the use of Carron's firing range and of their skilled crew of workmen.[38] Thus, Anderson settled his bill sheepishly and took his gun away from Carron, explaining to Captain Shand that it was better to try the weapon under field conditions, although it was still 'College-time' in Glasgow. Yet he admitted that he had intended to have the experimental firing at Carron, 'but the ill usage which I have lately received from the Carron Company' had caused him to change his mind in favour of a country venue near Glasgow. This gloss on his dispute with Stainton was clearly more diplomatic than truthful. To avoid any inconvenience – and possibly to influence the report to Richmond – Anderson offered Shand and Thompson hospitality at his house in the

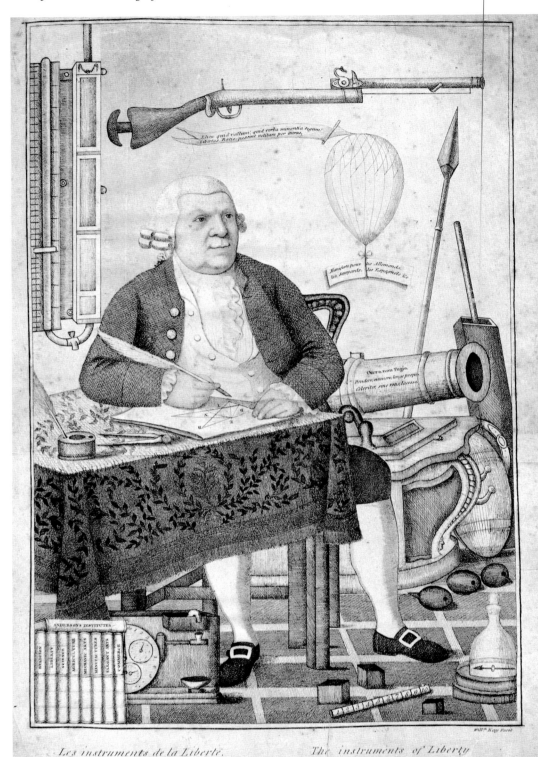

Les instruments de la Liberté.
Des mains de la Science.

The instruments of Liberty
From the hands of Science

1 Engraving by William Kay (29 December 1792) of John Anderson, conveying his interest in the art of war. Note the 'carabine' hanging on the wall which Anderson carried in the defence of Stirling during the Jacobite Rising of 1745, a representation of his six-pounder with bombs (to Anderson's left) which the French perfected and used at the Battle of Jemappes, and the natural philosopher's instruments. Published in January 1793 before Britain and France went to war, the reference to 'the instruments of liberty from the hands of science' reveals Anderson's initial sympathies with the French revolutionaries and may explain why he destroyed the original. His ideals and interests are shown beneath his Institutes (bottom left).

College: 'I can make sure of a good bed, wholesome fare, genuine wine and a hearty welcome'. Ever practical, he also pointed out that the lightness of the gun and its carriage – 800 lbs. – allowed for portability; it could be carted, transported by horse-drawn litter or manhandled over rough and hilly ground by trained gun crews.[39]

Progress was impeded by a change of military personnel, but Anderson continued to make arrangements for ammunition and workmen for the trial.[40] A notice about John Anderson's gun, no doubt a leak inspired by Stainton, appeared in the *Caledonian Mercury* in May 1789; Anderson was much concerned, perhaps needlessly.[41] Meanwhile the French were taking an interest in the gun, and Frederick of Brunswick had been informed of its potential.[42] At best, the British government's response could only be described as niggardly; the Duke of Richmond indicated to Anderson that the government would not meet any costs.[43] Anderson was left with little choice: the alternatives were either to pay for the testing or to communicate his invention, possibly within the frail protection of a patent enrolment.

John Anderson's resolution was not easily shaken: his new alloy gun was superior to brass cannon in common use, but its construction was not exceptional; it was the gun carriage (350 lbs. lighter than Army issue) which was a major innovation, 'light and snug', portable and, because of an ingenious compressed air shock absorber, with little recoil when the gun was fired. Moreover, gun and carriage together cost less than those currently in use. He therefore confidently offered to pay for a trial firing in London before specialist witnesses.[44]

Correspondence with Richmond continued into July, and eventually seven referees were agreed upon: Richmond named Major Paterson, Major Bloomfield and Captain Lawson, all of Woolwich Arsenal; Anderson named Sir Joseph Banks, President of the Royal Society, General Roy and Sir Archibald Campbell. These six met Anderson at Sir Joseph's house on 23 July 1789; they saw a model of the gun and agreed that the design was original. Two days later, Anderson met the Duke of Richmond and offered him the opportunity to be the seventh referee. Richmond refused but enquired what reward Anderson expected. Boldly, John Anderson asked for £1,200 per annum from the Scottish Civil List but was given little encouragement: 'we parted not only with Civility but with merriment, though with me it was all external'.[45]

Over the next couple of days John Anderson's field piece was unloaded from the *Minerva* (which had brought it down from Leith) and taken to the Royal Arsenal. On 27 July 1789 Anderson went to Woolwich and supervised its unpacking. A firing crew of eight men (as compared with a normal gun crew of fifteen) with a Sergeant and a Corporal had been assembled for the range trial, and on the following day field practice began – with the gun and its carriage being returned to a locked store that night. On 29 July, 1789 Anderson was concerned about overnight breaches of security; the gun had suffered minor damage while being inspected by persons unknown, but probably Woolwich personnel. However, test firing took place successfully on 30 and 31 July.[46] On 1 August at the official trial before the referees and 'a great number of people' the gun fired successfully, but there was some recoil, a great surprise and disappointment to Anderson. This failure to fulfil the claims made for his gun was probably due to minor technical hitches in a prototype, but it ended further government interest.[47]

A revised edition of Anderson's book on field artillery was translated into French and appeared in Paris in 1791. He went to France with his field piece and was fêted by the revolutionaries. The gun was, in fact, also inspected by Louis XVI, and the French manufactured it, later employing numbers of them in defeating the Austro-Prussian armies at Jemappes in November 1792.[48] Anderson was made an honorary citizen of the French Republic by the National Convention and one of his guns hung for a time in their meeting place carrying the inscription 'The Gift of Science to Liberty'.[49]

Another observer of Anderson's field piece was John Paul Jones, the celebrated American admiral, who quickly noticed the advantages for his navy of a gun with little recoil. Anderson, a great admirer of the spirit of the American militia which really was the equal of most British regular regiments during the War of Independence, was to seek in August 1793, unsuccessfully, an appointment to take charge of a federal arsenal, offering also to provide teaching and training for its workers. George Washington did not reply.[50]

From 1779 Anderson was devising new cannonballs and fuses. He was clearly ahead of his time – perhaps eighty years in his idea of a gun with an air recoil check mechanism and rather less in the case of time fuses and 'spheroid' shells. His grasp of ballistics and current military technology was far greater than might have been expected of an academic. This may well have made the British military establishment sceptical of his usefulness. George Washington might perhaps be forgiven; the first major expansion of federal arsenals occurred after the War of 1812.[51] Whether Anderson's efforts constituted 'research' is less doubtful. Advances in military technology are central to a nation's survival and may well have alternative peacetime applications; time fuses, for instance, were to offer considerable advantages in mining and quarrying.

When his former pupil and boarder of 1766, William Windham (1750-1810), became Secretary of War in 1794, Anderson took fresh hope. After the early military disasters of the French Revolutionary War, there was need for reform, and Windham was a reformer and not without personal resources and influence. In 1795 Anderson wrote a very lengthy letter to Windham offering to go to France to try to negotiate peace, which he thought was in Britain's interest. He explained that his *Essays* of 1788 had been revised and translated into French and that the Revolutionary Government might be prepared to give him a sympathetic hearing: 'The Artillery of my invention and the Military Advices which I gave to the French have made me a favourite with them, and in Paris'. Windham, perhaps wisely, thought the prospects for such a plenipotentiary unpropitious and therefore did not treat this idea seriously.

Anderson's other suggestion that the Department of Ordnance required reform was undoubtedly timeous. However, his root and branch approach was too radical for Windham. Anderson advocated the recruitment of a Board of Science whose main task would be to seek out worthwhile inventions; this almost certainly reflected his disappointing experience with Richmond and the Woolwich Arsenal earlier. As war became more sophisticated, the idea of a scientific civil service within the War Department seemed less far-fetched.[52]

Anderson was well aware of the inherent moral problems of a scientist interested or employed in improving weapons of war. He justified his own position by advancing the proposition that rational statesmen would recognise the implications of improved military technology and be more reluctant to involve their countries in war. Earlier wars had produced more casualties, he thought, because of the hand-to-hand nature of much of the fighting. Improved artillery and munitions, despite increased destructive power, might well produce fewer total casualties. We have the hindsight of experience from twentieth-century wars fought with technology beyond Anderson's dreams. Perhaps, one might accept the first part of his concluding proposition in the French version of his first essay: 'every improvement in field pieces will not only give victory to the army which first uses it, but after improvement is generally known, it will diminish the carnage in battles'.[53] The optimism of the second part reflected commonplaces in Enlightenment rationalism, and these were ill-founded.

Teaching and research, including publication and experimental work, absorbed much of Anderson's time but they were not his whole life. From 1753 he was a member of the Glasgow Literary Society which was dominated by university professors, serving as Secretary for five years between 1757 and 1762 and afterwards as President for a time. Like other members, he suggested topics for discussion and gave papers. These reflect his wider interests. Glasgow Literary Society discussions were wide-ranging and encompassed classical, moral, political, aesthetic and literary topics. On 10 May, 1765 his topic was concerned with how to test the truth of physical and political events and whether contemporary philosophers such as David Hume provided real guidance on this matter. Two years later on 20 March, 1767 his topic was 'Does a circulation of Learning by Reviews, Magazines, Newspapers etc. in every department of science tend to the real improvement of any science?'[54]

In the early 1770s he read two papers to the Society about the Roman Wall (1770 and 1773), using a map of the Forth and Clyde Canal survey to indicate where the *vallum* of the Antonine Wall ran, and giving detailed accounts of recent 'finds' and where they came from. Excavations for the Canal led to several discoveries which were examined by Anderson and reinforced contemporary interest in classicism.[55] In April 1777 he discoursed on professorial salaries and the idea of a university. On 7 November 1777 it was reported that 'Mr Anderson proposes to give next meeting the continuation of his discourses ... on pronunciation', clearly an interest based upon his early language teaching.[56] His Almanac of 1772, apart from containing a list of preachers in the College Chapel over the session, reveals his interest in church music.[57]

One of his great heroes was George Buchanan (1506-1582), and he gave a paper in November 1781 to the Literary Society about erecting an obelisk to his memory on the grounds of his distinction as a 'Poet, as a writer in Defence of Liberty, as an Historian, and as a Man of Genius who experienced great vicissitudes of Fortune'. Anderson thought the column should be placed at the top of Buchanan Street, be 150 feet high and probably cost about £200. George Buchanan, according to Anderson, anticipated in his *De Jure Regis apud Scotos* eighteenth-century views on liberty and the sovereignty of the law, teaching also that kings were raised above their subjects to administer justice and to promote their happiness. A king who did not perform these worthy functions could be deposed.[58]

Anderson's politics became more radical the longer he lived. The Whig commitment to a constitution where despotism was restrained by a system of checks and balances was under great strain as the eighteenth century proceeded. Anderson sympathised with the American colonists but did not believe in the violent overthrow of governments or societies; indeed he was a loyalist to the end. Nonetheless, he was passionately committed to the freedom of the Press and was, therefore, hostile to the persecution and attempted gagging of Tom Paine. It was not what men said or wrote which the law should be used to condemn but criminal or seditious behaviour. Thus, Anderson thought the transportation of Thomas Muir of Huntershill for treasonable talk was a major mistake, likely to lead to more popular unrest rather than less.[59]

Essentially, John Anderson began his adult life as part of the moderate Enlightenment consensus within Glasgow, modified only marginally by his devout Presbyterianism. Gradually, he moved to a more populist position. The notion that learning should simply enrich the individual gave way, in his mind, to the idea that knowledge should be used in the service of society. Thus his commitment to practical science and wider access to education became more marked. On this pivotal change in his ideas, Anderson's alliance with the mercantile and skilled artisan classes was based. Like these social groups he was less interested in moderate religious stances and more committed to 'old style' Calvinism than the majority of his academic colleagues. A pious Presbyterian, regularly in attendance at chapel, he was anti-Catholic – but not violently so. Anderson was aligned with a radical, law-abiding and law-worshipping segment of the enlightened classes and represented a fundamental challenge to the ideas and personalities dominant within Glasgow College. He enjoyed good food, fine wine and strong snuff, but otherwise his was a simple bachelor existence, often entertaining visitors to the city and College such as Boswell and Johnson (1773) after visits to the Highlands and Islands. James Boswell had been a student at Glasgow College in 1759-60, and Anderson had shown him and Dr Johnson around the city in 1773; Anderson sent Boswell a copy (now in Yale University Library) of the French edition of his *Essays* (1791) inscribed 'To James Boswell Esquire from his friend The Author'.

Glasgow professors in the eighteenth century were a quarrelsome and litigious group, possibly a consequence of their relatively closed existence. The College's exemption from the jurisdiction of City of Glasgow courts inevitably led to legal processes in the Court of Session, a waste of time and resources very often. John Anderson pursued a number of cases and was a defendant in others, sometimes alone but also in concert with others. As the classic work on the University remarks ' ... the administrative bodies stood in need of reform ... ' Few of these cases were personal; most were concerned with the College's affairs and Anderson's belief in the need for reform.

One exception was the persistent, personal quarrel between Anderson and James Moor, Professor of Greek. Moor developed a reputation for idiosyncrasy, moodiness and a liking for strong liquor but was also a scholar of great distinction. On 27 June, 1760 Moor and Anderson quarrelled in a Glasgow tavern. Having lost his temper, Anderson picked up a chamber pot but Moor threw a porter jug first and cut Anderson's face. The following day Anderson challenged Moor to a duel. Both were fined £20 and temporarily suspended from office during the vacation. Moor was no saint; Dr Trail, Professor of Divinity, took him to the Court of Session on one occasion, and he was admonished three times by the College Faculty for transgressions.[60]

Soon after the tavern brawl Moor published his book, *On the End of Tragedy according to Aristotle* (1763). It was well received, and the *Scots Magazine* carried a particularly favourable review in 1764. Shortly afterwards an anonymous *Letter to the Author* appeared, referring to Moor's book as 'a bundle of Pedantry and Nonsense; the author of which seems equally ignorant of Greek and incapable of writing good English'. Anderson was suspected of being the author of this scurrilous squib – and not only by Moor.[61] This caused Moor to pursue a vendetta against Anderson, irrespective of the merits of the issues in particular situations. No one contradicted Anderson when he later alleged: 'It is well known that Dr Moor was often Drunk and sometimes mad in the latter period of his life'.[62]

Much more irritating for his colleagues were Anderson's attempts to reform the university. It mattered little that he was often right; for most that only made him a more difficult colleague to endure. At first there was a reforming group to which Anderson belonged, but gradually he lost support within the university, although he gained it in the city. Disputes about College finances had intermittently erupted for about fifteen years before Anderson was appointed to the Chair of Natural Philosophy, the accounts often being disputed or protested by professors. Matthew Morthland, the College factor, was appointed in 1745 at a fixed annual salary of £60 but never presented or settled his accounts timeously. In 1760 Dr Robert Trail, supported by Professors Miller, Cumming, Williamson and Wright, had begun a case in the Court of Session with the object of ending financial maladministration, but this lapsed as Morthland promised to mend his ways.[63]

This promise was not sustained, and Trail began another action in the Court of Session in the summer of 1766 against the Principal, William Leechman (1706-85) who was his predecessor as Professor of Divinity, alleging that Morthland's misbehaviour was being condoned. This case lasted five years, and up to this time John Anderson had not bothered himself with the university accounts, 'being fully occupied with the business of his Profession and having entire confidence in those who took the management of the College revenue upon them'. After at first supporting Leechman, who had argued that total College revenues should be under the control of the Principal and professors and audited by the Visitors, John Anderson came to the conclusion that Morthland was negligent, and that the financial clauses of the Constitution of the University established by royal visitation in 1727 were being flouted. This Constitution of 1727 had fixed proper financial procedures for the factor to follow and for the Faculty to enjoin upon him.[64]

Anderson first sought a Declarator in the Court of Session in 1771 to determine the legal standing of the Constitution of 1727. The Court favoured Anderson's view, but the accounts of 1772, for instance, were not passed by the Faculty till 1775. In 1772 Anderson sought a further Declarator 'concerning the Management of the Revenue of Glasgow College'. His criticisms were soundly based, and some of his colleagues supported him. Yet his methods could be criticised, and he lacked the trimmer's skills of tact, discretion, and regard for internal procedures which would have maintained that support and possibly brought success. For example, it could be readily demonstrated that his fondness for the Court of Session prevented proper process through the University's Visitors. That argument made it possible for his opponents to detach the 'reasonable' men who naturally looked for a quiet settlement. Anderson would have argued, no doubt, that without the threat of a Court of Session case, he would not have been taken seriously.

Significantly, Thomas Reid, Professor of Moral Philosophy and Adam Smith's successor, supported Anderson and presented an additional paper to the Visitors. However, they were opposed by a powerful caucus headed by Principal Leechman. Anderson, convinced that he was right, provided the Visitors with evidence on how the factors at the universities of Aberdeen and St Andrews operated.[65] Essentially the 'master and steward' method of book-keeping was inadequate and, following the practices of the Glasgow tobacco merchants and the rest of Glasgow's commercial community, Anderson sought a proper double-entry mercantile system.

On 12 October, 1775 a meeting of the Visitors was held at Shaw Park, the home of Charles, ninth Lord Cathcart (1721-76), Rector of the University of Glasgow. This confirmed the statutes of 1727 which had not been kept by the factor or the Principal and professors. The Shaw Park decrees were a total victory for Anderson: the accounts had to be kept 'in the regular way of Bookkeeping'; the factor had 'to keep an exact cash book, Journal and Ledger'; many provisions were made to ensure proper accounting according to best practice; and 'from henceforwards the Statutes ought to be rigidly observed, and enforced by the Faculty'.[66]

Unfortunately, no matter what the Court of Visitors decided, Principal Leechman and his supporters were not prepared to accept and to operate these decrees. The dispute was still raging in February 1776, and Professors Reid, Wilson and Anderson formed a committee to defend the Visitors' verdict. A further memorial signed by these three and Professors Hamilton, Richardson and Young was prepared but not presented. Meetings of the Faculty continued to receive inadequate accounts, and Anderson's complaint of 1775 that 'We have not been able to learn that there are any accompts of any Corporation in the Kingdom, which are in such a state as those of Glasgow College' continued to be true. Morthland, the College factor, eventually became bankrupt, owing the College thousands of pounds.[67]

It would be mistaken to imagine that Anderson was the only trenchant critic that the Scottish universities in general – and Glasgow College, in particular – faced. The 'Academy' or 'Science' college movement started in Perth in the 1750s and expressed in practical terms dissatisfaction with existing curricula in school and university and was resonantly echoed in the West of Scotland, where it was commonplace for the sons of merchants to spend a year or two in Glasgow College. Reverend John Bonar of Perth West Church emphasised the place of the practical sciences in the curriculum and assumed that there was a close relationship between the economic 'superiority' of nations and their support for the sciences: 'as the scale of science rises or falls, that of the kingdom rises or falls with it'. Science, because of its emphasis on real life and work, improved the morality of societies, diverting 'youth from idleness, play and debauchery'. Bonar proclaimed the educational needs of the rising commercial and manufacturing classes; Perth Academy's two masters began teaching a 'relevant' curriculum in 1761.[68]

In the West of Scotland the most bitter attack on the Scottish universities came from Reverend William Thom of Govan, whose main target was his *alma mater*, Glasgow College. He produced a series of pamphlets from 1761 onwards, beginning with the self-explanatory *Letter to J–M–, Esq., on the Defects of an University Education and its Unsuitableness to a Commercial People* ... Thom was withering in his condemnation of a whole year (the second year at Glasgow) spent on Logic and Metaphysics and wanted more emphasis on 'practical' mathematics, history, natural history, geography, the history of commerce and 'practical morality'. He felt that the Glasgow curriculum required modernisation and that the College should follow the example of Marischal College, Aberdeen, which in the 1750s had introduced reforms. Lack of local competition for students, he declared, made the Glasgow Faculty reluctant to change; in Aberdeen, Marischal was faced with the alternative of King's College.[69]

Because Glasgow's professors were paid a small stipend and made up the bulk of their income from student fees, Thom thought they were often venal, prevailing upon students to take too many classes in one session and pretending to provide excellent private tuition for students who boarded with them but received no general pastoral guidance. They established extra classes and to gain income exerted moral pressure on students to attend them and yet they did not pay sufficient attention to the quality of their teaching and distanced themselves from personal contact with students as much as possible:

> A place [i.e. a Chair] in a university is considered as easy, honourable and lucrative. It is almost looked upon as a sinecure: it is not ordinarily the most ingenious and able for teaching that is pitched upon, but he who is connected or whose friends are connected with and can serve the men in power; and this seems to be growing more and more in fashion ...

He thought a new academy in Glasgow was the best means of remedying these deficiencies.[70]

Thom was well known to Anderson, but when the latter took up his first chair in 1755, he was part of the polite establishment – an insider – in the University of Glasgow. It was precisely because Anderson challenged their complacency and corruption and supported Thom's criticisms that his colleagues eventually believed he was beyond the pale.

Anderson did not pick his ground well. Despite his popularity as a lecturer and with graduates, he was a stickler for student discipline and principle and probably poor in detecting the difference between high jinks and malice. Moreover, because he lacked diplomacy and tact, he was inclined to defend his stance through the legal process rather than by negotiation. A short fuse to a bad temper did not help either. Disputes with students involved his colleagues for two reasons. They took in student boarders, some of whom fell foul of Anderson, and they were members of the *Jurisdictio Ordinaria*, a major faculty committee which included student discipline within its remit. The Principal and professors found Anderson a difficult colleague and they quite reasonably treated appropriate student cases as part of a wider legal game to control him.

Sometimes students provoked Anderson by their *gaucherie* or unruliness. For instance, in 1773 James Prosser, a wild Irish student, wanting to take a short cut in the 'Experiment' room, stepped over a rail into an area forbidden to students. Anderson pushed him back, and Prosser fell and sustained a minor injury. At the end of the demonstration the student was apologetic but boldly said that he thought Anderson should apologise too. Anderson refused. Taking umbrage, Prosser left but not before uttering threats. Anderson learned that Prosser intended to return next day with his friends who would be armed with bludgeons, that he would demand a public apology at the lecture and, if it was not forthcoming, threatened physical violence.

Forewarned is forearmed. Next day Anderson assembled a group of men from the town in a side room off the lecture theatre, and when Prosser appeared, they seized him, on orders from Anderson, dragging him through the College courts and along the streets to jail. There he was detained for several hours with common criminals until Professors Miller and Hamilton secured his bail, although Anderson had sent a note to the Sheriff asking him to refuse it. Still in a temper, Anderson started a short-lived case in the Court of Session but realised Prosser was being used by his colleagues in 'College politics'.[71]

In 1782 John Anderson was *Preses* of the *Jurisdictio Ordinaria*, and in December windows were broken during a disorderly rampage. Three students of Dr Hugh Macleod, Professor of Church History, were accused. Anderson discussed the incident with Principal Leechman who thought there ought to be an inquiry into their misbehaviour. Macleod, in defence of his boarders, dissented and was abusive about Anderson: 'not content with incessant litigations in his own Name, makes the Injuries and Offences of his Neighbours, the Pretence for raising Prosecutions, fomenting Disturbance and diffusing Scandal'. Thus a minor case of student indiscipline became a bitter argument between professors.[72]

Macleod and Anderson proceeded to conduct an undignified slanging match in which passion and prejudice replaced reason. Indeed, Macleod complained that Anderson had 'thrice raised and shaken a Loaded Cane at him in Presence of the Court, and after the Cane was lodged in another Gentleman's hand, ... calling him a Liar and many other opprobrious names'. Anderson admitted having a walking stick and pointing it at Macleod but denied threatening him with it. The Principal and five professors witnessed this incident, and one of them, Professor Reid, recollected that 'Mr Anderson was in great agitation and looked *very fierce* at Dr Macleod'. Later, Anderson 'burst out into a Second Fit of Passion and violent Expressions against Dr Macleod'.[73] Despite Anderson's obvious anger and extreme language the evidence suggests that Macleod, in attempting to protect his students from proper discipline, was economical with the truth and thereby provoked Anderson but was not in danger of physical assault. However, Anderson was suspended from the *Jurisdictio Ordinaria*, pending a Faculty hearing.

Among the three accused students was Warren Fitzroy (1768-1806), a boy of fourteen who happened to be the fourth son of the newly created first Baron Southampton. Anderson, while visiting a family in the city, had learned that Fitzroy, a student of Professor Macleod, had stolen a watch from John Dalzell Martin, his fellow boarder, and had sold it to Angus MacDonald, 'Toyman in the Saltmarket'. On his return to college, Anderson questioned Martin, found that he had indeed lost a watch and advised him to inquire of MacDonald. This Martin did and found that his watch had been sold by Fitzroy.[74]

Fitzroy had been in trouble before; Macleod knew of his 'irregular behaviour' and had once beaten him for using 'a false key'. Theft went far beyond normal high spirits, but Macleod claimed that Fitzroy had left the College, while, in fact, he was hiding in the house of James Williamson, Professor of Mathematics. There was a deliberate but ineffectual attempt to hush up this unsavoury affair; the story of the stolen watch was widely known in the town. To add insult to injury — as far as Anderson was concerned — Macleod, while claiming that Fitzroy was no longer a student and therefore beyond the power of the *Jurisdictio Ordinaria*, allowed him to mix with his classmates.

John Martin was put under heavy pressure by the Principal who was clearly concerned to stamp on any notion that the college had a thief among its students. Martin signed a precognition at the Principal's behest which made no mention of the stolen watch, and among the witnesses was Hugh Macleod. Realising that fair play from the *Jurisdictio Ordinaria* and the Faculty was unlikely, Anderson decided to take the case to the Court of Session.[75]

Meanwhile Anderson, because of his suspension from the *Jurisdictio Ordinaria*, could not take part in the internal discussions of the case. After several absences from the court set up to deal with Macleod's complaints against him, Anderson appeared on 29 January 1783 and offered apologies to the Principal and the Faculty in order to settle the issue. It is worth noting that Macleod had earlier pursued a number of quarrels with colleagues, but this was his first dispute with Anderson. However, when Macleod's complaints against him were about to be heard, Anderson was asked to leave the room; this he did under protest. In a private letter to the Principal, Anderson complained of the treatment he had received: 'Things have been said to me *in the faculty room* which no man dares to say to me out of it. Where is the Statute that makes that place *a Sanctuary for illiberal Treatment?*'[76]

Anderson's Bill of Advocation against Macleod was denied by the Court of Session on 30 April 1783 and, therefore, he had little option but to seek a settlement of their differences by the Faculty. He asked for a delay in Faculty proceedings and suggested that Macleod and he should both retract any statements which offended the other. Macleod, realising that he had a majority in the Faculty, was unwilling to accept this compromise, and on 6 May, 1783 at their meeting with the Faculty Anderson appeared with his lawyer. His requests for a delay in the proceedings during the meetings of the General Assembly (of which he was a member) were denied, and the Faculty insisted upon the total privacy of its meetings. On 26 May, 1783 Anderson felt compelled to enter a second Bill of Advocation against Macleod in the Court of Session and thereby reinforced his reputation for litigiousness. The Court believed that professors should settle their differences through university procedures wherever possible and decided that the dispute between Anderson and Macleod was such a case. When Anderson believed that a student had suffered a miscarriage of justice, he exercised his right to say so. James Wilson was accused of 'jumping' in the College Garden during the Fitzroy affair and was chastised by Professor Richardson, despite having a record of good behaviour in the previous two years. Anderson thought the student had been treated harshly, sent an account of the incident to his father which indicated that Wilson was merely one of several offenders, the others not being disciplined. His father felt that Anderson had treated his son fairly, but he thought that Richardson had not. His son had claimed that like the Honourable Mr Fitzroy he was no longer a student, 'but it seems the same rule could not be applied to the case of plain James Wilson'.[77]

Underlying this dispute was the need to establish the principle of proper student discipline and equal treatment of malefactors, no matter what their social standing. But Anderson handled the Fitzroy case badly and, no matter how much he was provoked, should have remained calm. This counsel of perfection, unfortunately, he did not follow, and in consequence he lost any power to influence academic procedures in the College.

Anderson's final suspension from the *Jurisdictio Ordinaria* arose from his attempt to discipline Andrew Crawford in 1784. Crawford had refused to present himself 'at the hour for examination', and Anderson therefore expelled him from his class. Anderson placed great store on structured assessment of his students: 'the hour of examination' was matched by 'the hour of prelection'; *viva voce* examinations and written exercises were equally important. Thus, his popularity as a teacher was not based on a lackadaisical attitude to his main duty. Examinations then did not possess the standing that they enjoy now, and Crawford successfully appealed to the

Faculty which insisted that the student be readmitted. Anderson's obduracy, once the Faculty decision was known, led his colleagues to summon him to appear before them; after much heated discussion about procedure, they declared that he had failed to behave properly as a professor and suspended him. Anderson remained in Coventry, debarred from attendance at the *Jurisdictio Ordinaria*, till 1792.[78]

During these years Anderson was left with no alternative but to harness external forces favouring reform. In the rectorial election of 1784, Edmund Burke, the sitting tenant, whom some students believed had supported Anderson's suspension, had to beat off a campaign against his re-election.[79] The Faculty, having accepted Anderson's gift of £20 in February 1770 to establish prizes for the best essay on a Natural Philosophy subject and for Elocution, decided unilaterally in 1784 to abolish this scheme and replace it with one of their own: 'They withdrew permission for Mr Anderson's Institution', forbidding him to continue with meetings of the Masters of Arts who decided who should receive the prizes. This arbitrary action and the wording of the decision may have caused Anderson to reflect on the merits of creating a new institution to compete with Glasgow College.[80]

Naturally, the graduates were affronted and so were many of the students. Anderson, therefore, became the head of a university reform movement intent on petitioning the King for a Royal Visitation. Assisted by many students, he organised fifteen petitions, some of which were widely circulated in the city and signed by large numbers. The Trades House with its fourteen incorporations petitioned the King to reform the University and sought a Royal Commission, mentioning the 'violent Dissentions, discords and animosities among the Professors, between them and the Students and among the Students'. Petitions signed by over 150 current students complained of abuses: faction; partiality against students; interference in rectorial elections by faculty; non-appearance of professors at the stipulated times for their lectures. The Irish students (40-50 strong) sent a separate petition making much the same points. The most impressive petition came from the city's merchant traders and manufacturers; this by April 1785 contained about 3,000 signatures. The graduates complained that the Principal and Faculty 'have stopped mooting' for the prizes in Elocution and Natural Philosophy. Ten petitions came from individuals who claimed some damage by the University. Anderson's own, dated 1 May, 1785, repeated his charges of financial maladministration, non-adherence to the Statutes of 1727, unjust proceedings by the Faculty against students and himself, and lack of regard for proper student discipline.[81]

Anderson also approached the local member of parliament, Islay Campbell (1734-1823), who became Lord Advocate in 1784, but he did not favour a Royal Commission. The petitions were conveyed by Anderson to London where he again met Islay Campbell MP, Lord Sydney (1733-1800), the Home Secretary, Lord Graham, Chancellor of the University, and the Rector, Edmund Burke. Anderson argued the case for root and branch reform and a Royal Commission into the affairs of Glasgow University. However, the petitions were denied. A further case in the Court of Session followed between 1785 and 1787; Anderson sued the Chancellor, the Rector, two Visitors, the Principal and some of his colleagues and sought £6,100 in damages – but all to no avail.[82] It is easy to decry these efforts as quixotic, but clearly, Anderson had touched a popular nerve in the civic consciousness of Glasgow.

Lest it be thought that Anderson was simply an idiosyncratic populist and not to be treated seriously, it should be noted that in 1792 he was asked by Reverend Dr Walker, Professor of Natural History in the University of Edinburgh, to delineate his views about the duties of professors and students and to suggest what the General Assembly should enact about the university training of divinity students. Anderson clearly took the opportunity to suggest the

2 The first page of John Anderson's Will contained in the first Minute Book of Anderson's Institution, 1796–99. This was probably entered by John Parsell, Anderson's 'operator' and amanuensis during his last illness. Probably the first trustees of Anderson's Institution wanted this copy made so that it was available to be used as an indication of Anderson's intentions.

level of entry of students, the curriculum, the hours of teaching they should enjoy and the methods of their assessment:

> It is of great importance for a Student of Divinity to reside at an University, not only for the sake of the Professors' lectures and examinations; but of books, society and literary conversation: And as he is to be a public speaker with a theological Character, it is highly proper for him to be exercised in the Debates of a Club ...
>
> ... these Rules are necessary in order to make our Clergy respectable and useful; by keeping away stupidity, and illiterate impudence ...

After the Faculty removed his suspension from the *Jurisdictio Ordinaria* in 1792, Anderson rarely attended its meetings, preferring to deal with his colleagues by correspondence. As time passed, he became more infirm and in 1795 was granted an assistant, William Meikleham. That summer he spent much time in Edinburgh, but he was very weak. In December he took to his bed, and under the care of Dr Peter Wright and Widow Watson, died in his seventieth year on Wednesday, 13 January, 1796 about midday and was buried on Saturday 16 January.[83] Wright, who 'saw him breathe his last', described Anderson as 'A man of general knowledge and Zealous in his profession'. He was certainly worthy of that short eulogy.[84]

Anderson's will dated 7 May 1795 opens with a reference to his 'soundness and vigour of mind tho' reduced in strength of body by sickness'. He had gathered valuables, family memorabilia and his grandfather's papers with an inventory into 'a painted Chest with three locks in the Red Room of my House in Glasgow College'; these items were left to his family beginning with his brother, Andrew, and laying down an order of inheritance after him. The locks had been sealed, and the three keys were – one each – in the care of Dr Wright, John Wilson, Town Clerk, and Mr Burns, Minister of the Barony parish. This chest was to be taken from the College house by Andrew and opened when he was alone.

The rest of his property John Anderson gave 'to the Public for the good of Mankind and the Improvement of Science'. He willed the foundation of 'Anderson's University' which was to be managed by 81 trustees. Anderson had organised and named these trustees in nine classes – Tradesmen; Agriculturalists; Artists; Manufacturers or Merchants; Mediciners, 'an old Scotch word' covering doctors, surgeons, apothecaries and druggists; Lawyers; Divines; Natural Philosophers; Kinsmen or Namesakes. The conduct of the trustees was to be monitored by nine Visitors – the Lord Provost and eldest Baillie of Glasgow, the Dean of Guild, the Deacon Convener of the Trades House, the *Preses* of the Faculty of Physicians and Surgeons, the Dean of the Faculty of Procurators, the Moderator of the Synod of Glasgow and Ayr, and the Moderators of the Presbyteries of Glasgow and Dumbarton – of whom six would form a quorum 'to enjoin and enforce faithful administration'. The trustees were to meet four times a year in March, June, September and December, and at the June meeting they were to elect a committee of nine managers by ballot for one year only – but they could be re-elected. The managers were to choose a President and a Clerk by ballot, and they were to meet every month 'and oftener if necessary'. In addition, there was to be a School or Academy under their close control.

The trustees had ultimate power over the university 'or Studium Generale for the improvement of Human Nature, of Science and of the country where they live'. Trustees missing six general meetings lost their places; vacancies were to be filled by election. Anderson deliberately chose the name 'Anderson's University' because it would not be appropriate to attach to it the name 'Glasgow': 'that would make a constant confusion between it, and the Old University, and College of Glasgow'. In any event, he felt that it had 'a better title to my name on account of the property bequeathed, than Mr Stirling's small Donation of Books had to perpetuate the name of Stirling's now Extensive Library'. Like Walter Stirling, John Anderson regarded his bequest as the beginning of a fund-raising exercise among those who supported his objectives.

Anderson clearly intended that his university should cover a wide, modern curriculum and award degrees. There were to be four colleges or faculties – Arts, Medicine, Law and Theology – each consisting of nine professors. Each college would have as its president, or dean, the senior professor. The Senate was to consist of all thirty-six professors, nine of whom would form a quorum, and the senior dean would be its President. Degrees would be awarded by the Senate on the recommendation of each college. Anderson also prescribed the titles of the various degrees and nominated all thirty-six professors and the four deans.

His choice of titles for the chairs is an indication of intended academic coverage. In Arts these were Physics, Ethics, Logic and Rhetoric, Greek, Senior Latin, Junior Latin, Civil History, Mathematics and Chemistry. In Medicine the chairs were in the Institutes or Theory of Medicine, Practice of Medicine, Anatomy and Theory of Surgery, Practical Surgery, Obstetrics, Materia Medica, Clinical Cases, Botany and Natural History. In Law Anderson's chairs were Roman Law, Law of Scotland, English Law, Law of Nature and Nations, Roman Antiquities, Scottish Antiquities, Ecclesiastical Law, Commercial Law, and the Practice in the Scottish Courts. In the College of Theology Anderson nominated chairs in Systematic Divinity according to the Church of Scotland, Critical Explanations of the Scriptures, Church History, Oriental Languages, the Burgher System of Divinity, the Anti-Burgher System, the Relief System, the Gaelic Language, and Sacred Music. Clearly, Anderson's populist brand of evangelical Presbyterianism was to be well represented.

John Anderson thought it likely that some nominees would not accept, but he believed it right to provide a complete academic plan for his university, 'and in the course of time, perhaps from these small beginnings, this Institution may become a Seminary of Sound Religion; Useful Learning; and Liberality of Sentiment'. He also provided for the filling of professorial vacancies; new appointments were to be made by the general meeting of trustees from three suitable candidates nominated by Senate. All such proceedings were to be by ballot. If the trustees did not fill a vacancy within three months, the power to act rested with the appropriate college. If these professors did not act within nine days, 'their right shall devolve to the Junior Professor, or the last made Professor of the whole Senate', a provision guaranteed to secure earlier action!

No one connected in any capacity with the University of Glasgow could serve in Anderson's University:

> Thus ... the almost constant intrigues, which prevail in the Faculty of Glasgow College about their Revenue, and the Nomination of Professors, or their Acts of Vanity, or Power, Inflamed by a Collegiate life, will be kept out of Anderson's University; and the irregularities, and neglect of duty in the Professors of Glasgow College, will naturally, in some degree, be corrected by a rival school of Education ...

No one concerned with the governance of the City of Glasgow – except in the Tradesmen class – could hold office in Anderson's University, so that the arrangements for Visitors would not be compromised. The Professors were not to be incorporated, as they were at the University of Glasgow, except for academic and disciplinary purposes. They did not own the property of the university nor could they serve as trustees or managers, so that there could be no conflict of interest. The trustees were to give 'every encouragement to such as are laborious and active in doing their duty' but they were not to permit professors 'as in some other Colleges, to be Drones

St David's (Ramshorn) Church, Ingram Street, where John Anderson and his grandfather are buried. Memorial stones to both men were built into the tower (east wall) and maintained after the rebuilding by Thomas Rickman in 1824. During restoration work prior to the church's conversion to the University Drama Centre in 1992-3, the stones were removed for cleaning and then returned. The Ramshorn Theatre, home of the Strathclyde Theatre Group, is a major venue for cultural events in Glasgow.

or Triflers, Drunkards or negligent ... '. The managers had powers to remove professors by proper procedures, but there was a right of final appeal to the plenary body of trustees.

An account of John Anderson's property as bequeathed to his university was given in the codicil to his will (4 January, 1796), but he was expecting donations to make up the necessary fund. He provided for annual accounts and proper auditing and gave further guidance in rules and regulations. He expected that the first appointment would be the Professor of Natural Philosophy and nominated William Meikleham. This professor was to give two courses, the 'Mathematical' and the 'Ladies' Course' in which no mathematical reasoning was to be used. Essentially, this latter course was to be open to men and women 'with the idea of making the ladies of Glasgow the most accomplished ... in Europe'. Entry to lectures was to be by ticket ' ... no men may be admitted who are disorderly, talkative, ill-bred or intoxicated; and no women that are giddy or incorrect in their manners. If they do not like these Conditions, they need not apply for Tickets'.

John Anderson advised his trustees to apply to the City Council for a charter or seal of cause so that they could be legally incorporated. After completing this very detailed will, which even took account of the disposal of his property if insufficient trustees could be found to carry out his intentions, Anderson nominated his executors and instructed them to act in accordance with his codicil which dealt with arrangements after his death. His funeral was to be quiet and to take place in the Ramshorn Churchyard; his executors were to settle his affairs with his brother and with Glasgow College, to pay all his debts and to recover various named items. His books and apparatus were to be catalogued; his furniture was to be brought out of Glasgow College and properly stored; arrangements for beginning a lecture programme were to be made. Finally, the executors were to set up two tablets of properly treated Kilsyth stone in the south-east wall of the Ramshorn Church – one to the memory of his grandfather and one for himself.[85]

What might be regarded as a ridiculously grandiose plan for a university should be taken as John Anderson intended it. He expected that his university would begin small but believed that he should put his lifetime of experiences in Glasgow College at the disposal of his trustees. What was really significant was not the generous coverage of his proposed curriculum or the number of chairs; it was the lack of professorial control over resources. His alternative to the University of Glasgow and its arrangements was governance by an effective laity recruited locally, the model indeed for the later reform of Scottish universities.

Wider access to classes, especially for women, was central to his academic plan. Thom's ideas of useful education coined in the 1760s converged with John Anderson's own; this idea of a university and of the nature of learning was in sharp contrast with the orthodox Enlightenment concept that knowledge enriched the soul but had no other social purpose. John Anderson left his executors with major tasks; these could only be undertaken by testing the generosity of those like the petitioners of 1784-5 who shared the vision of Jolly Jack Phosphorus.

REFERENCES

1 James Muir, *John Anderson, Pioneer of Technical Education and the College He Founded* (ed. J. M. Macaulay) (Glasgow, 1950).

2 C.G. Wood, 'John Anderson's *Vis Matrix* – his Actuating Spirit throughout the years of conflict and dissidence', *96 Group Paper*, 1994. I am most grateful to Mr. Wood for his kindness in allowing me to see this paper and for the many discussions I have had with him about John Anderson.

3 C.G. Wood, 'John Anderson: Some Fresh Aspects', *96 Group Paper*, 1959; C.G. Wood, I.F. Clarke, *et al*, 'John Anderson', *96 Group Paper*, 1966.

4 Strathclyde University Archives [SUA], A2/1 Letter, John Anderson to Gilbert Lang, 13 Feb. 1750.

5 SUA, A3 Letter, John Anderson to Gilbert Lang, 27 Dec. 1750; *Burke's Peerage and Baronetage*.

6 C.G. Wood, *96 Group Paper*, 1994.

7 National Register of Archives (Scotland), 0217 Moray Muniments, John Anderson to the Earl of Moray, 21 March, 1752. I am grateful to C.G. Wood for this reference.

8 C.G. Wood, *96 Group Paper*, 1994.

9 Andersonian Library Rare Books Department [ALRBD], MS3, John Anderson's Common Place Book, 1754-5; SUA, AX/2/2 Letter, John Anderson to Gilbert Lang, 16 January 1755.

10 ALRBD, MS/1 John Anderson's Common Place Book 1748-56, p.15.

11 SUA, AX/2/2.

12 C.G. Wood, *96 Group Paper*, 1994. The Bishop of Armagh wrote to the Principal (25 January 1755) in support of Anderson's request to postpone his starting date as Professor of Oriental Languages (University of Glasgow Archives) and was merely one of Campbell's influential acquaintances who did the same. Anderson was given leave till November 1756.

13 *Glasgow Journal*, 25 October, 1756.

14 David Murray, *Memories of the Old College of Glasgow* (Glasgow, 1927), pp. 20 and 113.

15 SUA, A/8, Account of transaction between Anderson and the Fund.

16 Ibid., A/10, Account of Instruments, 14 June, 1756.

17 ALRBD, MS7 Copy of a list of Instruments in the Physical Apparatus of Glasgow College, 26 June, 1760. This ignored by John Cable, 'Early Scottish Science: The Vocational Provision', *Annals of Science* (1973), pp. 186-7.

18 James Patrick Muirhead, *The Life of James Watt* (1859), pp. 92-3 and 226; *Bicentenary of the James Watt Patent* (ed. Robert Donaldson) (Glasgow, 1970), pp. 18-19; Murray, p.112; George Williamson, *Memorials ... of James Watt* (Edinburgh, 1856), pp. 134 ff.; R. Olson, *Scottish Philosophy and British Physics 1750-1850* (Princeton, 1975); Birmingham Reference Library, James Watt Papers JWP 3/37 No.16.

19 For example, *Glasgow Journal*, 29 March, 1756.

20 Murray, p.108.

21 'Anti-toga': students without gowns, admitted without matriculating from 1727; *Glasgow Mechanics Magazine* (March, 1825), p.98.

22 John Anderson, *The Institutes of Physics* (Glasgow, 1795), Preface.

23 *Glasgow Mechanics Magazine* (March, 1825), pp. 97-104; ALRBD, MS/30.

24 ALRBD, MS/41; Robert Reid [Senex], *Glasgow Past and Present*, (Glasgow, 1884), Vol. i, li; ii, 123 gives 1784 as the year of opening of the Gaelic Chapel.

25 *Glasgow Mechanics Magazine*, iii (1825) p.v.; v (1826), pp. 182, 201, 209, 334; Scottish Record Office, Acts and Decreets DAL 23 November 1787.

26 Both James Coutts, *A History of the University of Glasgow ...* (Glasgow, 1909), pp. 286 ff. and David Murray express this view. Cable, p.187.

27 ALRBD, MS/15 Rain Gauge Records, 1784-92; MS/15/2, Essay on Rain Gauges, 1780; C.G. Wood, 'John Anderson's Rain Gauge', *Philosophical Journal*, vol. 5, no. 2 (1968), pp. 138-150; *Idem, 96 Group Paper*, 1994; MS/26, John Anderson on Barometers; John Anderson, 'Of a new Rain Gage, of a weather register and of rainy climates', Letters and Papers of Royal Society, 1792.

28 SUA, A/5, Benjamin Franklin to John Anderson, 18 August, 1788.

29 Murray, pp. 55 ff.; *Glasgow Mechanics Magazine*, ii (1825), p.198.

30 ALRBD, MS/8, Journal of Experiments, 1782; C.G. Wood, 'The Anderson six pounder field piece', *Philosophical Journal*, 10 (1973), pp. 37-54.

31 ALRBD, MS/8, John Anderson to the Duke of Richmond, 1 September, 1782; SRO, Newhailes MSS, 476/1, John Anderson to Lord Hailes, 8 July 1782.

32 Ibid., Richmond to Dundas, 24 September, 1782.

33 ALRBD, MS/16, John Anderson to the Duke of Richmond, 10 March, 1789.

34 For Stainton, cf. R.H. Campbell, *Carron Company* (1961), pp. 161 ff.

35 ALRBD, MS/16, Joseph Stainton to John Anderson, 11 April, 1789.

36 Ibid., John Anderson to Joseph Stainton, 14 April, 1789.

37 Ibid., Duke of Richmond to John Anderson, 16 April, 1789.

38 Ibid., John Anderson to Joseph Stainton, 19 and 24 April, 1789; Stainton to Anderson, 20 and 23 April, 1789.

39 Ibid., John Anderson to Shand, April, 1789.

40 Ibid., Shand to Anderson, 14 May, 1789; Anderson to Shand, 17 May, 1789.

41 *Caledonian Mercury*, 18 May, 1789; ALRBD, MS/16, Anderson to John McNab, W.S., 20 May, 1789; John Robertson to Anderson, 21 May, 1789.

42 ALRBD, MS/16, Copy of R.E. Prospé to Professor Merian, 7 June, 1789.

43 Ibid., Duke of Richmond to Anderson, 10 June, 1789.

44 Ibid., Anderson to Richmond, 17 June, 1789.

45 Ibid., MS/16, pp. 119-123, Anderson's own account of his visit to Woolwich, 1789.

46 Ibid., pp. 124-31.

47 Ibid., p.148. It is true that Anderson was asked to put his gun to further trials but the estimated cost was £900 and beyond his purse. [British Library, Windham Papers, Add MSS 37845].

48 C.G. Wood, *Philosophical Journal*, 1973.

49 Muir, p.12.

50 C.G. Wood, *96 Group Paper*, 1994.

51 Ibid.; Muir, pp. 52 ff.; J.J. Farley, *Making Arms in the Machine Age*, (Philadelphia, 1994), Chapters 1 and 2.

52 SUA, K10/5, C.G. Wood, 'John Anderson: some fresh aspects', *96 Group Paper*, 1959; Edinburgh University Library, Laing MSS lv 17, John Anderson to William Laing, his bookseller, 28 February 1795.

53 ALRBD, MS/17, John Anderson's Military Sketches, and MS/23, John Anderson's Military Essays.

54 C.G. Wood, I.F. Clarke *et al, 96 Group Paper*, 1966.

55 ALRBD, MS/22; Coutts, p.332.

56 C.G. Wood, I.F. Clarke *et al*, *96 Group Paper*, 1966; Cable, pp. 190-1.

57 ALRBD, Almanack 1772.

58 Ibid., MS/25.

59 C.G. Wood, *96 Group Paper*, 1994; John Gray, *Biographical Notice of the Rev. David Ure* (Glasgow, 1965), p.22.

60 Muir, p.17; ALRBD, MS/41, p.126; Yale University Library, John Anderson, *Essais sur l'artillerie de campagne* (Paris, 1791); Coutts, p.290.

61 Murray, p.382.

62 ALRBD, MS/41, p.175.

63 ALRBD, MS/41, Professor Anderson's Law Plea (Matthew Morthland).

64 Ibid., Act Regulating the University of Glasgow, 1727; MS41/1, Process of Declarator 1775.

65 Ibid., MS41/3, pp. 1-14.

66 Ibid., pp. 38 ff.

67 SUA, A/13, Memorial to the Visitors; SUA, K10/3/3, D.A.R. Forrester, 'John Anderson's Views on Accounting', *96 Group Paper*, 1974; *idem. Philosophical Journal*, 1975; *idem*, 'Universities and Auditing' Typescript, 1963; Edinburgh University Library, Laing MSS II, 99/60, John Anderson to unknown correspondent, 14 December 1790.

68 D.J. Withrington, 'Education and Society in the Eighteenth Century', in *Scotland in the Age of Improvement* (ed. N.T. Phillipson and Rosalind Mitchison) (Edinburgh, 1970), Chapter 8, especially pp. 179-181; R.B. Sher, 'Commerce, Religion and the Enlightenment in Eighteenth Century Glasgow', in *History of Glasgow*, vol. I (ed. T.M. Devine and G. Jackson), (Manchester, 1995), Chapter 8.

69 William Thom, *Works* (Glasgow, 1799).

70 Ibid., pp. 284 f.

71 Murray, p.382; ALRBD, MS/41, p.127.

72 ALRBD, MS/41.2, Extract of Faculty Minutes, 17/19 December, 1782, pp. 10-11.

73 Ibid., pp. 14 ff.

74 Ibid., pp. 53 ff; *Burke's Peerage*.

75 Ibid., pp. 54 ff; Copy letter, John Anderson to Principal Leechman, 20 January, 1783.

76 Ibid., pp. 159-196.

77 Ibid., pp. 31, 39, 53, 81 ff; SRO, Acts and Decreets DAL, 23 November, 1787.

78 C.G. Wood, *96 Group Paper*, 1994.

79 Murray, p.238.

80 C.G. Wood, *96 Group Paper*, 1994.

81 ALRBD, MS/19.2 contains copies of petitions; Muir, pp.21 ff.

82 ALRBD, MS/19.2; C.G. Wood, *96 Group Paper*, 1994.

83 Muir, pp. 27-8.

84 Edinburgh University Library, Laing MS, 352/1; ALRBD, Dr Peter Wright's copy of John Anderson's *Institutes of Physics*, end papers.

85 Copies of John Anderson's will are available in Muir, pp. 126-162 and in SUA, B1/1, Minute Book of Anderson's Institution, 1796-99.

CHAPTER TWO

From Institution to University, 1796-1830

'Philosophy as it has been exalted and adorned by the discoveries of Newton and Lavoisier is now in every polished nation an object worthy of the homage and regard of the great and illustrious.'

Professor Andrew Ure, Minute Book B1/2, 1799-1810,
pp. 127-8, 21 March 1805.

After the interment of John Anderson on 16 January 1796, eight of his nine executors met in his house in Glasgow College. John Wilson, Town Clerk of Glasgow, produced Anderson's will and codicil and read them to the rest – Peter Wright, physician, James Monteath, surgeon, William Meikleham, Anderson's assistant, James Crichton, instrument-maker, William Reid, printer, James Fram, wright and cabinetmaker, and John Parsell, Anderson's amanuensis and 'operator'. Without reservation, they all agreed to act on the will: the painted chest was delivered to Anderson's brother, Andrew; the will was recorded in the Books of Council and Session in Edinburgh by Wilson; Reid agreed to print 300 copies of the will; one copy and a circular letter was to go to each trustee; they examined Anderson's repositories and found £278.40p. in bank notes and gold and silver coins from which they intended to pay his debts and lodge any balance in a bank.[1]

Six days later on 22 January 1796 they met again in Anderson's house at 9 p.m. Parsell, acting as their clerk, agreed to make a fair copy of the will and codicil, probably that recorded in the first minute book of the Andersonian Institution. William Meikleham (1771-1846) and Parsell agreed to check Anderson's library against his own catalogue and to compare his furniture and apparatus with the inventories.[2] By 12 February the circular letter and an extract from the will were prepared; £58.82p was authorised as Anderson's funeral expenses, and his servant, Helen Bishop, was given £6 in lieu of wages and one guinea as travelling expenses to Edinburgh. Anderson's horse was sold, and Parsell's wages as his 'operator' paid.[3]

Notices of the first meeting of trustees and executors to be held in the Tontine Tavern on 23 March 1796 were sent out by Parsell. Thirty-nine people attended, representatives from eight classes of Anderson's trustees, as indicated in Table 2.1. No kinsmen attended, and two executors were not trustees – William Meikleham, whom Anderson had nominated as the first professor, and John Wilson, his lawyer, who was associated with the governance of the city of Glasgow and thereby debarred under the terms of the will.

Apart from the clergy, lawyers and doctors, the developing commercial and industrial structure of the city was mirrored in the attendance. Alexander Oswald (1738-1813) of Shieldhall had been a tobacco merchant before purchasing his estate in 1783 and was a partner in the South Sugar House and the Linwood Cotton Company. He and his son, James, established in 1783 the leading cotton manufacturing firm in the city. In addition, he was a leading speculator in urban

TABLE 2.1   The first meeting of Anderson's Trustees, 23 March 1796

Class	Designation	Number Attending
1	Tradesmen	5
2	Agriculturalists	7
3	Artists	5
4	Manufacturers / Merchants	6
5	Mediciners	4
6	Lawyers	4
7	Divines	2
8	Natural Philosophers	4
9	Kinsmen	0

Source: BI/I Minute Book of the Andersonian Institution, 1796-99, pp. 53-5.

land and a radical in politics.[4] David Dale jr. represented another leading firm of cotton spinners and his father was the leading yarn dealer in Scotland.[5] William Gillespie of Anderston was a large-scale bleacher, dyer and calico printer with interests in the Woodside cotton mill and a shareholding in the Royal Bank.[6] John Geddes, managing partner of the Verreville crystal glass and pottery works, was keenly interested in Natural Philosophy and Chemistry and almost certainly one of Anderson's anti-toga students and certainly shared his martial interests.[7] The most famous of the others were George Macintosh and his son, Charles, pioneers of the chemical industry in the city.[8] However, there was support from the Trades House, the Chamber of Commerce, the Faculty of Procurators and the Faculty of Physicians and Surgeons. Generally the trustees who attended this first meeting were supporters of liberal causes in the city and beyond; for instance, a substantial group favoured parliamentary reform.

The meeting resolved to carry out Anderson's wishes as far as funds allowed and agreed to raise subscriptions and donations. They elected nine managers to serve till the June meeting. These were William Lang, smith, William Scott, gardener in Gorbals, John Geddes, Hugh Cross, merchant, John Scruton, surgeon, William Marshall, writer (lawyer), Reverend James Stewart of the Relief Congregation in Anderston, James Spreul Esq. (formerly a merchant), and William Gillespie. They were empowered to find accommodation for John Anderson's furniture, library, apparatus and other effects, to arrange for a lecture room, to decide who should be the first professor after discussion with William Meikleham and to apply for a seal of cause to incorporate the trustees.[9]

Thereafter, Hugh Cross became President and, following Anderson's will, John Parsell the clerk. Jointly with the executors, the managers asked the City Council for two rooms in the Grammar School in George Street, one for Anderson's apparatus and the other for lectures. Wilson had also put in a petition for a seal of cause 'erecting the Trustees into a Body Corporate'. Both these requests were granted, and rooms on the second storey of the Grammar School were provided rent-free for a year. A committee of five was established to seek further accommodation and to discuss ways of raising funds; another group of five was responsible for removing Anderson's effects from Glasgow College. The two lawyers, Wilson and Marshall, tried to recover debts due to Anderson's estate, including a sum from Mr. Humphries of Virginia.[10]

William Meikleham had settled in as Anderson's successor at Glasgow University and therefore on 7 May indicated that he would not accept Anderson's nomination. The managers decided to seek a 'respectable Professor of Natural Philosophy', and advertisements were placed in the Glasgow, Edinburgh and London papers. A circular seeking subscriptions was drafted and

4 Dr Thomas Garnett (1766-1802), first Professor of Natural Philosophy in Anderson's Institution, 1796-99. This painting was donated to Anderson's University by James Smith F.R.S. of Jordanhill, President between 1830 and 1839 and a major benefactor. Garnett, a very able lecturer, became the first professor in the Royal Institution in 1799.

signed by the great and the good of Glasgow, headed by David Dale of New Lanark. Thus, by the time of the first annual meeting of the trustees on 21 June 1796 much had been achieved, and funds were beginning to accrue. Vacancies in the ranks of the trustees arising from resignations (17), deaths (2) and movement away from Glasgow (1) were being filled.[11] This practice of prompt replacement or election of trustees brought fresh ideas and additional vitality to the institution.

The assembled trustees elected the nine managers for the coming year, gave them permission to meet on any convenient day (Anderson had prescribed Saturdays) and heard of the search for a suitable professor, 'being satisfied that the success of this Institution depends chiefly upon getting a man of Science and of Address to fill this Office'. They discussed the question of his payment, and after the meeting twenty-seven trustees and twenty friends dined at the Star Inn in John Street 'and passed the evening with much sociality and respect in commemoration of the philanthropic Professor'.[12]

By 2 July 1796 the managers were meeting in the library of the Andersonian Institution, as they had agreed to call it. Hugh Cross was re-elected President, Dr. John Scruton became Secretary and James McIlquham of Anderston, cotton merchant and manufacturer (but in Anderson's agriculturalist class), treasurer. Three relatively long-lived committees were established: Hugh Cross and Peter Wright were to be jointly in charge of the museum; James Monteath and John Geddes to be responsible for the apparatus, assisted by James Crighton and James Fram; Scruton and Reverend James Stewart were to review the advertisement and the further particulars relating to the professorship. Subscription forms had been printed by William Reid and placed in the Tontine and Star, in the Royal Bank and in the Andersonian library.[13]

During the summer the managers decided to appoint Dr Thomas Garnett (1766-1802) as their first professor.[14] Garnett, a pupil-apprentice of the celebrated John Dawson, surgeon and apothecary at Sedbergh, where he had been at school, graduated from the University of Edinburgh in 1788 and pursued a career of physician, scientist and itinerant lecturer. Recommended by Dr Duncan of Edinburgh and Dr Thomas Percival F.R.S., of Manchester for his 'private character and professional abilities', Garnett discussed salary and 'accommodations' before accepting the post on 12 September, 1796; he was to be paid £200 for teaching in the winter and spring from 1 November to 1 May. These arrangements were confirmed by the plenary meeting of the trustees on 21 September.[15]

Garnett duly arrived in Glasgow on 19 October and was temporarily ensconced in a house in Duke Street which the managers had earlier rented at £27 per year to accommodate John Anderson's effects. His classes were swiftly advertised in the local press. The first was a course of lectures 'on Arts and Manufactures' connected with Natural Philosophy and Chemistry and illustrated by working models and experiments; manufacturing processes, such as bleaching, dyeing, calico-printing, etching, engraving, and metallurgy, were to be demonstrated. This class was to meet in the hall of the institution (which would hold at least 150 students) in the 'New Grammar School Buildings' in George Street, daily at 8.30 a.m. beginning on Tuesday, 8 November, 1796. The second class followed Anderson's wishes precisely: 'A Popular Course of Lectures on Natural and Experimental Philosophy', in which 'abstract mathematical reasoning will be as much as possible avoided'. There were to be copious experiments and demonstrations, 'the whole calculated to afford at once instruction and entertainment to those whose occupations have not allowed leisure for investigating these subjects, and to refresh the memories of those who have'. This class was to be held weekly in the Trades Hall beginning on 8 November at 8 p.m. Garnett's third offering was a 'Popular' Chemistry class, illustrated by experiments and also held in the Trades Hall on Fridays at 8 p.m. beginning on 11 November. All these classes were to last till early May 1797.

Following the wishes of John Anderson and the managers, the last two classes were open to women, and the transferable class tickets were intended for a lady and a gentleman or for two ladies. The fee structure was relatively simple: the first class cost two guineas, and the other two, one guinea each. Anyone wishing to attend all three classes was offered a discounted fee of three guineas. The main objective was to educate young men for industry and commerce but also to provide a liberal education in science.[16]

The first session went well. The Trades Hall cost £31.50 to rent, and Garnett more than covered this from receipts for his general introductory lecture, given on 26 October, which produced £36.35. By the end of the session 972 students (about half of whom were women) had attended the three classes, the popular evening classes naturally attracting most, and this figure was 'exclusive of many visiting strangers'. The support from women, Garnett found particularly gratifying: he was personally committed to the educational emancipation of women; the Andersonian was 'the first regular institution in which the fair sex have been admitted ... on the same footing as men' and this represented ' ... an era in the annals of female education'.[17]

Much of this success was due to Garnett, who was at the height of his powers as a lecturer. He was largely responsible for implementing a curriculum for which John Anderson had provided the broad guidelines. The managers were very reliant on his advice and skill, and Garnett was regularly invited to their meetings. His aptitudes and interests closely resembled those of Anderson, and Garnett recognised that in two particular ways: he constantly referred, as did the trustees, to Anderson's will as the source of academic authority and he clearly intended to make Anderson's ideas and work more widely available through publication.

Anderson's executry took an eternity to settle. Much of the early income went to meet his debts, and thus the financial picture was more clouded than the academic vista. Yet the managers were sufficiently impressed with Garnett's commitment to allow him to live rent-free till May 1797. For the second session, 1797-8, he continued on a salary of £200 with the possibility of a performance-related bonus, once fee income was known.[18]

Academic diversification was also mooted. Reverend Robert Lothian, Anderson's nominee for the Chair of Mathematics and currently a teacher in the city, offered to teach Mathematics. This conflicted with Garnett's wish to teach the subject 'for his own emolument'. The managers prevailed upon him to offer one additional practical class in Chemistry for two nights a week instead, from which he would receive half the fee income. Meantime Lothian's offer was not accepted.[19]

Student attendance in 1797-8 declined to about 500, and the trustees were told of the likelihood of a deficit. By March 1798 a change to Garnett's terms of employment had become imperative because of a shortage of funds. Two options were touted: Garnett could receive the net proceeds of his lecture fees after all expenses had been met or a fixed salary of £100 and half the net income. Garnett did not find either alternative attractive and agreed that he would wait till income and expenditure for 1798-9 were known before agreeing his salary. The managers lacked the funds to mount the following year's classes, and therefore sought the approval of the trustees before accepting Garnett's generous offer.[20]

Financial constraints had earlier in 1796 caused the managers to reject overtures from John Burnside who tried to sell them the disused flesh market in John Street next to the Star Inn for 1,000 guineas. However, they knew that they needed more space. The March 1797 meeting of the trustees was told that a group of friends of the institution were keen to provide a building which they hoped to convey at some future date at a reasonable price or rental.[21] They were

5 Dr George Birkbeck (1776-1841), the second Professor of Natural Philosophy in Anderson's Institution, 1799-1804. This portrait was commissioned by the Mechanics' Class in 1823 and is now in the possession of the University of Strathclyde. Birkbeck, a pioneer of Mechanics' Institutes, went into private practice in London but continued to support adult education in the capital; hence his name was given to Birkbeck College.

interested in the 'fleshmarket', a large building, recently built as a speculation by Robert Smith on the west side of John Street, and completed its purchase from Fullarton, Hamilton and Company on 26 September 1798 for £1,520.

Twelve trustees had combined resources to make this purchase – William McNeil, a merchant and President in 1798-1802, William Gillespie, Alexander Oswald, President in 1797-8, Alexander Allan, a merchant, John Semple, bleacher of Finnieston, John Geddes, Robert Thomson jr., cotton manufacturer, John Pattison (1747-1807) of Kelvingrove, cotton spinner and merchant, Andrew Clarke, merchant, and three doctors, James Monteath, William Anderson and William Nimmo. This partnership launched a share issue of £2,000 made up of 100 shares at £20 each, offering a maximum dividend of five per cent or less to be covered by the Andersonian's income.[22] Thus, private speculation in urban land served a wider educational interest.

The size of the new premises made renting it to outsiders relatively simple. The congregation of the Relief Church – which was being built in John Street – required a temporary Sunday meeting place till their church was finished and paid a rent of two guineas a week. In addition, class numbers began to recover. By 6 December 1798 Garnett reported that he had received £170 for class tickets and another £10-15 was outstanding. Lothian, who had been allowed to lecture in Mathematics and Geography, had collected another £86.[23]

Soon afterwards Garnett suffered a devastating personal loss: his wife died in childbirth at Christmas.[24] Despite the emotional turmoil which this tragedy naturally produced, Garnett persisted with the second quarter in the New Year. He lost Parsell, who felt that he could obtain a better post elsewhere, and appointed as his second 'operator' a Mr Steel at a salary of £20.[25] In June 1799 he proposed to offer a new course in session 1799-1800, 'The Philosophy of Natural History', about the evolution of the earth; but the managers, sensing the possibility of a clash with Lothian, decided to defer a decision about its implementation. The trustees at first favoured Garnett and then, by a majority of only one, reversed their decision. Although they were unable to provide him with the security of a fixed salary, the managers and trustees were limiting the possibility of improving his income. Garnett had also considered returning to private practice as a doctor, but ultimately favoured a move elsewhere. After dallying in Newcastle lecturing to the Literary and Philosophical Society in the summer of 1799, Garnett accepted the remunerative Chair of Experimental Philosophy, Mechanics and Chemistry in the new Royal Institution, proffered his resignation to the managers of the Andersonian on 15 October, 1799 and moved to London.[26]

Garnett recommended Dr. George Birkbeck (1776-1841), a young Yorkshire Quaker who had recently graduated in Edinburgh, and also a pupil of the remarkable John Dawson of Sedbergh. Birkbeck was favoured by the managers, who received references from Dugald Stewart and John Playfair, but was only one of several candidates put to the trustees. They elected him by a majority of twenty-two. Birkbeck arrived in Glasgow in early December and quickly accepted the existing curricula and classes.[27] Revenue declined during Birkbeck's first quarter to £181.95, and most of this was spent on new apparatus.[28] However, in March 1800 he came forward with his own plans for the morning and evening classes for the following session and also offered an extra class for working tradesmen on 'mechanic power' free to students.[29] This was not the first class to admit mechanics and artisans – as Birkbeck later claimed – for Anderson and other Glasgow professors had 'anti-toga' classes earlier. Parsell, Anderson's amanuensis and operator, knew from personal experience that Anderson had taught mechanics and often dispensed free class tickets, and W.G. (probably William Gardner) analysed Anderson's class registers and found many examples of craftsmen from widely differing trades

TABLE 2.2   Trustees' Gifts and Loans, 1803

Designation	Class	Number of Donors	Gifts £	Loans £
Tradesmen	1	2	2.10	10
Agriculturalists	2	4	5.25	10
Artists	3	4	7.35	20
Manufacturers / Merchants	4	4	5.25	120
Mediciners	5	7	10.50	20
Lawyers	6	1	1.05	
Divines	7	5	5.25	
Nat. Philosophers	8	8	10.50	
Kinsmen	9	5	6.30	20
Total			53.55	200

Source: B1/2 Minute Book of the Andersonian Institution, 1799-1810, pp. 76-8.

being taught in the 'anti-toga' class. Before any controversy arose about the origins of mechanics' institutes, it was declared in 1806 by those who knew Anderson well that he had given lectures to artisans 'for many years previous to his death'.[30] What was new – and did not last long – was that Birkbeck's Mechanics' Class was free.

Birkbeck was clearly not impressed with the state of the Andersonian's apparatus; hence much of the revenue was consumed in making good deficiencies. After a faltering start the Mechanics' Class became a great success with about 500 in attendance.[31] Whether it was because the class was free, or because Birkbeck demonstrated great skills as a teacher, or a combination of both these characteristics, will never be satisfactorily settled. Recollections years later do not provide the sure ground that judgement would require.

In April 1801 Anderson's executors lent the institution £100, and the deficit on the session was only £47.74p with some income outstanding. However, this accounting made no reference to paying Birkbeck. His first salary instalment was £100, paid early in May and raised by the managers from their own pockets, and the new managers elected in June were enjoined to find another £100. In the September Steel resigned as 'operator', and James Kessen, a joiner and cabinetmaker, became Birkbeck's assistant.[32]

When Birkbeck reported on the 1801-2 session, he commented that the subscription tickets sold with a life of five years had just expired and that receipts were only £132. Yet great economy had been practised, and Kessen had worked well. Particularly gratifying was the attendance at the 'operatives' class; over 500 had attended with 'striking regularity, good order, with the most ardent attention'. Entry was no longer free: a nominal 5p was charged for each ticket, and since income from this class was £24.50p, a paying audience of 490 is indicated. The fee for this class rose to 25p in 1802-3, and by then Birkbeck had extended his classes: there were two morning chemistry classes and a new class in elementary Geography and Astronomy, and modifications to the Mechanics' Class.[33]

On 22 December 1802 Birkbeck gave a progress report to the trustees: the popular class in Natural Philosophy was better attended than in the previous session, but the numbers for Chemistry and Geography were disappointing, and in the latter subject fewer young people had attended than expected. Total receipts from class tickets were much the same, but he was hopeful of an improvement in the second quarter. Expenditure had been restrained by the good state of the apparatus and day-to-day economy.[34]

Accumulating debt was a major problem for the managers and trustees at this juncture. At the beginning of the session total debts had reached £260. Alexander Oswald offered to lend £100 and suggested that each trustee be asked to lend £10 to eliminate debt and provide working capital. In this context it is not surprising that the mechanics should be expected to pay something for their class. Oswald's offer was accepted; eight other managers offered £10 each, and the trustees were circulated for gifts of any size and/or loans of £10 or more. A revaluation of the Institution's apparatus produced a value of £339.12p. When in May 1803 the managers received the annual accounts, all current costs had been met from revenue, and Birkbeck had received a salary of £140 but was owed £87.40p 'for former labours'. By then, as Table 2.2 reveals, the trustees had subscribed £200 in loans and £56.70 in donations, about sixty per cent from the two classes, merchants and manufacturers (Class 4) and mediciners (Class 5).[35]

The short-lived Peace of Amiens gave way to a renewal of hostilities with France and a clouded economic horizon. The managers, headed by John Geddes, a colonel in the Glasgow Volunteers, submitted a loyal address to George III which included the following:

> While the Students who attend this Seminary are instructed in arts and sciences, the Professors will not fail to inculcate in their minds loyalty to their King, love to their Country, and submission to the Laws.[36]

The economic downturn had its deadly effects upon the academic session 1803-4. When Birkbeck gave his usual progress report on 21 December 1803, he admitted that attendance at the Chemistry lectures had been abysmal and, therefore, the course had been discontinued; the classes in Geography, Astronomy and Natural History were continuing but with poor attendances; the popular class in Natural Philosophy and the Mechanics' Class were better attended, but numbers were lower than in earlier sessions. By March 1804 the Chemistry class had been restarted and was being attended by forty 'Ladies and Gentlemen'. Total receipts to that date were only £135.65p.[37]

The managers respected Birkbeck's efforts and were sorry that they could not pay him better. Although his family provided him with sufficient income to make his salary simply an extra, Birkbeck was looking for a more secure post with better prospects. This the managers suspected, and therefore they instructed the Secretary on 4 April 1804 to find out his intentions. Birkbeck was at first indecisive in his response and indicated that since he could not think of better ways of increasing attendances and, therefore, revenue and because 'the Institution cannot afford a very considerable remuneration to the Professor', he wanted to develop a career as a physician as well as giving lectures. By July he had still not made up his mind, and they decided to give him till the trustees' meeting on 9 August 1804. On 5 August he resigned and left on what seemed cordial terms.

These did not persist. Birkbeck went to Birmingham to give lectures and wanted Kessen to work for him for a lengthy period. At first the Secretary of the Andersonian had given Kessen permission, thinking that only a few weeks' leave was required; then this decision was countermanded. Birkbeck was clearly angry in consequence, but Kessen had been appointed on 2 July 1804 to act as clerk to the managers as well as 'operator' to the professor and could not be spared for a longer period. This misunderstanding soured relationships and makes Birkbeck's later stance of private and public attacks upon the managers in the 1820s and 1830s intelligible.[38]

Three candidates presented themselves in answer to wide advertisement of the vacancy, one of them a trustee, Dr James Corkindale. Corkindale had completed a medical degree at Edinburgh and also studied Languages and an Arts curriculum in Glasgow. A fine scholar who had won first prizes in almost every class, he had particularly distinguished himself in

6 A pencil sketch (by an unknown artist) of Dr Andrew Ure F.R.S. (1778-1857), Professor of Natural Philosophy in Anderson's Institution, 1804-30. Ure was particularly interested in the application of science to industry and became a major eulogist of the factory system in classic works which are still quoted. After 1830 he moved to London and became a consultant.

Mathematics and Natural Philosophy. A student of John Anderson, Corkindale had also studied Chemistry for five years in Edinburgh and London. In Edinburgh he had been President for two years of the Royal Medical Society and of the Natural History Society, offices in which he was the immediate successor of George Birkbeck. His main rival was Dr Andrew Ure (1778-1857) who was, in fact, successful on 21 September 1804 in obtaining the post mainly because of his superior 'Talent for public speaking'. Both men had excellent references and on account of their residence in Glasgow were well-known to the trustees. Corkindale became an outstanding physician and continued to serve the Andersonian as a trustee and later as a manager.[39]

Ure had an excellent reputation as a chemist and was employed on the basis of receiving fee income but paying a rent for his lecture theatre and the operator's wages and other expenses. He very rapidly prepared his lecture programme. The Natural Philosophy class was to meet on Tuesdays and Fridays in accordance with 'an arrangement nearly the same as the Course formerly delivered by the Founder of the Institution', and Anderson's *Institutes* was to be the set text. The Chemistry class was to be held every Monday, Wednesday and Thursday at 8 p.m. The course for 'operative mechanics' was to begin in January. By the end of 1804 Ure was reporting reasonable progress, and in March 1805 fee income was £194.50p.[40]

Ure's strategy was unashamedly to attract a wealthy audience in the hope that 'the leading families in Glasgow' would ' ... take an interest in its success'. Varying the content from year to year was important and a popular teaching style essential:

> Further as Science no longer wears the repulsive and gloomy garb of ancient times it will be Doctor Ure's endeavour to exhibit her in these forms which may be calculated to amuse and fascinate.[41]

He was always ready to complain. The backlog of subscribers' tickets impeded the growth of revenue; his interest in the Mechanics' Class was at best lukewarm and his provocative commitment to *laisser faire* and the unqualified merits of the factory system likely to alienate skilled artisans, committed to unions, factory regulation and higher wages. Ure's attempt to interest industrialists and their skilled employees in Chemistry and Physics and his summer vacation visits to the great English factories were eminently praiseworthy and were gradually repaid by rising fee income. For 1805-6 revenue was about £250, eighty per cent of which came from the Natural Philosophy class.[42]

In 1805 Andrew Oswald was once again President and offered the building to the trustees for £2,000: £1,000 had been provided by fifty subscribers who wanted permanent class tickets for their money and the other £1,000 was available as a loan against the security of the property. This offer was accepted by the trustees in June 1806.[43] More details of this financial arrangement occur in 1809. The list of shareholders was heavily dominated by industrialists: the Gillespies of Anderston and Woodside, bleachers and cotton spinners, Henry Monteith, manufacturer and dyer, Robert Thomson jr. of Camphill, cotton manufacturer, Henry Houldsworth of Anderston mills and foundry, Hugh Baird, maltster and engineer of Port Dundas, John Geddes of Verreville glassworks, Charles Tennant of St Rollox chemical works and his partner, James Knox, John and James Robertson, engineers, who were to build the engine for Henry Bell's *Comet*. There was also a sprinkling of doctors and a group of merchants such as James Spreul and Walter Logan. Forty-two trustees took £20 shares which gave each of them a ticket for two, and Richard Oswald and five others took a £40 share and doubled their entitlement to tickets. Thus, in 1809 fifty-four permanent tickets were in circulation representing 108 student places.[44] The loan of £1,000 was raised on bond from Miss Coulter's estate.[45]

Meanwhile, further progress was made. Attendances at the Natural Philosophy classes continued to increase, and the Mechanics' Class was also impressive in the commitment demonstrated: 'Their Deportment during the Lectures would do Honour to the most polite audience in Great Britain'.[46] In 1806-7 Ure removed Pharmacy from his Chemistry course because he had started a supplementary morning lecture series concentrating on pharmacy and physiology. This was intended for medical students and was a direct consequence of the appointment of Dr John Burns (1775-1850) in June 1800 to lecture on the Principles of Surgery and also on Midwifery and women and children's diseases. A surgeon of some distinction, Burns retained his dissecting room in College Street, but as Anderson's nominee he represented the beginning of a significant academic diversification. He was well regarded by the main examining body, the Faculty of Physicians and Surgeons of Glasgow, which was prepared to accept Ure's certificates of attendance and performance for the new class.[47]

The depression of trade following Napoleon's protectionist decrees of Berlin and Milan and the Orders in Council badly hit classes in the Andersonian. Attendance at the Mechanics' Class was halved in 1807-8, although there were 'Numerous and genteel Audiences' for the other courses. A reading room and Mechanics' Library was created, and trustees were generous with gifts of books and periodicals. Among the 170 attending the Natural Philosophy class were 50 women. By 1809 the managers were co-operating with Glasgow Astronomical Society: the Society wanted to meet in the Andersonian, and the observatory which was being built was freely used by Ure.[48]

Printed attendance certificates for Chemistry students were added to those provided to medical students; the latter were being signed by Ure and countersigned by doctors among the managers.[49] Ure believed that a Mathematics class was necessary to support the other science classes and recommended John Cross, 'an eminent Mathematician' whom he was prepared to pay. Cross was appointed to teach Mathematics and Geography in January 1811 and began in the summer: Junior Mathematics daily from 12 to 2 pm; Senior Maths 10 to 11 am; and Geography 5 to 6 pm, 'The class for Young Ladies' being on separate days from that for boys. Geography had been closely associated with Mathematics because of its physical dimension, but Ure envisaged that Cross would make it the basis for developing transferable skills:

> The Geography Class is intended to Comprise a compleatly new System of education, particularly directed to teach young persons accuracy of thought, and propriety of diction, at the same time as they acquire a knowledge of the surface of our Globe, and its productions animate and inanimate. Peculiar pains will be taken with the Boys to explain the Commercial and Manufacturing relations between Great Britain, her Colonies and the various Regions of the Earth.

Clearly, these emphases had practical significance in the education of a commercial, maritime and industrial élite. The summer Maths class also had a strong practical element, including surveying and navigation as well as standard mensuration.[50]

James Cleland, the Superintendent of Works for the City and author and social statistician, became President in 1811 and immediately encountered cash-flow problems with the onset of the American War of 1812.[51] However, class sizes did recover, and accounts were gradually settled. Cross's appointment by the managers and his payment by Ure were adjudged improper by the trustees, intent on clinging to the letter of Anderson's will. The first of several disputes between Ure and other members of staff raised this question. Ure wanted total control of the building for his room rent was £100, and any clash of hours he deemed as being to his detriment. He was also seeking a fixed salary which the managers could not provide and therefore was actively seeking other posts between 1813 and 1815. He also disputed the terms of his original appointment. To settle this question and hopefully to placate Ure, in 1816 the managers agreed to arrange a new contract. He was given his classroom rent-free, and his operator was paid by the managers as was the cost of advertising his classes.[52]

Some revenue had been earned by day letting of parts of the building. For instance, the hall was used on Sundays by Neil Douglas on a two-year lease. Douglas had a respectable radical pedigree: he was a former member of the British Convention and an ardent republican; in 1816-17 he was a preacher of the Universalist sect, 'old, deaf, dogged, honest, and respectable', hot on denouncing George III and the Prince Regent, 'a poor infatuated devotee of Bacchus'. For these and similar sentiments in various 'prayers, sermons and declamations' he was tried at Edinburgh for sedition in late May 1817 but unanimously found not guilty.[53] The Andersonian managers attempted to give him notice but failed.[54]

In March 1816 Dr William Cummin was appointed Professor of Botany on an annual basis but soon ran into trouble with Ure who actually interrupted his class in April 1817, involving the managers in yet another demarcation dispute. Botany class times were fixed on Monday, Wednesday and Friday at 8 a.m. and 3 p.m. Other lectures in Law and Elocution were given in 1817 by James Galloway and John Crosbie respectively, but no appointments were made; the lecturers added to the revenue of the Andersonian by paying room rents.[55]

Dr. John Burns, Professor of Anatomy and Surgery, resigned to become Professor in the University of Glasgow in 1817, and Granville Sharp Pattison (1791-1851) applied to succeed him. Pattison, the son of a deceased trustee, John Pattison (1747-1807) of Kelvingrove, was a raffish character, perhaps a consequence of his interest in Anatomy. He had been in 1809 an associate of Allan Burns, the brother of John, who had been debarred from the profession of anatomist for grave-robbing. In the College Street Medical School Pattison was a popular teacher and surgeon, a member in 1813 of the Faculty of Physicians and Surgeons of Glasgow by examination and probably the active leader of student grave-robbers intent on obtaining subjects for practical anatomy. In 1814 Pattison had been tried for grave-robbing; the circumstantial evidence was very strong, but the verdict was not proven. He returned to the College Street Medical School and became its leading light and sole owner of its museum. In addition, he held an appointment at the Royal Infirmary but in 1816 quarrelled with Hugh Miller, the senior staff surgeon, and was censured by its managers.[56]

Pattison intended to concentrate on teaching and specialist surgery after his appointment in 1818 to the Andersonian, but the trustees were certainly taking a risk. In the summer months he visited medical schools in France, Germany and Italy, the pioneers of advanced surgery. On his return he prepared a popular course of lectures in Anatomy which was the cause of some concern to Ure who was using the same lecture theatre for Chemistry and thought his students might be affronted by the sight of anatomical specimens. Pattison's class was fixed for three evenings a week and he undertook to remove the specimens promptly. Ure even thought of using his own house for Chemistry lectures but found that his tack did not allow this. Compelled to be away from his home and wife at times known to Pattison, Ure was at a considerable disadvantage. Pattison certainly found Ure's wife, Catherine, attractive and regularly visited her in her husband's absence. She became pregnant and confessed to Ure that she had committed adultery with Pattison. Ure thereupon sued her for divorce, naming Pattison as adulterer.[57]

On 15 April 1819 the notarial extract of the Decreet of Divorce obtained by Andrew Ure against his wife, Catherine, arrived at the Andersonian for quiet consideration by the managers. Each of them read it in turn and returned it to John Geddes, the President. At their next meeting on 6 May they had a full discussion and 'were unanimously of opinion that it demands there [sic] interference'. A copy of this minute was sent to Granville Sharp Pattison at his house in George Square, and he was asked to appear before them on 13 May at 6 p.m. He responded in a letter dated 8 May but not delivered till 11 May, offering his resignation: 'I cannot bear that my name should be associated with Dr Ure's in any institution'. He claimed that there had been collusion between Ure and his wife to obtain a divorce, proclaimed his own innocence but did not specifically deny adultery. Although his resignation made it unnecessary for the managers to sack Pattison or to comment further on the Ure divorce case, they clearly did not believe him, and neither did the divorce court; the managers formally expressed 'their abhorrence of his conduct' and declared 'that he is unfit and ineligible ever to hold any position in this Institution'. The trustees, never content to rubber stamp decisions of the managers, significantly approved unanimously of their treatment of Pattison.[58] And so Pattison left Scotland for a tempestuous and brilliant career in London and the United States.[59]

Applications for his vacant chair were sought, replies circulated, and ultimately William Mackenzie (1791-1868) was appointed on 6 October, 1819. Mackenzie had been practising in London and submitted certificates as to his abilities from eminent London surgeons and Professor Beer of Vienna; he held the diploma of the Royal College of Surgeons of London and earlier had worked at the London Eye Infirmary and at the Royal Infirmary in Glasgow. One of the most distinguished ophthalmologists of the nineteenth century and a major author in this field, Mackenzie was co-founder with George Monteath (1788-1828) of the Glasgow Eye Infirmary in 1824.[60] However, he had trouble immediately with Ure about a possible clash of lecturing hours since both thought beginning at 8 p.m. was best for their classes. Mackenzie decided to begin his lectures in May 1820 when Ure's class had finished.[61]

When Ure reported on his classes in December 1819, he remarked that student numbers had been declining for several years till the current session because of the double-occupancy of the hall by the anatomists and himself: 'The Ladies ... constitute a larger proportion of the Class than they have done for any season during the last fourteen'. The previous winter the class had disintegrated by December, 'relieved from the horror and disgust of putrid dissections and human Anatomy', which the ladies found particularly repulsive. The popular Chemistry class had eighty students, 'a large number considering the commercial depression of Glasgow at present'.[62] In the spring of 1821 James Galloway began his Law course on feudal conveyancing and on rights and deeds of heritable property, using the hall at 8 a.m. on three days per week and paying ten guineas in rent.[63]

The following session saw unrest in the Mechanics' Class. This group had its own committee of twelve empowered to negotiate with the managers. A memorial of 19 January, 1822 referred to problems with their library and 'certain models' which had been constructed by members of the class. A room behind the class library for models and apparatus was set aside, and managers and class committee agreed that 'in no case whatever shall the Mechanics' class, their apparatus and Library ever be separated from the general management of Anderson's Institution'. This pious statement disguised the distrust the class felt towards Ure who was inclined to treat them cavalierly, and this led the mechanics to seek formalistic agreements which the Professor was inclined to ignore unless pressed by the managers. By March 1822 the agreement set out many particulars which Ure found irksome. The mechanics appointed a subcommittee of four to communicate directly with the managers about Ure's class. He was to provide fifty lectures between November and May on Saturday evenings at 8 p.m. '& such other night as shall be fixed by the managers'. The class fee of 50p was to be collected by the subcommittee; 40p was to go to Ure and 10p remain with the treasurer of the Mechanics' Class for approved expenditure on books and apparatus. For every hundred tickets sold, five apprentices over the age of fourteen were to be admitted to the lectures free.[64]

A fresh agreement was necessary in October 1822. Fee payments were made easier since an

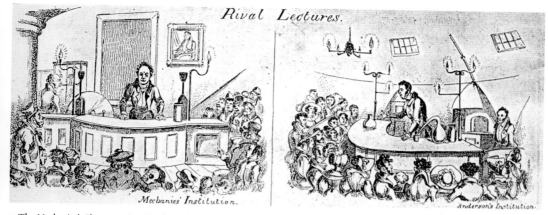

7 The Mechanics' Class was riven by discord, much of it provoked by Ure, and in 1823 one group left to form the Glasgow Mechanics' Institution, the first in Britain. This cartoon, 'Rival Lectures', appeared in *The Northern Looking Glass* in 1825. The artist clearly thought that the better provision and audience were at Anderson's Institution.

instalment plan was introduced, thus putting the class within the reach of anyone able to pay half-a-day's wages four times a year. All those who attended the class for five sessions were eligible, for an annual fee of $12\frac{1}{2}$ p, to be admitted to the library and museum. More regulations did not deal with the basic problem of Ure's attitude to the class and his unwillingness to negotiate with them. On 20 April 1823 matters came to a head. The managers listened at great length to the complaints made by the class committee and Ure's responses to them. Afterwards, they decided 'to terminate and quash all further discussion on the subject, as tending to no good'. They insisted that they had the best interests of the class at heart, would abide by the signed agreements and would not allow irrelevant matters to be introduced into the course.[65]

The managers claimed that they had no wish to interfere in how the class administered its affairs, but there were signs that they did not like the solidarity or organisation which the mechanics deployed. In turn, the mechanics were sensitive – perhaps over-sensitive – to what they believed to be condescension and paternalism. More widely, the skilled working classes in Glasgow in the 1820s were intent on controlling their workplaces, and so why should an élite of them not attempt to control their own education, especially when they were paying for it?

On 3 July 1823 the committee called a plenary meeting of the Mechanics' Class; the class split, one part remaining with the Andersonian and the other deciding to establish the Glasgow Mechanics' Institution. In this schism Birkbeck played his part, encouraging the class to take control of their own education and agreeing to be patron. On 5 November 1823 John Steele of Paisley began the first lectures in the new institution, and 600 tickets were sold. But debt accumulated over the next few years, and George Birkbeck was prevailed upon to lend £200. Fees were kept low and costs were generally fixed; the depression of 1826 cut attendance, revenue, and lecturers' earnings. Numbers never did return to those of the first session during the period up to 1830.[66]

Those who remained in the Andersonian's Mechanics' Class still quarrelled with Andrew Ure. In 1825 he was proposing to sell some apparatus and they disputed his right to do so. The managers met yet another delegation from the class and asked Ure to respond to their complaints; like the class they wanted the professor to provide a proper course with the appropriate apparatus to support it. Ure was dilatory in making an adequate response to this attack and eventually knuckled down, promising to revive his Mechanics' Class 'and give such a course of illustrations as shall not be equalled in Glasgow'. He would provide chemicals and apparatus as necessary and refrain from comments which 'may have tended to produce irritation in the class'. His adversaries were temporarily satisfied but they did not trust his good nature. The managers agreed that their case against Ure should remain on record till he proved that he intended to deliver his side of the bargain.[67]

Co-operation at this level produced worthwhile results. In the summer of 1826 some members of the Mechanics' Class assisted the managers' Committee on Apparatus to number and arrange properly the Institution's collection; this consisted of 434 complete pieces of apparatus of which one half were for the Mechanics' Class.[68] Student numbers in Ure's classes did not match his expectations; in 1827-8 his total fee income was about £150: 'I regret very much having opened my class this Season, as my time and professional talents, by which my family are to be maintained, will be consumed without any remuneration'.[69]

On 14 November, 1828 and on several occasions in 1829 the managers learned of further trouble between Ure and the Mechanics' Class. Their patience was virtually exhausted. The Secretary was instructed to prepare an *aide mémoire* of past and present cases involving Ure where they had felt it necessary to intervene; they also wanted to know about the present state of his classes and what were the likely causes of declining student numbers in his academic areas with suggested 'remedies'. An offensive letter complaining of 'extortion' and inadequate apparatus arrived from Ure on 22 December, 1829; they called him in, and he agreed to retract.[70] One method of solving the problem was to limit Ure's responsibilities. In the spring of 1830 the managers decided to create two posts, one the chair in Natural Philosophy, which Ure had held, and the other a new chair in 'Scientific Chemistry' into which they expected him to move. After accepting this change in May, Ure resigned in a one-sentence letter the following September.[71] His service had been long but increasingly acrimonious; yet he had published a *Dictionary of Chemistry* (1821), translated Berthollet's classic on dyeing (1825), applied an electric shock to a dead body to assess its effect and prepared notes for two major publications – his *The Philosophy of Manufactures* (1835) and *The Dictionary of Arts, Manufactures and Mines* (1837), both significant milestones in the intellectual progress of industrial capitalism. He went off to London to become a technical consultant.[72]

Finance was a central concern throughout the early decades of the Andersonian's history, but the value of its property was appreciating. Total non-academic income in 1818 was £175 per year and expenditure about £100: 'the Institution, if not very flourishing, is at least independent'. The managers thought the property could be improved and

> ... [the] liberal intentions of the founder ... promoted, if by a more profitable application of the property, the means could be found of extending the branches of public education in the institution and meeting the demand for more varied modes of instruction, which the increased wealth population and curiosity of this city every year exhibits.[73]

Discussions about the possibility of a new building followed. Other expenditure was curtailed; the Glasgow Gas Company connected the Andersonian to the mains supply and initially promised free gas for a period 'as a small tribute from the Company to the Institution'. This generosity may reflect the fact that James Beaumont Neilson (1792-1865), the manager, had received his scientific education at the Andersonian.[74]

Plans had been prepared 'for erecting three stories above the present ground story [sic]' which would occupy the whole front of John Street up to George Street. These plans were revised and refined, and estimates prepared by 'a very scientific respectable architect, and practical builder'. The idea of creating a building fund was aired and successful application for building consent made to the Dean of Guild Court.[75] In the winter months of 1818-19 a list of 'branches of

Education for which it appeared there was an effectual demand' was made and likely fee income assessed. Decisions about disciplines to be launched needed to be made so that the interior of the new building could be properly planned. To raise the necessary funds the trustees decided to circulate two subscription lists, one for donations to the building fund and the other for holders of debentures of not less than £25 each, secured on the property, transferable, and bearing five per cent interest, chargeable on the funds of the Andersonian.[76]

A specialist group of managers and trustees acted as a building committee, discussed changes in the plans and planned negotiations with the Star Inn proprietor about selling a servitude and with the Bank of Scotland about land needed for the extension. They intended to pay off the present bond due to Miss Coulter's estate (£1,000); the new building with land would cost £4,000 and apparatus and furnishings another £1,000. They calculated that 240 debenture-holders were needed, each contributing £25; the interest charge of £300 would be easily met from the annual rents of the cellars and ground floor, income from casual lets and from room rents paid by the professors.[77]

The resumption of gold payments in 1819 and dear money policies drove this scenario over the horizon; Scotland was gripped by radical fervour, and some thought a revolution inevitable. The managers tightened the Institution's belt, and one of the trustees, Reverend Dr. John Lockhart, minister of Blackfriars Church, was asked to persuade his son not to insist on the instant repayment of £1,000 due to Miss Coulter's estate.[78] The surplus funds from John Anderson's executry, £40, were finally added to the Institution's balance in June 1821.[79]

It was not till December 1823 that the new building committee was revived. Lockhart's bond was taken over by a private bank in September 1824; James Andrew Anderson (1785-1863), John Anderson's nephew and President (1824-30), later to be the first manager of the Union Bank, and leading banking spokesman, arranged this.[80] The short history and constitution of the Andersonian which appeared in 1825 was probably intended to raise shareholders' interest, but that boom rapidly collapsed. However, the Bank of Scotland was interested in the John Street property, and in 1826 this was valued at £5,000. A sale to the Bank was only feasible if the old Grammar School and additional ground on George Street was available for purchase, so that a new building could be erected.[81]

Satisfactory bargains were made: the Bank paid £5,000, and the old Grammar School was bought for £3,000. By March 1828 the plans for the new building were complete, and the foundations for an extension to the Grammar School were being laid along George Street. Robert Scott and James Watt were the architects and the main contractors; Bennet and Smith were engaged for the plumbing; the slating contract went to James Donaldson and the smithwork to William Lang and Son. The mason employed was James Gray and the wright was James Anderson.[82]

When the trustees met on 22 September, 1828, they decided to adopt the name 'Anderson's University' from the time that they occupied the new George Street building; they felt that this was consistent with the will of John Anderson.[83] The building was still unfinished in November, and the managers were calculating that they would need to borrow £2,500 on the property. However, in March 1829 they had a net deposit of £1,940 with the Bank of Scotland arising from the sale of the old building. In June 1829 the building was virtually complete, although the interior still required work. An Ionic portico of Robert Scott's design had been added to improve the appearance of the building; the previous practice of listing the teachers on a board at the entrance was not continued.[84]

After the dust had settled on the building work, their cost to April 1830 was £7,100, and raising a loan of £3,500 was being considered. Scott, the architect presented his final bill for ten

TABLE 2.3   New Building, 1828-31

Item	Cost (£)	Comment
Grammar School	3,000	
Conversion	500	Includes Portico
Extensions	4,700	£300 for old dome
Museum	800	
Total	9,000	

Sources: SUA, B10/1 Anderson University Report, 1832, p.4; T.A. Markus, 'Domes of Enlightenment: Two Scottish University Museums', *Art History*, Vol.8, No.2 (June, 1985), p.175.

guineas and indicated that he regarded this as his subscription to the new museum which had not then been started. James Smith F.R.S. of Jordanhill, a very wealthy *rentier*, whose family had accumulated wealth through West and East Indian trade, was a fervent supporter of the museum project and produced the first sketches of what it would look like on 7 April, 1830. It was to have a great dome with a gallery containing the library within a semi-circular extension which also included 'The Saloon', and two additional rooms. Built to the centre rear of the George Street building and using the dome from the John Street building, it was completed ready for the official opening on 22 March, 1831, after which a celebration dinner was held.[85] The total costs are set out in Table 2.3.

From 1824 onwards the free-enterprise curriculum offered by lectures at the Andersonian widened. Robert Wallace lectured in Mathematics to the mechanics and was appointed to a chair in December, 1824.[86] Thomas Atkinson, a radical bookseller whose apprentice was Daniel Macmillan, the founder of the London publishing house, lectured on Craniology.[87] In 1826 Wallace also offered evening classes in Geography and Astronomy and started a summer course in Mathematics.[88] Inevitably, he quarrelled with Andrew Ure in the winter of 1826-7, and his courses were not given.[89]

When the new building was being constructed from 1828, applications for new professorial appointments multiplied. Posts in Mathematics, Classical Literature, Latin and Greek, Geography and many medical specialisms were sought, and the main criterion used to determine the academic shape of Anderson's University was the founder's will.[90] Dr Robert Hunter, an eminent anatomist in the city, sought accommodation for a medical museum in the new east wing, offering £55 per year in rent for a lease of $10\frac{1}{2}$ years. He followed this by seeking a chair in Anatomy and Physiology, suggesting diplomatically that he would retain his dissecting room in Portland Street or elsewhere 'out of the Institution's Buildings and be bound that nothing shall occur in the buildings that shall give just ground for offence to the Managers'. The managers recommended his appointment and those of Dr Hannay as Professor of the Theory and Practice of Medicine and Dr. Armour as Professor of Midwifery and Medical Jurisprudence.[91] Added to the existing appointment of William Mackenzie, these new professors laid the foundations of a very powerful Medical Faculty.

Later in 1828, Alexander Watt, a trustee and a teacher at Glasgow Academy, became Professor of Astronomy and Geography. Peter Wilson replaced Robert Wallace as Professor of Mathematics and Dr Andrew Buchanan (1798-1882) became Professor of Materia Medica.[92] The report of student numbers in the classes of 1828-9 showed a quantum leap because of these additional appointments and is summarised in Table 2.4.

In April 1829 advertisements were placed for chairs in Logic and the Practice of English

Table 2.4   Report of Student Numbers, 1828-9

Professor	Subject			Student Numbers
Hunter	Anatomy			183
Armour	Midwifery and Medical Jurisprudence			54
Hannay	Theory and Practice			73
Wilson	Mathematics			50
Watt	Astronomy and Geography	Ladies	Winter	33
		Ladies	Spring	43
		Gentlemen	Winter	20
		Gentlemen	Spring	9
	Popular Astronomy			15
Ure	Chemistry			50
	Popular Chemistry			70
	Natural Philosophy		Winter	200
	Mechanics		Spring	150
	Total			950

Composition, Natural History and Mineralogy, Drawing and Painting, and Modern Languages. Some of these were filled during the course of the year: William Ross was elected Professor of the Theory and Principles of Painting and Sculpture; Dr John Scouler became Professor of Geology, Natural History and Mineralogy and became responsible for the new museum; B. Jourdain was appointed Professor of Modern Languages.[93]

In August 1829 Dr James Smith Candlish was appointed as an additional Professor of Surgery but died of typhus before he could take up the post. His successor, elected by a single transferable vote, was James Adair Lawrie (1801-59): the 'increased prosperity of the university has attracted an Extensive and keen competion [sic] from six candidates'.[94] Meanwhile, the first dozen student prize-winners in the newly created Medical School were reported in the Glasgow press: their house residences, apart from Glasgow, included Paisley, Stewarton, Irvine, Leicester, Norwich and Ireland.[95]

1830 saw staff changes and additional appointments. William Ross did not stay long and was replaced in the Chair of Drawing and Painting by John A. Gilfillan (1793-1864). William Hunter was elected to the newly created Chair of Logic and English Composition and J.P. Cheetham became Professor of Veterinary Surgery. Following Andrew Ure's resignation, Thomas Graham was appointed to the new Chair of Chemistry and Dr. William Heron became Professor of Natural Philosophy.[96]

There were two other interesting developments in 1830. Glasgow Philosophical Society sought a closer association with Anderson's University in April, and that matured over time. Secondly, Robert Connel, a respected teacher of Mathematics who had provided a temporary home for the Mechanics' Institution after the schism of 1823, – 'one who highly respects and fondly cherishes the memory of Dr. Anderson' – wanted to bring together the two mechanics' classes within Anderson's University because he felt that neither was viable on its own. The managers did offer him the olive branch, but coolly, for they knew that the Glasgow Mechanics' Institution had debts at least equal to its assets.[97]

Perhaps this opportunity should have been seized, but much had been achieved and the temptation to play safe must have been great. Science for the masses was an objective of some of the trustees but not all of them. United, they had created many assets since the first days after John Anderson's interment. The education of middle-class women and of skilled artisans had begun, and these aspects of the radical vision had taken shape in substantial modern premises. Consolidation and further expansion were the next goals.

REFERENCES

1 SUA, B1/1 Minute Book, 1796-99, p.45.

2 Ibid., pp. 46-7.

3 Ibid., pp. 48-9.

4 T.M. Devine, *The Tobacco Lords* (Edinburgh, 1975), pp. 24, 36, 45, 182 and 188; *Biographical Sketches of the Lord Provosts of Glasgow 1833-1883* (Glasgow, 1883), p.18.

5 For David Dale sr. see G.Stewart, *Curiosities of Glasgow Citizenship* (Glasgow, 1881), pp. 45-64 and D.J. McLaren, *David Dale of New Lanark* (Glasgow, 1985).

6 Guildhall Library GH 11937/38 Sun Fire Assurance Company Policy Registers, Policy 714224, 21 January 1801 insures £7,500 of assets.

7 J. Arnold Fleming, *Scottish Pottery* (Glasgow, 1923), pp. 95 ff; John C. Logan, 'The Dumbarton Glass Work Company, *c*.1777-*c*.1850', unpublished M.Litt. thesis, University of Strathclyde, 1970, p.129.

8 Clows, pp. 246 ff; A.E. Musson and E. Robinson, *Science and Technology in the Industrial Revolution* (Manchester, 1969), pp. 293 ff; G. Macintosh, *A Memoir of Charles Macintosh F.R.S.* (Glasgow, 1847); D.W.F. Hardie, 'The Macintoshes and the Origins of the Chemical Industry', *Chemistry and Industry*, June 1952.

9 SUA, B1/1, p.56.

10 Ibid., pp. 59-62.

11 Ibid., pp. 64, 67-72.

12 Ibid., pp. 73-4.

13 Ibid., pp. 75-8. For Anderson's Library see Muir, pp.70 ff and J. Malcolm Allan, 'John Anderson and his books', *96 Group Paper*, 1993. Anderson's 2,000-plus books were insured for £300 in July 1796 and his apparatus for £500.

14 The best treatment of Garnett is S.G.E. Lythe, *Thomas Garnett (1766-1802)* (Glasgow, 1984). See also Musson and Robinson, pp. 101, 107, 111, 129, 146-7, 162, 181, 349.

15 SUA, B1/1, pp. 76-84.

16 Ibid., pp. 91-3; Lythe, p.23.

17 SUA, B1/1, pp. 99 and 115.

18 Ibid., pp. 102-8.

19 Ibid., pp.113-5.

20 Ibid., pp. 170-2.

21 Ibid., pp. 107-110.

22 Ibid., pp. 198-205.

23 Ibid., pp. 209-12.

24 Lythe, p. 26.

25 SUA, B1/1, p.222.

26 Ibid., pp. 227, 232, 236-7; B1/2 Minute Book of the Andersonian Institution, 1799-1810, p.3; Lythe, p.26.

27 B1/2, pp. 5-10; the best biography is Thomas Kelly, *George Birkbeck, Pioneer of Adult Education* (Liverpool, 1959).

28 B1/2, p.14.

29 Ibid, p.13.

30 Kelly, pp.27 ff; see below, pp. 38-40; John Parsell, 'Memoir of Professor Anderson', *Glasgow Mechanics Magazine* (1825), pp. v-ix and (1826), pp.182-4; W.G. in *Scots Mechanics Magazine* (1825), pp. 97-104.

31 Kelly, pp. 30-1.

32 B1/2, pp. 25-33.

33 Ibid., pp. 36-47.

34 Ibid., pp.48-50.

35 Ibid., pp. 45 and pp. 51-78.

36 Ibid., p.83; *London Gazette*, 6 December 1803.

37 B1/2, pp. 87-9.

38 Ibid., pp. 90-102 and 105-8; Kelly, pp. 35 ff.

39 B1/2, pp. 110-19.

40 Ibid., pp. 123-7.

41 Ibid., pp. 128-30.

42 Ibid., pp. 131-148.

43 Ibid., p.154.

44 Ibid., pp. 234-5.

45 SUA, B1/3 Minute Book of the Andersonian 1811-30, p.116.

46 SUA, B1/2, p.157.

47 Ibid., pp. 15 and 160.

48 Ibid., pp. 210-39.

49 Ibid., p.251.

50 SUA, B1/3, pp. 1-5.

51 Ibid., p.9.

52 Ibid., pp. 12-25, 29, 38, 66 ff, 86-90.

53 H. Cockburn, *An Examination of the Trials for Sedition in Scotland* (1888), vol. ii, pp. 192-203.

54 SUA, B1/3, pp. 92 and 95.

55 Ibid., pp. 77 and 95.

56 Ibid., p.109; F.L.M. Pattison, *Granville Sharp Pattison, Anatomist and Antagonist, 1791-1851* (Edinburgh, 1987), pp.1-74. I am grateful to Dr. James McGrath for this reference.

57 SUA, B1/3, pp. 110 and 135-7; Pattison, pp. 76 ff.

58 SUA, B1/3, pp. 160-5.

59 Pattison, pp. 80 ff; Kelly, pp. 154, 157-60, 282-3; W.S. Miller, 'Granville Sharp Pattison', *Johns Hopkins Hospital Bulletin* (1919), pp. 98-104; J.J. Walsh, *Dictionary of American Biography*; *The Lancet*, 1829-30, ii, pp. 740-5, 799-800, 974-5 and 1830-1, ii, p.694.

60 SUA, B1/3, pp. 165-177 and 180; Olive Checkland, *Philanthropy in Victorian Scotland* (Edinburgh, 1980), pp. 191-2; A.M.W. Thomson, *The Life and Times of Dr William Mackenzie, founder of Glasgow Eye Infirmary* (Glasgow, 1973).

61 SUA, B1/3, pp. 179-81 and 188.

62 Ibid., pp. 181-2.

63 Ibid., p.196.

64 Ibid., pp. 294-7; Mitchell Library MS C311730 View of the Constitution and History of Anderson's Institution, 1825. I am grateful to Dr. W. H. Fraser for this reference.

65 SUA, B1/3, pp. 212, 217-19.

66 Ibid., p.220; SUA, C1/1, Glasgow Mechanics' Institution Minute Book 1823-24, *passim*.

67 SUA, B1/3, pp. 233-46.

68 Ibid., p.265.

69 Ibid., p.282.

70 Ibid., pp. 301 and 340-4.

71 Ibid., pp. 352, 358-9, 366.

72 W.S.C. Copeman, 'Andrew Ure', *Proceedings of the Royal Society of Medicine* (1951), pp. 655-62.

73 SUA, B1/3, pp. 115-118.

74 Ibid., pp. 129-30 and 134; T.B. Mackenzie, *Life of James Beaumont Neilson F.R.S.* (Glasgow, 1929), p.7.

75 SUA, B1/3, pp. 127-8 and 140.

76 Ibid., pp. 141 and 152.

77 Ibid., pp. 154-6.

78 Ibid., pp. 183-5 and 188.

79 Ibid., pp. 196-8, 201.

80 Ibid., p. 222; R.S. Rait, *The History of the Union Bank of Scotland* (Glasgow, 1930), pp. 234-5. Anon., *Memoirs and Portraits of One Hundred Glasgow Men* (Glasgow, 1886); Vol. 1, pp. 9-10; Norio Tamaki, *The Union Bank of Scotland* (Aberdeen, 1983), p.12.

81 SUA, B1/3, pp. 271, 178 and 281.

82 Ibid., pp. 284-90.

83 Ibid., p. 295.

84 Ibid., pp. 301, 314.

85 Ibid., pp. 350, 352; B10/1 Anderson University Report 1832, *passim*; B1/4 Minute Book of Anderson's University, 1830-64, 2 March 1831.

86 SUA, B1/3, pp. 228 and 232.

87 Ibid., p. 230.

88 Ibid., p.256.

89 Ibid., pp. 269-73.

90 Ibid., pp. 290-1.

91 Ibid., p. 293.

92 Ibid., pp. 299-301.

93 Ibid., pp. 311, 314, 372.

94 Ibid., pp. 320 and 346.

95 Ibid., p.311.

96 Ibid., pp. 357, 364, 369, 371-3.

97 Ibid., pp. 354-6.

CHAPTER THREE

Consolidation and Progress, 1830-60

' ... The committee can state that of a great number of individuals who
were for a number of years regular attendants on the lectures and readers
from the library few remain in the ranks of operatives which they then
occupied but with very few exceptions they are either managers of works in
their respective trades or, as is the case in many instances, succeeding in
business on their own account.'

Tenth Annual Report of the Glasgow Mechanics' Institution, April 1833

Since John Anderson's death there had been rapid social and economic changes in Glasgow, and
although the pace slowed, the transformation of the city into a major industrial centre and port
continued throughout this period. The population rose from about 77,000 in 1801 to over
202,000 by 1831 and more than doubled to over 420,000 in 1861. Urbanisation was an uneven
process, the decades 1821-41 showing particularly rapid growth, but about 7,000 inhabitants per
year were added net to the city's population up to 1861.' Social and economic strains on the
fabric of the city were very considerable: outbreaks of smallpox, cholera, typhus and typhoid
tested the skills of doctors and the readiness of municipal public health services; overcrowding
and homelessness were rife as the housing stock could not cater for the demographic expansion;
other essential public utilities such as water supply and sewage lagged behind urban growth and
contributed to a maelstrom of urban problems.

Glasgow became the industrial powerhouse of Scotland in this period. Its dominance in cotton
textile production had already been established by 1830, but the growth of engineering industries
linked to changes in transport, symbolised by steamships and locomotives, diversified the city's
economy. A range of small firms supported the largest companies in textiles and the metal trades:
machine-makers, coppersmiths, iron founders, brassfounders, and woodworkers. Middle-class
consumer demands aided the service industries and the food and clothing trades, and these
gradually responded to the opportunities presented by the mass market. Brewing and distilling
rapidly achieved economies of scale in flow production, as did many of the chemical firms, led by
Tennant and Company of St Rollox. All required skilled labour, and several presented
entrepreneurial opportunities for the technically trained; hence the obvious paean of self-
congratulation implicit in the tenth annual report of the Glasgow Mechanics' Institution of 1833.

No aspect of social policy invited wider debate in the 1830s than education. The Scottish
parish school system had clearly broken down in Glasgow, and the earlier endeavours of
Thomas Lancaster and Robert Owen to spread the word for a national system of education and
teacher training occasionally found local imitation but were generally ignored by politicians. In
Glasgow, J.C. Colquhoun of Killermont, MP for Dunbartonshire, was an exception and
introduced an Education Bill in 1834 which eventually, under pressure, he withdrew on grounds

of cost. Nonetheless, he was instrumental in the formation of the Glasgow Educational Association (later the Glasgow Educational Society) which attracted considerable support from the Presidents, managers and trustees of Anderson's University – James Smith of Jordanhill and James Andrew Anderson became its first vice-presidents. The leading light on the committee was David Stow (1793-1864), the first successful advocate of teacher training and the creator of the 'Normal Seminary'.[2] When the foundation stone for the 'Seminary' was laid on 14 November, 1836, one account relates:

> An unusual procession is threading its way through a greatly interested multitude; it embraces upwards of five hundred of the leading citizens including the Dean of Guild, the members of the Merchants' House, the members of the Trades' House, many of the clergy, the professors of the Andersonian University, with their distinguished President, James Smith Esq., of Jordanhill and the office-bearers of the Educational Society. It was a notable day for Mr. Stow and notable in the educational history of the City.[3]

The President and trustees of Anderson's University clearly embraced appropriate good causes which might underpin the work of their own institution. However, their main achievements in these years were the consolidation and expansion of the Andersonian. There were considerable pitfalls which they managed, sometimes with difficulty, to avoid. Having provided a new building, they added to net assets and recruited a staff which attracted a greater student following from a wider geographical area. Never immune from downturns in the trade cycle, especially in the 1840s, the Andersonian endured its share of disappointments. Yet in 1860 it was a stronger institution measured in terms of student numbers, material assets and reputation than it had been in 1830.

Its strongest area of study was its medical school. Its specialist medical library was started with a loan of £100 from the managers in 1830.[4] The death in 1831 of Dr James Armour who had combined the teaching of Midwifery with Medical Jurisprudence led to the separation of these two subjects and the creation of a Chair in the latter.[5] George Watt became the first Professor of Medical Jurisprudence and also inaugurated lectures in Forensic Science.

The trustees were concerned to introduce medical degrees as soon as possible, and in November 1831 instructed the managers to investigate this possibility.[6] The managers asked the views of the medical professors, and Robert Hunter, Professor of Anatomy, on their behalf responded, saying that in terms of John Anderson's will it was necessary to establish the Medical Faculty formally before degrees could be conferred. The professors favoured seeking degree-granting powers because it 'would be highly conducive to the welfare of the Medical School and prosperity of the University'. Maintaining proper academic standards was all-important:

> The Professors would consider it both their interest and duty to render these honours [degrees] as respectable as possible and would be happy to cooperate with the Managers in any way which may seem to them best calculated to ensure that important result.

They had also considered regulations. They believed that the title of Doctor of Medicine of the Andersonian University, Glasgow [MD AUG] should be conferred on those who would normally receive the university's medical diploma and assured the managers 'That none shall receive this *honour* but those who give satisfactory evidence of superior Medical and Literary attainments'. The examination should be strict and professional, practical and theoretical. Students who received prizes in all the medical classes should be entitled to the degree without examination and free of any additional expense. All other candidates would be subjected to 'searching examinations' in every subject.

The professors planned to examine candidates at three stages: Anatomy and Surgery first; Chemistry, Materia Medica, Botany and Medical Jurisprudence second; and Institutes of Medicine, Practice of Medicine and Midwifery as the finals. The examinations were to be conducted publicly, practicals by the medical professors in the presence of the President, Managers and Mediciner class of trustees. They proposed a scheme of differential fees: ten guineas was the graduation fee for those who took the examinations but did not take all the classes in the Andersonian and five guineas for those who attended all the medical classes in the institution. The fee income was to be divided equally between the university and the medical faculty. They also suggested that graduates should enjoy free use of the library and the museum and any additional privileges conferred by the managers and trustees. The medical professors also advised the managers to establish a Faculty of Arts beginning with a Chair in Civil History. The two faculties should include all the professors currently on the staff of the institution, and clearly they thought that a Senate should then be formed to provide an effective constitutional means whereby the academic staff as a whole could communicate with the Managers and Trustees.[7]

The trustees were in favour of creating the Faculties of Arts and Medicine and also of awarding degrees.[8] Further progress was delayed for two reasons. First, the Faculty of Physicians and Surgeons of Glasgow challenged teachers in the University of Glasgow's right to teach and to practise surgery unless they submitted themselves to examination by the Faculty; in consequence of this claim graduating students had to meet the same requirement. Eventually the Faculty attempted to enforce its monopoly by recourse to the Court of Session, the final case ending in its favour in 1834.[9] While this case was proceeding, the Andersonian managers wisely decided not to offend the Faculty with another degree proposal which included surgery. A Parliamentary Select Committee was appointed in 1834 following the Court of Session decision and the inquiry into the state of the universities of Scotland in 1831. The Committee's particular interest was medical education. The city was apparently well served for tuition in medical subjects. Apart from Glasgow University Medical School there were four other centres – the Andersonian, Portland Street Medical School, College Street School of Medicine and the Clinical School of the Royal Infirmary. The Andersonian and Portland Street provided instruction in all branches of the subject which were required for medical degrees in the Scottish universities or for a diploma in any of the medical corporations in Britain. The Andersonian taught the same curriculum as the University of Glasgow with the addition of 'Medical Jurisprudence and Police', Natural History, Comparative Anatomy, 'Mechanical Philosophy', Veterinary Surgery and instruction in Anatomical Drawing.

In making their submission to the Select Committee, the managers detailed subjects, fees, teachers, student numbers, and hours of instruction. There were 590 students studying twelve different subjects, and five years later the University of Glasgow medical school had a smaller class of over 400 students. All classes received five lectures per week except students of Natural History and Mechanical Philosophy who attended three times per week. Summer courses were offered from May to October in the main medical subjects, and the course in Practical Chemistry lasted three months and was limited to twenty-five students. All lectures were given in the Andersonian's buildings with the exception of clinical lectures which took place at the Royal Infirmary.

Many students of Glasgow University attended lectures at the Andersonian, presumably because they believed that they were being offered better teaching. However, certificates of attendance at the Andersonian were not recognised by Glasgow University. Students were regularly examined, one suspects in line with the proposals made in 1832 to the managers, and certificates were given only for good performance and regular attendance. Medical teaching and certificates were recognised by the Faculty of Physicians and Surgeons of Glasgow, partly because the Professors were all well respected members, by the Royal Colleges of Surgeons of London and Edinburgh, by the Army and Navy Medical Boards, and by the Apothecaries Company of London. Both the University of Aberdeen and the University of St Andrews accepted the teaching and certificates of the Andersonian Medical Faculty.

The obvious but totally explicable anomaly was the attitude of the University of Glasgow which was clearly intent on defending its own Medical Faculty. The Andersonian professors and managers had sought recognition for their teaching and certificates but had been refused. At the same time the University of Glasgow accepted certificates of private teachers in London and Dublin for credit towards diplomas and degrees. The Andersonian managers were quick to point out the apparent paradox of recognising 'distant teachers' whose qualifications and practices were difficult to validate while refusing to accept Glasgow-based instruction where the teachers and their qualifications were well known. Medical teaching at Glasgow University lasted for three months in the year whereas at the Andersonian the course was taught for six months and more lectures were given per week.

The facilities for study at the Andersonian were very good. Medical students were admitted to the museum free of charge, and together with the specialist Anatomy and Pathology museum it provided a superb resource centre with excellent illustrative material. These museums were valued at £4,000 in 1834. Four new classrooms were available for medical teaching, a chemistry laboratory, an apparatus room, and 'a hall for dissection'. The medical professors were paying one hundred guineas a year in rent for these facilities because the university lacked adequate endowment income, but the trustees hoped to dispense with this charge in the future.[10]

This initial approach to government for recognition of the medical classes was followed in 1835-6 by memorials suggesting that a central board for medical education should be established and be responsible for recognising institutions and courses.[11] Later, in 1836 there was an attempt via the Lord Advocate to secure recognition from London University for all certificates issued by the Andersonian.[12] However, the Medical Faculty had to be content with the recognition of the Faculty of Physicians and Surgeons of Glasgow.

Within the institution the medical professors met as a Faculty with a chairman and secretary and there can be no doubt that they were a strong force in determining academic policy and appointments. For instance, when Thomas Graham accepted a post at University College, London in 1837, they favoured the appointment of Dr Gregory to the vacant chair of Chemistry, and the trustees duly elected him. Similarly, in 1841 when Dr Robert Hunter resigned the Chair of Anatomy the medical professors recommended Dr Moses S. Buchanan as his replacement, and their choice, once approved by the trustees, was an outstanding success as a teacher.[13] When they sought the implementation of John Anderson's will in the matter of constituting a senate, they were disappointed because the managers felt that the Faculties needed to have a full staff complement before that change could be introduced.[14] The division of the Theory and Practice of Medicine into two separate academic areas was agreed in 1840 after the Faculty had suggested it, and the first incumbent of the new chair of Theory of Medicine was their nominee, Dr Andrew Anderson, 'a relative of our illustrious Founder and young Gentleman of the greatest promise'.[15]

Anderson in due course became the Secretary to the Medical Faculty and communicated regularly with the managers on a range of subjects. His colleagues were keen to maintain high standards of teaching and pastoral care. When Dr Crawford, Professor of Medical Jurisprudence, fell seriously ill and concealed his condition from his colleagues in 1856, for

TABLE 3.1   Medical Faculty: Student Numbers, 1830-60

Session	Anatomy	Theory & Practice	Materia Medica	Surgery	Midwifery	Medical Jurisprudence	Institutes of Medicine	Natural History	Veterinary Surgery	Total
1831-2	190	82	33	42	40	15				402
1833-4	218	41	22	60	25	11				377
1834-5	153	90	29	103	44	15				434
1836-7	335	45	20	60	26	12				498
1839-40	180	50	-	70	70	16			48	434
1841-2	80	36	-	59	37	13	14			239
Dec. 1842	170	45	30	59	26	18	26	8		382
Dec. 1843	213	45	39	50	49	39	26			461
1844-5	190	35	40	50	50	24	28			417
1845-6	140	35	45	76	30	17	22			365
1846-7	189	46	40	84	34	20	21			434
1847-8	220	56	-	76	41	23	37			453
1848-9	233	55	52	86	42	23	-			491
1849-50	255	68	51	96	43	30	25	20		588
1850-1	276	61	45	70	56	32	29	17		586
1851-2	205	66	41	67	-	29	16	13		437
1852-3	188	40	47	64	28	15	27	-		409
1853-4	192	40	40	65	30	23	17	30		437
1854-5	204	60	42	74	32	30	29	40		511
1855-6	249	52	-	74	26	28	37	47		513
1856-7	384	60	-	80	93	37	48	54		756
1857-8	366	74	54	102+15*	68	40	51	60		830
1858-9	358	74	50	90	100	69	47	61		849
1859-60	324	66	40	82	57	69	51	61		750
1860-1	370	60	57	109	40	40	47	61		784

*   15 for Military Surgery

Source: SUA, B1/4 Minute Book of Anderson's University, 1830-64.

instance, the Medical Faculty instructed Anderson to indicate to the managers that they did not want him re-elected to his chair, because of student complaints and his many unexplained absences. In fact, Crawford was dangerously ill and could not complete his lectures; his colleagues rallied round and did his work without further complaint.[16] When a new post in Military Surgery (following the Crimean War) was being considered, the Faculty was consulted, and a lectureship rather than a chair was eventually created.[17]

Despite the insecurity posed by annual re-election, dependence on tuition fees for income and the requirement to pay rents for classrooms, the Medical Faculty recruited some very able young doctors, several of whom served for long periods.[18] Robert Hunter, for instance, served in several capacities from 1828 to 1860; Andrew Anderson from 1840 to 1863; and Moses Buchanan died in office in 1860, having been appointed in 1841. Ten or more years' tenure was commonplace as Appendix 1 reveals, and such service contributed an intellectual cement to a Medical School where brilliant individuals such as William Mackenzie passed through to more prestigious posts in university medical schools.

The University of Glasgow's medical school gained several professors – apart from John Burns (1815) and Mackenzie (1828) – from the Andersonian. Andrew Buchanan (1798-1882) M.D. completed his degree in Glasgow in 1822, studied in Edinburgh and Paris, had three years

TABLE 3.2   Total Student Numbers

Session	Total
1796-7	972
1828-9	950
1831-2	1175
1832	1249
1835	1408
1837-8	1512
1838-9	1313
1839-40	1431
1840-1	1036
1841-2	1495
1842-3	1524
1843-4	1466
1844-5	1123
1845-6	912
1846-7	1263
1847-8	1380
1848-9	1084
1849-50	1239
1850-1	1302
1851-2	1106
1852-3	1367
1853-4	1462
1854-5	1685
1855-6	1920
1856-7	2255
1857-8	2395
1858-9	2450
1859-60	2249
1860-1	2349

Source: SUA, B1/4 Minute Book of Anderson's University, 1830-64.

as a resident assistant surgeon in the Royal Infirmary and also maintained a practice in the Wynds – one of the poorest districts of the city – when he took the Chair of Materia Medica at the Andersonian in 1828. He contracted typhus three times, the first occasion in 1829 when his friend Dr James Candlish died of the disease. He was the first editor of the *Glasgow Medical Journal*, the main periodical of the West of Scotland's medical profession in the nineteenth century. During the cholera epidemic (1832-3) he worked night and day in the specialist temporary hospital, trying his best to help the afflicted and garnering the data for his later publications about the disease.[19] In politics he was a Liberal Whig, a stance which commended him to Lord Melbourne's government and partly explains why he was preferred in 1838-9 to Dr Harry Rainy, a Tory, for the Glasgow University Chair in the Institutes of Medicine.[20]

Another Andersonian stalwart during the cholera crisis was Dr James Adair Lawrie (1801-59), Professor of Surgery from 1829 to 1850. Educated at Loudon parish school in Ayrshire and the University of Glasgow where he graduated M.D. in 1822 and then became a resident medical officer in the Royal Infirmary, he went out to India to work for the East India Company. However, his health suffered in Bengal and he returned to Glasgow in 1829 and was appointed the same year to the Chair of Surgery in the Andersonian. When cholera struck Glasgow, he

TABLE 3.3   Mechanics' Classes, 1830-60

Session	Mathematics	Chemistry	Natural Philosophy	Anatomy & Physiology & Natural History	Drawing	Composition
1826			946			
1831-2	101		238			
1835-6			346			
1839-40	281		250			
1840			76		36	
1841-2	200	200	130			
1842		150	150			
1845-6		91	67			55
1846-7		53	73			18
1847-8		47	50			
1848-9		30	25	15		
1849-50		50	75	45		
1850-1		36	56	47		
1851-2		25	57	32		
1852-3		33	95	30		
1853-4		110	280	110		
1854-5		125	360	126		
1855-6		194	400	163		
1856-7		219	400	163		
1857-8		364	400	171		
1858-9		415	400	168		
1859-60		356	400	92		
1860-1		360	424	116		

Source: SUA, B1/4 Minute Book of Anderson's University, 1830-64.

worked hard and long with his friend and academic colleague, Dr Andrew Buchanan, both in the cholera hospital and in private practice. This experience greatly added to his reputation as a capable and devoted practitioner and also attracted both patients to his practice and students to his classes. He was an excellent lecturer, and as Table 3.1 indicates, his class was highly popular, so much so that when Professor John Burns was drowned in the *Orion* in 1850, the University of Glasgow elected Dr. Lawrie to the vacant Chair of Surgery.[21]

James Alexander Easton (1807-65) M.D., the inventor of 'Easton's Syrup', a famous Victorian tonic mixture of iron, quinine and strychnia, became Professor of Materia Medica in the Andersonian in 1840 and served the institution for fifteen years. As Table 3.1 indicates, he did well by his subject during his tenure and clearly attracted students. His lecturing style was not to everyone's taste but he was always very well prepared, a man of wide factual knowledge and considerable learning. Thus, he was an excellent candidate for the Regius Chair in Materia Medica at the University of Glasgow in 1855.[22]

Student numbers in exclusively medical subjects are given in Table 3.1. These exclude Chemistry, partly because this subject was taken by many who had no intention of embarking on a career in medicine. Yet it should be remembered that many medical students did take this subject, and at least one professing it, William Gregory (1837-9), a pupil of Justus von Liebig, was elevated to the Chair of Medicine in Aberdeen before going to the Chair of Chemistry in Edinburgh.[23] These student numbers do not reflect the strength of the student body in the

TABLE 3.4   Science: Student Numbers, 1830-60

Session	Chemistry	Natural Philosophy	Mathematics	Natural History	Geography	Astronomy
1831-2	128	343	208			
1833-4	107	33		45		
1835	125	379	188		15	
1839-40	87	200	81		38	
1840	104	34	76			
1841-2	293	173	135		17	
1842	222	174	47	8	16	
1843	102	200				
1844-5	205	102	41			15
1845-6	123	25				
1846-7	99	32	140			
1847-8	102	23	127			
1848-9	153	28	92			
1849-50	164	31	100			
1850-1	179	28	120			
1851-2	160	32	120			
1852-3	143	33	120			
1853-4	161	35	146			
1854-5	174	40	150			
1855-6	169	13	160			
1856-7	241	20	130			
1857-8	252	20	110			
1858-9	239	12	130			
1859-60	237	20	185			
1860-1	269	9	150			

Source: SUA, B1/4 Minute Book of Anderson's University, 1830-64.

Medical School for it was possible to take several classes in the same year; they reflect class attendance by subject and in total. Sometimes, a dip in the attendance in one subject was offset by increases elsewhere; broadly, total attendances conform closely to the trade cycle, rising when the city's economy was prosperous and declining in depressions. 1841-2, for instance, marks a low-point as does 1851-3, but the long trend was upwards. The decade of the 1850s witnessed particularly rapid expansion, with numbers in Anatomy and Surgery being especially buoyant. Clearly, the Andersonian was supplying an expanding market for doctors.

Growth was occurring elsewhere but was generally more volatile and difficult to chart because of the poor quality of the statistical evidence. Total student numbers, given in Table 3.2, show a substantial increase between 1830 and 1860, with non-medical classes representing a fairly constant 35 to 40 per cent. Returns were often incomplete and therefore these annual totals tend to underestimate actual attendance. The growing prosperity of the 1850s was reflected in the sharpest increases in student attendance; by 1860-1 numbers were double those of 1831-2.

The Mechanics' classes (Table 3.3) went through the doldrums in the 1840s and early 1850s, but from 1853-4 there was a marked upturn in the Chemistry and Natural Philosophy classes. These two areas represented the bedrock of the Andersonian's non-medical endeavours (Table 3.4), but diversification into other areas such as Mathematics, Modern Languages, Logic, Rhetoric and Ethics, Drawing and Painting, Classics and Commercial Law was well established

TABLE 3.5   Additional Classes, 1830-60

Session	Music	Drawing & Painting	Phren-ology	Anatomical Drawing	Book-keeping Writing	Vetinerary Surgery	Phono-graphy	English, Logic & Ethics	Classics	French	German	Oriental Languages
1831-2		94										
1833-4				10								
1835		175				48		34				26
1837		268						20		91	18	21
1839-40		157			217			15			–	
1840		120			115			26				
1841-2		75			114			12	42	27		
1842	340	88			114				38	70	33	
1843	450	39			114			14	20	60	16	
1844-5	80	45					80					40
1845-6		30			38			55			40	
1846-7		100	25		234			55			18	
1847-8		118			250			20		40		
1848-9		82						25		40	32	
1849-50		61			52			25		40	9	
1850-1		65			36			64		70	15	
1851-2		40			40			50		80	8	
1852-3		67			40			22		116	9	
1853-4		37			42			12		69	13	
1854-5					60			19		102	18	
1855-6					109			35		95	23	
1856-7					101			52		96	45	
1857-8					106			32		78	32	
1858-9					75			44		78	40	
1859-60					74			38		45	52	
1860-1					95			36		65	41	

Source: SUA, B1/4 Minute Book of Anderson's University, 1830-64.

by 1860-1 as Table 3.5 indicates. Details about numbers of women students in this period are scanty and are summarised in Table 3.6.

The arrangements for the Mechanics' classes were laid down in 1831. Professor Heron, the new incumbent of the Chair of Natural Philosophy, taught his subject on Tuesdays and Saturdays at 8.15 pm; Thomas Graham, Professor of Chemistry, gave instruction on Wednesdays at 8 p.m. and Professor Peter Wilson gave his Mathematics course on Saturdays at 8 p.m. Fees remained modest, since the Andersonian faced price competition from the Mechanics' Institution: 50p for the full course and 25p for a half course. Entry to the Mechanics' Library cost 10p, if a course was not being taken.[24] Although there was never the trouble between this class and the professors which had been relatively common in the 1820s, Professor Heron fell foul of the students in 1832. The managers were firm but were intent on dissipating unrest while maintaining communication with the class committee:

> no proceeding or discussion tending to interrupt the peace or injure the discipline of the Class – or weaken the authority of the Professor – shall be permitted in any meetings of the Class. But whatever proposition or complaint the Committee may have to make must be submitted to the Managers – and not made the subject of discussions before the other members of the Class …

TABLE 3.6   Ladies as Students, 1831-42

Session	French	Chemistry	Natural Philosophy	Geography	Drawing	Mathematics	Composition
1831-2		50	81				
1839-40				18	42		
1840			130		54	97*	
1841-2	8				33	83	5
1842						47	

*   Not taught in Anderson's but by the Professor.

Source: SUA, B1/4 Minute Book of Anderson's University, 1830-64.

Heron and the class committee were at odds over the issue of tickets for the Library, and they also sent a circular letter to all the trustees 'denouncing in no measured terms the incompetency of the Professor of Natural Philosophy for teaching his Class'. It was surely reasonable to address complaints to the managers in the first instance and imperative that they should settle grievances rapidly.[25] A month or so later the dispute about class tickets for the Library was in the process of being settled, but Heron's competence was more difficult to assess or improve.[26] He resigned in 1833.

Meanwhile, the managers prepared a report on the Mechanics' Class for the trustees recommending a division of labour and responsibility. Professors were to take charge of disposing of tickets of admission, advertisements and the printing of handbills; the Mechanics' Library continued to be managed by the class committee. Library purchases were to be funded from the proceeds of an annual lecture given in turn by the professors and a capitation fee of $2\frac{1}{2}$ p per student for every half course. The class committee was to be elected: four from each class.[27]

Problems occurred because of the earlier division of the Mechanics' Class and the emergence of the Mechanics' Institution. There were a number of attempts to encourage Andersonian professors to give lectures in the Mechanics' Institution; they stood to gain materially but were probably generally sympathetic to the cause of working-class education. According to Anderson's will, professors were only to give lectures within his institution. Professor Robert Hunter had corresponded in 1832 with the President, James Smith, about giving a class in Anatomy and Physiology in the Mechanics' Institution and because of the fact that the course had been advertised was allowed to give it.[28] In 1836 Peter Wilson, by then Professor of Natural Philosophy, had agreed to give lectures in the Gorbals Popular Institution and was allowed to do so because of advertisements in the Glasgow press, but when his course was requested again in 1837, permission was refused, although he had attracted an audience of two hundred and fifty.[29]

Rebellion against the refusal to allow professors to lecture elsewhere was fuelled when the trustees overruled the managers in 1838 and allowed Wilson to lecture in the Gorbals Popular Institution.[30] In 1840 when Hugo Reid left the Mechanics' Institution for a post in Liverpool, on request F.W. Penny and P. Wilson were allowed to finish his lecture courses.[31] However, Penny decided that he did not wish to give the second half of his Mechanics' course, and although he was pressed to give it, the managers felt teaching for the Mechanics' Institution had induced his reluctance to do so.[32] John Hart (d. 1851), a long-standing trustee and former pupil of John Anderson, favoured a policy of combining all the 'popular' work in physics and chemistry 'under one lecturer'. This proposal was discussed at great length, but its implication was the reunion of the Andersonian and the Mechanics' Institution.[33]

After they had finished Hugo Reid's courses, Penny and Wilson wanted to continue to lecture in the Mechanics' Institution, but the managers opposed this. A dispute about the division of the fee between the Mechanics' Committee and Penny and Wilson in 1842 had to be settled by the managers, and probably inflamed the professors further.[34] They were clearly in the market for more teaching, for when the new 'Ladies Academy called Queens College' first advertised its courses, Wilson, Penny and Andrew Donaldson, Professor of Drawing and Painting, were listed among its teachers. Penny, when pressed by the managers, agreed to withdraw, but Wilson and Donaldson had been paid an advance and agreed a contract. However, all three were allowed to teach for the session 1842-3, but they were told that if they continued, they must resign their chairs at the end of that session. Donaldson, in fact, did resign.[35]

When Penny and Wilson were once again denied by the managers the opportunity to lecture in the Mechanics' Institution in 1844, they decided to appeal to the trustees and, if necessary, the Visitors. The medical professors supported them, and memorials were submitted to the trustees. After a heated debate the trustees by a majority of one decided that the prohibition was unreasonable and rescinded it. Forthwith the President, James Andrew Anderson, the Secretary, John Douglas, and one of the managers, Andrew Macgeorge (1774-1857), a distinguished Glasgow lawyer, resigned as managers. At the following quarterly meeting on 22 September, 1844 the remaining managers resigned, only for some of them to be re-elected, including Macgeorge.

Walter Crum (1796-1867), cotton manufacturer, calico printer, chemist and F.R.S., clearly was a leading light in the opposition to the old managers and prevailed upon the trustees to instruct the new ones to seek an amalgamation with the Mechanics' Institution provided any terms for such an outcome did not conflict with the will of the founder. William Murray (1790-1858) of the Monkland Iron and Steel Company and the new President of Anderson's University, James McLelland (1799-1879), the senior manager and gifted city accountant, and Crum met the Vice-President of the Mechanics' Institution, William Ambrose, to discuss the possibility of a merger. He was positive, but the Board of Directors was divided, the majority indicating that they would not favour joining the Andersonian until it was free of debt. Thus were the roles reversed compared with similar discussions in 1830.[36]

However, one positive result of these talks was the recruitment of Ambrose as the first permanent administrator, assistant to Walter Crum, Honorary Secretary. At his first managers' meeting in October 1844 Ambrose was assigned his duties: he was to be university factor and book-keeper for the Secretary and Treasurer; he was required to be in daily attendance, to call meetings, to keep minutes, to let rooms, to receive rents and other payments, to seek donations in money or kind, to correspond with the professors to raise student attendances – and presumably, fee income – all for the princely sum of £40 per annum, which the managers raised among themselves.[37]

The low-point of the Mechanics' classes, as Table 3.3 indicates, was reached in 1848-9, and the growth in numbers for Chemistry, Natural Philosophy and a class covering Anatomy, Physiology and Natural History was clearly evident from 1853-4. By then the new name of 'Popular Evening Classes' had become well established, and the first adjective fully justified. Penny became increasingly reluctant to teach the Popular Chemistry class for his energies were widely spread. In 1854 he suggested that his assistant, William Wallace, should replace him. Although the managers were willing to agree to this change, the trustees favoured Penny's retaining a foothold of at least one lecture per week. To this suggestion Penny assented, although the Popular Evening Class President and his committee colleagues wanted to test the new man before accepting him as the only possible *locum tenens*. In 1856 they sought to appoint Penny's replacement, if he was not available, and were suggesting a new class in Political

Economy, an idea not pursued by the managers. However, a dissenting student group favoured Wallace as their teacher, and he continued to serve in session 1856-7. By this date Penny was in delicate health, and his other classes were very large (see Table 3.4), but in 1857-8 he returned to teaching Popular Chemistry.[38] By 1860 the Department of Science and Arts examinations had become available to all the Mechanics' classes and supplemented the Andersonian's own class tickets.[39]

This period was remarkable for the growth of the Andersonian's reputation in Chemistry. The choice of Thomas Graham (1805-69) as the first professor in 1830 was inspired. The son of a Glasgow textile manufacturer who had made money in the West Indian trade, Graham graduated in the University of Glasgow in 1826 and then moved for postgraduate study to Edinburgh where he first began to lecture in Chemistry, having been unsuccessful in obtaining an appointment in the Glasgow Mechanics' Institution. On his return to Glasgow in 1828, he became an industrial consultant. In September 1829 he was elected in the place of the ill-fated Dr McCandlish to lecture on Chemistry and Mechanics by the committee of the Mechanics' Institution. He certainly impressed his class:

> The number, Variety and Brilliancy of his chemical experiments have shewn him to be completely master of his subject and must have convinced every one that he possesses very high qualifications as a Teacher of that useful and intricate science.

Having been re-elected in April 1830 after teaching 287 students in the previous session, Graham was an obvious candidate for the Chair of Chemistry in the Andersonian and was duly appointed.[40] He successfully maintained his place against his old teacher, Professor Thomas Thomson, of the University of Glasgow. The mainstay of his classes was the medical students but he also attracted those intent on other careers. Graham borrowed from Thomson the institution of laboratory practical classes for all his students when this training was not generally available in Britain.

During his stay at the Andersonian Graham produced twenty-nine research papers, according to the Royal Society's Catalogue of Scientific Papers. Quantity and method may not be true indicators of scientific quality, but in his laboratory Graham began his work on gaseous diffusion and completed his investigations into the nature of phosphates. Following Thomson who published John Dalton's views on atomism before Dalton managed to put them into print, Graham was a thorough-going atomist vitally interested in the effect of the motion of atoms in gases and liquids. Thus 'the father of colloid chemistry' began the creation of his international reputation in the Andersonian. Two papers singled him out quite early as an exceptional researcher. The first, 'On the law of the diffusion of gases', was read before the Royal Society of Edinburgh in December 1831 and published in the *Philosophical Magazine* in 1833. This paper won for Graham the Keith medal, the highest award of the Royal Society of Edinburgh. The second, 'Researches on the arseniates, phosphates and modifications of phosphoric acid' (1833) made him a great reputation immediately and won for him the Royal Medal of the Royal Society in 1838 and possibly his election to the Fellowship, two years earlier.

Graham was probably not at his best with elementary classes. According to Lyon Playfair (1818-98), one of his students and a great admirer, 'he was unable to keep discipline … and his expository powers were not of a high order'. However, he was an exceptional experimentalist and an inspirer of good research by others. This explains why so many of his more earnest students revered him. According to A.W. Hofmann, one of the greatest chemists of the nineteenth century, 'Graham was one of those singular minds which create and open new roads of science'. His laboratory was peopled with talent: James Young (1811-83), his assistant and

8 Portrait of Dr Thomas Graham F.R.S. (1805-69), the First Professor of Chemistry, 1830-7, in Anderson's University. 'The father of Colloid Chemistry', Graham moved to University College, London in 1837 and later became Master of the Mint.

9 Among Graham's students in the 1830s was David Livingstone (1813-73), the medical missionary and explorer. This photograph was taken by Thomas Annan of Glasgow c.1864. Livingstone was a prime example of the working-class student educated at Anderson's University in the first half of the nineteenth century.

later the founder of the shale-oil industry; Lyon Playfair, educationalist, politician and the first Professor of Technical Chemistry in the University of Edinburgh; David Livingstone, the missionary-explorer; Walter Crum F.R.S., recognised in Germany as one of Europe's greatest dyestuffs experts and later President of the Andersonian; J.H. Gilbert, an outstanding pioneer of agricultural chemistry; Sheridan Muspratt, educationalist-scientist; and many others who later made their names and fortunes in commerce and industry.

However, students could not obtain a degree, no matter how long they studied with Graham. He provided them with certificates of attendance issued by the Andersonian and, no doubt, wrote innumerable references. Most students did not trouble to graduate at this time, but this deficiency in the Andersonian's status, as we have seen, did concern the professors and the trustees and managers. Thomas Graham in 1837 decided to move to University College, London, where this problem did not exist.[41]

William Gregory succeeded Graham but only stayed at the Andersonian for two sessions before taking up the Chair of Medicine at Aberdeen University; he had been the choice of the medical professors.[42] In his first session, 1837-8, he had only 58 students and had departed by April 1839.[43] His successor, Frederick William Penny (1806-69), was unanimously elected in July 1839 on the recommendation of Thomas Graham who thought his analytical skills were exceptional.[44] He was greatly supported by the trustees and managers who found money to free him from room rents and also to expand his teaching facilities. The lack of a stipend before 1861 encouraged Penny to undertake industrial consultancy; during his career at the Andersonian his practice became very extensive and certainly militated against a strong commitment to research. For some years before his death 'his professional income exceeded £6,000 a year and it was progressing ... ' He had been an expert witness in a number of patent cases, in public enquiries and in ' ... criminal cases on behalf of the Crown ... ' His calmness under cross-examination was legendary; he was terse, precise and always inclined to keep additional evidence in reserve so that, if pressed by counsel, he reinforced his earlier statements by additional factors or reasons.[45] His greatest moment in criminal cases occurred during the trial for murder of Dr. E.W. Pritchard (1866) who twice applied unsuccessfully for posts in the Andersonian. Pritchard poisoned his victims using antimony and aconite for which there was no absolutely accurate test before 1882; Penny tried minute doses of these poisons on himself and was able to describe the symptoms, which the victims had complained about, from personal experience, no doubt a particularly enlightening experience for the jury and the bench alike.[46]

The growing strength of Penny's practical experience attracted many students, especially the sons of chemical manufacturers, to his classes. His practical classes were reputedly the largest in Britain by 1860, and after 1847-8, as Table 3.4 reveals, the story was one of steady expansion. The change in the Popular Chemistry classes to the examinations of the Department of Science and Arts, which Penny and his assistant, Wallace, supported, was the beginning of a long process to raise the quality of general scientific and technical education.[47]

The only blot on Penny's career at the Andersonian before 1860, apart from minor legalistic controversies, was a paternity case raised against him by Janet Jardine, the daughter of the janitor, whose family was housed in the Andersonian buildings. This case arose from allegations first made in October 1848 and was not settled till 1851. The managers and trustees, while not wishing to assume that Penny had fathered Janet Jardine's child, felt it necessary to keep him on short notice during this long period.[48]

The experience of Natural Philosophy and the other sciences was much less favourable than that of Chemistry. The Popular class in Natural Philosophy increased its numbers significantly from 1853-4 but the full-time day classes faltered, as it was no longer an examinable subject for

10 The original partners in the Hot-Blast Patent and their lawyers after the great trial involving William Baird and Company (1839-42) in Edinburgh which brought them a fortune in royalties. The inventor and former student, James Beaumont Neilson, is sitting far left, and next to him is Charles Macintosh, the celebrated chemist. Standing are Colin Dunlop and James Aitken of Clyde Ironworks and sitting are John Wilson of Dundyvan Ironworks (centre) and the lawyers, Kirkwood and Bannatyne (right). Several of these men were trustees of Anderson's University. This painting c.1843 is in the collection of the University of Strathclyde.

medical students by 1860. The straitened financial circumstances of the Andersonian in this period did not help, for apparatus was a constant but essential drain on resources.

After William Heron resigned in 1833, Peter Wilson moved into the Chair of Natural Philosophy, but his main interest remained Mathematics, especially since no additional appointment was initially made.[49] Wilson took over all the teaching for the Mechanics' Class in session 1835-6, and the class initially seemed to prosper.[50] He was undoubtedly a popular and effective teacher, but his range of teaching was too wide, encompassing – apart from Chemistry and Natural History – most of science including Geography and Astronomy. Moreover, taking account of the need to develop the market for skilled technicians and managers, the ties between Natural Philosophy and marine and other forms of mechanical engineering required exploitation. Whether Peter Wilson was the ideal man for this task is open to doubt, although he certainly tried his best.

When John Gilfillan resigned, the advertisement to attract candidates for the Chair of Drawing and Painting made special reference to the teaching of drawing for architecture, 'machinery' and the designing of patterns, the latter no doubt to exploit the cotton goods trade in printed calico and sewed muslin.[51] This is a clear indication of the importance which the managers and trustees attached to the notion of 'useful knowledge' and the connections between disciplines. The tradition of recruiting employers and managers from advanced firms as trustees – such men as David Elder, Robert Napier, three generations of Edingtons, John J. Griffin,

11 Interior of the Anderson Museum, a water colour *c.*1831 by John Alexander Gilfillan, Professor of Drawing and Painting (1830–41). Opened in March 1831, the Museum was a substantial learning resource for students and an attraction to visitors. Its principal promoter was James Smith of Jordanhill but it attracted major donations from William Euing and other wealthy Glasgow businessmen.

Matthew Perston Bell, Robert Freeland, James Young, Archibald Orr Ewing, J.B. Neilson and his son, Walter, George Thomson and William Tod – ensured that cotton and pottery manufacture, chemical manufacture and chemical engineering, shipbuilding and marine engineering, dyeing and printing, iron-founding, machine-making and locomotive building were represented in the strategic thought of the Andersonian management.

When Peter Wilson resigned to become Rector of Inverness Academy in 1845, the managers examined the position of Natural Philosophy and Mathematics closely. Alexander Bain was appointed to replace Wilson, and work was started on repairing and replacing apparatus.[52] However, when Bain resigned in 1846 at the end of his first session, George Greig took responsibility for Geography, having previously held the Chair of Rhetoric and Belles Lettres for one session.[53] Alexander Laing became the new Professor of Mathematics and brought to that discipline much needed stability and growth.

Later than summer Dr John Taylor was elected to the Chair of Natural Philosophy. He found that his day classes suffered as medical examiners no longer prescribed his subject as compulsory. Increasingly, he concentrated his efforts on the Popular Evening Class audience which grew considerably in the 1850s (see Table 3.3). Significantly, the student committee of the Popular Evening Class programme complained about others but never about Taylor. In 1856, after the Royal College of Surgeons in Edinburgh dispensed with their requirement for Natural Philosophy, Taylor favoured abandoning his day class, but the managers asked him to continue, but his day student numbers never rose above twenty (see Table 3.4).[54]

Day and evening classes developed, sometimes by design but occasionally by accident. Raising income by renting classrooms was a necessity for the managers, and the most obvious tenants were those prepared to offer teaching not already available in the Andersonian. Logic, English Composition and Ethics, French, German and Italian, the Gymnasium under the renowned François Foucart, formerly an officer in Napoleon's Imperial Guard, Music, Classics, Phrenology, Writing and Book-keeping, Phonography and Stenography found homes, as can be gathered from Appendix 2. Continuity is a crude test both of viability and student interest: there were significant numbers over a long period for French, English, Logic and Ethics, German, Writing and Book-keeping, Drawing and Painting (Table 3.5). The trustees favoured the formation of a Faculty of Arts in 1832 and created a Chair of Oriental Languages the following year to add to English, Art, and French.[55]

Because all professors only held tenure for a year at a time and received no fixed stipend, staff turnover in these Arts areas tended to be high. Some like Gilfillan, Professor of Drawing and Painting, served for over ten years, but this was exceptional. Monsieur B. Jourdain who taught French and Italian stayed for four years between 1829 and 1833, but a few simply appeared for one session. For instance Mr Wolski, teacher of Modern Languages in the High School, taught French to ladies in session 1841-2, and Herman Jonas gave German lessons in 1842-3. The longest-serving of the linguists was Professor Koerner, who began teaching German in 1843-4, was elected to a Chair in 1847 and was still teaching in 1860. French classes progressed under Professor William Anderson (1846-53) and Professor Nathan Meyer (1853-60). English went through the doldrums after James Robertson (1847-52) retired. Two appointments came to grief but James Brown, appointed in 1854, restored the subject's reputation in the Andersonian.[56]

Pressure on space was mounting in the late 1850s, and English, the other languages and Writing and Book-keeping were selected for removal by the managers and trustees. Penny of Chemistry was demanding extra accommodation and there were plans for extending the Museum. In 1859 Brown, Meyer, Koerner and McLean of Writing and Book-keeping were not re-elected at the annual round because it was thought that their rooms would be needed. Meyer was chairman of the Popular Evening Class committee but this position won him no favours, possibly because earlier he and his committee had lost the university seal. However, plans for expansion did not immediately come to fruition and so these teachers continued in office.[57]

From its opening the Museum attracted many donations from trustees, students, teachers and others to add to Anderson's gifts. There was a fine collection of stuffed birds, and the collection of 'coins, antiquities and other curiosities ... is Extensive and Valuable'. James Smith of Jordanhill not only designed the interior but was a munificent benefactor of coins and medals; Thomas Edington II presented mineral specimens to add to Anderson's extensive fossil collection; animals and birds from the Cape, Australasia and the South Seas, and South America could be seen; the gallery devoted to birds included 2,000 specimens bought from Joseph Sabine F.R.S.; comparative anatomy found a space, and when he retired in 1860, Professor Robert Hunter gave a thousand anatomical specimens.

After the British Association for the Advancement of Science met in Glasgow in the summer of 1840, John Grier Brown, a muslin manufacturer, and Walter Crum successfully negotiated for possession of the collection of fossils and minerals and models exhibited at the meeting. The Glasgow Dilettanti Society offered its collection of models on permanent loan in 1845. Professor Frederick Penny had collected about 1200 samples of chemicals and salts and gave these to the Museum in 1848. Although the Honorary Curator was James Smith (from 1848), the responsibility for the collections rested with Dr John Scouller who gave his own valuable collection of Natural History specimens to the Andersonian in 1849. In 1852 Dr. James Couper gave about 1150 mineral specimens, 500 foreign shells, 140 British shells, and some corals. The eminence of the Museum can be gathered from the fact that the Lord Commissioners of the

Treasury presented a group of Roman, Anglo-Saxon, and ancient Scottish coins, treasure trove discovered in 1851-2. One of the ancient canoes, discovered in 1849 at Springfield opposite the Broomielaw, was on permanent display at the Andersonian Museum.[58]

William Euing, a considerable benefactor to many good causes, made several gifts – coins, Roman pottery and ancient Scottish seals.[59] He it was who proposed the building of an extension to the Museum in 1856, and the plans were prepared by J.T. Rochead, a distinguished architect and trustee.[60] Euing and his friend, Robert Freeland, also found the money, and the final reordering of the Museum and the refitting of its cupola was in progress by November 1862.[61]

The Museum was not only a significant educational resource supporting the Andersonian's teaching but also a place for visitors on Wednesdays and Saturdays and on public holidays. Soirées were held in the 1830s to attract support and donations, but entrance charges brought in a significant income.[62] The normal cost of entry in the 1840s was $2\frac{1}{2}$ p and 1p on public holidays. Even these prices did not lead to great numbers of the working classes seeking admission. A family outing could be expensive in these days of large families, and therefore the Museum attracted the respectable middle classes. In 1852 the trustees experimented with a special Saturday evening entry charge of one old penny (less than $\frac{1}{2}$ p), and this certainly attracted many working-class visitors. Between 6 November and 22 December, 1852 the Museum attracted 5,391 visitors, an average of 770 per day; the smallest number on any one day was 653, and the largest, 1,088. £76.50 was raised in admission charges and donations in the first week.

The Museum Committee, inspired by this marketing success, decided to open on New Year's Day and during holidays at this special price. Between 22 December, 1852 and 22 March, 1853 there were 6,245 visitors. The number on New Year's Day, a Saturday, was 1,915, and on Monday, 3 January, a public holiday, there were 1,367.[63] The Museum became an increasingly popular attraction for the rest of the 1850s.

The doubling of student numbers, the growth of existing and new academic disciplines within the Andersonian, the development of the Museum and the extension of the institution's property and assets were achievements of the trustees and managers. It was a struggle to cope with the problems which growth generated and a great test of managerial skill. James Smith of Jordanhill, President (1830-9) F.R.S., was a wealthy and gifted geologist with catholic interests and magnificent ambitions for the Andersonian. The Museum gave him particular pleasure and he presided over its initial period of development. In 1839 he resigned abruptly because ill-health enforced absence from Glasgow and was succeeded *pro tem* by James A. Anderson, who served for a second term till the major crisis in 1844 arising from Professors Penny and Wilson wishing to teach in the Mechanics' Institution.[64]

A long period of stability followed with William Murray (1790-1858) of Monkland Iron and Steel Company as President till his death in 1858. Born in Glasgow, Murray became a partner in the Monkland Steel Company in 1824; this firm had been founded by his father, Francis, who had made money in the West Indian trade, and John Buttery *c.*1805. William Murray acquired considerable experience in colliery management at Banknock near Denny supplying the Monkland firm with its best coal. In 1826 that firm added pig iron to steel production and expanded its local coal supplies; the outlying collieries were sold off in 1835 and by 1840 Monkland works was a major producer of malleable iron. Murray's election and interest arose from the fact that he had attended the Chemistry and Natural Philosophy classes in the Andersonian; his principal interests were Geology and Mechanics. He was an energetic President, raising money and urging on improvements in the practical rooms for Chemistry and Anatomy, the necessary prelude to increasing the class sizes in these subjects. Elected to Glasgow Town Council in 1850, Murray took a great interest in the Loch Katrine Waterworks

TABLE 3.7   Balance Sheet (£) of the Andersonian, 1830-60

Year	Assets	Liabilities	Surplus	Current Income	Current Expenditure	Balance
1833	13,540.94	5,506.92	8,034.02	287.82	253.81	34.01
1844	15,322.77	6,822.45	8,500.32	479.64	462.89	16.75
1845	15,352.35	6,960.37	8,391.98	463.83	434.26	29.57
1858		3,832.16				

Sources: SUA, B/11/1-4 Financial Statements; Minute Book B1/4.

Scheme and for a time acted as chairman. On 2 November, 1858 he left for his Coatbridge house after a busy day at the hustings – he was the candidate for the twelfth ward – and when the train reached its destination, he was found dead in the carriage.[65] Walter Crum was elected to replace Murray and served out this period.

The office of President brought with it considerable influence and power, and these individuals expected to determine academic strategy as well as to deal with issues such as finance and property. Academic expansion and property development brought financial problems with them, and these were permanent throughout this period but did not prevent progress. A review of finances since 1828 led the managers to conclude that in 1831 a loan of £5,000 was required, and this was borrowed from the Bank of Scotland and formed the main liability shown in the balance sheet of 1833, details of which are given in Table 3.7.[66] Gifts came in from individuals but were generally designated for particular purposes. One significant gift was the rental income from the Isle of Shuna, in the Firth of Lorne, but a legal dispute delayed its acquisition. However, by 1844 Shuna was in the books as worth £1,000 to the Andersonian, the main reason for the increase in assets shown in Table 3.7.[67] Soirées were held to raise money, and the insistence that professors paid room rents is explicable in terms of attempting to reduce debt.

Several trustees and at least one manager, James Andrew Anderson, believed that it was best to give the professors their classrooms rent-free. To that end Anderson gave fifty guineas in 1826 to start a fund, and he favoured the use of any projected surplus in providing stipends for professors. James Smith, Thomas Edington II and William Smith added a further £50, but there was never enough to secure the objects intended.[68] Rents became a great issue for professors; many paid late or even accumulated arrears until dire action was threatened.

Expenditure on building behind George Street and on the iron gates to replace the 1828 Ionic portico was authorised, but these minor works and a western extension increased the debt owed to the Bank of Scotland and shown under liabilities (Table 3.7) for 1844 and 1845.[69] However, one purpose in seeking donations from the Glasgow public in 1839 was to be able to let rooms to professors rent-free and another was to create a minor capital works fund:

> This most valuable and interesting Institution is not so generally known and appreciated as it deserves ... it now has 13 teachers ... and 1313 students.

Small groups of trustees solicited donations by personal calls on their acquaintances. Walter Crum tried his friends in the local chemical industry, specifically seeking support for the Chair of Chemistry. In consequence, Frederick William Penny never did pay an economic rent for his accommodation even in his more affluent days.[70]

Hard times in the early 1840s caused the Bank of Scotland to examine closely the Andersonian's account. The managers preferred to stay with the bank which had served the institution well and therefore endeavoured to deal with its concerns. They prepared a report on the property pledged to the Bank, and an up-to-date valuation was sent to the Cashier. But the Bank still wanted its bond for £5,000 repaid at Martinmas 1841. In 1842 the managers sent a memorial to the Lord Provost and Council seeking the city's financial support. They claimed that there was a growing belief in the value of education, that it was no longer seen as a 'danger to the Institutions of the country' and that they were torn between the desire to provide cheap tuition and the idea of being able to pay good teachers. This appeal fell on stony ground after its reference to a council committee.[71]

After a temporary respite, the Bank of Scotland again demanded the redemption of its bond in May 1843. Andrew Macgeorge, a manager who was well acquainted with the Bank's agent, undertook to seek a further delay in repayment. The managers then turned to trying to raise rental income up to £600, a forlorn hope in the circumstances. The President, James Anderson, thought of a debenture issue at 3 per cent which could be used to repay the Bank of Scotland and at the same time give the managers a period of grace. This idea came to nothing, but Anderson managed to operate the bankers' 'old boy' network to secure delay in 1844.[72]

Meanwhile, James Anderson reviewed in detail the accounts for 1841-4. The current balances shown for 1844 and earlier did not even meet the interest on the debt. Using 5 per cent as the standard interest rate, Anderson calculated that the Andersonian required a further £92 to achieve a proper balance, including servicing the debt. Since the Bank of Scotland was clearly intent on retrieving its loan and did threaten to sell the Andersonian's property, there were only two possibilities: the trustees could raise £100 or more per year and pay off a small amount of the debt; or the managers could achieve the same effect by seeking a new loan at $3\frac{1}{2}$ per cent instead of 5 per cent. In any event, prompt payment of room rents by professors was essential; if they did not pay within two months, they were threatened with dismissal.[73] The economic circumstances were not propitious: city firms even in advanced sectors such as cotton and engineering were in difficulties in 1844, and raising donations or a fresh loan was not an easy task.

Yet trustees tried to raise subscriptions within their nine classes, going around the city in pairs. After Anderson resigned over the Mechanics' Institution teaching question, the new President, William Murray, raised £893 quickly and paid off the arrears of interest owed to the Bank of Scotland, which in October 1844 was pressing for repayment and threatening legal proceedings. Murray then canvassed other banks about taking on the Andersonian debt at a lower rate of interest; he also talked to the Bank of Scotland.[74] The following March he gave the Institution two wagons of coal and told the trustees that he had managed to reschedule the loan owed to the Bank of Scotland. That bank, the British Linen Company, the Commercial Bank, the Union Bank and the Western Bank had agreed to lend £1,000 each and the City of Glasgow Bank £500. Thus, a fresh loan of £5,500 could be raised for five or seven years at 3 per cent 'in order to allow the University to clear off its present debt'.[75]

Several of these banks were relatively new foundations, and at least one of them, the Western Bank, pursued ambitious expansionist policies which antagonised the older Edinburgh institutions.[76] The fall in student numbers in the 1840s not only reflected the economic difficulties encountered by the urban economy but also adversely affected current income. Because of the financial circumstances of the institution in May 1848 Ambrose agreed to accept half of his salary (£20) till prosperity returned.[77] Throughout 1848 and 1849 the evening classes were not paying their way, and the class committee which administered them would have withdrawn had they not been bailed out by the managers.[78] Meantime, the professors tended to accumulate large arrears in room rents.[79] By the middle of the 1850s student numbers had increased substantially (see Table 3.2), once more the students were asserting their independence, and James McClelland was preparing a scheme for liquidating the university's debt.[80]

Apart from the annual subscriptions of managers and trustees, endowments, often for specific purposes, began to appear. John Ferguson of Cairnbroch left £1,500 in 1857 to fund four bursaries; John Freeland gave £2,000 for the improvement of the Museum. Ferguson's capital sum was, in fact, used to liquidate part of the institution's debt, although bursaries were provided according to his wishes. Freeland and William Euing also provided money to provide extra accommodation for Chemistry students. The bequest from Ferguson was most fortuitous: the collapse of the Western Bank in 1857 led its liquidator to seek repayment of £1,000 borrowed in 1845, and the fragile City of Glasgow Bank was also in need of £500 and sought repayment of its loan. The managers had little option but to reduce the institution's debt to just over £3,800.[81] Thus, the Andersonian entered the 1860s with a smaller debt but still in straitened circumstances.

Favourable agreements were made with the Glasgow Philosophical Society which enriched the Andersonian's library. The Glasgow Phil. included in its membership many of the Andersonian's trustees – James Cook, the engineer, James Cleland, William Dixon, ironmaster, John Geddes, Henry Houldsworth, cotton spinner and machine-maker, Charles McIntosh – and the agreements in 1832 and 1840 provided for the Society to use a room in the Andersonian for its meetings and in exchange the library received the Society's books.[82] Support was given to the study of Geology by Professor John Taylor and James Smith of Jordanhill.[83]

The managers' main failure was the lack of a proper legal base for Anderson's University which may have restricted endowments and certainly prevented the conferring of degrees. Since most students did not graduate, the lack of degree-granting powers may not have seemed significant in the period 1830 to 1860 but it was vital thereafter. The failure to attract government support was not the managers' fault: they submitted a memorial to the Home Secretary in 1840/1 seeking a government grant, but the Education Committee of the Privy Council denied their claim.[84] Working-class elementary education was its sole remit. The trustees supported the institution with their money and time; the managers even more so. They had their idiosyncratic lapses in, for instance, supporting the Victorian craze of Phrenology. However, they had carried the torch for scientific and technical education, when pioneers were very few.

REFERENCES

1   S.G.E. Lythe and J. Butt, *An Economic History of Scotland, 1100-1939* (1975), p.245.
2   Sir Henry P. Wood, *David Stow and the Glasgow Normal Seminary* (Glasgow, 1987), pp. 2 ff; L.J. Saunders, *Scottish Democracy, 1815-40* (Edinburgh, 1950), pp. 296 ff.
3   Wood, p.31.
4   SUA, B1/4 Minute Book of the Andersonian University 1830-64, 22 December, 1830. This library was insured for £80 in 1832.
5   Ibid., 10 October 1831.
6   Ibid., 5 November 1831.
7   Ibid., 7 June 1832.
8   Ibid., 22 June 1832.
9   Saunders, pp. 339 ff.
10 SUA, B1/4, 11 June 1834.
11 Ibid., 22 December 1835 and 2 March 1836.
12 Ibid., 22 December 1836.
13 Ibid., 6 and 22 September 1836; 7 August and 3 September 1841. Similar instances regarding academic appointments followed up to 1860.
14 Ibid., 6 September 1836.
15 Ibid., 29 May 1840 and 22 June 1840.
16 Ibid., 23 and 27 June, 22 September 1856.
17 Ibid., 22 June 1857; 14 and 28 July 1857.
18 See Appendix 1.
19 *One Hundred Glasgow Men* (Glasgow, 1886).
20 Murray, pp.160-2.
21 *One Hundred Glasgow Men.* vol.II, pp. 171-2; Murray, p.158.
22 Murray, pp. 236-8.
23 SUA, B1/4 Minute Book of the Andersonian, 1830-64, 22 September 1837 and 22 March 1839; R.H. Nuttall, *The Department of Pure and Applied Chemistry: A History, 1830-1980* (Glasgow, 1980), p.5.
24 SUA, B1/4, 10 October 1831.
25 Ibid., 17 and 21 March 1832.
26 Ibid., 17 April and 3 May 1832.
27 Ibid., 22 September and 5 October 1832.
28 Ibid., 2 November 1832. James McConnechy, the usual lecturer in Anatomy, had resigned; SUA C7/1, Mechanics' Institution Letterbook, 1824-42, 26 June 1832.

29 SUA, B1/4, 2 November 1836 and 22 June 1837.

30 Ibid., 19 October 1838.

31 Ibid., 22 December 1840.

32 Ibid., 13 and 22 January 1841.

33 Ibid., 6 February 1841.

34 Ibid., 18 June 1841; 9 and 16 February 1842; 7 and 22 March 1842; 4 May 1842.

35 Ibid., 28 September 1842; 12 October 1842; 22 December 1842; 20 April 1843.

36 Ibid., 22 June 1844; 10 and 17 July 1844; 22 and 25 September 1844.

37 Ibid., 14, 16, 18, 30 October 1844.

38 Ibid., 8 and 22 September 1854; 5 October 1854; 22 September 1855; 23 June 1856; 17 and 22 September 1856; 22 June 1858.

39 Ibid., 11 October 1860.

40 SUA, C1/1 Minute Book of the Glasgow Mechanics' Institution, 1823-34, 7, 10 and 28 August 1826; 4 September 1826; 9, 11 and 28 September 1829; 28 April 1830; 6 and 8 October 1830; B1/3 Minute Book of the Andersonian, 1811-30, p.371; B1/4 5 July 1837; H.H. Browning, *The Andersonian Professors of Chemistry* (Glasgow, 1894), pp. 15-28; T.E. Thorpe, *Essays in Historical Chemistry* (1894), pp. 160-235.

41 J. Butt, 'James Young, Industrialist and Philanthropist', Unpublished Ph.D. thesis, University of Glasgow, 1964, pp. 7-11; Nuttall, pp.4-5.

42 SUA, B1/4, 6 and 22 September 1837.

43 Ibid., 22 December 1837; 22 March 1839.

44 Ibid., 1 July 1839.

45 Butt, 'James Young', pp. 416 ff; Murray, p. 240.

46 *The Trial of Dr. Pritchard*, edited by William Roughead, (Glasgow, 1906), pp. 173-88.

47 Nuttall, p.5.

48 SUA, B1/4, 17 April 1849; 22 and 28 June 1849; 22 September 1849; 11 October 1849; 14 December 1849; 3 April 1850; 13 May 1850; 22 June 1850; 24 July 1850; 23 September 1850; 20 January 1851; 2 April 1851.

49 Ibid., 22 June 1833.

50 Ibid., 22 September 1835. See Table 3.3.

51 Ibid., 22 December 1840; 22 March 1841.

52 Ibid., 22 June 1845; 15 October 1845.

53 Ibid., 18 and 22 June 1845; 24 July 1846.

54 Ibid., 24 July 1846; 5 August 1846; 23 June 1856.

55 Ibid., 25 April 1833, 22 June 1833; 4 July 1843.

56 See Appendix 2.

57 SUA, B1/4, 22 June 1859; 3 August 1859; 22 March 1860; 22 June 1860.

58 SUA, B10/1 Anderson's University Report, 1832, pp. 2, The first major donation of stuffed birds was made by [McLachlan in 1831. B1/4, 2 November 1831; 22 Septemb 1840; 23 May 1845; 22 September 1848; 14 December 184 23 September 1850; 5 May 1852; Senex, vol.ii, p.348.

59 SUA, B1/4, 22 September 1855.

60 Ibid., 22 and 29 October 1856.

61 Ibid., 24 November 1862.

62 Ibid., 5 October 1836. The managers arranged a fortnightl series of soirées on Mondays.

63 Ibid., 22 December 1852; 23 March 1853.

64 Ibid., 23 September 1839; 17 July 1844.

65 Ibid., 22 December 1858; Anon., *The Lord Provosts Glasgow* (Glasgow 1883), p.181.

66 SUA, B1/4, 22 June 1831; 21 July 1831; 15 August 1831; 2 May 1832.

67 Ibid., 22 June 1832; SUA, B/11/3 Financial Statemen 1844.

68 SUA, B1/4, 4 January 1836.

69 Ibid., 4 February 1839; 3 April 1839.

70 Ibid., 22 March 1839; 13 November 1839.

71 Ibid., 8 and 22 September 1841; 13 October 1841; November 1842; 22 December 1842; 11 January 1843; February 1843.

72 Ibid., 10 May 1843; 19 July 1843; 8 November 1843; 2 December 1843; 14 February 1844; 22 March 1844.

73 Ibid., 22 June 1844.

74 Ibid., 22 June 1844; 25 September 1844; 14 October 184 23 December 1844; 22 December 1858. This detail given b Walter Crum in his eulogy of William Murray.

75 Ibid., 22 March 1845; 2 April 1845.

76 S.G. Checkland, *Scottish Banking* (1975), pp. 325 ff an 448 ff; J. Butt, 'The Industries of Glasgow c.1830-1912', i *History of Glasgow*, vol.2, ed. by W.H. Fraser and I. Mave forthcoming.

77 SUA, B1/4, 17 May 1848.

78 Ibid., 22 June 1848; 22 September 1848; 22 September 1849

79 Ibid., 3 April 1850.

80 Ibid., 21 March 1856; 23 June 1856.

81 Ibid., 22 June 1847; 16 September 1847; 22 December 1857 22 March 1858.

82 Ibid., 23 January 1832; 6 April 1832; 14 December 1840.

83 *History of the Geological Society of Glasgow, 1858-1908*, e by Peter McNair and Frederick Mort (Glasgow, 1908 pp. 9, 14-15, 23-4, 26, 172, 202 ff, 204-7.

84 SUA, B1/4, 22 March 1841.

CHAPTER FOUR

New University or Technical College, 1860-86

'My idea is this, that ... they should teach chemistry as a branch of general education, which every man ought to know ... I am very anxious that scientific instruction should be advanced or disseminated as widely as possible ... '

James Young, President of Anderson's University, 1872.

After the Great Exhibition of 1851 demand for a new type of university and criticism of the old institutions increased. The supporters of change came generally from the industrial and commercial middle classes with some assistance from the 'aristocracy of labour'. 'Promotion campaigns' also included members of the nobility and occasionally the monarchy. Prince Albert formally opened the Museum of Practical Geology in South Kensington which he hoped would become the nucleus of an 'Industrial University'. But after the appointment of Sir Roderick Murchison as Director in 1855 this wider vision was lost, despite the excellence of the teaching staff.[1] To the Prince Consort and several of the Commissioners of the Great Exhibition, the need for a new type of institution required little demonstration:

... a rapid transition is taking place in Industry; raw material, formerly our capital advantage over other nations, is gradually being equalised in price, and made available to all by improvements in locomotion, and Industry must in future be supported, not by a competition of local advantages, but by a competition of intellect ...

According to Lyon Playfair, alumnus and James Young's friend, the establishment of industrial colleges for scientific research and teaching was the best answer that Britain could provide to such a competition.[2]

On the continent the competition had already begun. By 1831 Germany had six *Technische-Hochshulen*: Karlsruhe founded in 1825, Darmstadt in 1826, Munich in 1827, Dresden in 1828, Stuttgart in 1829 and Hanover in 1831.[3] One British pioneer of the Industrial University, J.A. Lloyd, F.R.S., looked enviously at the French system of technical and scientific education and in 1851 proposed that models of the École Polytechnique should be established throughout Britain,[4] although a generation earlier, Baron Charles Dupin had urged the French government to note and copy the Andersonian as one of 'the institutions which conduce to the progress of industry and of the knowledge that directs it'.[5] James Hole, Secretary of the Yorkshire Union of Mechanics' Institutes, favoured state grants for the better type of Mechanics' Institutes, which he thought could become constituent colleges of the proposed Industrial University.[6] This was well in advance of continental thinking.

But apart from the Andersonian, Owens' College, the University of London and the South

Kensington colleges, little was being done to integrate applied sciences and technology within the curriculum of Higher Education, although modern theoretical sciences had begun their march to proper status in some of the existing universities.[7] A few technical colleges were founded by local enterprise, for example in Wigan in 1858. The idea generally faded in the 'fifties and revived in the late 'sixties after the passing of the Second Reform Bill. By that time James Young was a senior figure in the Andersonian's management and in the interest of the rights of that institution and for the advancement of applied science more generally was prepared to take sides in any new debate.

Why did the idea of technical universities and colleges recede? Lack of state support was probably the most important reason, but state apathy was merely a reflection of prevailing social and economic attitudes. British commercial and industrial prosperity combined to reinforce the worship of market forces, and in that climate a radical re-examination of scientific and technical education was unlikely to occur. Training on the job was thought to be superior to any college course or, as T.H. Huxley put it in his address at the opening of Sir Josiah Mason's Science College, Birmingham:

> ... the practical men believed that the idol whom they worship – rule of thumb – has been the source of the past prosperity and will suffice for the future welfare of the arts and manufactures ...

But the practical men could perhaps be excused. Few had graduated to industrial management via formal higher education. Without a cadre of the highly trained in charge, British industry was unlikely to encourage educational innovation. If industrialists did not regard technical and scientific education as important, they were unlikely, in sufficient numbers, to urge their middle managers and skilled workers to attend classes nor would they reward by promotion those who did so. There was a widespread fear that wider educational opportunities might encourage the footloose and make trade secrets common property. Even the more progressive believed that an elementary education system was a crying necessity; scientific and technical education was an unaffordable luxury for aspiring foremen.[9]

If British industrialists were generally unenthusiastic about scientific and technical training for their workers, the trades unions were equally remiss. But then, they were infant organisations with more directly utilitarian industrial objectives. Workmen of left-wing persuasions might ask themselves whether it was worthwhile acquiring a technical and scientific education, if according to the nature of society, the main profits of their endeavours would go – in the absence of adequate rewards – to their employers. Individuals, indeed, were not likely to be interested in science and technology *per se*; they were also, if they believed in education at all, likely to be concerned about the political and economic theory underpinning British society. Courses in Politics and Economics were not generally part of the curriculum of the few scientific and technical institutions that did exist, despite their advocacy in Scotland by Dr Thomas Chalmers.[10]

Supporters of a wider curriculum including science and engineering at the high table had to convince the rest of society that their ideas were valid and their activities essential for the welfare of the country. They had to convince industrialists, politicians and trades unionists; they had to reform old institutions and create new; they had to undermine the prevailing political, social and economic dogma, for there were many Liberals – even Thomas Chalmers[11] – who worshipped the Smilesian doctrine of self-help and feared that government grants for scientific and technical education would deprave the individual and act as subsidies to otherwise inefficient industries, preparing the path to greater state intervention in the future and greater personal taxation. From debates about education practical men had to produce practical results.

12 James Young (1811-83), student and assistant to Professor Thomas Graham in Anderson's University and in University College, London. Young made a fortune in the Scottish shale-oil industry during the period 1850-70, became a trustee in 1858 and served as President from 1868 to 1877. A major benefactor, he endowed the Young Chair of Technical Chemistry in 1870 and attempted unsuccessfully to secure a Charter for Anderson's University in the early 1870s.

James Young (1811–83) became a trustee of Anderson's Institution on 22 September 1858[1] and served as President from 1868 to 1877. By position and custom the President of the Andersonian enjoyed great authority. As we have seen, Anderson's constitution was designed to eliminate professorial control and bickering and to give power to a large lay body of trustees; in practice the committee of managers and the President had most of the authority and all the power to administer the institution. From the beginning Young was a strong President, if only because of the unanimity of his election. His wealth, in an age of self-help and no government grants, made him indispensable. Although there were many radicals among the trustees, it was only when he became very adventurous that there were attempts to control his use of power – and these generally developed not from resentment but from timidity.

Nowhere did Young leave a memorial of his ambitions for the Andersonian, and therefore it is impossible to be categorical about what his plans were. When he addressed meetings, his remarks were rarely reported fully; indeed, he did not enjoy speech-making sufficiently to preserve many of his notes. He was far more at home in the small committee meeting or bringing shrewd pressure to bear behind the scenes. But when he took the chair at the trustees' meeting for the first time on 22 September 1868, the Secretary of the Andersonian reported that Young made 'some excellent remarks on the importance of Scientific Education' and thanked the assembly for the honour they had done him in appointing him President. He spoke feelingly of the 'great benefit he and the public generally had derived from the instruction given in this University' and he stated that he hoped that 'in the future as in the past the University would prove a powerful auxiliary in Scientific and useful education'.[13] From the policies he pursued, it is clear that Young intended to leave his mark on Anderson's University by ridding it of debt, endowing it with funds, securing its legal status at the highest level that others more politically powerful would allow, extending its curricula, widening its student catchment area, appointing men of brilliance to its Chairs and providing it with buildings and facilities which would ensure its direct relevance to Scotland's industries.

Finance was the key to the whole future: without endowments and gifts it would be impossible to rid the University of its debts, to provide for more students, to attract the right kind of professors or to regularise its anomalous constitution. The assets of the University rose remarkably during Young's presidency, because Young either found the money personally or he sought money from those who had it – not always with the success that he would have liked. When he became President, the buildings and other assets of the Andersonian were worth about £9,000, and this included the recent gift of the Model School by William Euing, the immediate Past-President.[14] There was no general capital reserve fund and the University owed £4,000 to four banks: the Bank of Scotland, the Commercial Bank, the British Linen Bank and the Union Bank.[15] Current expenditure was met by student fees, subscriptions from trustees and managers, normally in the range of one to three guineas each, and very largely by extracting room rents from its professors and teachers, who were also generally responsible for paying local rates and taxes.

Because the trustees were not legally incorporated, there was no absolute security of the University's funds, and this did not encourage simple donations of any size. Instead substantial gifts came protected by separate and often very detailed deeds of trust. Young himself followed the examples of John Freeland and William Euing when, in July 1870, he finally endowed the Young Chair of Technical Chemistry with £10,500 by separate deed of trust.[16] Euing and Young together had cleared the debt of £4,000 in September 1868, each contributing £2,000.[17] By session 1872-73 University property and other fixed assets stood at over £26,000, and cash reserves were approaching £11,000.[18] By that stage the University's managers were advancing considerable sums on the security of property, providing the institution with a steady and relatively secure income from investments. By 1876 there was a cash fund of over £22,000 of which over a half was available for general purposes.[19] On the day-to-day income and expenditure account there was also a transformation: on 22 March 1878, three months after Young's resignation from the Presidency – he remained a manager until his death in 1883 – the Secretary reported that there had been an annual average surplus on current account of £129.70 over the past eight and a half sessions.[20] The surplus for 1876-77 session, Young's last as President, was over £271, more than twice the average over the period of his tenure of office.[21] James K. Dempster, the University architect, set a demolition value on the whole site but not including Young's laboratories for Technical Chemistry in 1878 of £16,000.[22] When Young died in 1883, the total assets of the Andersonian, including the Young Chair and its buildings were worth nearly £68,000.[23] Despite this very considerable advance in the University's fortunes, by then current expenditure was beginning once again to exceed income, the Medical Faculty, in particular, becoming more expensive to administer because of its declining student fee income.

How was it that from the 'sixties to the 'eighties the finances of the Andersonian improved so significantly? Young's generosity was, of course, of major importance. The Young Chair and its buildings cost over £20,000 – and these were by no means the only gifts made by the President. His example undoubtedly stimulated the generosity of others, although men like William Euing had already established a reputation for philanthropy. Thus John Freeland, who had already give £7,500 by deed of trust in 1861, was prepared to promise £2,000 for the 'Chair of Practical Natural Philosophy', and this sum was received in May 1873;[24] when he died in 1878, by his will dated 8 June 1868 he left a further £5,000 to the University.[25] The gifts of Euing and Freeland, taking account of their long association with the Andersonian, would probably have come to the University, no matter who was President, provided he appeared reasonably competent.

But Young's initiative and energy in fund-raising attracted wider support, perhaps most easily illustrated by considering the endowment of the Chair of Applied Mechanics. The concept of the Chair probably derived from Joseph Whitworth's scholarship scheme. In June 1868 it was reported to the managers' meeting that one of Whitworth's exhibitions, valued at £25, had been allocated to Anderson's University;[26] a copy of Whitworth's scheme to create 'a faculty of industry analogous to the existing faculties of Divinity, Law and Medicine' was entered in the Minutes, and then it was particularly recorded that Whitworth believed that it was vital for the country's continuing prosperity that departments of Applied Mechanics should be established in every major academic institution.[27] With Whitworth's sentiments the managers agreed, and in September 1869 they planned to appoint a teacher of Mechanical Drawing as a beginning.[28] In 1872 a course of evening lectures on Marine Engineering was given by Laurence Hill; this proved a great success. Hill reported:

> ... The little Hall was nearly full ... My second lecture went off very well and I was told afterwards was very well liked ... . I hope these lectures will prove the success the directors wish ... [29]

Thus the independent association between the Andersonian and Mechanical Engineering began, and education was linked with heavy industry on Clydeside, just at the time when the river became the leading centre for shipbuilding in the world. Meanwhile Young collected money for the Chair. John Tennant of St Rollox contributed £1,000;[30] James White and his brother, both chemical manufacturers, put up £500 each;[31] Robert Freeland another £500.[32] John Freeland gave £2,000;[33] Young himself offered £1,000[34] and David Laidlaw £100;[35] offers of bursaries, amounting of £300, were also received.[36] By September 1875 nearly £1,200 was still required and Young agreed to make this sum up. On 29 May 1876 the managers reported to the trustees that 'This Chair ... suggested by your President about four years ago' was to be instituted forthwith.[37]

Young's successful fund-raising was the product of good personal relations as well as the institution's excellent standing in the local industrial community. His friends far and wide rallied to his appeals, and so often he personally reported additions to the funds to the managers. His leadership inspired confidence in his fellows. Dr. John Stenhouse campaigned for money extensively and secured many bursaries.[38] When Young was cruising in the Mediterranean in the Spring of 1875, he called to see John Freeland in Nice:[39] on 24 March 1876 he took breakfast with James Duncan on Duncan's yacht *Pinico*; over the meal they agreed to provide a student with a bursary for one year.[40] Thus any opportunity to present the Andersonian as a worthy cause for philanthropy was taken — and there were many successes.

Economic circumstances did not favour fund-raising in the late 'seventies because of a severe slump. Young tried in 1879 to raise £4,000 locally for the endowment of lectureships in Natural History and Geology, having already offered £1,000 himself. The managers gave him their support but not their money: they hoped that 'the amount required for these lectureships will be speedily raised'.[41] John Lennox Kincaid Jamieson, President (1879-83), the Secretary and Young went canvassing for the money but without any appreciable success; on 11 August 1879 it was agreed to defer further canvassing until replies had been received 'from some of the parties called on'.[42] By October 1879 it was deemed inadvisable to press the matter, and it was agreed that 'when business revives further efforts should be made to raise the required sum of £4,000'.[43] In fact, this money was never raised.

Another basic problem of Anderson's University was the anomaly of its legal status and in particular its right to use the title 'university'. Moreover, without a royal charter its funds were only protected if they were trustee endowments; lack of adequate legal safeguards for the institution's funds was likely to prove a deterrent against attracting more general gifts.[44] In addition one of the past secretaries had died owing the Andersonian money, and there was nothing that could be done. An enterprising President and committee of managers could be accused of acting *ultra vires*, if they infringed the terms of Anderson's will, for example by creating Chairs in subjects or disciplines which Anderson had not catered for. Professor Penny almost prevented the emergence of the Young Chair in Technical Chemistry by exploiting these tactics in 1869. Incorporation of the trustees was the answer — and, if with it went a royal charter conferring university status, fund-raising would be made so much easier.

There were grounds for hope since in other parts of Britain new university colleges were evolving — but not in the same town or city which already had an established university. Matthew Arnold had a real visionary insight in 1868:

> We must plant faculties in the eight or ten principal seats of population and let the students follow lectures there from their own homes.[45]

John Scott Russell favoured a great federal technical university with one hundred Chairs at the central college and twenty-five Chairs in fifteen local colleges in the main industrial cities.[46] But the redbrick universities grew from much smaller beginnings. The Newcastle College of Physical Science, backed by steel, shipbuilding, mining and heavy engineering interests, had opened its doors in 1871; by 1874 textile and mining industrialists had led the way in promoting the Yorkshire College of Science in Leeds; Josiah Mason rallied the hardware trade into a new university college in Birmingham by 1880; a College of Science for the West of England was established at Bristol in 1876; a university college in Liverpool in 1882; in Nottingham and

heffield university extension movements fathered new colleges. In Wales a university college
/as opened in Aberystwyth in 1872.[47] Why should there not be similar changes in Scotland?

Young and his fellow managers of Anderson's University decided to rely on the Royal
Commission on Scientific Instruction. With the Liberals in power, the reform of education was
eing widely canvassed, and the Andersonian's tradition of self-help in scientific and technical
ducation going back to 1796 seemed likely to attract support; it seemed inevitable that there
/ould be radical changes. The Devonshire Commission was Gladstone's answer to the external
ressures upon his government.[48] In December 1868 Edward Baines, Liberal editor of the *Leeds
Mercury*, was advocating that the colleges at South Kensington should be made into a technical
niversity, and in January 1869 a conference of interested parties was called.[49] Joseph
Whitworth launched his philanthropic scheme of national scholarships in Applied Sciences in
March 1868 and he clearly hoped that these would provide the incentive for the development of
aculties of Industry in the existing universities and colleges. By 1871 there was an active
ommittee campaigning for a National University for Industrial and Technical Training. Inside
arliament E.T. Gourley and J.M. Carter urged Gladstone to support this National
University.[50]

The prospect of raising finance for this venture through additional taxes deterred many
iberal members until J.R. Taylor turned public attention to the wealthy guilds and companies
f London, whose endowments had been intended to provide craft and technical training.[51] It
/as in this atmosphere that James Young, James McClelland (1799-1879) and Alexander Harvey
1796-1876) gave evidence to the Royal Commission on behalf of the Andersonian on 8 March
372. McClelland, an accountant, gave evidence first. He dealt with many questions on finance,
tudent numbers and staff and then openly stated that 'we were as much entitled to a charter from
he Government as any school for the teaching of science in Great Britain'. When asked if he
roposed that there should be an additional body in Scotland established to grant degrees,
McClelland was clearly nonplussed. He imagined a federal examining board 'from whom might
manate degrees for the whole nation'.[52] He also thought – and this was more likely to appeal to
he Commissioners – that Anderson's University should become the nucleus for the training of
cience teachers in Scotland, for 'you are powerless to conduct scientific education until you
ducate teachers in science'.[53] This was one self-perpetuating weakness in the state system of
lementary education.

When Young was examined, he agreed with everything that McClelland had said and went
ven further. He declared that he favoured teaching general science to all classes and that it was
ital to the economy and to the community to develop advanced classes in Applied Sciences.[54]
e thought government grants should be made to colleges throughout Britain, for 'I cannot see
better application of money than by teaching science'.[55] Lack of suitable endowments had, in
is view, been the great drawback to the work of Anderson's University: 'We have been a
aining school for professors. London and the University of Glasgow have taken some of our
est'.[56] He expected to recruit professors who could do fundamental research as well as teach. In
is view, the best teacher was also an original researcher: 'If he is not, I think it would be a great
isfortune'.[57] Young evidently thought that a charter and adequate remuneration, partly backed
y government grants, would enable Anderson's University to attract and retain this type.
cience and research would flourish and so would student scholarship.

Anderson's University could make no immediate use of the evidence given by its
epresentatives until the Report of the Royal Commission was laid before Parliament, because of
s confidential nature, but McClelland, while recognising this, favoured applying to the
overnment for a charter incorporating the University. However, when the managers met, they

decided to wait until the Report was available.[58] Meanwhile they proceeded to strengthen their case by acquiring more land and accommodation; this was necessary because of increased student numbers. In October 1873 the Secretary made the first of a series of attempts to purchase the High School which was behind Anderson's University, but by February 1874 it became clear that this would not succeed.[59] However, by September 1874 a new Physics laboratory had been built for Professor Forbes who was given power to spend up to £500 on equipment, if he so desired.[60] Great improvements were also made to the Medical School's dissecting rooms.[61] The managers were then thinking of the complete rebuilding of Anderson's University; Young was to head the sub-committee appointed to direct this major project.[62]

There was also pressure from below. In 1875 the Medical Professors were anxious about the state of Anderson's Medical School, 'which ... was a little behind the requirements of the day'. New classrooms and laboratories were urgently needed. A deputation met the managers and urged them to consider selling the existing university buildings and erecting a new Medical Faculty building in the neighbourhood of the new Royal Infirmary, which, they thought, should be absorbed by Anderson's University. The last suggestion of the Medical Faculty was especially significant: Anderson's University should seek a Royal Charter and adopt a new name, such as Anderson's College of Science. There was considerable discussion, and the managers promised to reflect on these suggestions later.[63]

The most pressing grievances of the Medical Faculty related to the refusal of Glasgow University to accept Anderson's Medical School certificates as valid; these were referred to the Royal Commission on the Scottish Universities in 1876.[64] Young's trustees were negotiating in 1876 for adjacent property, the Jewish Synagogue, which it was proposed should be turned into additional laboratories.[65] Young was away on the Continent, and the managers decided, in his absence, to limit the cost of any new building to £2,000. They were loth to risk their general reserve of just over £12,450 and calculated from their experience of the previous six years that to meet an expenditure of about £500 per annum, their total general fund had to be invested at 4 per cent.[66]

Once the Report of the Royal Commission was laid before Parliament, the managers decided, on McClelland's suggestion, to reprint privately the evidence given on their behalf. As a booklet it was to be circulated to all members attending the meeting of the British Association for the Advancement of Science in Glasgow in 1876.[67] The booklet was printed and circulated in July; the Andersonian's buildings and Museum were painted and decorated specially for the occasion and then thrown open to the members of the British Association and their friends.[68] But the campaign for a Royal Charter was not successful. The Royal Commission's Report did not recommend this course.[69]

Young, therefore, decided to apply for a private Bill of Incorporation and instructed the Secretary accordingly. The managers then discussed the matter and unanimously decided in favour of that course of action.[70] Grahame and Wardlaw, the Parliamentary Solicitors, prepared the draft Bill;[71] by December 1876 the Bill had been received by the Private Bill Office and by January 1877 the Glasgow MPs and Sir Edward Colebrooke, MP, had been lobbied.[72] On January, 1877 the managers were discussing Lord Redesdale's comments on the Bill: he suggested that the number of trustees should be reduced and that there should be some residential qualification for managers. The managers were opposed to both of these suggestions for very practical reasons: any reduction in the number of trustees would diminish both the funds obtainable from subscriptions and also the wide area of enlightened support which Anderson's eighty-one had ensured; they considered that attendance by managers was a better test of interest than residence, a perfectly reasonable position to take.[73]

In Young's absence opposition to the Bill came also from the Senatus Academicus of the University of Glasgow. On 5 February, 1877 a conference took place between the managers and a deputation from the Senatus. The Very Reverend Principal Caird prefaced the discussion by stating that:

... there might exist the most cordial relations between the University and Anderson's Institution. They both existed for the promotion of learning and Science, and they could have no interest save in forwarding and acting in friendly relations ...

Yet the Senatus felt that they must oppose the Bill. They objected to the name 'Anderson's University', and therefore wanted a title containing neither the words 'University' nor 'College'. John Anderson still inspired some hostile reaction: he was ' ... not in very friendly favor towards the University ... he obviously intended to set up what might prove ultimately a rival university ... ' This they intended to prevent. The Private Bill should renounce the managers' right to establish Anderson's University as a 'mimic university'; they should disclaim any right to grant degrees.[74]

The managers responded with comments and speeches which varied from the ambivalent to the candid. Mr McKinlay said that he could not imagine that the Andersonian would ever seek to be a rival institution to the University of Glasgow.[75] But McKinlay must have known that he and his fellow managers, under Young's leadership, had been pursuing a university-promotion campaign; perhaps he believed the Andersonian's concentration upon pure and applied sciences would not infringe upon the intellectual boundaries of the University of Glasgow. It was futile and indeed fraudulent to deny that Anderson's managers had intended to secure university status and degree-granting powers, since the evidence, given by McClelland, Young and Harvey before the Royal Commission in 1872, was in print, and those members of the Senatus who had attended the British Association's meetings in 1876 must have received it. The ambitions of Anderson's University were certainly known to a small section of the Senatus – those Medical professors who had been recruited by the University of Glasgow from Anderson's University. Whatever the source of information – from Parliamentary Papers, hearsay in the City, or from well-informed individuals – it seems most likely the main grounds of the opposition to the Bill were based on the belief that Anderson's University wished to grant degrees and exercise the other functions of a university.

Mr Cunliff followed McKinlay and openly stated that:

... one of the principal objects in applying for the bill was to obtain the effect of a Charter, and to place them in a proper relation with the University and they were always seeing that objection was taken to the tickets of the Medical School being accepted by the University on account of its assuming the title of a University ... [76]

'That was why the managers were prepared to drop the name 'University' in favour of 'Anderson's College, Glasgow'.[77] They certainly would have preferred to have degree-granting powers in a peaceful, unchallenging world but did not believe it was worthwhile to sacrifice their Bill for them; indeed, they had made no mention of degrees in their draft, but they were most anxious to ensure that the qualifications of their medical students were recognised under the terms of the Act of 1861.[78]

There were several reasons why Anderson's College, Glasgow, Bill made no reference to degree-granting powers. Apart from medical students and those intending to take up appointments in industry and commerce, they had very few students likely to want to take degrees in science. Medical students were provided for under the terms of the Act of 1861; the others were generally not so degree-conscious as future generations of students were to become. Should it happen that governments decided to support the expansion of scientific and technological education, degree-granting powers might follow or be organised on a national federal basis. The managers expected that all such powers would ' ... be taken from all Educational Schools and given to an independent body ... '[79] This belief should be seen in terms of the City and Guilds Industrial University movement, which was being officially canvassed; to the central examining body in London, it was proposed to link provincial colleges in a system of examinations at various levels directed at testing competence and ability in applied sciences and vocational subjects. Throughout 1877 and 1878 – and even later – there was considerable public interest in and controversy about this scheme, but no 'Industrial University' developed in Great Britain.[80] Mistakenly, as it turned out, the managers were gambling on the assumption that an Industrial University would be founded, to which Anderson's University would be affiliated.

However, a deliberate insertion in the Private Bill disclaiming degree-granting power obviously could do little harm, and it might, by improving relations with the University of Glasgow, do some good. The managers were adroitly manoeuvred into this action, once they admitted that they themselves did not intend to apply for degree-granting powers. The deputation from the Senatus were then able to suggest that a disclaimer would suit both parties, for they thought that Anderson's will was far too definite in its requirements of his trustees: as Professor Allen Thomson inaccurately put it: 'The Will of Anderson directed the Trustees to found a literal copy of the University'.[81]

Four days after this meeting, on 9 February, 1877, the University representatives sent in their list of suggested modifications to the Bill, as the managers had requested.[82] On 19 February the Secretary of Anderson's University replied, after consulting the Parliamentary Solicitors and legal opinion in Glasgow. The managers were not prepared to drop the title 'Anderson's College, Glasgow'; nor were they prepared to call their professors 'lecturers', as the Senatus wished, but they were prepared to disclaim degree-granting powers, which they had never enjoyed.[83] No reply was received to the Secretary's letter, but the ten days' delay in sending it may have convinced the Senatus that Anderson's University was using obstructionist tactics in the hope of preventing the University of Glasgow from protesting against the Bill. In fact, on 2 February, 1877 a petition against it containing seven points of objection was presented to the House of Lords by the University of Glasgow, signed by Principal Caird on behalf of the Senatus Academicus.[84] Hastily the Secretary and managers mobilised their defences against this petition by lobbying MPs and influential friends of Anderson's University and by preparing to send witnesses from the Faculty of Medicine and from the trustees.

The Bill was due to be heard before a Committee of the House of Lords on Monday, 6 March. On the previous Saturday, 4 March, 1877, the Secretary received a letter from Professor Blackburn, who was leading the University of Glasgow's objections to the Bill, asking for a meeting between the managers and a deputation from the Senatus Academicus. Although there was no time for this meeting to be held before the first hearing of the Bill – and Blackburn indeed, had left Glasgow for London to support the University's petition before his own letter had been delivered – it seems likely that the Senatus were seeking a compromise. On Sunday, 5 March, 1877, the University's counsel approached the solicitors acting for Anderson's trustees privately, and a settlement was reached: in exchange for a slight rewording of one clause the University agreed to allow the Bill to pass unopposed. Thus, on the following day, 6 March 1877, the Lords referred the Bill to Lord Redesdale, Chairman of the Committee of Unopposed Bills.[85] It quickly passed its three readings and by 22 March, 1877 had been read for the first time in the House of Commons; it received royal assent on 17 May.[86]

The Anderson's College, Glasgow, Act of 1877 incorporated the trustees, changed the name of the institution and remodelled the powers and duties of both the trustees and managers. Funds were safeguarded by giving the trustees the right to sue and be sued; gifts could be elicited much more readily when they were protected by law; investments could be readily changed in the interest of running a more modern portfolio as economic circumstances dictated, but security was not sacrificed. Thus financial regularisation was achieved.

The Chair of Technical Chemistry, founded by James Young in 1870, was permanently associated with Anderson's College, thereby strengthening for ever the teaching of applied sciences in Glasgow and the West of Scotland. Trustees and managers were no longer disqualified by membership of, or association with, Glasgow University or the government of the City of Glasgow. This clause paved the way for closer and closer co-operation between the higher educational institutions and also the City authorities.[87]

However, the sub-clause[88] disclaiming degree-granting powers in practice placed the University of Glasgow in the dominant position in any negotiations about degree courses which occurred later. Although at this stage Young was not in the best of health, he had had enough experience of legal disclaimers in business to recognise the weaknesses of such a sub-clause — perhaps his absence was critical. On the other hand the managers could not be expected to anticipate the failure of the technical university movement in Great Britain in the late 'seventies and 'eighties nor had they our gift of hindsight. Moreover, the expenses of the Private Bill procedure were well known; this Act cost £613.57p,[89] and had it not been unopposed, it would have cost much more. It seems that Young's fellow managers, in his absence, were likely to consider very carefully the costs of retaining a principle which the College, they felt, was unlikely to need — after all the immediate problems of their medical students had been overcome! In any case the Technische Hochschulen, which they fervently admired, did not at this stage have degree-granting powers either; they were operating at the same level and in the same academic areas which the managers intended for their own College.

The control of the trustees and managers over academic appointments and policy was made clear and complete by the Act. The trustees were to appoint new professors ' ... without any recommendations from the Senate ... ' They were given powers to alter lecture courses, to abolish existing professorships or to institute new ones, if they so desired; Anderson's will was no longer their sole authority. Also they were to have a new common seal.[90]

From 1860 onwards there was a clear attempt to attract good — and generally young — professors at appropriate times. Walter Crum in 1856-7, for example, tried unsuccessfully with Young to bring the great Justus von Liebig to Scotland to found a School of Agricultural Chemistry.[91] After lengthy discussion James Galbraith, writer in Glasgow, was appointed to the Chair of Commercial Law in 1861.[92] Improvements were made to the accommodation, including the creation of a large new lecture theatre which impressed a raw young Professor of Natural Philosophy, George Carey Foster, who recalled it thirty years later. The equipment was not so impressive:

> Physical apparatus at the Andersonian on my arrival was most of it conspicuous by its absence, and a good part of what did exist consisted of contrivances for producing curious or surprising effects, veritable tricks, rather than apparatus for instruction ... [93]

The arrival of Carey-Foster in 1862 was occasioned by the resignation of Professor John Taylor (1846-61), a year earlier. Crum, Euing and McClelland conducted a head-hunting exercise in London, believing that a young man trained in Physics with a chemical laboratory background would serve their purposes best. There was also the need to cater for a Popular

Evening Class audience to be considered. As it happened, University College, London, where Carey-Foster was assistant to Professor A.W. Williamson (1824-1904), had a science curriculum which included heat, light and electricity within Practical Chemistry. As the managers were told by Crum:

> As to the power of any of the Candidates [for the Chair of Natural Philosophy] to interest a popular audience, it is yet in a great measure to be tried ... But in this Institution we have repeatedly run such risks, having faith in the searching investigation we have made into the powers of the Candidate – his strength of mind, and dignity and steadiness of character – his general as well as his special acquirements – the work he has done, and the power he has of expressing himself clearly.
>
> Some of us can declare from experience that that plan has been followed in the choice of every young man who has been elected by Anderson's Trustees from Thomas Graham downwards, and the result ... has been not only to fill this school with able men but to make it the means of introducing not a few who have afterwards occupied elsewhere high academical positions in pure science and in medicine.[94]

Carey-Foster took time to find his feet, but his first Popular Evening Class attracted 248 students, all men. He was reminded of rule 2 of Article 9 of John Anderson's will which prescribed the provision of a class for women and began offering a day class in 1863-4.[95] In 1865 he resigned to return to University College as Professor of Experimental Natural Philosophy.[96]

No appointment immediately followed. Edward Maxwell Dixon (1829-89), a mathematician at the Church of Scotland Normal School, gave lectures in 1865-6, as did Dr Adams of Merchiston Castle Academy, Edinburgh. Alexander S. Herschel, who had been a candidate when Carey-Foster was successful, was eventually appointed to the Freeland Chair of Natural Philosophy in September 1866.[97] The Freeland stipend of £100 per year and the income from student fees net of room rents was augmented by the provision of a technician at James Young's expense, but it was not sufficient to retain the young, mobile and intellectually able. Herschel resigned in 1871 to take the founding Chair in Natural Philosophy at Newcastle, a more secure position in several respects.

The vacancy was difficult to fill. Seven unsuitable candidates presented themselves, and Young and William Euing attempted to raise additional endowments to support the Chair. Private searching led them to James Prescott Joule (1818-89) F.R.S., pupil of Dalton and a man of private means with a laboratory at Whalley Range, Librarian (1844), Secretary (1846), Vice-President (1851) and President (1860) of the Manchester Literary and Philosophical Society. Having established the mechanical equivalent of heat, Joule, an acquaintance of Young, would have been a great catch for the Andersonian; he was prepared to accept the Chair 'provided he was appointed without an application on his part an [sic] secured an Income of £300 or thereby and that from £500 to £1,000 be expended as required on Philosophical Instruments'. Unfortunately, the money could not be raised, and there were no classes in Natural Philosophy in 1871-2.[98]

The time-honoured practice of appointing an able young man was then followed. George Forbes, the son of the late Principal of St Andrews University (James David Forbes (1809-68)), just down from Cambridge, was appointed in October 1872. Forbes was prolific during his time at the Andersonian, producing about fifty papers on a variety of subjects pertaining to theoretical and applied physics. An electrical engineer of considerable prowess, he later became an inventor with many patents and consultant on the Niagara hydro-electric scheme. His projects included work on the telephone, fire-damp, gas in mines, the measurement of alternating current, electric lighting and power transmission; he was a keen astronomer and accurately predicted in 1880 the existence of an ultra-Neptunian planet; Pluto was, in fact, discovered in 1930.[99]

When Forbes resigned in August 1880, he was succeeded by James Blyth, MA, F.R.S.E, who received a basic stipend of £200 per year and contributed to the very successful Popular Evening Class programme as well as providing daytime classes. Some of his students succeeded in the examinations of the Department of Science and Art, and Blyth, as a consequence of the government policy of payment by results, received £39 at the end of his first session and £123 in 1883. One of his more substantial purchases paid for by the managers in 1882 was a dynamo driven by a gas engine.[100]

One of the clearest indications of how Anderson's University fostered talent is demonstrated by the career of James Croll (born 1821). Appointed in February 1860 as the janitor after John Jardine retired through ill-health on a pension of £20 per annum, Croll earned a salary of £1 per week, but he had, in addition, a university house within the building with free coal and gas, and local taxes paid. He obviously made great use of his access to the University Library and the Library of the Glasgow Philosophical Society. An early member of the Glasgow Geological Society which met in the Andersonian after its foundation in 1858, he displayed tremendous talent and research capability. His main papers dealt with the probable causes of climatic change over geological time, and his first which appeared in 1864 so impressed Sir William Thomson (Lord Kelvin), Sir Andrew Ramsay and Sir Archibald Geikie that they later sponsored his successful candidature as Secretary to the Geological Survey in Scotland in 1867. Academic honours came to him later in life as his major researches appeared in one volume, *Climate and Time* (1875). He died an LL.D. and F.R.S.[101]

In Mathematics there was continuity: Alexander Laing, appointed in 1846, conducted very successful elementary and advanced classes in the day, fighting off unfair competition from teachers of copperplate writing and accountancy, both of whom infringed on his territory because of their interests in double-entry book-keeping. His evening classes were very large, generally 140 or more strong. When he resigned in June 1881, he raised the question of a 'retiring allowance' with the managers, but they believed that he had fared well enough. It would have done him little good for he died about a year later, leaving his books and their 'presses' to the College. His classes were taken by James Blyth until the appointment of William Raitt after the merger with the College of Science and Arts in 1886-7.[102]

Major growth occurred in Chemistry. The additional Chair in Technical Chemistry was offered in 1869 to W.H. Perkin, the inventor of the first coal-tar dyes; tenure was to be for a period of not less than five years at a salary of £300 per year. Although Perkin accepted the post, the opposition of Professor F. W. Penny and his threat of legal action against the managers and trustees, on the grounds that Anderson's will did not provide for two professors of Chemistry, deterred him from taking it up. Penny claimed that he had transformed a department of 58 students into a school of over 800; but this simply indicated that there was room for another appointment. The controversy ended with Penny's death in November 1869.

Perkin was replaced in 1871 by Gustav Bischof, son of the eminent Professor of Chemistry in Bonn, who was not able to exploit the opportunities which the regional chemical industry offered. The Young Chair and Laboratory were intended to support a more practical, industry-based education which, its promoters believed, was badly needed:

... As Chemical education stands at present, manufacturers know that, if they engage a young man as a Chemist, although he may have certificates of proficiency for years of study in the

TABLE 4.1　Student Enrolments in Technical Chemistry, 1871-86

Session	Number	Increase / Decrease
1871-2	14	
1872-3	17	+.
1873-4	11	-(
1874-5	8	-
1875-6	25	+1
1876-7	39	+1.
1877-8	40	+.
1878-9	28	-1:
1879-80	28	(
1880-1	81	+5:
1881-2	112	+3:
1882-3	149	+3:
1883-4	179	+3(
1884-5	43	-13(
1885-6	58	+1

Source: Annual Reports of the Young Chair, 1871-86.

Laboratory, when he enters the Factory he has to begin an apprenticeship, and for a year or two i of little use to his employers.

As Table 4.1 indicates, development was slow up to 1875-6. Bischof had the disadvantage of teaching in a foreign language but he made a real attempt to relate the intellectual content of the course to local industry's needs. He lacked the skills needed to market the course and therefore did not achieve the results expected of him. A tuition fee of £20 *per annum* did not help recruitment; anyone able to afford that was likely to go to one of the great continental schools of Chemistry, for the distinction of continental qualifications and experience was outstanding.

Unfortunately, Bischof was a subject of ridicule among his students because his English was very poor. He tended to leave laboratory instruction and supervision to his assistants, Otto Hehner and William Ramsay, who, although brilliant by most standards, had at this stage in their careers very little teaching experience. According to Hehner, both were dissatisfied: ' ... neither of us could obtain advice or stimulus from our professor ... Chemically, our life at the Andersonian was unsatisfactory'. Yet Ramsay learned gas manipulation techniques in the Young laboratory which the joint discoverer of 'inert' gases later put to good use, and it could be reasonably agreed that he became Glasgow's outstanding chemist. Hehner became a famous analyst and industrial consultant in London. R.W. McIvor went to Australia and became a leading agricultural chemist. Significantly, all three made their reputations outside Scotland.

Bischof did not lecture in the evenings. This was his major mistake, for evening courses for skilled workmen and supervisory grades had proven successful in other subjects and because of their cheapness would have attracted those who could not afford to attend a full-time day class. However, his linguistic difficulties might have militated against success, and he certainly realised that too many students lacked a sound basic education.

The fortunes of the Young Chair began to revive with the appointment of Dr Edmund Mills F.R.S. (*c.*1840-1921), who succeeded Bischof in 1875. A pupil of A.W. von Hofmann at the Royal College of Chemistry, Mills gained industrial experience with Dr John Stenhouse and

TABLE 4.2   Student Enrolments, 1861-66

Session	Medical	Arts	CLASSES Popular Evening	Other Classes	Total
1861-2	631	376	844		1851
1862-3	565	347	975		1887
1863-4	633	463	841		1937
1864-5	575	520	860		1955
1865-6	639	480	993		2112
1866-7	551	561	1001	283	2396
1867-8	564	534	1271		2369
1868-9	581	569	1400		2550
1869-70	584	645	1312		2541
1870-1	565	618	1457		2640
1871-2	438	269	1110	397	2228
1872-3	460	327	1370	349	2523
1873-4	380	318	1457	344	2510
1874-5	331	253	1324	367	2283
1875-6	306	159	1240	525	2255
1876-7	199	234	1082	544	2098
1877-8	310	281	992	313*	1978
1878-9	352	296	1021	323	2020
1879-80	415	497	827	352	2119
1880-1	768	406	1008	307	2164
1881-2	357	743	790	519	2521
1882-3	375	710	1153	511	2749
1883-4*	307	577	1071	530	2664
1884-5	350	724	1070	428	2615
1885-6	329	635	941	403	2370

1. Total includes Technical Chemistry from 1871-2 (see Table 4.1).
2. Where no entry for Other Classes, these were often included with Popular Evening Classes.
*   Incomplete.

Sources: Annual Reports, 1861-86; Minute Books, 1861-86. Gilmorehill (1870) and the rise of the Royal Infirmary Medical School (1876).

then came to Glasgow University in 1863 as a tutor before returning to London to University College. An energetic man with broad experience, Mills was and remained a prolific researcher, employing team methods of investigation. His lectures were delivered very early in the morning and therefore ' ... attracted the attention of young men in business'. He instituted works visits for his students, collected a small technical library and developed good industrial contacts, encouraging the use of the laboratories by industrial chemists. Perhaps the most brilliant – and original – research worker in the Young Laboratory during the tenure of Mills (1875-1901) was a bursar, James Bannatyne Hannay, an early crystallographer and the first man in the world to make artificial diamonds. Hannay's 'diamonds' were forgotten amid other interesting objects in the British Museum and he was scoffed at till the late 1940s; X-ray crystallography has vindicated his reputation. Up to 1886 a wide range of research was undertaken in the Young Laboratory: in brewing and fermentation, by-products recovery at ironworks, dye chemistry, glass formation and explosives. Maintaining the support of British industry was a major task, especially during depressions, and many students like McIvor left the country.

After Penny's death, the Chair of 'Scientific' Chemistry was taken by T.E. Thorpe of Owens'

College, Manchester, who did not manage to attract students on the scale of his predecessor but still had about seventy students in attendance at his lectures in the early 1870s and a full practical class. His experience was first-class, having worked with Bunsen and Kekulé before joining Roscoe in Manchester. Thorpe resigned in 1874 to become the first Professor of Chemistry in the new Yorkshire College of Leeds.

Before Thorpe's appointment, James Young had been approached by William Dittmar with his latest offprint and a gentle inquiry about the possibility of succeeding Penny. Thus he was a ready-made successor to Thorpe and had similar experience – formerly with Kekulé and latterly as assistant to Roscoe. Dittmar made a reputation as an analytical chemist and, apart from a substantial number of learned papers, produced standard texts on quantitative and qualitative analysis. During his tenure (1874-92) his students were well prepared for entering the chemical and other industries – for he did not really recognise any academic boundary between 'Scientific' and 'Technical' Chemistry, sometimes alarming Professor Mills. There was a range of provision for students, but most attended evening classes, and a minority took the examinations of the Department of Science and Arts.[103]

The new chair in Applied Mechanics was filled in 1876 by William T. Rowden who was recruited from Elswick Mechanics' Institution, Newcastle-upon-Tyne. Rowden was an Associate of the Royal College of Mines and a graduate of London University, and he had sixteen years of teaching experience – four at Bristol, four at Woolwich and eight at Elswick – before coming to Glasgow. In the examinations of the Department of Science and Arts his Elswick students had achieved the best results and the most prizes in the whole of Britain, a fact known to the Andersonian's managers and a principal reason for his appointment.[104] Rowden certainly lived up to his reputation, rapidly building an academic area which served all the local industries comprising heavy engineering: by 1878 he had 156 students in his classes, which were often disturbed by the choir practices in St Paul's Church. By 1881 payment by results, arising from examination successes recognised by the Department of Science and Arts, brought him over £500, a very significant component in his professorial income; in 1884 he received £622 from this source and £71 from the City and Guilds of London Institute examination successes.[105] Rowden's earlier experience in Newcastle of shipbuilding and allied industries and locomotive engineering evidently prepared him well for the Glasgow phase of his career (1876-1904).

As Table 4.2 makes clear, student enrolments increased between 1861 and 1886, but the experience of academic areas varied significantly. Arts enrolments – Mathematics, Natural Philosophy, Chemistry and Applied Mechanics – nearly doubled; a miscellany of 'Other Classes', as they are described in the Annual Reports, responded remarkably to student demand; the Popular Evening Classes in Chemistry, Natural Philosophy, Anatomy and Physiology and other subjects attracted the largest numbers. These three areas contrast markedly with the experience of the Medical Faculty which, apart from the pressures induced by downturns in the regional trade cycle common to all – 1871-2, 1875-8 and 1884-6 – was severely hit by the transfer from the High Street of the University of Glasgow Medical School to Gilmorehill (1870) and the rise of the Royal Infirmary Medical School (1876).

Pioneering in Medicine continued. The Glasgow Ophthalmic Institution (1868-92) was associated with the Andersonian Medical School from 1869, when Dr John Reissburg Wolfe (c.1830-1904), its founder, was appointed to a lectureship. Wolfe, born in Breslau but a Glasgow graduate (1856), had travelled widely in Europe, working in Salonika and Paris, becoming Senior Surgeon to Garibaldi and an Inspector of Italian Military Hospitals before returning to Scotland first to an appointment in Aberdeen and then returning to Glasgow c.1868. His experience and methods in Ophthalmic Surgery were continental – and, *ipso facto*, to local doctors, doubtful; many thought him a trickster and others a dangerous charlatan. Yet his results with cataract operations were exceptionally good, and he also tried treating some wounds with skin grafts. Inevitably, his appointment was controversial, and there was some delay before the trustees approved it.[106] However, Wolfe proved to be a successful teacher, and his Ophthalmic Institution a useful centre for the practical training of students: in the 1870s his classes regularly attracted about fifty students.

In January 1878 the Medical Faculty wanted to establish a dispensary where the city's poor could be treated free. The managers approved of this, partly because it was argued that student doctors would gain a great deal from experience in staffing it and visiting the sick in their homes. It proved to be a great success at relatively small cost. James Burn Russell (1837-1904), Glasgow's outstanding Medical Officer of Health (1872-98) and eventually Medical Member of the Local Government Board for Scotland (1898-1904), was a strong supporter of this dispensary and became a trustee of the Andersonian. When the managers heard that Russell intended to give some lectures on public health in 1878 they offered him the great hall, but he preferred to use Corporation property. Dr James Christie was then appointed to a lectureship in Public Health.[107] Another specialist appointment in 1879 was Dr Thomas Barr to a lectureship in Aural Surgery.[108]

In the spring of 1879 Professor James Morton (Chair of Materia Medica) suggested that the Medical Faculty should diversify into the academic and practical study of Dentistry associated with the foundation of a Dental Hospital. Under the Dentists' Act of 1878 the Faculty of Physicians and Surgeons in Glasgow and the Royal College of Surgeons in Edinburgh were given powers to set examinations in Dental Surgery and to award diplomas to successful candidates. The close relationship particularly between the Glasgow Faculty and the Andersonian probably explains Morton's interest; the managers and trustees were sympathetic when they were informed that of the thirteen classes required by the Faculty, nine were already provided and another was available at the Royal Infirmary. Thus, three new classes were needed in order to provide a complete course; the managers advised that the trustees should make appointments of practising dentists. Three appointments, all for one session in the first instance, followed in May: Dr J. Cowan Woodburn (Glasgow M.D.) to a lectureship in Dental Surgery and Pathology; James R. Brownlie L.D.S., R.C.D.E. (London) to a lectureship in Dental Mechanics and Metallurgy; and John Crooks Morrison to a lectureship in Dental Anatomy and Physiology. Accommodation was provided not only for teaching but also for the first Dental Hospital, but no additional funds 'for operating chairs and spittoons' were provided. Fee income and philanthropy became its main sources of income. Morrison died in 1881; by then he was recognised as a professor; in the Chair of Dental Anatomy and Physiology he was succeeded by Dr David S. Allan. The academic study of Dentistry and the Dental Hospital was associated with Anderson's College till 1885 when the dental staff rented premises, removed operating chairs and spittoons to the top floor of 56 George Square and opened the independent Glasgow Dental Hospital and School on 4 May.[109]

The departure of the Dental Hospital and the teaching staff marked the end of a protracted process in the strategic planning of the Andersonian. Space constraints in the boom of the early 1870s caused a fundamental re-examination of the George Street site and its uses. In 1873 there was an unsuccessful attempt to purchase the High School building. However, by September 1874 Professor George Forbes had a new laboratory for which Sir William Thomson (later Lord Kelvin), a former student in the Mechanics' Institution, made a donation of £100, and great improvements were made in the dissecting rooms of the Medical School. The Managers were then thinking of a complete rebuilding of the University, and a sub-committee was appointed to direct development.

After the removal of Glasgow University to Gilmorehill, the opportunity to teach its undergraduates disappeared except in the summer session. Student enrolments in the 1870s were noticeably lower than in the previous decade (see Table 4.2). The Medical Professors were convinced that degree-granting powers were essential and appropriate. Their most pressing grievance was the refusal of Glasgow University to accept Anderson's Medical School certificates as valid, and the managers successfully referred this issue to the Royal Commission on Scottish Universities.[110]

The failure to get degree-granting powers in the Act of 1877 which changed the institution's name to Anderson's College was critical. Thereafter the Medical Faculty sought to move westwards close to Glasgow University and the new Western Infirmary, but could not persuade either the trustees or their other academic colleagues and the Popular Evening Class committee (which represented the largest group of students) of the correctness of this action. The managers in 1878 established a fund-raising committee chaired by James White of Overtoun, a leading chemical manufacturer, to create a substantial endowment fund for the Medical Faculty, but the sharp depression at the end of that decade made its work impossible. A new Medical School in the vicinity of the University of Glasgow was priced at a minimum of £6,500, and the separation of the Medical Faculty was agreed. In the whole institution it was felt that an endowment of about £40,000 was needed to cover the cost of Professors, laboratories and equipment. By 1879 stark economic realities in the shape of the worst depression to afflict Glasgow since 1819 stalled the reconstruction of the College and the Medicals' move westwards.

A further attempt was made to amalgamate the Medical Faculty with the Royal Infirmary Medical School in 1881, but discussions were at first inconclusive and then the terms of a possible settlement unacceptable.[111] Instead, the Medical Faculty began to raise money to support a move westwards, but the first site – at the junction of Church Street and Byres Road – 534 square yards at £2 per square yard was felt by the managers to be insufficient, but a suitable building would have cost £5,000. Meanwhile the Royal Commission on Technical Education was visiting the city, and the Educational Endowments Commission (Scotland) Bill was about to receive royal assent. In May 1883 the managers decided that Anderson's College should become a 'leading feature in a General Technical College' for Glasgow and that the Medical Faculty should be separated completely from it and retain the name of Anderson's College Medical School.

Following evidence to the Educational Endowments Commission making this policy clear, the future lay in amalgamation with the College of Science and Arts (formerly the Mechanics' Institution), Allan Glen's School, the Young Chair of Technical Chemistry and the Thomas Atkinson Institution. The draft scheme prepared in consultation with the interested parties took several years before it was finally accepted – and even then the attempt to retain Anderson's name in association with the new technical college only failed after a stubborn fight. The Anderson College Medical School, aided with a grant of £5,000, was separately incorporated under the limited liability company regulations in 1886. Henry Craik, the newly appointed Secretary of the Scotch (sic) Education Department, a staunch supporter of technical education, pressed through inevitable compromises, and final approval by the Privy Council came on 26 November, 1886. The trustees nominated six permanent governors of the Glasgow and West of Scotland Technical College and nine directors of Anderson's College Medical School. The managers met for the last time on 9 June 1887, and instructed the Secretary to hand over all books, deeds, papers, moveables and cash balances to the Board of Governors of the new college.[112]

Amid these complicated negotiations teaching and student life continued. Both staff and students were consulted about the draft scheme for the new technical college. Professors Blyth, Dittmar, Mills and Rowden suggested that a council representing the teaching staff should be

13 Dr Henry Dyer (1848-1918), student and Whitworth Scholar at Anderson's University, 1863-8, and graduate of the University of Glasgow, was appointed the first Principal and Professor of Civil and Mechanical Engineering in the Imperial College of Engineering,Tokyo,1873-82,and became a trustee of Anderson's University and Life Governor of the Glasgow and West of Scotland Technical College and Royal Technical College,1887-1918.

recognised by the new Board of Governors.[113] This was the origin of the later Board of Study. The opportunities for new courses, which the merger offered, required close investigation, but a strengthening of academic provision seemed likely.

Most students attended only one class; it was calculated in 1883 that only seven per cent attended two or more, but elementary classes were not examined closely.[114] Yet student life and societies began to flourish. The medical students had a smoking room before the professors had managed to prevail upon the managers to give them a senior common room. Technical Chemistry students in 1879 obtained the use of a room for gymnastics, including fencing, and formed a student club on the German model. Two years earlier, in 1875 the Young Laboratory Students' Society had been founded to hear papers of technical interest and to discuss abstracts of recent publications; this was the earliest non-medical departmental student society.[115] Significantly, it was Professor Mills who took the initiative in seeking a professorial common room – also in 1877 – because he felt that otherwise the opportunity to meet colleagues was very limited.[116] Certainly, he might have found it difficult to meet Professor A. S. Wilson (Chair of Botany) who doubled as Pastor of the Free Church in North Queensferry.[117] The Andersonian Natural History Society was formed in 1885 and met regularly in the managers' room but was asked to pay for heat, light and cleaning.[118] In 1886 a Microscopical Society fared better: its preliminary meeting cost its members nothing![119] Later in 1886 the Andersonian Chemical Society was formed with an initial membership of seven for the reading and discussion of papers on chemical and allied subjects.[120]

Most students were male, although Botany, Chemistry, Natural Philosophy and Mathematics attracted a trickle of women. The first female winner of a bursary was Miss Anne L. Church of Hillhead, who was appointed to a Kerr Bursary in Botany in August 1886.[121] Most attended in the evenings, usually choosing one class from the many on offer. The vast majority combined a job with studying, and from the 1830s and possibly earlier the winter full-time session from late October or early November to early May made 'sandwich' type arrangements possible where the student intercalated study and work.

Although an overwhelming proportion of students lived and worked within a short geographical radius of the city centre, improvements in public transport led to a widening of the catchment area. A number of Irish and English students seeking medical qualifications had studied in the Andersonian's Medical School, and a few had come to train as medical missionaries. After 1860 there was a change to the pursuit of applied science and technology, and the possibility of technology transfer became very real.

In 1863 five young Samurai of the Choshu clan were smuggled out of Nagasaki, Japan in a ship belonging to Jardine and Matheson. They were part of an élite intent on overthrowing the Shogunate, restoring the Meiji dynasty and gaining knowledge and experience which would assist Japan to industrialise. After spending two years at University College, London, one of them, Yamao Yozo (1837-1917), came to Glasgow and attended evening classes at Anderson's University at the same time as Henry Dyer (1848-1918), an apprentice engineer (1863-8) with the firm of James Aitken, foundrymen and engineers of Cranstonhill. Yamao obtained an apprenticeship at the great Clyde shipyard of Robert Napier, the first Japanese apprentice in the western world. In 1866 Yamao combined this job with attending Alexander S. Hershel's lectures on Natural Philosophy and in subsequent sessions he attended other science classes including Professor Penny's class on Inorganic Chemistry and Metallurgy. By the time that Yamao returned to Japan in early 1870, the Meiji dynasty had been restored, and he joined the Ministry of Public Works. Yamao and Ito, the leader of the original five Samurai and now (1871) Minister of Public Works, drew up plans for the vocational training of engineers and technicians in a school of engineering, modelled on Yamao's Glasgow experience. Meanwhile, Dyer completed a brilliant career at the University of Glasgow (1868-73), graduating M.A., B.Sc.C.E. as a Whitworth Scholar. Other Japanese students at the Andersonian included Torajiro Ishimaru (1866) and Hachico Umawatari (1866).

Delay in the recruitment of foreign experts for the Imperial College of Engineering worked to Dyer's advantage. He was recommended to Hugh Matheson, agent for the Japanese Ministry of Public Works in London, and spent ten years as the first principal (1873-83). While there he systematised the 'sandwich' course training, established a fine School, and was the real source of ideas for the Japanese to apply in building their new Higher Education system.[122]

Most Japanese students came to Glasgow after Dyer's return in 1883, but one turned up in Professor Mills's Young Laboratory in 1879-80. His name was J. Takamine, and he obtained an apprenticeship at Tennant's St Rollox Chemical Works, the largest firm in Scotland.[123] Thus, Anderson's College played a significant part in Japan's drive to industrialise, not simply through its training of students but also because of the key importance of Yamao and Henry Dyer.

The years, 1860-1886, saw many changes, none more striking than the emergence of the Glasgow and West of Scotland Technical College, the first merger in the history of a mature educational institution. Anderson's name had gone — save from the Medical School which maintained an independent and successful existence till after World War Two. The schism inaugurated in 1823 by the Glasgow Mechanics' Institution was forcibly settled by the Educational Endowments Commission. Pressure from foreign competitors was gathering force: Glasgow as an exporting city in a free-trade nation required to invest more in scientific and technical education.

REFERENCES

1 W.H.G. Armytage, *Civic Universities* (1955), p.196.
2 Lyon Playfair, 'The Chemical Principles involved in the Manufactures of the Exhibition as indicating the Necessity of Industrial Instruction' in *Lectures on the Results of the Great Exhibition of 1851* (1852) I, p.193.
3 Armytage, p.234.
4 J.A. Lloyd, *Proposals for Establishing Colleges of Arts and Manufactures* (1851).
5 Baron C. Dupin, *The Commercial Power of Great Britain, exhibiting a complete view of the Public Works of the country* (1825), II, pp. 235ff.
6 James Hole, *History and Management of Literary, Scientific and Mechanics' Institutes* (1853).
7 D.S.L. Cardwell, *The Organisation of Science in England* (1957), p.71.
8 T.H. Huxley, *Science and Education: Essays* (1893), p.137.
9 S.F. Cotgrove, *Technical Education and Social Change* (1958).
10 Thomas Chalmers, *On the Christian and Economic Polity of a Nation* (Glasgow, 1839), III, pp.104 ff.
11 J.Wilson Harper, *The Social Ideal and Dr. Chalmers' Contribution to Christian Economics* (Edinburgh, 1910), pp.363ff.
12 SUA, B1/4, Minute Book, 1830-64, 22 Sept., 1858.
13 SUA, B1/5, Minute Book, 1865-81, p.72.
14 Ibid., p.167.
15 Ibid., p.73.
16 Ibid., p.159.
17 Ibid., p.73.
18 Ibid., p.278.
19 Ibid., p.385.
20 Ibid., p.484.
21 Ibid.
22 Ibid., p.502.
23 Reports of the Committee of Governing Bodies giving Technical and Science Teaching in Glasgow, 30 June, 1883. The total funds and assets available in the City amounted to nearly £127,300.
24 SUA, B1/5, Minute Book, 1865-81, p.258.
25 Ibid., pp. 191 and 479-80.
26 Ibid., p.55.
27 Ibid., p.59.
28 Ibid., p.245.
29 Ibid., p.248.
30 Ibid., p.236.
31 Ibid., p.247.
32 Ibid., p.249.
33 Ibid., p.258.
34 Ibid., p.283.
35 Ibid., p.354.
36 Ibid., pp.222 and 289.
37 Ibid., p.395.
38 I have been able to trace £1,800 which came to the Andersonian as a result of Stenhouse's efforts.
39 SUA, Pocket Diary of James Young, 27 April, 1875.
40 Pocket Diary of James Young, 24 March, 1876.
41 SUA, B1/5, Minute Book, 1865-81, p.551.
42 Ibid., p.564.
43 Ibid., p.570.
44 BPP Royal Commission on Scientific Instruction and the Advancement of Science, 1872, Q. 9,994-6.
45 M. Arnold, *Schools and Universities on the Continent* (1868), p.276.
46 J.S. Russell, *Systematic Technical Education for the English People* (1869).
47 Armytage, p.222.

48   Ibid., pp. 226 ff.
49   Cardwell, pp. 85 ff.
50   Armytage, p.227.
51   J.R. Taylor, *Reform Your City Guilds* (1872).
52   Royal Commission, Q. 9,991-3.
53   Ibid., Q. 10,015.
54   Ibid., Q. 10,030.
55   Ibid., Q. 10,053.
56   Ibid., Q. 10,047.
57   Ibid., Q. 10,050.
58   SUA, B1/5, Minute Book, 1865-81, p.219.
59   Ibid., pp. 281 and 290.
60   Ibid., pp. 294 and 302.
61   Ibid., p.302.
62   Ibid., p.318.
63   Ibid.
64   Ibid., p.400.
65   Ibid., pp. 390 ff.
66   Ibid., pp. 385-6.
67   Ibid., p.392.
68   Ibid., pp. 407-8.
69   Royal Commission Seventh Report, p.22.
70   SUA, B1/5, Minute Book, 1865-81, pp. 409-410.
71   Ibid., p.411.
72   Ibid., pp. 429 and 432.
73   Ibid., p.433.
74   Ibid., pp. 435-7.
75   Ibid., p.437.
76   Ibid.
77   The example of the title, 'Anderson's College, Glasgow', was derived from Owens' College, Manchester.
78   21/22 Vict. c.83 allowed Medical Professors of Anderson's University to be regarded as private teachers of Medicine; the certificates which they issued to students, successful in their examinations, were as valid as a university degree.
79   SUA, B1/5, Minute Book, 1865-81, p.437.
80   Cardwell, pp. 98-103.
81   SUA, B1/5, Minute Book, 1865-81, p.438.
82   Ibid., pp. 440-1.
83   Ibid., p.441.
84   Ibid., pp. 442 ff.
85   Ibid., pp. 443-6.
86   40 Vict. c.12.
87   Ibid., clauses 4-9.
88   Ibid., within clause 4.
89   SUA, B1/5, Minute Book, 1865-81, p.467.
90   40 Vict. c.12 clauses 12-15.
91   Liebig to Lyon Playfair, in *Memoirs and Correspondence of Lyon Playfair*, ed. T. Wemyss Reid (1899), pp. 169ff.
92   SUA, B1/4 22 December 1860; 24 January, 18 March, 10 April 1861.
93   G. Carey-Foster, F.R.S. to A.H. Sexton, 9 September 1893; SUA, B1/4, 16 August 1861: £3,000 had been raised for new building and part of the High School playground purchased for £100. A.H. Sexton, *The First Technical College* (Glasgow, 1894), pp.58f.
94   SUA, B1/4, 19 November 1861; 15 and 23 July 1862; 19 August 1862.
95   Ibid., 22 June 1862; 22 December 1863.
96   Ibid., 9 August 1865.
97   Ibid., B1/5, 22 September 1865; 22 December 1865; 22 September 1866. For E.M. Dixon's later career as a pioneering headmaster of Allan Glen's School, see Olive Checkland, *Philanthropy in Victorian Scotland* (Edinburgh, 1980), pp. 122-3 and n.
98   SUA, B1/5, pp. 202-7, 227.
99   Ibid., p.235; Butt, Ph.D. thesis, pp.446-7; Royal Society Obituary Notices, vol.ii (1936), pp. 283-6.
100 SUA, B1/5, 9 August 1880; 27 September 1880; B1/ Minute Book 1881-7, 12 December 1881; 22 September 188
101 SUA, B1/5, 31 January 1860; 1 February 1860; September 1867. *History of the Geological Society of Glasgow 1858-1908* (Glasgow, 1908), edited by P. McNair and Mort, pp. 67 and 204-6.
102 SUA, B1/5, 13 June 1881; 29 August 1881; B1/6, December 1882.
103 Butt, Ph.D. thesis, pp.407-45; James Adams, *Biographic Sketch of the late Frederick Penny* (Glasgow, 1870), *passim* Sir William A. Tilden, *Sir William Ramsay: Memorials his Life and Work* (1918), p.42; M.W. Travers, *A Life of S William Ramsay* (1956), pp. 27 and 37; Sexton, p. 196 f Nuttall, pp.5-7.
104 SUA, B1/5, 29 May 1876.
105 Ibid., Annual Report 1878-9; B1/6, 12 December 1881; June 1884.
106 Ibid., B1/5, 22 December 1868; 22 March 1869; 2 Apr 1869; O. Checkland, pp. 192-3.
107 SUA, B1/5, 14 January 1878; 9 December 1878.
108 *Public Health Administration in Glasgow* (Glasgow, 1905 edited by A.K. Chalmers, *passim*; SUA, B1/5, 11 and 2 March 1878; 20 October 1879; O. Checkland, p.204.
109 SUA, B1/5, 20 March 1879; 28 April 1879; 6 and 12 Ma 1879; 16 February 1881; 22 March 1881; B1/6, 12 Marc 1885; O. Checkland, pp. 196-7; T.B. Henderson, *T History of the Glasgow Dental Hospital and School, 1879-195* (Glasgow, 1960).
110 Butt, Ph.D. thesis, pp. 396f.
111 SUA, B1/5, 22 March 1878; 13 and 31 May 1878; 6 and 2 June 1878; 9 September 1878; 20 March 1879; 14 Marc 1881; 13 and 27 April 1881; 9 August 1881; B1/6 February 1882; 13 March 1882; 12 June 1882.
112 SUA, B1/6, 10 July 1882; 10 August 1882; 11 Septembe 1882; 9 October 1882; 21 and 28 May 1883; 7 June 1883; 2 July 1883; 13 August 1883; 27 February 1884; 19 Marc 1884; 28 April 1884; 12 May 1884; 9 June 1884; 19 Marc 1885; 13 and 30 April 1885; 25 May 1885; 4 and 2 September 1885; 13 October 1885; 1 March 1886; 12 Ma 1886; 16 and 22 June 1886; 9 and 22 September 1886; 1 and 22 December 1886; 13 and 19 January 1887; February 1887; 21 March 1887; 9 June 1887; Minutes Evidence given before the Educational Endowmen Commission, 3 April 1883, Q.2738-2795.
113 SUA, B1/6, 8 July 1886.
114 Statement by J.L.K. Jamieson before Education Endowment Commission at Glasgow 3 April 1883.
115 SUA, B1/5, 14 May 1877; JBC (Author's collection Calendar of the Glasgow and West of Scotland Technica College, 1898-9, p.317.
116 SUA, B1/5, 9 November 1877.
117 Ibid., 14 March 1881.
118 SUA, B1/6, 13 August 1885.
119 Ibid., 7 April, 1886.
120 JBC, Calendar GWSTC 1898-9, p. 317.
121 SUA, B1/6, 12 August 1886.
122 SUA, General Notes/68 List of Japanese students prepare by Sami Kita, 1980; W.H. Brock, 'The Japanes Connexion: Engineering in Tokyo, London, and Glasgo at the end of the nineteenth century', *British Journal for th History of Science*, Vol.14, No.48 (1981), pp. 227-43; Grac Fox, *Britain and Japan, 1858-83* (Oxford, 1969), *passim*.
123 SUA, General Notes/68.

The First Merger and the Emergence of the Royal Technical College, 1887-1914

'That this meeting of citizens of Glasgow and neighbourhood, having considered a report upon the nature of the widely separated buildings occupied by the Glasgow and West of Scotland Technical College, their obsolete and unsuitable character, and their insufficiency to provide for the very large and increasing number of students seeking admission to the College, heartily approves and commends to the generosity of the public the scheme for providing new and adequate buildings for this deserving institution.'

Motion put to a public meeting by J.G.A. Baird, M.P., 20 December 1900.

COMPONENTS FORMING THE GLASGOW and West of Scotland Technical College represented different aspects of philanthropy and each had a singular history. Anderson's College had the longest record and greatest assets, especially when the Young Chair of Technical Chemistry and its building were added by James Young's will in 1883. The College of Science and Arts had emerged from the Glasgow Mechanics' Institution and its association represented the end of a schism begun in 1823. It operated under many disadvantages until John Leadbetter (1788-1865) in 1831 provided a building in North Hanover Street. Leadbetter, the self-made son of a wright, who became a merchant's clerk in Glasgow and then founded his own firm c.1815, had attended evening classes at the Andersonian. He was very successful in the linen trade, establishing branch houses in Dundee and Belfast and by 1832 belonged to Glasgow's merchant élite, entering municipal politics as a radical Tory supporter of Sir Robert Peel, and becoming Lord Dean of Guild in 1844, an active promoter of the Edinburgh and Glasgow Railway and other companies and a director of the Union Bank of Scotland.[1] In 1859 the North Hanover Street building was purchased by the Edinburgh and Glasgow Railway Company for £5,000 free of all costs to the Mechanics' Institution, and this sum was used to purchase a substantial property, 38 Bath Street, previously known as Harley's Byres, opened in 1862.[2]

The change of name in 1879 to 'College of Science and Arts, Glasgow' followed incorporation under the Companies' Acts of 1862, 1867 and 1877 and an annual grant of £600 per annum from the Hutcheson's Educational Trust. There was much duplication of personnel between Anderson's College and the Mechanics' Institution and its successor, especially in management and industrial liaisons. Its system of honorary councillors manned by leading industrialists led to the appointment of several entrepreneurs who were managers or trustees of the Andersonian, including James Young and Walter Montgomerie Neilson. Like the Andersonian it had provided a bridge followed by many artisans on the route to wealth and status. Most of the independently-minded spirits on the committee of 1823 had become wealthy.

14 and 15. The Glasgow Mechanics' Institution at 61 North Hanover Street provided by John Leadbetter (1788-1865). Note the statue of James Watt and his separate condenser for the steam engine on top of the building. This building was sold to the Glasgow and Edinburgh Railway Company in 1859 and the proceeds used to buy premises at 38 Bath Street (open in 1862). These continued in use after 1887.
(Right) Watt's statue from the original building is now in the foyer of the Royal College; for many years it stood on the stairs (first floor) inside the College.

Hugh Barclay (President in 1823, 1827 and 1829), for instance, had become Sheriff of Perthshire; James Watson (1824) was knighted as Lord Provost of Glasgow and after several ventures in business became the city's first stockbroker.[3]

The attendance of journeymen operatives had declined; most of the students by 1886 were clerks, warehousemen, apprentices and those who used it, like William and James Thomson, as a prelude to study elsewhere. Yet its evening class audiences exceeded 2,300 by 1871-2. As with the Andersonian, female students were very much in the minority, although there was a special class for women which specialised in the three Rs and attracted nearly 170 students in 1872-3. Among its staff there were some who could work at a much higher level in the merged institution: Principal Andrew Jamieson, C.E., F.R.S.E., who taught Mechanical and Electrical Engineering; William Raitt, M.A., B.Sc.(Edinburgh), who taught Mathematics; Alexander McLay, C.E., B.Sc., Professor of Mechanical Engineering Drawing and an expert in building construction; and Alexander Humboldt Sexton, Professor of Chemistry with a special interest in Metallurgy.[4] Its most important conceptual contribution to the new institution was its three-year certificate programme, established in 1879. Apart from Medicine, Anderson's College lacked this systematic structure, relying on one-year courses. The College of Science and Arts had devised a very sensible and progressive pattern of classes called Junior and Senior Science. Year 1 (Junior Science) included classes in Mathematics, Chemistry, Mechanics and Drawing. The following two years allowed for in-depth study according to occupation, and by Year 3 the technical

16 The Glasgow and West of Scotland Technical College photographed by Annan in 1902 before the great rebuilding. This building was built in 1828, and note Robert Scott's portico (centre left) was still the main entrance. The Young Laboratory of the 1870s can be seen at the far left.

content was paramount. Walter Montgomerie Neilson, the President (1866-74), was a staunch advocate of a unified Glasgow Technical College, and discussions had proceeded from 1883 onwards. The scheme prepared by the Educational Endowment Commission included the significant clause allowing the new governors to acquire ground near to Anderson's College and to sell the College of Science and Arts building.[5]

Thomas Atkinson, bookseller and stationer in Glasgow, by his will dated 17 September 1833, left his whole estate — with few exceptions — to Trustees who were instructed to accumulate a capital sum of at least £5,000 or an annual income of £400 before creating an institution for the education of artisans and members of the middle class. Atkinson regarded the Andersonian as 'too aristocratic' and the Mechanics' Institution as 'too democratic', and he was particularly interested in the provision of courses in languages and literature. His *via media* never became a physical reality; in 1861 a private Act, The Atkinson Institution of Glasgow Act, incorporated thirteen trustees and they continued to accumulate capital. This fund under the scheme of 1886 was the source of bursaries totalling not less than £300 per annum.[6] To this was added a minimum of £1,400 per annum from Glasgow City Educational Endowments Board and £800 from Hutcheson's Educational Trust.[7]

More visible because of its building was Allan Glen's School, a product of the bequest of Allan Glen (1778-1850), wright of Glasgow, and founded in 1853. Glen, a Unitarian, left his estate to provide a school for children of 'respectable parents of the industrious classes' which was built on land which he owned on the corner of North Hanover Street and Cathedral Street. In 1876 the

17 Interior of the Glasgow and West of Scotland Technical College, c.1902, showing the Natural Philosophy laboratory of James Blyth (1838-1906), Professor 1880-1906, who is seated third from the left. From left to right, the staff are Andrew Scobbie (mechanic); A. Macdonald; James Blyth; Dr James Muir (later Professor, 1906-38, historian of the College and biographer of John Anderson); and Vincent J. Blyth (the Professor's son who later went into industry).

Governors obtained Allan Glen's Institution Act which gave them powers to educate 'necessitous' boys, and the scientific and technical bias and distinction of the school was thereafter initiated, with Edward Maxwell Dixon (whom we have already noticed in connection with the Andersonian) as headmaster (1878-89). Clearly, the Endowment Commissioners intended that Allan Glen's School should be developed as a feeder institution for higher scientific and technical education in Glasgow; otherwise they would not have placed it under the governance of the Glasgow and West of Scotland Technical College Board.[8]

The scheme approved by the Privy Council specified the election of Governors and naturally these four major components were represented on the first Board as Table 5.1 indicates.

Apart from the professional men, there was a strong representation on the Board of Glasgow's advancing heavy industries. Alexander Stephen II (1832-99) of Kelvinhaugh and Linthouse, one of Glasgow's leading shipbuilders, became Chairman. From 1884 he had been a trustee of Anderson's College, not the only Board member who had previous connections with the College of Science and Arts or Anderson's.[9] Yet he represented the Merchants' House of Glasgow. Thomas Russell (d.1911) was an ironfounder and shipbuilder; David Rowan (1822-98), a marine engineer; Richard Greenshields Ross, an engineer and ironfounder; William Lorimer, a locomotive engineer and partner in the Glasgow Locomotive Works of Dubs and Company at Polmadie; Alexander Whitelaw, an ironmaster and partner in William Baird and Company of Gartsherrie. As vacancies occurred, the Board recruited other industrial leaders such as William Collins (1817-95) and Walter Wilfrid Blackie from paper and publishing, John Ward of the Leven shipyard, and Henry Alexander Mavor, the electrical engineer.[10]

TABLE 5.1   The Board of Governors of the Glasgow and West of Scotland Technical College

Electing Body	Governors Elected	Term of Office
Council of City of Glasgow	David Richmond	5 YEARS
	William R.W. Smith	
Senatus Academicus of the University of Glasgow	Sir William Thomson	5 YEARS
	Dr John Young	
Glasgow School Board	James Henry Kerr	5 YEARS
	Thomas Russell	
Glasgow City Educational Endowments Board	William Ure	5 YEARS
	James T. Tullis	
Governors of Hutcheson's Educational Trust	James McFarlane	3 YEARS
	Thomas A. Mathieson	
Merchants' House	Alexander Stephen	3 YEARS
Trades House	William Robertson Copland	3 YEARS
Faculty of Physicians	Dr Henry Muirhead	3 YEARS
Faculty of Procurators	Anderson Kirkwood	3 YEARS
Philosophical Society	J.J. Coleman	3 YEARS
Institution of Engineers and Shipbuilders	John Thomson	3 YEARS
Trustees of Anderson's College	Dr Andrew Fergus	LIFE
	Alexander Whitelaw	
	David Thomson Maclay	
	Robert Goodwin	
Trustees of Young Chair	John Young	LIFE
	Henry Dyer	
Trustees of Allan Glen's Institution	Rev. George Stewart Burns	LIFE
	Alexander Andrew Fergusson	
	Professor George Gilbert Ramsay	
	Richard Greenshields Ross	
Trustees of College of Science and Arts	David Rowan	LIFE
	William Lorimer	
Trustees of Atkinson's Institution	John Neilson Cuthbertson	LIFE
	John Wilson	

Source: JBC, GWSTC Minutes, 21 January 1887, pp.2-3.

These were multi-faceted individuals who like their colleagues had several philanthropic interests. John Neilson Cuthbertson was Vice-President of the Glasgow Foundry Boys' Religious Society, Vice-President of the Institution for the Education of the Deaf and Dumb and Vice-President of the Glasgow Athenaeum amid a busy social and political life. Alexander Andrew Fergusson was President of the House of Shelter, a society which provided homes for women prisoners on their release. Lorimer served on the Juvenile Delinquency Board and was one of the promoters of the Victoria Infirmary. James T. Tullis, a prominent leather manufacturer, was a founder member of the Scottish Leather Trade Benevolence Society. David Rowan was a director of the Western Infirmary, and Robert Goodwin (drowned 1911) a director of the Glasgow Foundry Boys' Religious Society. One might expect such activities of Rev. George Stewart Burns (d. 1896), a director of the House of Refuge and the Reformatory and Industrial Schools, but professional men and industrialists alike were often impelled by religious conviction into charitable work.[11]

Well-meaning voluntaryism was accompanied by a keen commitment to advancing the

TABLE 5.2   Glasgow and West of Scotland Technical College: List of Professorial and Teachers' Salaries and Other Staff's Wages by Institution, March 1887.

Institution	Name	Academic Area	Net Salary (£)	Expenditure on Post (£)
Anderson's College	James Blyth	Nat.Phil & Maths	568.25	101.61
	W.T. Rowden	Applied Mechanics	1,116.10	117.50
	W. Dittmar	Chemistry	616.26	543.11
	Colin Brown	Music	100	
	Murray	Vocal Music	18	
	J.C. Christie	Geology	55	
	A.G. Wilson	Botany	11.10	
	E.J. Mills	Technical Chemistry	378.30	150.50
	Peter Wright	Agriculture	26.00	
	Andrew Scobie	'Mechanician'	90.00	
	James Rowe	Janitor	80.00	
College of Science and Arts	Andrew Jamieson	Principal Engineering	760.11	
	William Raitt	Mathematics	610.85	
	Alexander McLay	Drawing	631.425	
	A. Humboldt Sexton	Chemistry	593.70	
	Thomas King	Botany	35.875	
	Macartney	'Sound, Light and Heat'	57.59	
	Brown	Naval Architecture	54.50	
	D.M. Mowat	Mining	46.50	
	E.E. Barker	Freehand Drawing	51.875	
	Francis Magauran	Curator	110.00	
		Principal's Assistant	19.25	
		Library Assistant	24.00	
		Charwoman	26.775	
Allan Glen's School	E.M. Dixon	Headmaster	600.00	
	James Struthers	Assistant	175.00	
	D.A. Low	Assistant	290.525	
	Thomas J. Primrose	Assistant	150.00	
	David Waddell	Assistant	140.00	
	John Brown	Assistant	164.00	
	Robert Montgomery	Assistant	120.00	
	D.S. McNair	Assistant	206.16	
	Miss Macphail	Assistant	90.00	
	Thomas S. Lambie	temporary		
	D. Mackinlay	Visiting Master	60.00	
	H. Krueger	Visiting Master	55.00	
	Francis Moncur	Workshop	80.00	
	R.J. Brown	Assistant	12.00	
	Andrew F. Bell	Assistant	12.00	
	William Robertson	Assistant	30.00	
	John Irving	Janitor	58.30	

1. Net Salary has to be added to Expenditure for Total Income.
2. Expenditures include payments to assistants for chemicals, apparatus, prizes, certificates.
3. Net Salary includes any payments from the Science and Art Department.
4. Appointments at Anderson's College dated annually from 31 October; those at College of Science and Arts from May; those at Allan Glen's School were for short periods, the maximum notice being three months.
5. James Rowe's appointment terms included a house.
6. Andrew Scobie's duties were essentially in the service of Natural Philosophy.

Source: JBC, GWSTC Governors' Minutes, 1887-8, Finance Committee, 30 March 1887.

TABLE 5.3   Property and Funds Under the Control of the Governors in 1887

Trust / Institution	Net Value of Property and Funds	Comment
Anderson's College	40,880.175	
Freeland Trust	8,260.36	
Euing Trust	3,135.15	Substantial liquid assets
Young Chair	8,531.31	Laboratories and liquid assets
College of Science and Arts	13,089:91	No liquid assets
Allan Glen's Institution	28,514:575	Liquid assets and building
Atkinson Institution	8,930.45	Totally liquid assets

Source: JBC, GWSTC Governors' Minutes, 1887-8, Finance Committee, 7 September, 1887.

regional economy. This purpose could be best served by ensuring a good supply of skilled and technically trained personnel leavened by a crop of managerial talent. Governors such as Stephen and Sir William Thomson knew the importance of the role of the Glasgow and West of Scotland Technical College and met privately to discuss how best to aid the regional and national economy. Thus, the formal minutes are no true guide to their educational thought. The Board built on the strengths of the components of the merger, and, in particular, they drew up curricula and courses through a consultative process in which Thomas Russell and Henry Dyer played a very significant part.

In the background lurked the syllabus of the Science and Art Department — and payment by results — which several of the Governors as well as many academics found too constraining. Yet it was impossible to ignore the revenue derived from the Department and its importance to professorial salaries. Rapid changes were, therefore, impossible. The assets provided by the merger required accurate measurement; finance and property were the keys to the door of desirable change. A rational rewards system for staff was needed, if only to retain and to recruit academics able to grasp the opportunities offered by the amalgamation of the two main institutions — Anderson's College and the College of Science and Arts. Allan Glen's School required new premises if it was to be an effective feeder to the Technical College, for expansion of pupil numbers was essential. The bursaries available to pupils and students needed efficient management to maximise the effects of the sums available. The insecurities, which merger betokened, had to be removed with sensitivity if innovation was not to be obstructed.

These questions undoubtedly engaged the attention of the temporary business committee appointed by the Governors on 21 January 1887. They recommended the creation of four standing committees — Finance, Teachers, Property and Bursaries — which with slight modification were set up and did most of the donkey work.[12] The former institutions were empowered to continue their administrations till the vesting date of 26 May 1887. Meantime, the Governors advertised for a Secretary, and appointed as their principal officer, John Young, M.A., B.Sc., of the Library, University of Glasgow, who had previously given Geology lectures in the Andersonian.[13]

William Raitt as Secretary of the Committee of professors and lecturers submitted to the Committee on Teaching and Staff, early in March 1887, full details of proposed classes, timetables and a list of fees for session 1887-8 and copies were made and circulated for discussion.

The Finance Committee obtained a note of all professorial and teachers' salaries, their sources and expenditures which are summarised in Table 5.2.

The data given in Table 5.2 illustrate that net earnings for full-time staff in Anderson's College and the College of Science and Arts – apart from W.T. Rowden's case – were roughly in the same range, and that bracket included Edward Maxwell Dixon, the Headmaster of Allan Glen's School. The objective of the Finance Committee was to find a formula for rationalising salaries, removing 'expenditures' on items that might be provided by the institution and thereby making academic staff more secure. Surprisingly, there was little duplication of academic effort and therefore, it was possible, assuming goodwill, to retain all the staff.

The average salary earned over the previous three years was calculated and virtually guaranteed. However, half of students' fees and grants from the Science and Arts Department were part of the wage bargain, so that professors and teachers had an incentive to teach well. Gradually, the process of annual salary review removed the reliance on fees and grants, but this was a slow process.[14]

The Finance Committee had the accounts of the various trusts audited, and their assets valued. The results are given in Table 5.3. The most substantial institution in terms of property and funds was clearly Anderson's College and its associated trusts, a conclusion made firmer by the inclusion of the Young Chair of Technical Chemistry.

The College of Science and Arts had no net liquid assets because of its overdraft with the Union Bank and its bond on its property owed to the City Educational Endowment Board. Allan Glen's Institution had substantial assets but its school needed considerable expenditure, and the Atkinson Institution was a milch cow – no substantial outgoings, no property but substantial sums lent out on bond.[15]

The Property Committee, after consulting the professors, received estimates for repairs and alterations to the Andersonian and the College of Science and Arts which at best slightly exceeded £1,550.[16] A substantial investment in extending Allan Glen's School was agreed in September 1887; this was based on the plans drawn up by James Salmon for the previous trustees and estimated at about £5,500.[17] After completion and furnishing with additions up to 1896 the actual cost was over £10,000.[18] This was the most substantial capital expenditure by the Governors in the first ten years of operation. Thus the basis was laid for turning a relatively small single-sex school into the major selective science high school in the city. Excellent headmasters and staff made this transformation intellectually possible, and the renown of Allan Glen's was secured rapidly by the policy of providing bursaries to attract able pupils from a wide area, even beyond the city's limits. When the school was transferred to Glasgow School Board in 1912, it had over 600 pupils and was the subject of a stream of highly complimentary inspectors' reports over the years.[19]

Arrangements were made by a specialist Committee to form a general reference library in the Andersonian, but the Euing Library of Music and Young's Chemical Library were kept separate, the latter because its catalogue was not complete.[20] To make room for the general library the Library Committee recommended that two major collections – Zoological and Ethnological – from the Museum should be given to the Hunterian Museum, and this was eventually agreed.[21]

After negotiations between the Teaching and Staff Committee and the Board of Studies, a unified programme of classes emerged, and a certificate and diploma system of awards evolved. This was largely based upon the model set by the College of Science and Arts, which by 1886 had constructed diplomas in Mechanical Engineering, Electrical Engineering, Chemistry and Naval Architecture, normally examined annually and obtained after three years of study combined with an apprenticeship. Henry Dyer, while not quite claiming credit for this innovation, certainly approved of it and later compared it with his system at the Imperial Engineering College in Tokyo.[22]

Where Dyer led the way was in urging the Governors to seek recognition of these courses by the Senate of the University of Glasgow, the beginning of a process which ultimately led to affiliation. He was supported by J.J. Coleman (1837-89), an early entrepreneur/inventor in the field of refrigeration. The Senate responded cautiously but favourably, no doubt partly because Kelvin was a Governor and an authoritative advocate but also on account of the generous gifts made by the Technical College to the Hunterian Museum. They preferred to await the deliberations of the expected Royal Commission on the Universities rather than an immediate agreement. Meanwhile, the University of Edinburgh recognised in 1888 the course in Agriculture as qualifying in part for the B.Sc. and was prepared also to recognise two years of appropriate day classes – but not evening classes – in other sciences. Shortly thereafter Glasgow University in 1889 recognised the diploma in Engineering as exempting Technical College students from the first two years of the B.Sc. course. The Governors began the illustrious record of the Associateship, which, they agreed on 16 May 1889, should be conferred upon all those who obtained the Diploma.[23]

The following September, Dyer and the Committee on Teaching and Staff were given the task of drafting an affiliation proposal in the hope that Glasgow University Senate would join in an approach to the Royal Commission on the Scottish Universities.[24] Although the Technical College gave separate evidence, the draft ordinance submitted to the Commission by Glasgow University and covering degrees in engineering science was more limited but made appropriate references to the Diploma and provided that holders required to complete a further three courses at the University, normally undertaken in one session. A degree in Agricultural Science, which allowed classes taught by Professor Wright and his colleagues to be credited, was also floated in 1892.[25] By 1895-6 individual Associates were reported as graduating at Glasgow University in Civil Engineering and Mathematics and Natural Philosophy, the latter with first-class Honours. Others were taking degrees of London University and examinations of a range of professional institutions.[26] Yet numbers in the diploma courses remained small before 1900, many students being content with one-year certificates.

For over a decade the recognition of diplomas for entry to the final year of a Glasgow B.Sc. seemed to satisfy the ambitions of the College; other issues such as the financing of a new building assumed higher priority, and when the question of affiliation was raised again in 1906, as Forrester has demonstrated, the initiative came from the University.[27] Principal Donald MacAlister joined the Board of Governors in 1907, showing the significance which the Senate attached to co-operation with the College. The University had made inquiries into the working relationship between the University of Manchester and the Manchester School of Technology, and possibly this example was the model for later developments.[28] Principal MacAlister's presence on the Board facilitated informal discussions which were further assisted by a very favourable report in 1909 about the work of the College made by Professor John Perry, F.R.S. to the Scotch Education Department in which he expressed the view that the College should have the power to grant a B.Sc. degree.[29]

Perry's report led to an approach to the University Court and steady progress towards affiliation by a new ordinance, a process which began in 1910. Both institutions wanted to retain a degree of separation, but both recognised the importance of arranging an effective system of academic co-operation. Proper standards had to be assured; examiners in both institutions had to work together, and yet there had to be a degree of freedom – and mutual trust – in arranging

TABLE 5.4   Student Numbers and Fee Income, 1887-1914

Session	Day	Evening	Total Students	Total Enrolments	Fee Income (£
1887-8	n/a	n/a	1,793	2,946	2,220.97
1888-9	124	1,882	2,006	2,874	2,089.0
1889-90	134	2,251	2,385	3,357	2,291.3
1890-1	149	2,453	2,602	3,693	2,860.9
1891-2	194	2,503	2,697	3,986	3,574.1
1892-3	196	2,604	2,800	4,312	3,666.12
1893-4	207	2,597	2,804	4,315	3,578.4
1894-5	229	2,878	3,107	4,652	3,734.6
1895-6	219	2,886	3,105	4,618	3,751.92
1896-7	251	3,076	3,327	5,061	4,237.92
1897-8	286	3,134	3,420	5,196	4,446.2
1898-9	263	3,442	3,705	5,553	4,479.82
1899-1900	527	3,869	5,025	5,759	5,144.12
1900-1	609	3,989	5,248	n/a	5,280.4
1901-2	596	4,394	5,651	8,575	5,174.0
1902-3	652	4,424	5,678	7,905	5,527.5
1903-4	489	4,149	5,333	7,848	5,716.12
1904-5	530	4,424	5,363	8,577	5,777.1
1905-6	535	3,758	5,012	8,261	5,577.6
1906-7	544	4,381	5,762	9,652	6,220.0
1907-8	605	4,621	5,918	10,009	6,295.72
1908-9	487	4,623	5,824	10,680	6,599.92
1909-10	523	4,944	5,517	11,277	7,157.7
1910-11	560	5,152	5,712	11,383	6,952.87
1911-12	572	4,691	5,263	10,777	6,661.5
1912-13	610	4,298	5,069	10,482	6,718.67
1913-14	669	4,342	4,908	10,737	7,481.0

1. Figures generally include Allan Glen's School up to 1912 but not consistently. Hence some disparities in total student numbers.
2. Country Centres are occasionally included after 1903 in totals.

Source: JBC, GWSTC, Governors' Minutes and Annual Reports; SUA, E1/1/3, 4, 7, 9 GWSTC, Governors' Minutes

curricula. Working relationships of this sort were advancing elsewhere: in Newcastle-upon-Tyne where the University of Durham had conferred constituent college status upon Armstrong College, in Bristol where the Merchant Venturers' Technical College became the Faculty of Engineering of the University of Bristol, in Leeds, Sheffield and Manchester. Many conferences took place between representatives of the College and of the University, culminating in affiliation by Ordinance No.12 (1912) which was approved by the Privy Council on 7 March 1913. The outbreak of World War I makes it impossible to assess the likely effects of affiliation and whether the outcome might have been the creation of a Faculty of Applied Science based upon the College. Such an academic rationalisation might well have been feasible, and the history of Anderson's institution and its successors might have become part of the record of the University of Glasgow.[30]

The increase in student numbers indicated in Table 5.4 (which also includes pupils at Allan Glen's up to 1912) reflects the strain on accommodation which became obvious as early as 1892. Most of the pressure was coming from evening-class populations, but day students increased in number during the 1890s and accounted for a disproportionately large percentage of fee income. Day classes in 1896-7 contained 251 students and produced fee revenue of just over £2,365 out of about £4,238.[31] Alterations in the Andersonian Buildings and a lease of premises adjoining the Science and Arts Bath Street premises eased the overcrowding temporarily, but these were makeshift changes and recognised as such. The Property Committee reported in favour of reconstruction in 1891 but had not yet reached the conclusion that a totally new building was necessary.

Expenditure up to £3,000 was authorised in June 1892, and a special committee appointed to examine the possibility of 'providing a new building adapted to the present and prospective requirements of the teaching of science in the community'.[32] But economic circumstances in the period 1892-6 were not propitious. The urban and regional trade cycle turned sharply down, and interest rates rose. Philanthropy on a substantial scale was an unlikely prospect, and without it, a new building was an impossible dream. The Governors sought help from the deceased: under the wills of the Misses Steven of Bellahouston a vast fortune had been left to aid charitable and educational institutions in the city – and the promotion of scientific and technical education was specifically mentioned. The Bellahouston Trustees were sent 'sketch plans of a new building' together with a memorial setting out the nature and work of the College and seeking a grant for new premises.[33] But they were not prepared to fund a new building without other supporters.

Instead they offered £25,000, and initially it was intended to use part of this to purchase land in North Street and thus to move from George Street. The Corporation of Glasgow agreed with the Bellahouston Trust to hold the site for up to two years in 1896, and a public appeal for funds was being planned.[34] But the time elapsed, and even Paisley possessed 'a Technical Institution with modern buildings beyond comparison with those of this College' by 1900.[35]

The revival of the city's economy at the end of the century led the Governors to revive the idea of a public appeal, although donations for the building fund had been accruing steadily since 1898. Property at the corner of George Street and Montrose Street was purchased in 1900 for £14,000, and steps were taken to appoint an architect. By 5 October 1900 the firms listed below had been invited to take part in an architectural competition:

> David Barclay
> Clark and Bell
> Honeyman and Keppie
> James Miller
> James Salmon and Son
> Thomson and Sandilands
> T.L. Watson

A rough estimate of 160,000 square feet for the new building was reached by obtaining schedules of space deemed necessary by the heads of departments.

A public meeting at the City Chambers was then called by the Lord Provost, when the case for support was put by J.G.A. Baird, M.P. on 20 December, 1900. The competing architects were then given detailed instructions to work within an initial budget of £120,000, and their designs had to be delivered by 19 April 1901 to a precise space requirement of 154,510 square feet. James Miller withdrew from the competition, and the remaining designs were displayed in the College. The Board of Studies was then asked to prepare a detailed report on the two best, and a skilled 'Measurer' to estimate costs selected. The Board of Studies was strongly in favour of David Barclay's design which laid out plans of rooms amounting to 164,526 square feet with another 69,728 square feet of corridors and staircases at an estimated cost of £154,667. Barclay was duly appointed by the Governors to build what became the Royal College Building on 17 June, 1901.[36]

This decision was not a moment too soon. An Inspector's Report to the Scotch Education

18 Sir William Robertson Copland (1838-1907), a civil engineer and Glasgow Councillor, served as a Governor (and latterly as Chairman) on the Board of the Glasgow and West of Scotland Technical College. The great rebuilding of the College and its extension took place during his chairmanship.

Department in 1901 was both laudatory about academic courses and condemnatory about the physical environment in which they were taught:[37]

> Nowhere else in Scotland is there a school which is so full, varied, and practical courses of study can be found in Mechanical, Electrical, and Civil Engineering, Building Construction, Metallurgy, and Mining, Chemical Industries, ec., as are offered in the Glasgow and West of Scotland Technical College, both in day and evening classes. The staff is worthily held in high reputation, and its members are distinguished not only on account of their scientific attainments, but equally by the zeal, ability, and success with which they conduct the work of their classes ...
>
> Reference has been made in previous Reports to the unsuitability, to say the least, of many of the present classrooms and laboratories for the purposes of the College. Personal inspection of the conditions under which the work is being carried on will convince anyone of the truth of this. The class-rooms are, as a rule, cheerless and ... without satisfactory ventilation. On a winter night more than one of these have been found packed with students working in a vile atmosphere, at a temperature of between 75° and 80°F. Good apparatus, models, and testing engines of different kinds are in plenty; but the laboratories are poorly fitted and exceedingly inconvenient places in which the students are often enough crowded, to the jostling of each other at their experiments.

The site consisted not only of the Andersonian Buildings but also included the City Public School and the Pupil Teacher Institute, all of which were owned by the College. Funds flowed in rapidly, adding to the residue of the old Building Fund. There were many small subscriptions, some organised by trade or occupational groups, and the industries upon which Glasgow's prosperity rested produced many substantial contributors. The Governors led by example, giving personally and also assisting the solicitations of the Chairman, William Robertson Copland (1838-1907), Civil Engineer and Glasgow Town Councillor, associated with a firm of engineers and boilermakers in Dobbie's Loan. The response to the public appeal was magnificent. By January 1901 over £79,000 had been raised, and the target had been raised to £150,000. By September following about £101,000 had been offered.[38]

Contracts were put out to tender in 1902, including those relating to the removal of existing buildings, a process which had to be phased in order to minimise disruption to classes.[39] Estimated costs were thrown awry during the course of 1902 because the boom was reaching its peak – materials had risen by fifteen per cent since 1900 and wages had gone up by 0.05 p an hour. By July 1902 it was estimated that the new building would cost £180,000.[40] The red sandstone came from Dumfriesshire quarries, and it was thought that the acres of white tiles in the corridors would be easy to keep clean.

Analysis of the first £175,000 raised by September 1902 allows certain generalisations. Gifts of over £500 were most important. Allowing just over £7,200 for accumulated interest, a further £150,000 came in these relatively large gifts. The largest donors were Andrew Carnegie, Scottish-American steelmaster and philanthropist, and the Bellahouston Trust who each gave £25,000. Substantial grants were made by the Scotch Education Department and the City of Glasgow. Gifts of £500 or more came from the shipbuilders, locomotive-builders, founders, engineers, iron and steelmasters, chemical manufacturers, carpetmakers and mining companies; the Scottish Association of Master Bakers, in the hope of a School of Bakery comparable with the London School, contributed £2,488.475 p, mostly in small sums but with the large firms, William Beattie, Bilsland Brothers, Macfarlane, Lang and Company, J. and B. Stevenson and the United Co-operative Baking Society giving £1,300 between them. Governors gave what they could afford, as did former students.[41]

On 14 May 1903 King Edward VII and Queen Alexandra visited the College, and the King

19 King Edward VII laying the foundation stone of the Royal College Building at the south-east corner of George Street / Montrose Street (183 George Street) on 14 May 1903. The King (holding the mason's gavel) was accompanied by Queen Alexandra (centre right in the platform party) with Sir William Robertson Copland behind the King.
20 (front endpaper) The completed building (architect, David Barclay) was the largest single educational complex in Europe at the time.

laid the 'Memorial Stone' of the new building. All the subscribers to the Building Fund were invited and representatives of public bodies. Seating was provided for 2,600, and 1,500 tickets were issued to students, staff and families which admitted them to higher parts of the site from which they viewed the ceremony. The Chairman of the Governors addressed the King and in his response Edward VII indicated his pleasure and also his recognition of the importance of advanced scientific and technical education. The proceedings ended with the singing of the National Anthem, led by a choir organised by Harry Colin Miller, Euing Lecturer in Music.[42]

The 'Royal College' Building took years to complete. The first section was nearly complete in September 1904, but it was not ready for occupation till Session 1905-6. It cost £140,000, and there was added expenditure on the site and on the purchase of St Paul's Church amounting to £44,654. Equipment was expected to cost about £40,000 of which over £18,000 had been raised by September 1904.[43] The collapse of the boom was glaringly apparent by 1904, and so fund-raising from local industry and commerce was difficult. Yet £209,763 was raised for this building and its equipment by September 1905, sufficient to complete it on time for the opening of the Session 1905-6, but with little left to start the second section. The Secretary of State for Scotland, the Right Hon. John Sinclair, M.P., formally opened the first section on 21 December, 1905 but it was already in use.

However, the Chairman of the Governors in his public remarks jocularly referred to the good work which had been done in completing this phase but admitted that his colleagues and he 'were at the end of their financial tether'.[44] A grant of £25,000 from the Scotch Education Department allowed the Governors to authorise the erection of the second section fronting George Street, and by September 1907 work had begun, and total sums raised approached £300,000.[45] Rapid progress was made after a slow start, and this centre block on George Street was completed and occupied by September 1908. The third section extending to John Street, estimated to cost £26,000, had been started, and an additional wing on John Street (the fourth section) was being planned.[46] These sections were finished in Session 1908-9 and 1909-10 respectively, five years after the first section was occupied. Thus, 'the largest building in the Kingdom devoted to education' was completed ten years after the launch of the public appeal, and the Governors were free of debt. The total floor space was 308,600 square feet or over seven acres. £272,320.375 p was spent on the building of these four sections; site costs and property purchases accounted for a further £46,153.60 p; equipment up to 1910 had cost £35,397.62p. The grand total was just over £353,880.[47]

This magnificent complex became the Royal Technical College in 1912. George V had visited India in 1910 for the Great Durbar and been impressed by the fact that many major engineering projects had been constructed by engineers trained at the Glasgow and West of Scotland Technical College. Ever since Edward VII had laid the foundation stone, the Governors had wanted the title 'Royal Technical College', and on George V's return they were advised that the moment was opportune to petition the Secretary of State for Scotland. This was done, and on 9 February, 1912 the Governors were informed by the Scottish Office that the King had acceded to their request.[48]

A change in title also reflected concomitant changes in type and level of work undertaken in the College. From 1887 to 1896 the departmental structure emerged and courses increased in number without much alteration in their category. Much effort was expended in preparing students for the Science and Art examinations, since College income and teachers' salaries were equally affected by the pass level. There were 16 day classes in 1887 and 39 by 1896; the number of evening classes rose from 34 to 65.[49] The momentum for new classes reflected the needs of industry as technical changes occurred. Sometimes, professors anticipated the market for new classes, but generally the voice of industry was loud and unequivocal. The nine departments 'of study' – Agriculture, Civil Engineering, Mechanical Engineering, Naval Architecture, Electrical Engineering, Architecture, Chemical Engineering, Metallurgy, Mining Engineering – taught day students for certificates and diplomas and also provided evening classes. To these were later added Chemistry, Mathematics and Natural Philosophy.

Agriculture moved in 1899 to join the Scottish Dairy Institute, Kilmarnock in forming the West of Scotland Agricultural College. Its place was quickly taken by other vocational subjects such as the Industrial Arts which expanded rapidly after 1896. Sub-committees consisting of employers and representatives of employees were formed to manage groups of evening classes geared to supply manpower to specific industries. These were a source of further momentum for creating new classes which industry required. Apart from industrial liaison these sub-committees often raised support, notably gifts of equipment or materials. Usually, a governor joined a sub-committee and also appropriate professors. In 1902, for instance such sub-committees were established for classes in Plumbing, Boiler-Making and Bakery. Mathematics and Natural Philosophy, Engineering, Chemistry and Metallurgy all developed the same organisation, gradually replacing the Standing Committee on Teaching and Staff. By 1912 twenty such groups were operating in the Royal Technical College.

This network was important in persuading major employers to systematise the sandwich course. As already indicated, many students attended College in the winter and obtained appropriate work in the summer which helped them financially. What was new after 1900 was pressure from parents – especially those with a professional background – to link apprenticeship formally with full-time study during the College session. Although many employers were initially reluctant to change their employment strategy, which postulated that apprentices should attend evening classes in their own time, slowly the sandwich system expanded. By 1912 the College Calendar listed 73 firms operating the 'sandwich' system. They came from a range of industries, including car and truck companies such as Argyll Motors Ltd., Alexandria and Albion

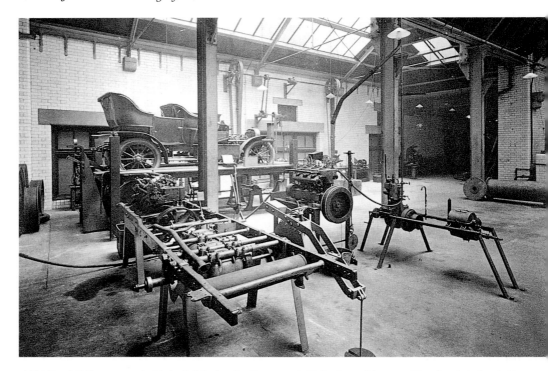

21 The Royal College c.1912: the Mechanical Engineering Department's Motive Power laboratory. Note the relatively primitive equipment and the Argyll motor car on the test rig at the back of the laboratory.

of Scotstoun as well as from shipbuilding and locomotive firms like John Brown of Clydeban' and the Caledonian Railway Company. Some had partners trained in the Royal Technica College and its predecessors, such as William Beardmore (1856-1936) of Parkhead, Georg Inglis of Pointhouse shipyard and many associated with the Fairfield Shipbuilding an Engineering Company of Govan.[50]

Year by year as the new building became operational from 1905 new classes were added including special vacation classes for teachers in physics, chemistry and electricity an magnetism. Specialist areas in electrical, mechanical and civil engineering were explored as nee became apparent, most concerned with building and the capital goods industries – Railways an Roads, Reinforced Concrete Construction, Sewage and Water Supply, Harbours and Docks. A few were concerned with service industries and consumer goods production – watch-making boot and shoe production, bakery and confectionery. The War Office asked for a class i Automobile Engineering in 1907, and a successful class was provided for non-commissione officers.[51]

As some industries and services required or acquired a scientific basis, so new classes o disciplines took root. The most obvious example was Bacteriology, which the Governor decided to introduce because of its industrial and social utility. Food-processing, brewing distilling and tanning were old industries increasingly geared to mass consumption; sewage an water supply were critical services in Glasgow by 1900 – all, the Governors thought, woul benefit from a more scientific base which Bacteriology provided. Peter Paterson began classes i 1901-2, but major development occurred under his successor, Dr David Ellis (1904), who also assumed responsibility for Botany for his annual salary of £170. The course which Ellis offere became part of the Diploma in Chemistry in 1906-7, and he rapidly became a head of departmen with responsibility for the School of Bakery and other classes associated with food and drink, and from 1909 Pharmacy, a subject requested by the Glasgow and West of Scotland Chemists' Association.[52]

The long-established subjects saw change and a growing emphasis on research. For some disciplines such as Chemistry and Technical Chemistry this represented no break in tradition, but even these produced more and grew in strength. Professor William Dittmar died suddenly in February 1892, and his successor, George G. Henderson, M.A., D.Sc., senior assistant to the Professor of Chemistry in the University of Glasgow, proved to be an inspired choice.[53] A young man of tremendous energy, Henderson raised the standard of teaching and research. He also made effective contact with many industrialists and leading lights in the chemical industry. Under his regime students took the Diploma, the Associateship of the Institute of Chemistry and occasionally the external B.Sc. of London University before gravitating to jobs in local firms, notably Nobel, Tennants of St Rollox, J. and G. Cox of Gorgie Mills, Edinburgh, and Scottish and Irish Oxygen Company (later British Oxygen Company) of Polmadie, as well as going south of the Border to public and industrial posts. Glasgow as the great centre of cyanide and ferrocyanide production (following Beilby's patent of 1890), output which was increasingly used in gold refining from the 1890s, also trained the assayers (from 1896) and chemists who went to South Africa, Australia, India, the United States and Canada where their skills were put to good use.[54]

Edmund J. Mills, as a consequence of the Governors' wish to unite the departments of Chemistry and Technical Chemistry in 1892 temporarily became 'Director' of Chemistry, an unfortunate experiment which failed. When he retired in 1901, after twenty-six years of service, his successor was appointed only after a period of reflection.[55] The Governors decided upon an interim lectureship which was filled by Thomas Gray in 1902; he became professor in 1903 and worked collaboratively with Professor Henderson as well as developing his own research niche in 'Fuels' and industrial safety in coal and oil-shale mines.[56]

William Raitt, Professor of Mathematics, also died in office in 1895 and his successor, George Alexander Gibson, gradually built up the department, starting with one assistant, John Miller, but relying on appropriate staff from Allan Glen's School to assist with the evening classes. When he resigned in 1909 to take the Chair of Mathematics in the University of Glasgow, Gibson strongly and successfully supported Miller's candidature for the vacant Chair.[57] Up to 1914 the work of this department increased, despite the movement of elementary classes to local authority control.[58]

Alexander Humbolt Sexton developed the department of Metallurgy after the merger of 1886-although for a few years he continued to teach evening classes in Chemistry at Bath Street. A Londoner, Sexton was trained at the Royal School of Mines and worked for a time in the Royal College of Science in Dublin before moving into industry, working for a number of metallurgical firms. Sexton developed the assaying course, already mentioned, which was so successful in placing students in careers throughout the world, and made effective liaisons with the main iron and steel producers in Scotland. After twenty-five years' service, Sexton retired in 1909, having produced standard texts on non-ferrous alloys.[59]

Major changes occurred in engineering. Some of these arose from the circumstances of the merger but most were reflections of market demand for students and research in the capital goods industries, which were expanding throughout the international economy in the period 1890 to 1914. Civil Engineering and Surveying continued to be taught at 38 Bath Street. Alexander Maclay, B.Sc., C.E., had worked for nearly four years for the Glasgow and South Western Railway before joining the staff of the College of Science and Arts. After the merger his main activity was teaching engineering drawing, and thus he gravitated to Mechanical Engineering and is so listed in the Calendar of 1889-90, increasingly concentrating on machine design up to his retirement in 1903. The first specialist part-time lecturer appointed after the merger was Arthur Watson Thomson, who had spent three years (1878-81) in Tokyo at the Imperial College of Engineering where Henry Dyer was Principal, followed by five years as Professor of Engineering and Land Surveying at the Royal Agricultural College, Cirencester. Thomson successfully launched the Diploma in Civil Engineering, but his specialist interest was in Applied Mechanics. When he left to become Professor of Engineering at the College of Science, Poona, India in 1890, Thomson had already a record of publication with Thomas Alexander, both being former students at Glasgow University under Professor W.J. Macquorn Rankine (1820-72), one of the most accomplished academic engineers of the nineteenth century.[60]

His successor, Gilbert Thomson, an Edinburgh graduate, started the institution's connection with public health and environmental health engineering, beginning with evening classes in 'Sanitation' in 1890-1. He was then appointed to mainstream Civil Engineering duties, still part-time position. Evening-class students naturally took longer to complete the Diploma which was first achieved in 1895, but some earlier students were content with certificates. Thomson maintained his part-time post for fourteen sessions, having a private consultancy practice as his main source of income, but he taught evening classes in Sanitary Engineering for a further thirty-three years.[61]

The first full-time appointment was George Moncur, B.Sc., A.M.Inst.C.E., a student at University College, Dundee and a graduate of Edinburgh University who had served his pupillage under Blackadder of Dundee and afterwards worked for the Caledonian Railway Company, before joining the Great North of Scotland Railway to take charge of design and erection of constructional work. Appointed as a lecturer in 1905 at a salary of £250 per annum, Moncur proved to be a prolific publisher and an energetic member of the College who worked long hours. In 1907 he began the surveying camp field excursion which became a feature of summer teaching and also aided the inauguration of the Civil Engineering Society. Much teaching effort naturally went into transportation topics, especially Railways. This department also dealt with major public utilities such as water supply, sewage, docks and harbours and railway signalling. Reinforced Concrete Construction became the responsibility of a specialist lecturer in 1911-12 after MacAlpine had pioneered its use on the West Highland line. Moncur became a professor in 1911, a just reward for a dynamic individual.[62]

Electrical Engineering began from a more privileged position, for Andrew Jamieson (1849-1912), the Principal of the College of Science and Arts, had an educational and industrial background which fitted ideally what was required in a professor. After Aberdeen University he worked for Hall, Russell and Company and then the Great North of Scotland Railway, joining Sir William Thomson and Professor Fleeming Jenkin in Glasgow in 1873. Jamieson became chief assistant electrician in companies abroad which these two academic entrepreneurs advised in the making and laying of cables, finally reaching the rank of Chief Electrician (1877-80) for the Eastern Telegraph Company which operated in the Mediterranean, off the cost of East Africa and in the Indian Ocean.

When he became Principal, Jamieson lectured on all aspects then known about Electrical Engineering but at the time of the merger he was simply described as Professor of Engineering. However, in 1892 he was designated Professor of Electrical Engineering and taught classes totalling about 500 students. He was an active publisher despite his teaching load and was also an active industrial consultant. At the time of his retirement in 1899 he had published 23 technical papers on a range of significant and mainly practical problems.

His successor, Magnus Maclean, was a Glasgow graduate from Skye who retained an interest in Celtic Literature and lectured and published on the subject – after his appointment to Glasgow and West of Scotland Technical College. Assistant to Kelvin from 1884 and University Lecturer in 'Pure and Applied Electricity' from 1895, Maclean was already internationally recognised as an outstanding scholar. He extended his foreign contacts, visiting continental universities and *technische hochschulen*. The department grew and absorbed very rapidly the significance of technical and industrial innovations, especially wireless telegraphy and radio. Students of the department were in great demand throughout the world, and many went to the United States and Commonwealth to take up lucrative posts.[63]

The lifeblood of Clydeside industry depended fundamentally upon injections from Mechanical Engineering in this period. Alexander Maclay, William T. Rowden and Andrew Jamieson made a formidable triumvirate in 1887, but the next quarter-century saw remarkable developments. John Gordon Longbottom was appointed lecturer in Mechanics in 1895 from 23 candidates; a Whitworth scholar, Longbottom rapidly acquired large classes totalling 1,107 enrolments by 1895 and nearly 1,250 in 1896. His need for assistance was clearly apparent, and by 1900 the payment of additional assistants was commonplace despite financial pressures induced by the prospect of the new building. Both Rowden and Maclay retired in 1903, and Longbottom became a professor.[64] William Henry Watkinson, a Yorkshireman and also a Whitworth scholar, had received his technical education in the College of Science and Arts and then had taken classes in the University of Glasgow where his talents drew him to the attention of Kelvin. An assistantship was followed by a short period as a teacher in Sheffield. He was appointed to teach about steampower and steam engines in 1893, subjects of vital moment to the Glasgow economy. This professorship was retitled Prime Movers to make its ambit comprehensive, but when Watkinson resigned in 1905 to take the Chair of Engineering in the University of Liverpool, much research was being undertaken in turbine design.[65]

Watkinson's successor was Alexander Lawson Mellanby, D.Sc., M.I.Mech.E., a graduate of Durham University College of Science (Newcastle). Mellanby had an extensive marine engineering background, having trained at the Central Marine Engineering Works and at Hartlepool with T. Richardson and Sons, marine and electrical engineers. His first research at Newcastle, and later at McGill University, Montreal, was on the relative efficiencies of multiple expansion marine engines; for this he received an M.Sc. from McGill and after further work a D.Sc. from Durham. He had been 'Chief Lecturer in Engineering' at Battersea Polytechnic and a lecturer in the Manchester School of Technology. His chair was renamed Motive Power Engineering shortly after his appointment, and he rapidly reviewed the state of the laboratories and sought fresh equipment. He quickly turned to investigate the effects of steam jacketing upon the efficiency of horizontal compound steam engines. Mellanby was also willing to learn from the best continental practice and visited many German technical institutions just before World War I. To Longbottom's 1,293 students in 1908-9, Mellanby added a further 635, an increasing number attending as full-time day students from the Clyde shipyards.[66] But Naval Architecture remained a Cinderella throughout the period, only a single lecturer being employed.

Another significant development was Mining Engineering, always a relatively small department with a succession of part-time staff in the 1890s but with a considerable reputation and influence from its earliest days. The regulation of mines by government inevitably placed strains upon the supply of trained skilled labour able to meet the requirements of the legislation. In 1902 Daniel Burns, M.I.M.E., was appointed lecturer in Mining; 35 years old, Burns had lectured for the Lanarkshire Education Authority for six years, the last three at Coatbridge Technical College. He faced a formidable task: an industry with a poor labour relations record

22 The School of Navigation's deviascope on the roof of the Royal College (City Chambers in background). This photograph first appeared in the Royal Technical College Magazine of March 1913. Students were taught to adjust the compass by using the deviascope, and here one is also being instructed in 'the rule of the sea lanes'.

and an ignorant labour force which often lacked even a basic education. Experience in the pit was essential to assess working problems, but the standard of the supervisory employee required substantial improvement. Burns recruited part-time, experienced tutors with the proper attitude towards mining safety and trained thousands of managers, overmen and firemen over the period to 1914. In 1909 he was appointed Professor.[67]

Architecture developed as a discipline from unpretentious origins. Charles Gourlay, B.Sc. F.R.I.B.A., F.S.A.(Scot.) was appointed to lecture in 1888 and in a period of hectic building booms in the city greatly developed his discipline. The Glasgow branch of the Institute of British Architects was keen to elevate the subject and also to gain a seat on the Board of Governors, but there were few full-time day students, Gourlay relying on evening classes for his work. His Building Construction classes were particularly well attended (185 students in 1895-6), and in consequence, he was appointed to a Chair in 1895 with a salary of £400 per annum. His publications perhaps were a diverting release from the mundane business of his teaching life; his articles show his speciality was the history of cathedral-building, and he was an expert on Glasgow Cathedral. A trickle of students took the examinations of the Royal Institute, a reflection of the small number of full-time day students before 1914, but evening classes were very popular, 525 students being enrolled in the department in the last session of peace.[68]

The composition of the student body became increasingly diverse during this period. Most evening students came from Glasgow and adjacent districts, but the day students came from further afield, including a growing number of postgraduates. Between 1890 and 1905 there were a further sixteen Japanese students and a significant number from India. The Japanese included Kajiro Mijashima (b. 1875) who had taken a course at the Imperial University Tokyo before

23 Among the electrical engineers educated in the Glasgow and West of Scotland Technical College was John Logie Baird (1888-1946). Baird completed his Diploma in 1914 and was already showing the promise of a distinguished career as an inventor. Here he is shown in 1945 holding the 'Telechrome', which he designed to show television pictures in colour and in three dimensions.

studying Naval Architecture. This was one of the popular choices of the Japanese, although most read Mechanical Engineering, and at least one, Senchi Matsuda (b. 1877) was a 'Japanese Government Student'.[69]

Student life, as day students' numbers rose to over 600 by 1900, reflected the growing complexity of departmental evolution. The Andersonian Chemical Society (1886) in 1908-9 had over 120 members; the Scientific Society (1892) had about 320 and discussed many contemporary issues affecting engineering firms – bonus systems, testing petrol engines, foundry problems – as well as listening to Frederick Soddy talk about the mysterious substance, radium. The Anderson Naturalists' Society (membership 331) was very popular, meeting monthly and with frequent field excursions. The Architectural Craftsmen Society (1896) had 118 members in 1908 and held eleven meetings and also visited buildings under construction. The Dialectic Society (1906) had seventy members and discussed and debated questions of general interest. The Bakery Students' Association had 90 members in its first session (1908-9), met on Saturday evenings and listened to work-related talks. The Civil Engineering Society (established in 1906) with a membership of over 200 was equally utilitarian but it also held social gatherings in the College. A Textile Society was formed in 1911 but there is no mention of social functions.

The Students' Representative Council was formed in 9 November 1893; it was elected by the students from all departments in the College and was the official body representing the students with Governors on all matters of general interest. By 1908-9 the evening students decided to organise their own committee, but that session both SRC and ESC jointly organised the College magazine, published monthly throughout the session and self-financing because its circulation rapidly reached over 2,000. The SRC had committees on athletics and amusements, and clearly stimulated the social life of the College community. The day students opened a union in 1911, after negotiations between the Governors and SRC over the period 1909-11. Papers, a billiard table, chess, draughts and dominoes were available, and the possession of a large room made student life more sociable. In 1912 the Association of Former Students was formed and was intended to supply to members information about their contemporaries and about living and working conditions and job opportunities in the country or area in which they were resident. Reunions were organised through collaboration with the SRC and the various student societies before 1912.[70]

On the eve of World War I the Royal Technical College had clearly escaped from the penury of the early 1890s. Aided till 1908 with 'whisky money' (from 1891) and private donations which arrived, fortuitously it seemed with every financial crisis, the College had become a favoured child of the Scotch Education Department. Designated a Central Institution in 1901, the College was served by feeder institutions providing continuation classes from which the best students made their way. After its absorption of the Weaving College in 1908, there was no comparable institution outside the universities in Scotland. Industry recognised its advantages, for the College generally responded when an educational initiative was suggested as, for instance, in the introduction of a lectureship in Sugar Manufacture in 1911. The division within the student community between middle-class recruits and ex-pupils of Board schools was remarked upon by John Charles Waltham Reid, who, as a student, hated his 'sandwich' experience at the North British Locomotive Company. John Logie Baird (1888-1946), in the same class in 1908 but much less of a 'Hooray Henry' than Reith was at that time, did not require to learn the lessons of classlessness which Flanders Fields and especially the Battle of the Somme were to teach. He intended to make use of his training as an electrical engineer and of his native genius to escape the poverty trap.[71] Reith as Director-General of the BBC and Baird as the inventor of television were both to play a major part in transforming the post-war world into a 'global village'.

REFERENCES

1   *One Hundred Glasgow Men*, pp. 173-6; Tamaki, pp. 10, 11, 13, 15, 22, 24, 25, 28, 37, 49, 56, 181, 182; T. Kelly, *George Birkbeck*, p.150.

2   SUA, C7/2 Letterbook of the Glasgow Mechanics' Institution, 1855-61, Secretary to W.G. Hodge, 8 March 1859, 16 August 1859; JBC, Calendar of Glasgow and West of Scotland Technical College, 1889-90, pp.20-1.

3   Calendar 1889-90, p.20; *The Lord Provosts of Glasgow, 1833-83*, pp. 295-9; SUA, C11/9 Annual Reports of the Mechanics' Institution, 1879.

4   SUA, C11/8 Annual Report, 1866; Annual Reports, 1869-74; C11/9 Annual Reports, 1876-81; C11/10 Annual Reports, 1881-6.

5   SUA, C11/8 Annual Report, 1874; Annual Report, 1879; B1/6 Minute Book of Anderson's University 1881-7, 12 February 1883; 13 August 1883; 4 September 1883; 7 November 1883; 27 February 1884; 9 June 1884; 21 April 1885.

6   SUA, DB3/4 The Atkinson Institution Act, 1861; JBC, Calendar, 1889-90, pp.21-2.

7   SUA, B1/6 Minute Book of Anderson's University, 1881-7, 28 April 1884.

8   39 and 40 Victoria, cap XIV, Allan Glen's Institution Act, 1876; J.A. Rae, *The History of Allan Glen's School, 1853-1953* (Glasgow, 1953), *passim*; JBC, GWSTC Governors' Minutes, p.3; O. Checkland, pp. 122-3.

9   J.L. Carvel, *Stephen of Linthouse* (Glasgow, 1950), pp. 38 ff, 54 ff, 67-91, Appendix A; SUA, B1/6, 21 March 1884.

10 JBC, Calendars 1887-1914; Post Office Directories of the City of Glasgow, 1887-1914; John Shields, *Clyde Built* (Glasgow, 1947), pp. 81 ff, 127; Butt, 'The Industries of Glasgow … '

11 Leslie L. Forrester, 'Technical Education and the Economy of the West of Scotland, 1870-1914', Unpublished Ph.D. thesis (University of Strathclyde, 1991), pp. 189-93. Cf. also O. Checkland, for the various charitable bodies.

12 JBC, GWSTC Governors' Minutes, 1887-8, pp. 4-6.

13 Ibid., pp. 4, 6, 7, 11, 13-14. His salary was £300 per annum.

14 Ibid., GWSTC Governors' Minutes, 1887-1914, *passim*.

15 Ibid., GWSTC Governors' Minutes, pp. 49-51.

16 Ibid., p.52.

17 Ibid., p.65.

18 Ibid., Annual Report, 1896.

19 Ibid., Bursaries Committee Minutes 1887-1911, *passim*; GWSTC Minutes, 1911-12, pp. 68, 96, 97, 109, 160, 181; Forrester, Ph.D. thesis, p.243.

20 Ibid., Secretary's Report, 18 January 1888.

21 Ibid., GWSTC, 1887-8, pp. 104-5, 109, 120-1.

22 Forester, Ph.D. thesis, pp. 207-9; Henry Dyer, *Technical Education in Glasgow and the West of Scotland* (Glasgow, 1893), p.5; Brock, 'The Japanese Connexion … ', pp. 227-8.

23 JBC, GWSTC Minutes, 1887-8, pp. 84, 98, 119-120, 157; Secretary's Report, 16 January 1889, p.3; SUA, E1/1/3 Governors' Minutes, 1889-90, Annual Report; 16 May 1889; Forrester, Ph.D. thesis, pp. 369-70.

24 SUA, E1/1/3 Governors' Minutes, 1889-90, 18 September 1889.

25 JBC, GWSTC Minutes, 1891-2, pp. 91, 106; Forrester, Ph.D. thesis, pp. 370-2.

26 JBC, Annual Report, 1895-6, p.3.

27 Forrester, Ph.D. thesis, pp. 373 ff.

28 JBC, GWSTC Minutes, 1907-8, pp. 104, 114 (the first meeting attended by Principal MacAlister was on 21 January 1908); Forrester, pp. 373-4.

29 JBC, GWSTC Minutes, 1909-10, pp. 50-2, 55.

30 Forrester, Ph.D. thesis, pp. 375-7; JBC, GWSTC Minutes, 1909-10, p.61; Ibid., Minutes, 1911-12, pp. 29, 30-8, 40, 54, 96, 198, 201; Ibid., Minutes, 1913-14, pp. 2, 8, 10, 12, 28, 34, 54, 67, 143, 158.

31 SUA, E1/1/7 GWSTC, Annual Report, 1896-7.

32 JBC, GWSTC Minutes, 1891-2, p.90; Annual Report, 1891-2.

33 Ibid., Annual Report, 1892-3.

34 Ibid., Annual Report, 20 January 1897.

35 Ibid., Annual Report, 16 January 1900.

36 Ibid., GWSTC, Minutes, 1899-1900, pp. 48, 66, 99; Minutes, 1901-2, pp. 5 ff, 8, 19, 20-1, 23, 24, 32-8, 41.

37 Ibid., Minutes, 1901-2, p.44.

38 Ibid., Annual Report, 1900-1, p.68.

39 Ibid., Minutes, 1901-2, pp. 131A ff.

40 Ibid., p.154.

41 Ibid., Annual Report, 1901-2, Appendix I, Building Fund.

42 Ibid., Annual Report, 1902-3.

43 Ibid., Annual Report, 1903-4.

44 Ibid., Annual Report, 1905-6.

45 Ibid., Annual Report, 1906-7.

46 Ibid., Annual Report, 1907-8.

47 Ibid., Annual Report, 1908-9 and 1909-10.

48 Ibid., GWSTC Minutes, 1911-12, pp. 53, 56, 95, 143, 152.

49 Ibid., Annual Report, 1896-7.

50 Forrester, Ph.D. thesis, pp. 204 ff; *A Goodly Heritage: A Hundred Years of Civil Engineering at Strathclyde University, 1887-1987*, edited by Alexander R. Buchan (Glasgow, 1987), pp. 3-23; Royal Technical College Calendar, 1912-13, pp. 37-9; J.R. Hume and M.G. Moss, *Beardmore, The History of a Scottish Industrial Giant* (1979), p.31.

51 Forrester, Ph.D. thesis, pp. 222-3.

52 Ibid., p.224; JBC, GWSTC Calendar, 1901-2; Minutes, 1903-4, p.177; Minutes, 1965-6, pp. 94, 132; Minutes, 1909-10, pp. 47, 48, 49, 61, 134, 160.

53 Select publications appear in the Annual Reports, and those for Chemistry increase substantially 1892-1914; JBC, GWSTC Minutes, 1891-2, pp. 77, 85-6, 91.

54 Nuttall, pp. 8-9; Butt, 'The Industries of Glasgow … '; see, e.g., Calendar 1910-11, pp. 286 ff for appointments taken up by former students.

55 JBC, GWSTC Minutes, 1891-2, pp. 79-80, 91.

56 Ibid., GWSTC Annual Report, 1900-1, pp. 74-5; GWSTC Minutes, 1903-4, pp. 71, 19, 29, 30, 45, 50, 119.

57 Ibid., GWSTC Minutes, 1909-10, pp. 111, 112, 119.

58 Ibid., RTC Minutes, 1913-14, Annual Report, p.7; D.C. Pack, *A Short History of the Department of Mathematics*, n.d. (c.1975), pp.4-5.

59 Ibid., Annual Reports, 1892-1909, *passim*.

60 Buchan, pp. 10-15; Ramsay, pp. 141-3.

61 Buchan, pp.15-16.

62 JBC, GWSTC, Minutes, 1905-6, pp. 49, 57, 97, 98, 120; Minutes 1910-11, pp. 6, 19, 21, 64; Buchan, pp. 19-25.

63 Department of Electronic and Electrical Engineering, *Centenary* (Glasgow, 1992), pp. 3-4; JBC, Calendar, 1887-8; Calendar, 1892-3; GWSTC Minutes, 1899-1900, pp. 14, 17, 45, 70, 76, 83; Annual Reports, 1899-1914.

64 JBC, GWSTC Minutes, 1895-6, Annual Reports; Minutes, 1903-4, pp. 64, 112, 120, 145.

65 Ibid., GWSTC Minutes, 1905-6, pp. 60-1.

66 Ibid., pp. 62, 97, 113, 142; Annual Report, 1906-7, p.188; Minutes, 1909-10, pp. 171, 180; Annual Report, 1908-9, p.2.

67 SUA, E1/1/9 GWSTC Minutes, 1901-2, 14 May 1902; Forrester, Ph.D. thesis, pp. 229 ff; JBC, GWSTC Minutes, 1909-10, pp. 7, 11, 26.

68 JBC, GWSTC Minutes, 1887-8, pp. 91 (election of John Honeyman, architect to Governors), 126, 133; Minutes, 1895-6, p.13; Annual Reports, 1895-1914.

69 SUA, General Notes/68, List of Japanese students prepared by Sami Kita, 1980.

70 Ibid., Annual Report ,1908-9; Calendar, 1912-13, pp. 475-81.

71 Ibid., GWSTC Minutes, 1891-2, p.61; Forrester, Ph.D. thesis, pp. 391 ff; JBC, GWSTC Minutes, 1908-9, p.52. *Reith Diaries*, ed. by Charles Stuart (1971), pp.22-3; J.C.W. Reith, *Into the Wind* (1950), pp.11-13; P. Waddell, *Man of Vision: A Jubilee Tribute to John Logie Baird ...* (University of Strathclyde, 1975), pp.2-3; Tom McArthur and Peter Waddell, *The Secret Life of John Logie Baird* (1986), pp. 28 46-7, 50, 54-62.

CHAPTER SIX

War, Peace, Depression and War Again, 1914-45

'The need of trained men in industries has never been more clearly recognised, and exceptional efforts have been made by local firms to co-operate in maintaining the system of engineering training, the so-called "sandwich" system, peculiar to Glasgow and adopted forty years ago, under which qualified apprentices spend three or four winters in attendance on College courses, returning to their practical work in the shops during the intervening summers. The success of this system is undoubted ... '

Annual Report, Session 1924-5

BY 1914 A MUTUALLY REINFORCING relationship existed between the Royal Technical College and the principal industries of Scotland which was symbolised by the 'sandwich' system. Moreover, the departure of students for the United States, Europe, Japan and the countries of the Empire and Commonwealth and their replacement by others from many countries, some of them graduates, created its reputation as an international centre of excellence in applied science and technology, although most students came from nearby. The strains of war and the advent of a depression which shattered the international economy roundly tested the resilience of the institution, its departments and personnel. How well it and they adjusted is the subject of this chapter.

Staff, students and alumni volunteered for the services in great numbers from the day that war was declared. Initially, it was proposed that the College should form a battalion of its own members, but Lord Kitchener personally requested that, 'in the interests of more speedy mobilisation', there should be co-operation with the Chamber of Commerce to form the 17th (S) Battalion of the Highland Light Infantry. The idealism that led a thousand students and members of the College to enlist before the end of 1914 requires some explanation. Haldane's Officers' Training Corps scheme was the nursery of many a martial ambition among students, alumni and staff. John Charles Walsham Reith had joined the Glasgow University contingent in 1908 and by 1910 was a sergeant. Commissioned in 1911 as a Territorial in the 5th Scottish Rifles, he was typical of many who later found themselves in France or Mesopotamia or at the Dardanelles, immoderately optimistic about the shortness of the conflict and completely confident of the outcome.[1]

The School of Navigation, established in 1909 to serve the needs of the major Glasgow-based shipping lines for officers, was rapidly placed on a war footing; Chief Petty Officer Alexander Macdonald, Instructor of the Admiralty Signalling Class, was called up on 1 August 1914.[2] The age structure of the student population partly determined their direction to the services; over 74

TABLE 6.1   Royal Technical College: Roll of Honour, 1914-20

Date	Officers	NCOs	Men	Total	Comment
12 June 1915	202	174	717	1,141	48 incomplete returns
15 June 1915	357	225	824	1,410	1 nurse and 3 sp. service
14 October 1915	468	331	927	1,736	1 nurse and 9 sp. service
7 February 1916	544	377	1,038	1,971	1 nurse and 11 sp. service
5 February 1917				2,300	
18 December 1917	903			2,504	
17 December 1918	1,128			2,757	
26 October 1920				3,225	Still incomplete

Source: JBC, RTC Governors' Minutes, 1915-20.

per cent of the day students of 1913-14 were between the ages of eighteen and twenty-six, and 73 per cent of the evening students.[3] The military were given special facilities in the College for the medical examination, enlistment, and equipment of the 17th Highland Light Infantry, and many volunteers came from the student body.[4] Benno Schotz (Mechanical Engineering), arguably Scotland's greatest twentieth-century sculptor, and John Logie Baird (Electrical Engineering) qualified in that last session of peace for the Associateship. At the Governors' Annual Meeting on 20 October, 1914 the Chairman, George Beilby, explained that because of the war the public distribution of diplomas and prizes had been abandoned, but the new Associates [ARTC], 'some of whom were in military uniform', were introduced and admitted to their special status.[5]

H.F. Stockdale, the Director since 1899, was given special powers to deal with any emergencies arising from a decline of about a third in the student enrolment and the departure of staff for the services. Some staff resigned without publicly declaring their intentions, but by October 1914 Natural Philosophy had lost two evening-class staff, one of whom was commissioned; Mathematics, two evening staff; Chemistry, all three Senior Lecturers, Second Lieutenants Wilson and Agnew and Captain Heilbron, and 'a laboratory attendant', G.T. Stewart, who was a Territorial; Technical Chemistry, two staff, Lieutenant-Colonel O'Connor and Trooper Hardie; Metallurgy, one member of the evening staff; Mechanics, two members of the evening staff; Electrical Engineering, its instrument-maker, Sergeant John Hossack; the School of Navigation, eleven commissioned officers and two instructors for the *Empress* training ship; and the Administration, two key people, the Chief Clerk, Lance-Sergeant John Douglas and the Head Janitor, Sergeant-Major John Downie. The outflow was massive: by 1918 only four staff of military age had been retained – in reserved occupations – to ensure that the College could continue to function. Attempts were made to deal with the gaps either by dropping classes or increasing their sizes and, infrequently, by temporary recruitment of those exempt, unfit or over age for military service.[6]

A Roll of Honour was kept which increased in size as the war proceeded. Its statistical details are given in Table 6.1, and it was maintained until 1920 as information about alumni accumulated.

RTC personnel served in each of three services and in every theatre of war. Casualties were considerable, mostly among those in attendance in 1913 and 1914; about one in five were killed: 287 officers and 328 NCOs and men. Another 53 had been taken prisoner, and a number were wounded in action, including John Reith.[7] The Governors regularly noted with a mixture of sorrow and pride the sacrifices made by College members and the honours won. The latter, as in early 1917, are summarised in Table 6.2.

TABLE 6.2   Honours won by RTC Alumni as at 5 February 1917 and 26 October 1920

Honours	1917 Number	1920 Number
Victoria Cross	2	3
Distinguished Service Order	2	
Military Cross	43	
Distinguished Service Cross	2	
Distinguished Conduct Medal	7	339
Military Medal	12	
Mentioned in Dispatches	49	
Commended for service in action	2	
Meritorious Service Medal	1	
Croix de Légion d'Honneur	2	
Croix de Guerre	2	
Médaille Militaire	1	
Russian Order of St Stanislaus	1	11
Al valore Militare	1	
King of Serbia's Gold Medal	1	
Montenegrin Silver Medal	1	
Total	129	353

Source: JBC, RTC Chairman's Committee Minutes, 5 February 1917; Annual Report 26 October 1920, p.2.

Other members, led by George Beilby, the Chairman of the Governors, contributed to the war effort their scientific and engineering expertise. Beilby became a member of the Admiralty Board of Inventions, the kind of body of which John Anderson would have approved; he was also heavily committed to selecting chemists for war work, made necessary by the lack of chemical imports from Germany.[8] Industrial mobilisation was just as essential as organising the services for war and produced many equally complex problems which only state intervention was slowly capable of solving.[9] An institution with a long record in the application of science and technology to production problems clearly had a part to play.

Professor Henderson was President of the Society of Chemical Industry (1914-15) and completing his work on terpene chemistry (for which he was elected F.R.S. in 1916) when the war began. He had cultivated industrial contacts and was widely consulted when chemical firms encountered problems in production. Many alumni occupied important positions in the industry, and the drive to improve munitions and to substitute British-made chemicals for German imports engaged their attention. Professor Thomas Gray and the Technical Chemistry Department became heavily involved in coal-tar testing by 1915, especially in analysis of gasworks output with a view to maximising supplies of toluene and benzene. This work continued throughout the war. Beilby took on the rôle of Director of the Fuel Research Board in 1917 and in 1918 recruited Gray on secondment for work at East Greenwich. Gray's earlier work on coal analysis for the Ministry of Munitions no doubt admirably fitted him for this new post. Henderson took over the supervision of coal-tar testing.[10] Generally, the Department's close connections with Nobel assisted in the general drive to increase the supply of explosives.

The Department of Textile Manufacture rapidly suffered a fall in its student numbers since it had a high proportion of Territorials; it is worth noting that Private Henry May (1st Scottish Rifles) who won the Victoria Cross 'For most conspicuous bravery near La Boutillerie' on 22 October 1914 was an evening student in this department (1909-12). It moved rapidly into war

TABLE 6.3   Student Numbers 1914-45

Session	Day	Evening	Total Student Numbers
1913-4	669	4,342	5,011
1914-5	445	2,583	3,028
1915-6	409	2,115	2,524
1916-7	453	2,134	2,587
1917-8	662	2,495	3,157
1918-9	981	2,178	3,159
1919-20	1,135	4,555	5,690
1920-1	1,290	4,356	5,646
1921-2	1,203	3,969	5,172
1922-3	1,160	3,812	4,972
1923-4	1,006	3,810	4,816
1924-5	936	3,817	4,753
1925-6	895	3,254	4,199
1926-7	934	3,235	4,169
1927-8	931	3,238	4,169
1928-9	967	2,939	3,906
1929-30	1,008	2,949	3,957
1930-1	903	2,880	3,783
1931-2	897	2,728	3,625
1932-3	878	2,549	3,427
1933-4	910	2,485	3,395
1934-5	908	2,698	3,606
1935-6	1,001	2,624	3,625
1936-7	1,026	2,665	3,691
1937-8	1,019	2,814	3,833
1938-9	1,087	2,704	3,791
1939-40	1,019	1,748	2,767
1940-1	941	1,438	2,379
1941-2	1,105	1,430	2,535
1942-3	1,197	1,587	2,784
1943-4	1,116	1,798	2,914
1944-5	1,266	2,227	3,493

Source: JBC, RTC, Annual Reports and Statistics, 1914-45.

work, testing thousands of textile materials – for tents, aircraft and airships – for the Admiralty and War Office as well as assisting firms supplying cloth for the services, most of which were working overtime, thereby also reducing student enrolments. There were only fourteen students in the day classes in 1915-16 (of whom thirteen were women from the College of Domestic Science), and although this was slightly better than in 1914-15 (thirteen students), it did not compare with peacetime numbers. There was also a steady fall in evening-class enrolments to 1917, common to all departments, as Table 6.3 indicates.[11]

Inevitably, the engineering departments were heavily involved in war work. Some critical classes had to be suspended for lack of numbers or instructors. Electrical Engineering had to give up evening classes in Motor Design, Electrical Wiring and Instrument Making and a laboratory class in Motive Power Engineering was lost by the Department of Mechanical Engineering, both for the session 1914-15. The Department of Mechanics had excellent testing facilities, and from May 1915 these were gradually exploited by government departments. Modification in laboratory courses became necessary as this work mounted, and some evening classes were suspended.

24 The War Memorial on the stairs in the foyer of the Royal College. The sculptor was Kellock Brown, the design by T.L. Watson who died before its completion (by Colin Knight) in 1921. It commemorates the sacrifice of 615 members of the College who gave their lives in the Great War of 1914-18.

Professor J.G. Longbottom divided this work into three elements: assistance to the Aeronautical Inspection Department; projects assigned by the Inspector of the Glasgow Munition Board; and jobs for local firms making munitions. The first division was concerned with testing aircraft structures and engines, often involving the design and construction of special apparatus. The second element was concerned with testing shells and shell parts and was very time-consuming, causing the staff to work Sundays and holidays. The third was similar to the second but conducted for private firms, sometimes testing new munition materials. Tests were running at about 1,200 per month by October 1916. A Brinell Testing Machine was lent to the Inspector of the Glasgow Munition Board because tests for hardness were being conducted on materials and objects which could not be brought to the College. It was so badly damaged that the Ministry of Munitions, after some haggling, agreed to replace it.[12]

The major effort went into training munitions workers, many of them women. This dilution of labour was needed for the war effort, but strongly resisted in some plants by trade unionists, an initial contribution to the myth of Red Clydeside. The Ministry of Munitions asked for the College's assistance in 1915, and there were initial questions about the practicability of instituting short-course training. In the autumn of 1915 H.F. Stockdale and Professor Mellanby visited the shell factories of G. and J. Weir at Cathcart and of Beardmores of Parkhead and then examined existing training classes in Manchester, Edinburgh and London. Local manufacturers were strongly in favour of the Royal Technical College becoming a trainer, and James Weir offered to take all the workers the College could train. Most of the early classes in other centres were exclusively male, and thus the industrial relations issue did not at first emerge. The initial plan was for twelve-day courses working seven hours per day in the hope of producing efficient lathe operators. Thirty-nine lathes were drummed up from all quarters, mainly from school workshops. By early 1916 forty (including one possessed by the College) were in constant use and a new course training women as oxy-acetylene welders 'to be engaged in the manufacture of trench bombs' had been started. A local firm with the bomb contract supplied three experienced welders as instructors, and the British Oxygen Company supplied free oxygen. College certificates were issued to those completing the course.

Once these training efforts proved to be successful, the Ministry of Munitions sought to extend them; the Governors agreed that the College would do as much as possible. Fuse-hole plugs for shells were made in the College by their thousands from 1916 onwards, and the staff and mechanics made gauges and dies to order for local munitions firms. Rooms were made available to Ministry personnel so that co-ordination of training and other activities was facilitated. Eventually, by 1918 the Ministry of Munitions had taken direct control of all this work. However, a course for women aircraft inspectors was established in March 1918, and thirty-six students enrolled. And thus, the emancipation of women from stereotypical female jobs was considerably advanced by the War and the College.[13]

The cost of war was reflected in two particular instances. In March 1917 the Chairman's Committee acceded to the request of the Glasgow Red Cross for use of a workshop in the College for the manufacture of crutches 'and other appliances in timber' required in the local hospitals.[14] More permanent was the War Memorial on the stairs which faces the doors of the Royal College. Plans were in hand as the Governors gave thanks for the cessation of hostilities in December 1918, and the Chairman's Committee was empowered to consider what form the Memorial should take. At first there was discussion of a stained-glass Memorial Window or Windows, but both the Staff Common Room Committee and the Students' Representative Council preferred a monument. So did some members of the Chairman's Committee, and a design based on the College seal was prepared by Thomas Lennox Watson, a former Governor nd one of the unsuccessful architects who competed to design the Royal College building. nitial plans for placing tablets on each side of the staircase containing the names of the dead vere discarded on account of cost. The sculptor was Kellock Brown, and donations were gradually received to meet the estimated cost of £1,600. The marble was supplied by John Youden and Son, and because of the death of T.L. Watson, Colin Knight completed his design of the bronzes with minor modifications. On 20 December 1921 the completed War Memorial was unveiled by Lady Beilby, and her husband, Sir George, addressed a large gathering of staff nd students.[15]

Thus, a generation of survivors commemorated the gallant six hundred, talents lost to cottish industry and learning, and the world economy. A very small minority are remembered n the prizes awarded as a result of endowments given by relatives. Madame Bourdon gave 0,000 francs to found the prize in the Glasgow School of Architecture in memory of her son, Professor Eugène Bourdon, Director of Architectural Studies (1904-16), Chevalier de la Légion 'Honneur, Croix de Guerre, Military Cross, Officier d'Académie, killed in action on the omme, 1 July 1916. J. Whitelaw Hamilton established a fund of £500 in memory of his son eslie, a student in the Glasgow School of Architecture who was killed in action in Mesopotamia n 15 October 1918.[16]

Some advances were made in the war. Collaboration between Glasgow University and the College further developed: classes were made available to students of both institutions when ither found it impossible because of the war to maintain teaching. A new ordinance in 1915 xtended the Glasgow B.Sc. degree to students of Chemistry, clearly a precedent for further co-peration.[17] The idea of a new development fund to support research was mooted just before the var and gathered pace. Essentially, the fund was originally designed to provide teaching ssistance to allow senior staff members more time for research, but its aims diversified over me.[18]

However, the problems of adjusting to peacetime conditions were very considerable. As Table 6.3 shows, there was a sudden increase in day students beginning in Session 1917-8 which eached its peak in 1920-1. Total student numbers peaked in 1919-20 at 5,690, and these early ears of peace placed strains on accommodation, staff and other resources. The examination hall nd ante-room were used in 1918-9 to house Ministry of Labour staff attempting to cope with emobilisation. Sir George Beilby and H.F. Stockdale joined a universities deputation to the Chancellor of the Exchequer to seek increased financial support, for the ravages of inflation were endering nonsensical pre-1914 levels of salary, and the costs of equipment and teaching materials (especially chemicals) were escalating. The fee structure required to be examined rgently.

Some students, half-way through courses when the war began, were in danger of being isadvantaged in the peace. The Board of Studies suggested to the Governors that special war ertificates should be issued to deal with these hard cases. The demobilised and unqualified equired some priority; the large number of staff who had gone to the colours or into war work eeded to be assimilated into a revised staff structure. Employers, including universities, were kely to poach the most talented, unless attractive salaries and working conditions could be rovided. Men, who had risen in the armed services, might or might not be sceptical about Lloyd George's claims that Britain would become a land fit for heroes to live in, but they were unlikely o accept the old status of assistant lectureships.

At first there was an attempt to hold down staff salaries, although some increases were ranted, but a revision of this policy became vital as disaffection grew and some staff voted with heir feet.[19] Lieutenant-Colonel I.M. Heilbron of Chemistry is a case in point. Heilbron, a

25 Sir George Thomas Beilby F.R.S. (1850-1924), Chairman of the Board of Governors, 1908-24, great technical chemist and inventor, successful businessman and enthusiast for advancing the status of the Royal Technical College. His distinguished war work won him many friends in the establishment and possibly influenced the Treasury to include the Royal Technical College in the first University Grants Committee list of recipient institutions.

26 The Organic Chemistry laboratory with staff and students c.1919. Included are Professor G.G. Henderson, who left in that year to take the Chair in the University of Glasgow, I.M. Heilbron who succeeded him, and F.J. Wilson who also became Professor of Organic Chemistry after Heilbron's departure to the University of Liverpool.

Glasgow man, Associate of the College (1905), and Young Exhibitioner (1907-9), had first become third assistant to Professor Henderson in 1909 and was offered the same post in 1919 after distinguished war service. One of his colleagues left for an industrial post at treble the salary, and Heilbron also offered his resignation in May 1919. In August Henderson resigned to take the Regius Chair at Glasgow at a time when student numbers in Chemistry were high and rising. The Governors decided to appoint Professor Thomas Gray of Technical Chemistry as Director of the largest School of Chemistry in Britain and to promote Heilbron to the Chair of Organic Chemistry as well as creating a new Chair in Inorganic and Analytical Chemistry for his colleague Dr. F.J. Wilson. Heilbron had begun his distinguished lifelong work 'in the application of advanced techniques to the elucidation of the properties of naturally occurring substances with a spectroscopic study of coloured materials' before moving to Liverpool University in 1920 and thereafter to Manchester and Imperial College.[20]

Since his own research had been in Organic Chemistry, Professor Wilson transferred to the chair vacated by Heilbron and was replaced in Inorganic and Analytical Chemistry by Dr. R.M. Caven, formerly a Senior Lecturer at University College, Nottingham and currently Principal of Darlington Technical College (since 1918). Several additions were made to the staff, including Dr. J.M. Cranston (the last man to identify a naturally-occurring element, protoactinium, and a gifted musician). Gray and Henderson (who was a Governor representing Glasgow University, 1925-38) found it easy to collaborate, and the new ordinance of 1915 worked reasonably well until the creation of the University of Strathclyde in 1964.

Throughout the inter-war years the staff of Technical Chemistry and Chemistry worked in unison, providing service teaching for many courses as well as supervising students for the

Associateship of RTC and the B.Sc. of Glasgow University. Fuel and dyestuffs research were the main specialities within Technical Chemistry while Wilson published many research papers, often in collaboration with Steven and Hopper, on hydrazines. Among his most successful students in Session 1918-19 was Taketsuru Masataka (1894-1979) who on his return to Japan established the Nikka Whisky Company and thereby became the founder of the Japanese whisky industry. Caven already had textbooks to his name – and original research papers – on appointment but added books on chemical analysis as well as papers on the properties of inorganic double salts.[21]

Unlike many other industries which the college served, chemical manufacture expanded in the inter-war period, and the emergence of the major petrochemical companies and Imperial Chemical Industries in 1926 increased the domestic demand for trained chemists. Successful students, however, continued to go abroad, especially to the United States, South Africa and Australia. Gray, Young Professor (1903-32), was replaced by Dr William Murdoch Cumming, Senior Lecturer in Organic Chemistry since 1920, who had industrial experience with British Dyers Ltd. as a manager and director of research. A prolific researcher, he was in 1933 joint author of two textbooks and had published about thirty papers.[22]

R.M. Caven died in 1934 in his last year of service at the age of 64. The vacancy was not filled. Instead there was some reorganisation, and Professor F.J. Wilson became Freeland Professor, a title revived in 1934 but in use before 1920. Total student enrolments remained well over 1,000 till World War II and from time to time approached 1,400. Staff held many external appointments including examinerships and maintained a strong publications record.[23]

Natural Philosophy faced many of the post-war problems of staffing, accommodation and resources already described in relation to Chemistry. The influx of new students (1,467 enrolments in 1920) in the boom up to 1921 necessitated several new appointments, but the Freeland Professor, James Muir, appointed in 1906, provided continuity of management throughout, only retiring in 1938. A special evening class for Pharmacy students was introduced in Session 1921-2 and collaboration with the engineering departments was close. Both had extensive industrial contacts and consultancy work. Muir researched with his assistants into the physical properties of steel. Students had to be content with College certification, the Associateship being the pinnacle of undergraduate endeavour. Yet even in the depths of depression student enrolments never fell below 1,000. Muir was succeeded by Dougald B. McQuistan, M.A., B.Sc., F.R.S.E., who had been Associate Professor in the Department since 1925. McQuistan, a distinguished graduate of Glasgow University, had extensive teaching experience at Allan Glen's School during which he was for six years external examiner in Natural Philosophy at his *alma mater*. The lack of differential between secondary school and university salaries explains this career pattern.[24]

In the first ten years of the *College Research Journal* which was initiated mainly because of Caven's enthusiasm for encouraging young research workers of all disciplines into publication, Natural Philosophy was the third department – after Mechanical Engineering and Chemistry – in the number of contributions made by staff, but Muir certainly did not believe in self-advertisement. Very few entries relating to the Department appear in other College publications. Alumni are the best testimony available to any department, and many Associates went on to take university degrees. One, David Anderson, a mechanical engineer, took his Glasgow B.Sc. with special distinctions in Mathematics, Natural Philosophy, Physical Laboratory and Engineering and Drawing. After his Ph.D. and extensive teaching and administrative experience in England he was to return to RTC as Director.[25]

Sir David Anderson's academic career also illustrates the place of the Department of

Mathematics. It was a major support to the Engineering departments, an ancillary subject in the Associateship and the B.Sc. degrees offered under the Ordinance of Affiliation of 1913. Professor John Miller, D.Sc., had been assistant to George Gibson, and, after Gibson's election to the Glasgow chair in 1929, became his successor, serving the Royal Technical College till 1934. Student enrolments were over 1,100 in 1921-2 and were roughly halved during the course of the Great Depression. Miller had the reputation of being a lucid and well-organised lecturer, but economic circumstances were very much against him after 1929. The advertisement for his successor emphasised the importance of close working relationships with the professors of engineering, but shipbuilding, marine and locomotive engineering and other capital goods industries, which had both supported and gained from the College, were in varying degrees of difficulty.[26]

Miller was succeeded by Professor Reginald O. Street (1934-51), a Fellow of St John's College, Cambridge who had graduated with distinction as a Wrangler in 1911. After graduation he had read Physics and spent a year in the Cavendish Laboratory working under Professor J. J. Thompson. Winner of the Rayleigh Prize in 1913, he joined the Royal Flying Corps (later the Royal Air Force) during the First World War and was attached to the Meteorological Section of the Air Ministry. After the war he joined the staff of University College, Southampton and thereafter moved to the Department of Applied Mathematics in the University of Liverpool where he published papers on Elasticity, Tidal Theory and Mathematical Geophysics. In short, he was the type of mathematician likely to commend himself to engineers in the Royal Technical College.

He rapidly undertook his own review of the department and its staffing needs, pointing out to the Governors' Committee (Mathematics, Natural Philosophy and Natural Science) in March 1935 'the large amount of lecturing work, and the preparation and correction of very numerous examination papers and exercises'. He clearly thought that members of the staff were overworked, unlikely to pursue research in current working conditions and unable to undertake extra undergraduate courses. He received authority to make an additional appointment at a salary of £300; the most suitable candidate, the Committee thought, apart from normal academic qualifications, would have interests which lay 'in the application of Mathematics to practical problems'.[27] This paragon was duly found and appointed.

Street himself offered an advanced class in 1935-6 in Mathematics as an aid for those studying 'Advanced Electricity', clearly aimed at Associateship level and higher, which continued for a number of years. The University of St Andrews rapidly recruited him as external examiner in Applied Mathematics in 1935, and advanced evening classes gradually showed an increase in enrolments. By 1936 he was Vice-President of the Edinburgh Mathematical Society, and President in 1937, and student enrolments, both day and evening, showed a marked recovery. In 1938 extra mathematics teaching was introduced into degree courses for engineers, chemists and metallurgists, and new appointments followed.[28] The recovery of the department was then interrupted by World War II.

In Natural Science, the main feature of the inter-war period was the growth of Pharmacy. Supported by the Glasgow and West of Scotland Chemists' Association, the idea of a School of Pharmacy reached the Governors in March 1920 and was immediately given serious consideration by the relevant committee. The Director and appropriate representatives of the Pharmaceutical Society of Great Britain met in the College on 24 March, 1920, and demand for courses, fees, and support from local pharmacists were discussed. Since the College was grossly overcrowded in 1920, H.F. Stockdale was naturally concerned about accommodation, especially laboratory space. Supporting departments were inspected by Major Peck of Cambridge,

Inspector of the Pharmaceutical Society, and presented no problems in terms of professional recognition of a course. Peck favoured beginning with one lecturer, a specialist in Pharmacy and Materia Medica.

By June a timetable had been drawn up, and Robert S. Glennie, formerly 'Chief Lecturer' in Pharmacy, Botany and Materia Medica, appointed. Dr David Ellis, lecturer in Bacteriology and Botany, became 'Superintendent of the School of Pharmacy', and purchases of apparatus and materials for classes were authorised.

Ellis organised day and evening classes designed to prepare students for the Qualifying Examinations of the Pharmaceutical Society, beginning in Session 1921-2. However, Glennie left under a cloud in 1921 just as the prospectus for the School of Pharmacy was being circulated. Recognition of a degree course was being negotiated with the University of Glasgow, but existing students were already taking the examinations of the Pharmaceutical Society. Glennie was replaced by Dr. James Prior Todd, Ph.D., with effect from 1 September, 1921. Todd held the Minor and Major qualifications of the Pharmaceutical Society, had about five years' experience in retail pharmacy, four years as a Teacher of Pharmacy and Materia Medica in the Glasgow School of Pharmacy and three years' Army Service during which he was Senior Pharmacist in the 23rd British Stationary Hospital, Baghdad, and a member of the Board of Pharmacy Examiners for Mesopotamia. An Assistant Demonstrator and two Student Assistants were also appointed. And thus J.P. Todd at the age of twenty-seven launched the School of Pharmacy.[29]

The Court of the University of Glasgow approved the degree of B.Sc. in Pharmacy before Session 1921-2 began, and enrolments proved to be satisfactory: 212, mainly in the day classes, probably representing about 70 individuals. The Depression of the early 1920s affected enrolments the following year, producing a decline to 178, but there was a sharp rise in 1923-4 to 316. Retail experience was usually gained after Part I of the Pharmaceutical Society examinations, and thus there was a lapse of up to three years before day students returned to College. Candidates for the Major examination, therefore, tended to be few in the early years of the School.

A junior lectureship in Botany to replace Miss Wanda Zamorska became necessary in 1926, and this post was taken by Miss Blodwen Lloyd, M.Sc., a first-class Honours graduate of University College, Aberystwyth (1922) with some teaching experience in her own department and also at Porth Grammar School. Miss Lloyd was to serve the College long and well and is now an honorary graduate. By that date more stringent regulations governing the training of pharmacists had been anticipated by the staff, large numbers of day students – relative to other centres – had been attracted, the B.Sc. in Pharmacy was reasonably established, and research was proceeding on the stabilisation of drugs and on the quantitative tissue variations in medicinal plants.[30]

By 1929 student numbers appear to have reached a plateau. David Ellis had been elevated to a Chair of Bacteriology in 1924 and remained Superintendent of the School till his death in 1937. He had managed the emergence from a group of classes in 1909 of a School of Pharmacy which by the early 1930s had become the largest in Britain. Progressively, research had also grown in quantity, and it was generally believed, in quality. A new four-years' Honours Degree in Pharmacy was introduced in Session 1932-3 to which most existing students decided to transfer. Recognition visits by the Pharmaceutical Society and London University came and went with satisfactory outcomes, but there were very few candidates for London degrees after 1928.

A post-graduate diploma course in Biochemical Analysis was introduced in 1934-5, taught by Dr. S. L. Tompsett, lecturer in Biochemistry at the Royal Infirmary. James P. Todd was appointed in 1937 to succeed David Ellis, and thus, the opportunity was taken to head the School with a qualified pharmacist, a desirable change in an era of growing professionalisation; Todd also became responsible for the Department of Bacteriology and Botany and by his example led the School in an effective research effort.[31] World War II was to prove a major testing ground and watershed in the development of Pharmacy, and it was fortunate that the School was headed by a man of considerable experience in peace and war.

The School of Architecture, jointly organised by the College and the School of Art, had lost its director, Professor Eugène Bourdon, killed in action in 1916, as has been noted earlier. There was an interlude before an appointment was made, but College students and staff did have Professor Charles Gourlay to supervise them. Enrolments were low in 1918-19, and thus the need for extra staff did not arise. The influx of new students in the following session showed a six-fold increase, as demobilisation took effect. James B. Fulton, F.R.I.B.A., was appointed as Director of Architectural Studies in 1920. A brilliant student of both the School of Art and the Royal Technical College, Fulton had wide experience with some of the best Glasgow and London architects and had taught in the London County Council School of Building under Professor Beresford Pite.

Fulton persuaded colleagues in both institutions that the curriculum for their Diploma should be substantially revised in order to gain recognition from the Royal Institute of British Architects. There was a clear attempt to copy the 'sandwich' system whereby day and evening attendances were combined to allow professional training in an architect's office to occur simultaneously with academic work. The Institute did recognise the revised Diploma, thus exempting those who had completed the five-year course from its final examinations. Unfortunately, Fulton was taken very seriously ill and died in 1922; it became necessary to take steps to find another Director of Architectural Studies.

Fulton's successor was T. Harold Hughes, A.R.C.A., A.R.I.B.A., a partner in Sir John Burnett's practice; his credentials were impressive: formerly head of the School of Architecture in Aberdeen (1910-14), which had a good reputation, he was a considerable prizeman and a medallist of the Royal College of Art. Yet he inherited from Fulton a very sound base upon which a very successful school could be built – over 300 students, most of them combining evening classes with practical experience in an architect's office.[32]

Hughes remained Director of Architectural Studies up to 1942 and was thus primarily responsible for meeting the needs of society for competent architects during two major building booms, 1922-9 and 1932 into the war. Locally, there were major additions to the housing stock in the 1920s and 1930s, and the growth of suburbia allowed full play for Art Deco. This was most clearly manifested in commercial buildings, such as department stores, hotels, restaurants, cinemas and ballrooms. From the mid-'30s, new factory building, road construction and urban renewal gathered pace, and Hughes' position as Superintendent of Building Classes became significant in organising a better supply of skilled labour, the main bottleneck, despite high levels of unemployment. Rearmament added to existing economic strains in the construction industry: there was a great demand for building labour as new aerodromes and coastal defences – including stations for the radio-location system (radar) – were built.[33]

Hughes encountered the tensions existing in any joint School of Study managed by two institutions. His specialist appointment at Glasgow School of Art was in Architectural Design, and he encountered demarcation difficulties with Charles Gourlay in the Royal Technical College in 1923. Hughes' authority over the School was upheld by the Joint Committee of Governors, and co-operation by Gourlay and other members was required. The task of mounting a university degree, B.Sc. in Architecture, led to the sinking of differences: in 1924

27 Civil Engineering students undertook surveying and other practical exercises at an annual summer camp. Here the party are shown at Loch Eck c.1920.

Glasgow University initiated this degree which was, however, only taken by a minority of students up to 1945. The first degree awarded was conferred on W.T.P. Bryce, M.A., in the summer of 1926. The majority preferred to take the diploma course which could be achieved by a combination of part-time and full-time study.

Gourlay died in 1926, and the Joint Committee discussed moving most of the teaching to the Royal Technical College in response to suggestions made during the accreditation visit of the Royal Institute's Board of Education, although there were some rumblings in the School of Art about Architecture's place as an Art. The teaching of Design and Construction in the same building was clearly desirable and strongly endorsed by Hughes, and the fact that the School of Art was not represented in any affiliation with the University of Glasgow was significant when discussing the location of degree classes. Proximity to a strong Civil Engineering group was also thought to be important. Hughes was then chosen to replace Gourlay as Professor of Architecture in the Royal Technical College and also retained the post of Director of Architectural Studies, the first time that both these posts had been held by the same person.[34]

A major review of the School next occurred in 1938, following a report from the Visiting Board of the Royal Institute. Essentially, the School of Art had housed most of the evening classes since 1927, and the day classes had been held in the Royal College. Both institutions had accepted the principle of co-ordination, but in practice they had behaved almost independently of each other. The day classes were very successful, according to peer review, but the Visiting Board was reluctant to continue the recognition of the evening classes, thought the lack of co-ordination was a substantial problem and implied that physical separation of the two divisions should be ended. They favoured locating the School in the Royal College. However, a Special Committee appointed by the Joint Committee reported in favour of the School of Art.

The School of Art lacked suitable accommodation, and a second visit by Darcy Braddell, Chairman of the Visiting Board of the Royal Institute, reaffirmed their preference for the Royal College. There was strong support for the School of Art from the Glasgow Institute of Architects, since they took the view that their profession belonged with the Fine Arts. Eugène Bourdon had the correct view of events in 1903 when he favoured an amalgamation of the School of Art and the Technical College. The whole area of industrial design might have grown faster and earlier, much to the potential advantage of the British economy. The Battle of the Somme took more than Bourdon's life in 1916; it prevented the emergence of an alliance between Art, Design, Architecture, Construction and Engineering, a vision which only an incomer like Eugène Bourdon would be capable of propagating successfully. Instead, a compromise perpetuating division was hatched: a certificate left in the School of Art and the rest of the Diploma taught in the Royal College.[35] Both remained under the aegis of Governors from both institutions operating as a Joint Committee until 1965.

Post-war recovery in the capital goods industries led to a massive influx of students intent on taking engineering courses. Civil Engineering, Mechanical Engineering, Mechanics, Electrical Engineering, Mining Engineering, Metallurgy, Economic Geology and Naval Architecture accounted in Session 1919-20 for 5,432 enrolments out of 13,475 (40 per cent), more than double the total for the previous session.[36] Thus, Table 6.3 indicates a broad story of a major boom in student numbers up to the economic recession of 1921 and an almost unrelieved decline till 1933-4 followed by faltering recovery up to the war of 1939-45.

Over-inflation of the heavy engineering industries during World War I was not sustainable in the harsh trading circumstances of the 1920s and 1930s. Foreign competition, protective tariffs elsewhere, and the failure of the international economy to grow, all attacked Glasgow's position of industrial leadership. Some industries such as shipbuilding, locomotive engineering and coalmining were in structural decline till given the kiss of life by World War II. Others had cost disadvantages either of labour or raw materials: iron and steel production, for instance, was hit not only by structural decline elsewhere but also by the depletion of raw material resources. The regional economy required a transforming agency generated by the domestic market for it was unlikely to come from overseas, despite the attempt to create a viable sterling area within the Commonwealth and Empire. National incomes within the Imperial trading area were not growing sufficiently to aid the capital goods industries of the West of Scotland. Falls in the prices of foodstuffs and colonial raw materials aborted the growth of demand. A consumer goods revolution was required at home: it began and was noticeable in the Midlands and south-east England, but it was missing elsewhere.[37]

Yet the solutions adopted in Scottish industry did keep up the demand for highly skilled, graduate-type labour. Canada, the United States and South Africa, previously magnets for College graduates and associates, remained so till 1929-30. Rationalisation and the emergence of large firms in British industry put a premium on training and skill, particularly if these were allied with experience, which, as the Annual Report of 1924-5 indicates, was the great attribute of the 'sandwich' course system. The explosion of numbers in 1919-20 and 1920-1 was largely a consequence of demobilisation programmes after 1918.

The recognition of the Royal Technical College in 1919 as a University College by the University Grants Committee of the Treasury was largely a consequence of two unrelated circumstances. The first, and possibly the more important, was the affiliation ordinance with Glasgow University; the second was the contribution made by College personnel (including the Chairman Sir George Beilby) to the war effort. Beilby was an adept and eminent scientist-administrator, a gifted inventor and patentee, a discreet and diplomatic man with unshakeable

28 Herbert Fitton Stockdale (1868-1951), Secretary/Treasurer of the Glasgow and West of Scotland Technical College, 1899-1904. On the advice of the Scotch Education Department, which conferred the status of a central institution on the College, the Board of Governors appointed H.F. Stockdale its first Director 1904-33.

resolve and clear objectives. Contemporaries close to events certainly gave him much credit for the way he conducted relations with the infant UGC. But he was admirably served by the Director, H.F. Stockdale.[38]

Engineering gained most from this recognition, partly because more of its costs were borne by the Treasury and partly on account of its longer, pre-affiliation, connections with the University of Glasgow. For the B.Sc. in Engineering had the largest student recruitment and covered more departments than any other degree. In the inter-war years public funding accounted for an increasing proportion of College income, the Scottish Education Department contributing about two-thirds and the UGC one-third of funds derived from Government. However, it should be noted that student fees made up about a quarter of total income and public funding nearly a half. It was the fairly constant stream of gifts in money and kind from industry and private individuals which kept the books tightly balanced.[39]

Much research in engineering had been war-related up to 1919, but this bias gradually changed. Professor Longbottom of Mechanics was not highly qualified academically but allied to excellent teaching ability a remarkable capacity for finding brilliant mathematical as well as practical solutions to engineering problems. His department did much testing of turbine pumps with a view to improving their working efficiency, and he was interested in engineering materials, experimenting with basic and acid steel and cast iron at high temperatures. His connections with local industry were very close.[40]

When Longbottom died in 1924, the Committee on Engineering in a joint meeting with the Chairman's Committee decided to incorporate Mechanics within the department of Mechanical Engineering; Professor Mellanby was appointed Professor of Mechanics and Mechanical Engineering, and Dr. Kerr (who, as Mellanby's research assistant, had been selected as a high-flyer) became Associate Professor, a rank deliberately designed to retain good, young and ambitious staff. Longbottom's laboratory, which he had jealously guarded for his own department's use, was opened to civil engineers, metallurgists and others who could make use of its facilities, although it was expected that the main users would be mechanical engineers.[41]

Mellanby had the ill-deserved reputation of being an ascetic, somewhat detached figure, ruthless in academic politics and rarely losing an important battle for power. When George Moncur retired in 1933, Civil Engineering was also absorbed by the Department of Mechanical Engineering, and Mellanby became Professor of Civil and Mechanical Engineering and Mechanics. The real explanation for these developments was not Mellanby's ambition to become a pluralist professor but rather the College's need in days of tight monetary policy and reduced government funding to keep administrative and departmental costs down. Significantly, the UGC Returns for these years show that the Royal Technical College had both a low endowment income and one of the lowest costs per full-time student equivalent (FTE). Considering the relative costs of students in science and technology, this does suggest a very deliberate attempt to be both highly efficient and exceedingly economical.[42]

Students performed well under Mellanby, and many made a considerable mark after graduation. Research was nurtured as was industrial consultancy. In 1921-2, for instance, work was commissioned by the British Marine Oil-Engine Manufacturers' Association, and there was co-operation with Metallurgy in examining different classes of cast iron under high temperatures. Much work in the early 1920s was concerned with turbine design blades and discs, and the working efficiency of particular types. David Anderson and William Kerr did much of this work under Mellanby's supervision. Experiments on evaporative condensers begun by O. Sneeden in 1920 were continued by J.C. Orkney (1921), David Anderson (1923) and later by A.W. Scott

TABLE 6.4   Graduates attending the Royal Technical College, 1913-38

Session	Numbers	Universities outside Scotland
1913-4	118	S; C; L; M; Cal; Punj; Copen
1923-4	115	O; C; L; M; Li; Le; D; McG; Cal
1925-6	148	L; D; Le; M; W; Cal; Punj
1926-7	123	L; Le; W; Bom
1932-3	102	C; L; Le; S; B; Cape; Wit; Ben; Bom; Kyoto
1936-7	100	O; C; L; D; R; B; D; To; Ben; Cal; Luck; Mad; Chiao-Tung, Tientsin
1937-8	104	O; C; L; D; R; B; D; Bom; Cal; Mad; Patna; Tientsin; Tsing Hua

1. Many of these students worked in firms as graduate apprentices and attended evening classes.
2. Recruits from all the Scottish Universities were commonplace.
3. Key to Universities outside Scotland: B = Belfast; Ben = Benares; Bom = Bombay; C = Cambridge; Cal = Calcutta; Cape = Capetown; Copen = Copenhagen; D = Durham; L = London; Le = Leeds; Li = Liverpool; Luck = Lucknow; M = Manchester McG = McGill; Mad = Madras; O = Oxford; Punj = Punjab; R = Reading; S = Sheffield; To = Toronto; W = Wales; Wit = Witwatersrand

Sources: JBC, Annual Reports, 1913-38.

(1929-30). Successful industrial contacts brought gifts of valuable equipment, sometimes from alumni in responsible positions in major companies, but much of the apparatus was made in the 'machine laboratory'.

The mid-'20s witnessed the developing problems of the coal, iron and steel, engineering and shipbuilding industries, most dramatically manifested in the General Strike of 1926; there had been 'a serious reaction on College affairs' and a sharp decline in student numbers, as Table 6.3 reveals. However, graduate numbers remained buoyant (see Table 6.4). The *College Research Journal*, begun in Session 1924-5, gathered pace, and external publication of research increased significantly. Metal 'creep'/fatigue joined the subjects under investigation in 1925-6 and the strength of materials group acquired a Japanese postgraduate, Masa Kitigawa, later (1929-30) an Engineer-Lieutenant in the Imperial Navy. This connection with the Japanese Navy was maintained by Suzuki Shigemoto (Associate in Mechanical Engineering, 1928) who by 1936 was a Lieutenant Commander in the Shipbuilding Department of the Admiralty in Tokyo. A new Dynamics laboratory was gradually commissioned in Sessions 1927-9, and work on the theory of lubrication was made more effective by new testing machines. A continuous feature of research in this department was its applicability to industrial problems as well as its advancement of theory.

As the outlook for the West of Scotland's basic industries further darkened from 1929-30, the fall in student numbers was obvious down to 1934-5, although the cohort of day students began to recover in the previous session (Table 6.3). Yet the sharp increase in unemployment did not markedly affect the College's graduates, and there was an absolute shortage of College metallurgists reported in 1930. Demand for mechanical engineers persisted also and was extended by the desire of firms to make their marketing departments technically qualified. Dr. A. W. Scott became involved with the Hannah Dairy Research Institute in collaborative work on milk-drying and produced an experimental plant for producing milk powder in Session 1929-30, but the full practical implications of this work were not to become apparent till World War II.

In 1932-3 the Scottish Education Department, under 'the Geddes axe' procedure to reduce public expenditure, cut the College grant, despite the UGC's exemption from this privation. Staff salaries over £2 per week were reduced by three per cent, not the full cut of ten per cent experienced in some other sectors of the public service. The Report of 1932 recorded the cold facts of the diminution in income but did not wallow in self-pity:

Notwithstanding the decrease in income, there has been no lowering of standards and no restriction of any field of work, while research in nearly every department has been prosecuted with energy and success. This has been possible only because of the hearty co-operation of the staff and their willing acceptance of the conditions imposed by the circumstances of the times.

Mechanical engineering felt the draught in two ways: there were no new significant academic developments, and industrial consultancy, the lifeblood of good academic engineering departments, temporarily declined sharply. Before the full effects of depression had struck, however, a new wind tunnel, supported by the Weirs of Cathcart, had been designed. A young research student, holder of the Greenock Research Scholarship, Adam S. T. Thomson (1908-) had also begun his researches into lubrication, which were eventually to lead him to the Chair in 1946. The contemporary comment, that 'His work had been notable for experimental ingenuity and the results obtained are of great interest', signified a promising career.

The wind tunnel was nearing completion in Session 1933-4, and preliminary experiments begun. Governing and control gear had to be manufactured according to the design of J. Caldwell, B.Sc., A.R.T.C. Mellanby retired in 1936 and was replaced by the much more extrovert William Kerr. According to one of his assistants (Professor Emeritus Robert M. Kenedi), he was an excellent teacher, brilliant raconteur and always immaculately dressed. Hard of hearing, he used this handicap to considerable advantage in College politics, only hearing what he wished to hear. His research credentials were first class, and his industrial experience and contacts considerable. He maintained existing lines of research and stimulated new ones. Aeronautical engineering came of age and studies of wing ailerons began in the wind tunnel in 1935-6.

The revival of the Scottish economy was faltering and inconsistent, but tests of materials increased significantly in 1936-7, there were more calls for opinions about engineering failures, constructional and design problems, and the range and number of inquiries began to strain staff resources. The Agricultural Research Council commissioned laboratory research on grass drying, there were new studies of marine propellers and further investigations of 'creep' and steam turbines. The construction boom led to many tests of materials – reinforced concrete and wire ropes being especially common – but there was a variety of industrial problems upon which staff were consulted – bearing failures, and shaft vibrations in deep well pumping being simply two common examples. Plant was designed for drying grass, and thus the Agricultural Research Council received value for money, and high-speed boiler research was being developed by 1939. Much of this research and consultancy activity had relevance for the teaching of undergraduates and their training for industrial posts. Student enrolments in the last full year of peace reveal that twenty-five per cent were in Civil Engineering, Mechanical Engineering and Applied Mechanics.[43] The following year brought war, and secrecy cloaked research.

The nucleus of Civil Engineering staff led by George Moncur till 1933 contributed to his pioneering series of the *Glasgow Text Books of Civil Engineering* which outlasted his tenure. Student numbers showed the cyclical trends already described, with the Diploma being more commonly awarded, because of the possibility of evening attendance, than the Associateship in the 1920s and 1930s. Higher degrees were earned, perhaps that of D.Sc. (1928) awarded to Alexander Thom being particularly significant, since he carried the Royal Technical College's expertise to the University of Oxford, where he later became Professor of Engineering Science. Teaching and research within the amalgamated department under Mellanby and Kerr were limited by student numbers, resources and laboratory space. Yet Drs William Hunter and Charles Moir kept the base of Civil Engineering intact and indeed strengthened it for later expansion and ultimately autonomy again.[44]

Electrical Engineering remained a buoyant sector throughout the interwar period because of its widespread applications and the capital investment (which the First World War probably delayed) in supply companies, the National Grid, railway electrification, and new consumer industries such as automobiles, radios and white goods. John Logie Baird's pioneering efforts in television led him to fresh areas of technical achievement, some of which remain within the realm of speculation about his 'secret life'. His manifold interests were to engage groups of scientists and engineers for the rest of the twentieth century: fibre optics, 'noctovision' (a detection system which closely resembled radar), long-range television transmission, and better television cameras, capable of achieving excellent colour definition.[45]

Both power engineering and the 'consumer goods sector' attracted attention from the Department of Electrical Engineering. Magnus Maclean's tenure of the Chair ended in 1924, and he was replaced by Stanley Parker Smith, a graduate of Armstrong College, Newcastle (1904), and an 1851 Exhibitioner, who had studied at Karlsruhe. Parker Smith expanded both the teaching and research activities of the department from a small base. Enrolments ran at 1,329 students in 1923-4, 822 in 1932-3 and 685 in 1937-8. This trend was deceptive, since attendance at day classes tended to increase in the 1930s, generally at the expense of the evening classes, and student hours rose. Employment remained good throughout the '30s, but generally students on graduation had to leave Scotland to work in England or overseas; Scotland's industrial structure was weak in terms of Electrical Engineering.

Industrial relevance remained a constant theme in the department, and thus Power Engineering saw most growth. M.G. Say was appointed as a research assistant with a project relating to railway electrification; later to become Professor of Electrical Engineering at Heriot Watt College, Say found few industrial connections in Scotland apart from Glasgow Corporation's Subway managers, for British railway companies experimented with electrification south of the Border. Yet his work was valuable for the future. Parker Smith and George Hibberd (later to become Professor of Mining Engineering) worked together on testing flameproof mining electrical equipment. Work had begun and been abandoned in Sheffield University; the electrification and mechanisation of Scottish pits ran ahead of the rest of Britain. Local firms also supported students concerned to find out more about the 'electrics' of automobile and lorry engineering. Albion Motors, in particular, were very supportive of this advanced course.

Parker Smith was very active in the Institution of Electrical Engineers, serving on the Council from 1926 and on many of its committees. He was an energetic publisher on subjects such as electrical equipment in automobiles; his most 'student-friendly' publication was *Problems in Electrical Engineering*, an edited text of tutorial problems with answers. Parker Smith was interested in oscillography which he expected would assist in fault location on high-power overland lines. This interest led him to visit German technical institutes in the 1930s, and in 1934 he met Dr. Constantin Szeghö in Aachen. Szeghö's Ph.D. thesis related to the cathode ray tube; his cold cathode could register 'single traces in a fraction of a microsecond' and was long-lasting. Parker Smith offered Szeghö a temporary appointment which he accepted, being anxious to leave Nazi Germany. Ultimately, Szeghö joined John Logie Baird's staff and emigrated to the United States to work for the American subsidiary, Baird Corporation.[46]

Metallurgy, tied to the apron-strings of Chemistry in 1914, gradually cut the knots and formed alliances with several other departments, notably Natural Philosophy and Mechanical Engineering. Its importance to major firms such as Colvilles was recognised by John Craig and others concerned with the restructuring of the iron and steel industry between the wars.[47] Rationalisation into larger units was commonplace in the British industry, and graduates and diplomates were in constant demand, despite the economic pressures on the industry. Alfred

Campion, appointed lecturer in 1909, became Professor of Metallurgy in 1911 and enjoyed the delight of small classes for the Diploma. He was active in consultancy, advising a local foundry on the proper charge of materials to achieve the best results, but paying £75 of his fee to the College for the privilege. Metallurgical analysis could be construed to be an activity for private firms not academics, but the Governors thought it valuable to solve problems for Glasgow firms.

Campion resigned in 1918, and was replaced by Cecil H. Desch, lecturer in Metallurgical Chemistry in the University of Glasgow, an appointment known to be popular with local industrialists. Desch began the re-equipment of the department and was interested in the heat treatment of high-speed tool steels. Student enrolments reached 242 in 1918-9, but Desch decided in 1920 to accept the Chair in Sheffield and, therefore, he had little time to leave his mark on the department.[48]

His successor, John Harold Andrew, was a Chemistry graduate of Manchester University who took postgraduate degrees in Metallurgy. He had excellent industrial experience, working for Armstrong, Whitworth & Co. from 1914 as research director, and a good publication record. Andrew cultivated industrial support and organised classes on demand, for instance in smith work and forging. By 1927-8 student enrolments stood at 338, but most of the teaching was in the day. The research of the department – by Hay, Higgins, Binnie and Andrew – increasingly concentrated on high-quality alloy steels. Undoubtedly, Metallurgy grew in stature and strength during Andrew's tenure, but he too was tempted by the Sheffield Chair and resigned in 1931.[49]

Andrew's replacement was Robert Hay who was educated at Alloa Academy and Glasgow University. His industrial experience included service with the Steel Company of Scotland, Stewarts and Lloyds, and government employment during the war at Nobel's Explosive Company, Ardeer and at the Gretna munitions plant. Hay joined the staff of the College in December 1919 as a lecturer, was promoted to senior lecturer in January 1921 and was also the 'Graham Young' lecturer in Metallurgical Chemistry. In 1926 he graduated Ph.D. at Glasgow University and produced a steady stream of research papers. Professor Hay remained in office till 1959 and created a small but well respected department. Among its associates was Harold Montague Finniston, who became a demonstrator for a short time after obtaining a distinction in his diploma examinations (1934).[50] This was the first significant step in a career which led to the Chairmanship of British Steel. It was difficult to retain staff in this department, because industrial appointments were both lucrative and relatively numerous.

Hay developed research co-operation with James Muir, Professor of Natural Philosophy, and with various members of the Mechanical Engineering department. He was also able to attract the support of Dr Andrew McCance, an industrial assessor in the department and the 'technical brains' at Colvilles, later Chairman of the Board of Governors. Professor Hay was very active in the iron and steel industry's research organisations and contributed a number of research papers of direct industrial relevance, especially on open-hearth steel practice. Both the British Iron and Steel Federation and the Department of Scientific and Industrial Research began to provide financial support for staff research.[51]

Mining went through travail in this period, never attaining again the significance which it enjoyed up to 1920. The rationalisation of the industry into larger units did stimulate the demand for highly trained mining managers, and the problems posed by increased mechanisation and deeper mines added to the need to apply science to production. Yet the industry was in structural decline, only arrested by the Second World War. Daniel Burns, appointed as a lecturer in 1902, became Professor of Mining in 1909 and remained in post till his retirement in 1932. Most of the students came to evening classes, and total enrolments in 1919-20 amounted to 668, but 150 day enrolments accounted for over 60 per cent of the hours taught. Support was sought from the

Miners' Welfare Fund, and grants of several thousands of pounds were given from 1924 onwards to aid the teaching and research of the department.

Student numbers fell in the day classes, so that by 1923-4 there were only 40 enrolments out of a total of 646. The session of the General Strike, 1925-6, was disastrous with only 15 day enrolments out of 472. The University of Glasgow and the College began to confer about the teaching of Mining when Burns was due to retire with the result that the discipline, apparatus and students were concentrated in the College. The degree was revised, a new laboratory created and fully equipped, and special evening courses preparing candidates for the Mine Managers' Certificate were provided.

The two institutions had agreed on the new James S. Dixon Professor of Mining, Andrew M. Bryan, a distinguished graduate of the University of Glasgow with teaching experience and military service to his credit. Most recently he had been Senior Inspector of Mines – since 1926 – and had been responsible for over 400 mines of various types in Scotland and the North of England. During his time in the inspectorate he had published research papers in appropriate professional journals. Thus, he combined a wealth of practical experience with research and teaching ability.

Gradually, student recruitment revived: 40 day enrolments in 1938-9 and 127 for evening classes. Bryan was in great demand as an external examiner, especially in the Universities of Leeds and Wales. He published on dust and other health and safety issues in the mines and with J. Smellie, Ph.D., A.R.T.C., won the Norman Henderson Prize for the best paper submitted to the Mining Institute of Scotland in 1937-8. Rearmament was beginning to revive the coal industry in Scotland, and opportunities for qualified men were improving.[52]

Student facilities improved in the inter-war period. Apart from the established societies a Dramatic Society was formed, but the main development was the acquisition of sports facilities and a new pavilion at Cambuslang. By the end of the '30s ten teams were regularly using the College sports ground at the weekends. Charities Week became a considerable institution by the early 1920s. As students were recruited from outside the city, the problem of residences emerged. Reminiscences do survive from this period. One Technical Chemistry student (1934-8) came from Elgin and he noticed the milling crowds of students, relatively few of whom were female. It was a cosmopolitan crowd with students from the United States, Egypt, South America and Germany. The Students' Union provided light relaxation and it became 'a most necessary part of college life'. 'Digs' were at first daunting: a widow as a landlady, a small bed-sit in a tenement and a tight budget. The course encouraged independent study, especially in the Associateship year when the project was the main task. Confidence and maturity were engendered by all these experiences: 'I came of age in many senses and still feel I owe a great debt of gratitude to the Tech, its staff, and its unique environment'.[53]

The Second World War distorted life in the College almost as much as the Great War of 1914-18 had done. Day student numbers, however, did not fall, and after the initial decline (see Table 6.3) in total numbers, recovery proceeded. Air-raid precautions were taken; fire-watch duty was arranged; some volunteered for war service; others were in reserved occupations. Although a new extension was being built, its future progress was problematical. A summer term was introduced, and a 'fast-track' Associateship and Diploma resulted.[54]

National Service affected staff and students. Three staff in Metallurgy and Technical Chemistry were working in the College full time for the Government, their salaries being recovered from the Ministry of Supply. The David Elder lectures in Astronomy held annually since the beginning of the century were suspended for the duration. Professor Andrew Bryan resigned on 30 May, 1940 on account of the development of the Ministry of Mines. No

29 War trainees lining the basement corridor on the occasion of the visit of King George VI and Queen Elizabeth to the Royal Technical College Emergency Training Centre for machine operators set up in the Mechanical Engineering Department for the Ministry of Labour, 5 March 1941. The King was accompanied by Sir Robert Robertson (1860-1949) who was Chairman of the Board of Governors, 1931-46.

replacement was immediately planned, for the number of students had fallen considerably. The School of Pharmacy, apart from teaching its students, was involved with war work organised by the Department of Health for Scotland. The Engineering Department began instructing munitions workers in ordinary machine operations and gradually extended its activities. Electronic equipment (unspecified) was lent to the Ministry of Aircraft Production without charge for the duration of the war.

The Department of Electrical Engineering began training army personnel and shipyard electricians for Yarrow's, John Brown's, Fairfield and Scotts' of Greenock. Essentially, most departments were training students for reserved occupations, which largely explains why student numbers remained relatively stable in the day classes.

Working under great pressure inevitably took its toll. Professor Kerr who was a diabetic was certainly under great strain from 1941. The Governors decided to appoint John C. Orkney as Associate Professor to undertake some of the burden arising from new classes and reduced staffing. Pressure on space also became an issue in 1941; departments where the number of students was comparatively small released space even if new timetabling became necessary. The failure to complete the extension was becoming critical.[55]

The shortage of skilled technicians encouraged Lord Hankey's Technical Personnel Committee for the War Cabinet to seek help from the Technical Colleges. 150 places were found for entrants prepared to take intensive training in the summer of 1942. Training programmes for women covering a range of mechanical skills had begun in June 1941; by January 1942, 300 trainees were enrolled. Machines were used day and night. Women production supervisors had also been trained, many going to work in Royal Ordnance Factories.

The Department of Electrical Engineering started courses in 1940 for R.A.F. trainees who were needed as wireless/radio mechanics: 546 were trained in 1941. Most of those who passed became radar operators, and the whole programme was supervised by Dr (later Professor) Eric Fairley. By the end of the war, over 10,000 trainees had passed through the department. A shortage of skilled men for the mines led to the introduction of an intensive course in 1943; students were nominated by the mine-owners who paid fees and maintenance grants. The Department of Pharmacy became the Central Depot for the National Blood Transfusion Service in 1942 and Professor Todd was appointed Regional Director for the West. Most of the blood – 9,000 pints in the year ending 31 March 1943 – was turned into plasma, and research work was proceeding on its processing and preservation. By 1945, 34,000 pints of blood were being collected and processed in the year. Work on the treatment of burns in collaboration with the Royal Infirmary and the Medical Research Council was also far advanced. Bakers were trained for the services by the School of Bakery: the cookhouse, often mobile, had to be much better organised than had happened in World War I.[56]

Many of the service trainees also did drill and physical training. Both were noisy. Pharmacy lectures, according to Dr Mary Dawson, were often interrupted in consequence. Tablet-making machines were not available to the would-be pharmacists; they were being used to compress explosives elsewhere.[57] Science and technology applied to production brought final victory in the summer of 1945, and not a moment too soon. The need for skilled men and women had never been so amply demonstrated before.

REFERENCES

1 Reith, *Into the Wind*, pp. 15 ff; R.C.K. Ensor, *England, 1870-1914* (1964), pp. 395-6.

2 JBC, RTC Governors' Minutes, 1913-14, p.167.

3 Figures calculated from Annual Report, 1913-14, p.22.

4 Annual Report, 1914-15, p.5.

5 JBC, RTC Governors' Minutes, 1914-16, p.3.

6 Ibid., RTC Chairman's Committee, 6 October 1914.

7 Ibid., Annual Report 1919-20, p.1; *The Reith Diaries*, p.25. Cf. also J.C.W. Reith, *Wearing the Spurs* (1937), *passim*.

8 JBC, RTC Governors' Minutes, 1915-16, *passim*; Annual Report, 1914-15, p.18.

9 Clive Trebilcock, 'War and the Failure of Industrial Mobilisation: 1899 and 1914', in J.M. Winter (ed.), *War and Economic Development* (Cambridge, 1975); Samuel J. Hurtwitz, *State Intervention in Great Britain, A Study of Economic Control and Response* (New York, 1949), Ch. 2.

10 JBC, RTC, Annual Report, 1913-14, p.5; Nuttall, pp.8-9; JBC, RTC, Governors' Minutes, 1915-16, pp. 51, 62, 73, 81, 84; Governors' Minutes, 1917-19, pp. 5, 18, 74-5, 76.

11 Ibid., RTC, Governors' Minutes, 1915-16, pp. 19, 27, 40, 62, 71, 85, 95-6; Minutes, 1917-19, pp. 23-5.

12 Ibid., RTC, Governors' Minutes, 1913-14, p. 172; Minutes, 1915-16, pp. 83, 93; Minutes, 1917-19, pp. 7,16.

13 Ibid., RTC, Governors' Minutes, 1915-16, pp. 36, 43-44, 73, 78, 91-2; Governors' Minutes, 1917-19, pp. 66, 76, 80; D. Kirkwood, *My Life of Revolt* (1935), pp.108-110; R.K. Middlemass, *The Clydesiders* (1965), pp. 61 ff.

14 JBC, RTC, Governors' Minutes, 1917-19, p.17.

15 Ibid., pp. 121, 138, 147, 156, 159, 169, 177; Governors' Minutes, 1920-1, pp. 17, 26, 46, 47, 58, 88, 90, 100, 106, 118,

133; Annual Report, 1919-20, p.1; Governors' Minutes, 1922-3, pp. 3, 4, 5, 11, 20.

16 Ibid., RTC, Governors' Minutes, 1917-19, pp. 145-6. Also among the dead, for instance, were HLI Major Marshall Downie (Associate 1896), B.Sc., who had been Managing Director of Duncan Stewart and Company (Annual Report 1914-15, p.1) and Captain James Lusk BA (Cantab), Senior Cert. of the College (1901), Director of Colvilles, who was the grandson of David Colville and expected to become Chairman (Calendar 1915-16), p.349 and P.L. Payne, *Colvilles and the Scottish Steel Industry* (Oxford, 1979), p.132).

17 Ibid., RTC, Governors' Minutes, 1915-16, pp. 6, 12, 23, 32A, 78.

18 Ibid., RTC, Governors' Minutes, 1913-14, p.158; Governors' Minutes, 1915-16, pp. 64, 73; Governors' Minutes, 1917-19, pp. 148, 156, 170, 175, 177, 178; Governors' Minutes, 1920-1, pp. 2, 5, 16, 19, 26, 46, 58, 88, 102, 106, 117.

19 Ibid., RTC, Governors' Minutes, 1917-19, pp. 116-17, 119-20, 124-6, 129, 139, 148, 162-5.

20 Ibid., Calendar 1915-16, p. 334; GWSTC, Governors' Minutes, 1909-10, p.114; RTC, Governors' Minutes, 1917-19, pp. 157, 170-1; Nuttall, p.9; JBC, Governors' Minutes, 1920-1, p.60.

21 Ibid., RTC, Governors' Minutes, 1920-1, pp. 60-1; Nuttall, pp.10-11; JBC, RTC, Annual Reports 1920-34. SUA, General Notes/68, List of Japanese students prepared by Sami Kita, 1980.

22 JBC, RTC, Governors' Minutes, 1932-3, pp. 59, 63, 75.

23 Ibid., RTC, Governors' Minutes, 1934-5, pp. 45, 58, 69-70, 78, 106; Annual Report, 1933-4, p.8; Annual Reports 1935-9.

24 Ibid., RTC, Governors' Minutes, 1920-1, pp. 12, 28, 33, 34, 92, 119, 144; Annual Report, 1920-1, pp. 2, 7; Governors' Minutes, 1922-3, pp. 28, 29, 53, 95; Annual Reports, 1929-36; Annual Report, 1937-8, p.9; Governors' Minutes, 1924-5, p.123.

25 Ibid., Annual Report, 1933-4, p.10; RTC, Calendars 1936-7, p.354.

26 Pack, p.5; JBC, RTC, Annual Reports, 1929-34; RTC, Governors' Minutes, 1934-5, pp.4-5.

27 Pack, p.5; JBC, RTC, Governors' Minutes, 1934-5, pp. 38, 49, 55, 98.

28 JBC, RTC, Governors' Minutes, 1934-5, p.105; Calendar, 1935-6; Annual Report, 1934-5, pp. 8 and 12; Annual Report, 1935-6, pp.3, 13, 15; Annual Report, 1936-7, p. 12; RTC, Governors' Minutes, 1938-9, p.28.

29 JBC, RTC, Governors' Minutes, 1920-1, pp. 33, 43, 35, 49, 57, 118, 130, 141.

30 JBC, RTC, Governors' Minutes, 1922-3, pp.2, 96; Annual Report, 1921-2, p.2; Annual Report, 1922-3, p.2; Annual Report, 1923-4, p.2; RTC, Governors' Minutes, 1924-5, pp. 48-50; Minutes, 1926-7, pp. 51, 53; Annual Report, 1925-6, p.16.

31 Ibid., RTC, Governors' Minutes, 1928-9, pp. 43, 98; Annual Report, 1927-8, p.3; Governors' Minutes, 1930-1, p.93; Governors' Minutes, 1932-3, pp.34-5, 87-8; Governors' Minutes, 1934-5, pp. 50, 113; Governors' Minutes, 1936-7, p.98.

32 I am grateful for a communication about the history of the School of Architecture from Hugh C.S. Ferguson (25 June 1982) who is researching this area. JBC, RTC, Governors' Minutes, 1917-19, pp. 91, 151, 164; Annual Report, 1918-19, p.1; Governors' Minutes, 1920-1, pp. 72-3, 127-8, 146; Governors' Minutes, 1922-3, pp. 6, 25-6, 34.

33 Cf. H.W. Richardson and D.H. Aldcroft, *Building in the British Economy Between the Wars* (1968), *passim*; J. Butt, 'Working-Class Housing in Glasgow, 1900-39', in *Essays in Scottish Labour History*, edited by Ian MacDougall (Edinburgh, 1979), pp. 143-169; Sidney Pollard, *The Development of the British Economy, 1914-90* (1992 edn.), pp. 120-1; B.Weber and J. Parry Lewis, 'Industrial Building in Great Britain 1923-38', *Scottish Journal of Political Economy*, Vol.8, No.1 (1961); Mark Thomas, 'Rearmament and Economic Recovery in the late 1930's', *Economic History Review*, Vol.36, No.3 (1983), pp. 564-5, 566; C.L. Mowat, *Britain Between the Wars, 1918-40* (1955), pp. 458-61.

34 JBC, RTC, Governors' Minutes, 1923-4, pp. 19-20, 41-2; Governors' Minutes, 1926-7, pp. 49, 70-73, 107, 108-9.

35 Ibid., RTC, Governors' Minutes, 1938-9, pp. 45-53, 56-63.

36 Ibid., Annual Report, 1919-20, p.5.

37 R.H. Campbell, *The Rise and Fall of Scottish Industry, 1707-1939* (Edinburgh, 1980), Part III; Pollard, *British Economy 1914-90*, pp. 37-114.

38 JBC, RTC, Governors' Minutes, 1924-5, pp. 3, 14, 62, 70; Annual Report, 1923-4, p.6.

39 Ibid., Accounts, 1920-39, *passim*.

40 Ibid., Annual Reports, 1919-20, p. 13; 1920-1, p.8.

41 Ibid., RTC, Governors' Minutes, 1924-5, pp.43-5.

42 UGC Returns 1921-2, 1934-5, 1937-8.

43 JBC, RTC, Annual Report, 1921-2, pp. 10-11; Annual Report, 1922-3, p.3; Annual Report, 1923-4, pp. 11-13; Annual Report, 1925-6, p.13; Calendar, 1929-30, p. 369; Annual Report, 1927-8, p.12; Annual Report, 1929-30, pp.1-2; RTC Governors' Minutes, 1932-3, p.72; Annual Report, 1932-3, pp. 1, 12, 14; Annual Report, 1932-3, p.18; Annual Report, 1933-4, p.16; Annual Report, 1934-5, p.17; Annual Report, 1935-6, p.22; Annual Report, 1936-7, pp. 19-22; Annual Report, 1937-8, p.83; Calendar, 1936-7, p.432.

44 Buchan, pp.31 ff.

45 J.C. Logan, 'Electricity Supply: Electrical Engineering and the Scottish Economy in the Inter-War Years', in A.J.G. Cummings and T.M. Devine, eds., *Industry, Business and Society in Scotland Since 1700* (Edinburgh, 1994), pp. 101-24. Idem, 'An Economic History of the Scottish Electricity Supply Industry, 1878-1930' (unpublished Ph.D. thesis, University of Strathclyde, 1983), *passim*; L. Hannah, *Electricity before Nationalisation* (1979), *passim*; Pollard, pp.43 ff; R.E. Catterall, 'Electrical Engineering', in N.K. Buxton and D.H. Aldcroft, eds., *British Industry Between the Wars, Instability and Economic Development 1919-39* (1979); McArthur and Waddell, pp. 11 ff.

46 *Centenary of Department of Electrical Engineering* (1992), pp.6-7; Annual Report, 1923-4, p.2; Annual Report, 1932-3, p.2; Annual Report, 1937-8, p.1; Research Reports within the Annual Reports, 1924-39.

47 John Craig (1874-1957), a self-made man of great talent, was a Governor during the inter-war period; cf. Payne, *Colvilles*, pp. 132 ff.; David Murray, *Sir John Craig: Sixty-seven Years with Colvilles* (n.d., c.1956), *passim*.

48 JBC, RTC, Governors' Minutes, 1915-16, p.82; Governors' Minutes, 1917-19, pp. 81-2, 129; Governors' Minutes, 1920-1, p.16.

49 Ibid., Governors' Minutes, 1928-9, p.35; Annual Report, 1927-8, pp. 4, 10; Governors' Minutes, 1932-3, p.6.

50 Ibid., Governors' Minutes, 1934-5, pp. 3, 46, 107.

51 Ibid., Annual Reports, 1932-9, *passim*.

52 Lythe and Butt, pp. 220 ff; JBC, Annual Report, 1919-20, p.5; Annual Report, 1923-4, p.2; e.g. RTC, Governors' Minutes, 1924-5, p.54: £2,250 was granted by Miners' Welfare Fund; Annual Report, 1925-6, p.2.

53 JBC, Reminiscences of Archie M. Pennie, Ottawa, Canada, 10 December 1973; Annual Reports, 1923-39, *passim*.

54 Ibid., Governors' Minutes, 1940-1, *passim*.

55 Ibid., pp. 31-2, 37, 40, 46, 56, 64, 69 ff., 101-2, 128-9.

56 Ibid., Governors' Minutes, 1942-3, pp. 6-7, 14-17, 18 ff., 71, 96.

57 Ibid., Memorandum: Dr. Mary Dawson to J. Butt, 11 April 1974.

CHAPTER SEVEN

The Movement to University Status, 1945-64

'The views ... of the academics on the nature of the structure and
governance of the university-to-be were very definite and they were clearly
much debated. They took trouble to propagate their opinions vigorously.
For example, they felt strongly that non-professorial staff should have a
substantial say in all matters concerning the academic and general well-
being of the institution; they advocated that the students should have some
say too in all matters of importance to students; by and large they wanted
to have a more democratic structure brought into being, certainly more
democratic than was operated in the existing Scottish universities.'

Sir Samuel Curran, *Issues in Science and Education: Recollections and Reflections*
(Carnforth and New Jersey, 1988), p.56.

THE PROBLEMS OF RECONSTRUCTING the British economy after 1945 encouraged government
of both major parties to review Higher Education and to pursue plans for expansion. Th
disruption and diversion of production during the war had been very serious, but there was littl
time to achieve peacetime efficiency, for Britain was bankrupt and, therefore, heavily reliant o
American loans.[1] The weaknesses in Britain's industrial structure required drastic action becaus
inadequacy could no longer be concealed behind a pillow full of foreign reserves. Expo
performance had to be greatly improved, the economic wounds of war healed, and socia
cohesion maintained. Emergency training programmes for the demobilised were introduced t
assist all three of these processes. Demand for skilled and educated people was buoyant in a full
employed society: industry, commerce, public utilities and social services required mor
graduates, and thus, the universities and colleges entered more centrally into government policy

Entering Higher Education in the post-war period was for those able to take advantage of th
opportunity a particularly enriching experience. Pent-up demand for places made expansio
inevitable, but the financial means was no longer such a hurdle for students because o
government grants. More importantly, the normal irreverence associated with student bodie
was reinforced and modified by men and women who had left the services or war work and wer
intent on making up for lost time. These were mature people who had had enough of rank an
authority, many of them having exercised responsibility beyond what their years woul
normally have allowed. They were keen to learn and not prepared to accept second-best fro
their teachers or anyone else in the new world of learning. They worked hard and played har
making student life for those straight from school a really illuminating and maturing experienc

Staff too were inclined to take an independent line. In the Royal Technical College th tradition of leaving management to the Governors, who often also stimulated academic initiatives, was longstanding and reflected the ideas of John Anderson absorbed by both Anderson's College and the College of Science and Art. Until 1895 the Board of Studies in the Glasgow and West of Scotland Technical College had included a substantial representation from the Board of Governors, but after 1945 this body acquired influence and an independent spirit.[2] Appointments, traditionally controlled by Professors and allowed as an expense against the Head of Department's name until the 1930s, could not be managed in a period of expansion in such a nepotistic fashion after 1945.[3] The organisation of a local branch of the Association of University Teachers reflected the realities of the need for more open procedures and a demand from some non-professorial staff for greater participation in decision-making.[4]

Old attitudes died hard, and those nurtured and promoted under the pre-war system found it difficult to listen to the growing voices of egalitarianism. Change occurred in a piecemeal fashion, but there were increasing numbers of new staff, some of whom quickly absorbed the existing commitment to widening access and opportunities for students represented in the traditions of the College and combined that with a vision that university status was essential and should be preceded by a more open system of government. Healthy debate was an inevitable consequence of the clash of two contradictory philosophies united only by the clear objective of achieving university status.

Changes in personnel occurred for a number of reasons. In October 1944 Professor Forsyth James Wilson of Chemistry died after thirty-eight years of service to the College, and Professor W.M. Cumming, the Young Professor, became Director of the School of Chemistry.[5] Instructors, recruited during the war in Engineering, returned to local authority employment or to their pre-war employers. College staff on war work elsewhere gradually returned, having often gained valuable industrial or research experience. The Director of the College, Sir Arthur Huddleston (1881-1948), appointed in 1933 in succession to Herbert Fitton Stockdale, retired after a period of illness in October 1945.[6] Wilson was replaced by Frank Stuart Spring as Freeland Professor of Chemistry; Spring, aged thirty-seven, was a Liverpool graduate with first-class honours (1928), Ph.D. (1930) and D.Sc. of Manchester (1937) and eighty papers to his name.[7] The new Director was Dr David Anderson (1895-1981), an alumnus of great talent, who had graduated B.Sc. of Glasgow University, with special distinction in Mechanical and Electrical Engineering, Mathematics and Physics, in 1920 and been awarded the Associateship with special distinction in Mechanical Engineering in 1921. He combined industrial experience with the North British Locomotive Company and Fullerton, Hodgart and Barclay of Paisley with conventional academic research at which he excelled. Anderson was a strategic thinker with experience as a Head of Department of Mechanical and Civil Engineering and Principal of Derby Technical College (1926-9) before becoming Principal of the Central Technical College, Birmingham (1930-45).[8] He soon recognised the intrinsic weaknesses of the relationship with the University of Glasgow but as a reasonable man was prepared to test its flexibility to the limit.

Another very significant change in 1946 was the retirement of Professor William Kerr (1886-1959), of Civil and Mechanical Engineering, exhausted by his efforts in the war years, compounded both by his unwillingness to delegate more to his senior staff and the fact that he was a diabetic.[9] His replacement, Adam S.T. Thomson (1946-73), a distinguished alumnus and member of staff who had been seconded during the war to work on rocket development, knew the importance of delegation in what rapidly became, in terms of students, a mammoth department. Professor Thomson had a major task in restoring a war-depleted department and took the view that Engineering was a 'Group' from which departments would naturally emerge provided he created a proper working environment. Apart from the revival of Clyde

30 The Central Office of Information issued c.1952 a series of photographs of Royal Technical College students undertaking practical work as part of a scheme to promote technical education. Here students of mining engineering are gaining practical training.

shipbuilding and engineering, he saw the 'Group' as serving the capital goods industries of the world, and students came from, and went to, every continent during his tenure. Committed to the notion that academic engineers needed to keep their industrial connections, he welcomed government and business initiatives, seeking research support or consultancy.[10]

New appointments in 1946 also included Ian Bridge in Naval Architecture, a small department with its main teaching load in the evening classes at that time, and Dr George Hibberd, an alumnus and member of staff, to the vacant chair of Mining, jointly held in the Royal College and the University of Glasgow.[11] After consultation with the University it was also decided to establish a Department of Industrial Administration with a remit to provide management training in engineering and applied sciences, including one-year postgraduate courses. This decision led to a closer working relationship with the Scottish College of Commerce and ultimately to merger.[12] The School of Architecture was reorganised, and W.J. Smith appointed Professor in the Royal College; urban and regional development was stimulating the profession and a growth in staff and student numbers.[13] After lengthy deliberations, George H. Thomson was appointed College Secretary early in 1947; he was to serve the College (1947-66) through most of the difficult years both following the war and also immediately preceding the conferment of university status. New posts in the administration supervised by Mr Thomson were quickly added: a Registrar and a Cashier, significant developments in the form which the central services would take over the next thirty years.[14]

Long-established departments like the Schools of Navigation, Bakery, and Textile Manufacture were revived, the last with a solid endorsement and £4,000 donation from Courtaulds. Their long-term futures were by no means certain, partly because of the Scottish Education Department's policy of concentrating other advanced work such as Town Planning in the Royal Technical College and also because of structural changes in the industries which they served. However, they flourished in the apparently favourable circumstances prevailing in the 1950s.[15]

Student numbers grew rapidly from 1945 onwards as ex-service personnel took advantage of educational opportunities and school-leavers sought training for a society committed to Beveridge's notion of full employment. The main contrast with pre-war was the increase in full-time day students; these had doubled in number by session 1947-8 compared with 1937-8. By 1948-9 evening-class student numbers had reached over 3,600 to add to 2,425 attending (many part-time) in the day, the total student population exceeding 6,000. The trend to more full-time day students and more overseas students continued throughout the 1950s; by 1958 there were 1,766 full-time day students and by 1964-5 the student population was 4,107, all reading for degrees and diplomas of the University of Strathclyde.[16] This expansion in full-time numbers was made possible partly by the continuing process of hiving off some activities to the local authorities[17] and partly by physical expansion which provided more accommodation.

Staff numbers after 1945 were a marked contrast with the previous history of the Technical College. In 1900 there were 29 full-time members of staff; by 1927-8, 93; in 1939-40, 160, to whom need to be added the Librarian, William G. Burrell, and three assistants, 16 laboratory staff and 15 other staff associated with the central administration. In 1945-6 there were ten professors, four heads of department, three lecturers-in-charge, 25 senior lecturers, 79 lecturers and two special cases of individuals responsible for organising Continuation Classes, a total of 123, before recruitment had started. In session 1961-2 the staff had more than doubled to about 330.[18]

The immediate problem in 1945 for most departments was that they generally had smaller staffs than pre-war, but student numbers and therefore classes were much larger. In Civil and Mechanical Engineering Adam Thomson developed a comprehensive long-term development plan; its major features included a considerable increase in staff and the subdivision of the 'Engineering Group' into a number of main sections, each of which would, subject to satisfactory progress, be capable of standing on its own feet and have its own professor. In addition, a completely new building was necessary.[19]

The Governors accepted these proposals in principle and over a short period of time. The incomplete extension in John Street was finished first, 'temporary' staff accommodation was provided in the vast corridors of the Royal College for more than two decades, and every possible space was used for teaching purposes. Shortage of building materials was a major constraint, and the John Street Building, originally intended partly to provide social and welfare accommodation for the students, was only authorised by the Scottish Education Department because it could be adapted to provide more much needed teaching facilities. Yet the Students' Representative Council was given space.[20]

What became the James Weir Building was long in the making. Structural steel was very scarce, and amounts initially available would not have been adequate to complete the building.

31 The Library of the Royal College of Science and Technology in 1957. It has been relocated twice since then, first to the McCance Building in 1964 and then to the Curran Building in 1979.

The Governors had in 1947 decided to appoint an architect to prepare a plan, taking account of all the land which might become available up to Cathedral Street and across to John Street. They took up Adam Thomson's suggestion that the first phase, which they initially expected to be built by 1952-3, should be assigned to the 'Engineering Group' but they were already anticipating further blocks for a completely new library, and to accommodate the Students' Union, Chemistry, Metallurgy and Textiles.[21]

In fact, the Montrose Street Extension first phase was not completed till 1956, but it was sufficiently spacious to accommodate a much larger 'Engineering Group' and included excellent laboratories.[22] Both the Scottish Education Department and the University Grants Committee made significant contributions both to the cost of the building and its equipment.[23] A second Associate Professor, Dr Alexander W. Scott, had been appointed in 1947 with special responsibility for Chemical Engineering, and he became Professor of that subject in 1956.[24]

A review of courses offered within the 'Group' in 1956 clearly took account of developments in industry. In Mechanical Engineering, undergraduate and postgraduate courses were to take account of Nuclear Power Engineering, including subjects such as nuclear fuels, reactors and power stations. A new four-year Associateship course in Production Engineering would be firmly based on the existing Mechanical Engineering course, with the specialisation occurring in third and fourth years – design for production, including aesthetics of design; jig and tool design; manufacturing processes; machine tools and metrology; automation; engineering metallurgy or materials; and other modules associated with Management Studies. Servo Mechanisms and Automatic Control were areas where additional training facilities were thought to be necessary because of the development of automation.[25]

Dr. William Frazer, Reader in Environmental Control Engineering and Resource Utilisation, was appointed to a revived Chair of Civil Engineering in 1956; such an appointment, agreed in principle in 1951, was anticipated by Professor Thomson in his earlier Report to the Governors. Developments in Civil Engineering followed thick and fast, once the move into the James Weir Building had been completed. The 'Group' name was altered to 'Mechanical, Civil and Chemical Engineering' in 1956 and it became a 'Division' in 1963. Postgraduate classes, begun in the evenings in Session 1952-3, were greatly extended: Structural Engineering, Hydraulics and Traffic and Highway Engineering featured in the Diploma from Session 1957-8. Reconstructing undergraduate courses was an inevitable consequence of the introduction of the three-term year in 1960-1, although 'sandwich' arrangements were retained in the third year of the course. In 1963 an autonomous Department of Civil Engineering emerged with 14 members of academic staff, including the section of Structural Engineering. By then an Inshore Oceanography project had been started with support from the Clyde Navigation Trust and the Department of Scientific and Industrial Research. Soon afterwards an outstation for Hydraulics was established at Meadowside Quay, and RV *Strathclyde* was acquired.[26]

After his appointment Professor Scott replanned the Chemical Engineering undergraduate programme which had previously depended heavily on classes provided for Mechanical Engineering. There was an extension of teaching in Thermodynamics to link with classes in Heat Engines and Chemical Thermodynamics. Emphasis was also placed on the chemical engineering aspects of Nuclear Power Engineering such as fuel supply and processing, corrosion and other engineering materials problems in reactors and associated chemical plants.[27]

Although the first phase of the Montrose Street Extension had added nearly 83,000 square feet to the College's accommodation, and had provided an infinitely better teaching and research environment for the 'Engineering Group', pressure of student numbers was inexorable, and the second phase extending to Cathedral Street, thus completing the James Weir Building, was

TABLE 7.1   Mechanical, Civil and Chemical Engineering: Student Statistics, 1946-1964

Session	1946-7	1963-
Total Undergraduates	340	80
Graduates in M. Eng.	51	13
Graduates in C. Eng.	22	6
Graduates in Chem. Eng.	3	2

Source: A.S.T. Thomson, 'Notes ... 1946-64', p.4.

begun in 1960. The Universities Grants Committee had agreed in 1958 to provide £250,000 per annum for five years beginning in 1960 to complete the James Weir Building and the new block to house Chemistry and Chemical Technology, now known as the Thomas Graham Building together with a new Chemical Engineering Laboratory which linked the Chemistry building with the Students' Union building.

These developments, completed in 1963-4, as far as the 'Engineering Group' is concerned, added a further 64,000 square feet to their accommodation and a new laboratory of 8,500 square feet.[28] Increased undergraduate numbers, contrasting 1946-7 with 1964, are given in Table 7.1 The increase in the output of graduates was only possible as a consequence of the completion of the Montrose Street Extension (first phase) and the deployment of greater financial resources by the College, by the Scottish Education Department and, increasingly, by the University Grants Committee.

Articulation between certificate and undergraduate courses was excellent in this academic area. Between 1955 and 1963, 324 former Higher National Certificate students gained the Associateship of the College in the 'Engineering Group': 109 with first-class Honours; 148 with second-class Honours; and 67 with a Pass award. In Session 1963-4 about 70 HNC students transferred to the third year of the Mechanical Engineering course, a reflection not only of the existence of appropriate articulation arrangements but also of the commitment of highly motivated students, many from backgrounds with no previous experience of Higher Education.

The 'Engineering Group' probably had the most satisfactory constitutional relationships with the University of Glasgow of all the College Departments. However, under the new Ordinance No.96 all Engineering degree students were required to attend classes for three terms beginning in Session 1960-1. Since College-trained degree students were awarded the same qualification as the relatively few University-trained students, wide disparity of practice was not possible, although the 'Group' was given power to set its own examinations. Two other circumstances also contributed to the break-up of the old formal 'sandwich' system. It became increasingly difficult to place all students with firms as numbers increased – and there were particular difficulties in the case of overseas students who were not potential employees but very likely to return to their own countries. Moreover, rapid developments in technology had to be taken into account in revised syllabi and teaching, augmenting pressure for a longer academic period of study. Yet there were substantial advantages in the 'sandwich' system, for theory and practice were never far apart. An intensive College-based practical training was, therefore, included in the new degree and associateship courses.[29]

Growth in postgraduate activity in Engineering escalated after 1955. Not only were more advanced instructional courses provided, but there were also more research students. Special evening courses were numerous in these years: advanced classes on thermodynamics, aerodynamics and vibration aspects of axial compressors, mechanical vibrations, automatic control, oil hydraulics, experimental stress analysis, and traffic engineering were but a few of those provided. Class sizes ranged from ten to forty students for these instructional courses. The postgraduate Diploma of the College was awarded for successful completion of courses in Civil Engineering, Mechanical Engineering, Power Engineering including Nuclear Power, and Production Engineering; these courses qualified under a new Ordinance for the M.Sc. of Glasgow University.[30]

Longstanding research and consultancy connections were maintained with industry. That with the British Shipbuilding Research Association began pre-war with an initiative of Professor Kerr. There was no shortage of good research available in the 1950s and '60s to the shipbuilders and repairers – on the lubrication of large marine oil engines; on the ventilation of cargo spaces; on corrosion fatigue in large water-cooled boilers; and on many other topics. The structural decline of the regional shipbuilding industry was not a consequence of inadequate academic underpinning; other reasons have to be sought. Research work was undertaken for the Cold Rolled Sections Association leading to the preparation of load tables for a wide range of conditions and the appropriate British Standard Specifications. Investigations into the strength of welded joints and sheet roof assemblies were also conducted. The Ministry of Aviation commissioned work on the causes of rocket nozzle erosion. The Scottish electricity boards sought advice on a range of matters including problems caused by power station cooling-water effluent, heat dissipation models and hydraulic model investigations on spillways, outfalls and river beds. Individual firms asked for materials and other forms of testing, but there were also substantial consultancies – in terms of time – relating to refrigeration, the optimum design of hones, the design of structural decking and cladding, and the division of flow in sedimentation tanks. The Medical Research Council sponsored work in Bioengineering, and the Department of Scientific and Industrial Research a major investigation of Inshore Oceanography.[31]

Bioengineering – simply defined as the application of engineering principles and techniques to the study of medical problems – began in 1957 when mechanical engineers and local clinicians became interested in using controlled hypothermia in operations. In consequence a Biomechanics Research Group was established under Dr. Robert M. Kenedi. Fields of research widened: investigations included the determination of skin tensions, so significant in grafting and plastic surgery, dynamic forces and deformations in the human body arising from work and other activity, the design of prostheses, the characteristics of human cartilage and its transplantation, and lung function analysis. Visiting Professor Tom Gibson and Dr John Paul joined Robert Kenedi in this group, and the base of future developments in Bioengineering, linking clinicians with engineers, was firmly set in 1963 when Kenedi was elevated to the Research Chair.[32]

Collaboration between Mechanical Engineering and the National Engineering Laboratory at East Kilbride began with an arrangement whereby Associateship students were allowed to conduct their research projects at NEL. For several years this worked well. In 1963 cooperative activity was greatly aided when five senior officers of the National Engineering Laboratory were appointed Visiting Professors – the Director, Dr Sopwith, the Deputy Director, Mr. Penny, the Superintendent of the Machinery Group, Mr Timms, the Superintendent of the Fluids Group, Dr Grunberg, and the Superintendent of the Materials Group, Mr. Phillips. Higher-degree students were able to work at NEL, and staff at East Kilbride could research for higher degrees of the new University of Strathclyde.[33]

Electrical Engineering was heavily involved in the war effort, as we have seen, and in Session 1944-5 had 1,265 enrolments of which 588 were in day classes. It was possibly the slowest department to recover a peacetime equilibrium because war trainee courses did not end till March 1946. The following session, 1946-7, there were 1,301 enrolments, but 563 in the day classes accounted for about 60 per cent of the teaching. As in the other engineering disciplines,

Electrical Engineering's staff taught a variety of courses, Higher National Certificate, Associateship and Degree. In 1947-8 six new appointments were made including J.T. Pender and James E. Matthews (student demonstrator), both of whom were to serve the Department long and well. In view of the development of Electronics Dr Eric Fairley was promoted to the first Senior Lectureship in the subject after a hectic period of war work. The end of an era came in 1948 when Professor Stanley Parker Smith retired at the age of sixty-four to become the educational adviser to the North of Scotland Hydro-Electric Board which was contemplating the creation of a Staff College.[34]

By due process Dr Frederick M. Bruce (1912-) was appointed Professor of Electrical Engineering. Educated at King's College, Newcastle and Queen Mary College, London, Bruce served a graduate apprenticeship with C.A. Parsons and Company, the pioneering turbine producers. Following his apprenticeship, he returned to King's to do research work for four years on behalf of the British Electrical and Allied Industries Research Association. On the eve of World War II Bruce was awarded a Sir James Caird Senior Scholarship to research on high voltage phenomena. The war interrupted this research career and provided another; Bruce worked for the Ministry of Supply's Armament Research Department for five years before proceeding to the Nelson Research Laboratories of the English Electric Company at Stafford where he was in charge of the High Voltage Laboratory.

After taking up his appointment Professor Bruce completed a review of research facilities in the department. He found major deficiencies arising from the impact of wartime services training. That work, although of major significance for the war effort, was of a relatively low standard in his view, and thus a new research tradition with modern facilities had to be created. He wanted a new Electronics Laboratory, the reconditioning of the existing high voltage and measurements laboratories, the provision of 'adequate staff accommodation' and the erection of facilities for advanced measurements and communications work. Modern equipment was needed, and the undergraduate programme had to be fundamentally revised. About personnel, his main thrust was simple: 'Lecturers must be men of the highest ability and qualifications ... who remain in very close contact with their industrial counterparts'.[35]

Professor Bruce recruited a number of high-calibre research engineers; Dr Henry Lamont later took a senior post in RCA Inc., and Dr Michael Potok eventually went to the Royal Military College, Shrivenham, as a Professor. Zygmunt Jelonek arrived in 1953 from the Polish College in London. He had escaped from Poland in 1939 where he had been in the service of the Polish Radio broadcasting system. By practical experience and inclination he was able to make a major contribution to the teaching of electronics in the undergraduate programme and also led a research team working on the basic problems and theories of control.

Bruce's own interest in high-voltage engineering and power led him to develop this aspect of research very rapidly after 1950. Research contracts were obtained with the Central Electricity Generating Board in 1954, and this collaboration became very significant. A major achievement was the effective planning and creation of a new High Voltage Laboratory which was opened in 1961, and this greatly aided research and industrial liaison, thereby adding to the Department's portfolio. Many young power engineers were trained under Bruce's supervision, some of whom were to play a leading part in the development of the department in the University of Strathclyde.[36]

Mining Engineering increased its tiny output of graduates between 1946 and 1964 and also developed many short courses for its major patron, the National Coal Board. Most associates and degree students worked for the Board at some time during their course and many of them afterwards. Postgraduate courses were developed in Ventilation, Strata Control and Subsidence, and Mining Geology. A major centre for studying means of preventing 'dust' diseases, the Pneumoconiosis Research Unit, was established in the Department in 1948 immediately after the Board began to control operations. Geophysical surveying, rock mechanics and mineral exploration were other research interests in what always remained a small department. Because staff were relatively few in number, they were always busy on a range of consultancy projects and providing short courses as well as the normal run of teaching.[37]

The Department of Naval Architecture was also very small, competing as it did with the better-endowed department at Glasgow University. It provided some service teaching for the School of Navigation, conducted evening classes for all stages of the National Certificate and taught a small number of full-time students for the College Diploma or Associateship. By 1964 there were three staff including the head of department, Ian Bridge, and the output of full-time students was eight to ten per year. This department, like others, attracted some very able Norwegian students, and by 1960 the College had about one hundred of these students in total. Unable to offer postgraduate qualifications, the department relied on support from outside firms to mount projects. Ian Bridge had served his apprenticeship (1932-7) with William Denny of Dumbarton and had afterwards been engaged in experimental tank work with that firm up to his appointment in 1946. This work remained his main research: between 1954 and 1957 he completed a detailed study of paddle-wheel propulsion and in 1962 he was responsible for the structural design of the plywood prototype of the Denny sidewall hovercraft with which most of the trials were conducted.[38]

The School of Architecture was very badly affected by the war, and because of the length of the undergraduate programme it was bound to take time to recover. Under Professor William J. Smith it greatly prospered compared with its position before the war. As Director of Studies, he managed growth without either confusion or trouble between the two constituent institutions. From 1947 the staffing problem began to ease as appointments were made. Before the war the number of students attending full-time day classes was 40, and there were about 100 part-timers. After considerable decline in the early years of the war there was a sharp recovery beginning in Session 1944-5 when total numbers recovered to 83 and in the following year to 148. The full impact of demobilisation was felt in Session 1946-7; hence the significance of four new appointments including John Murray, David Paterson and Margaret Brodie, all of whom were to serve long and well. In 1946-7 the total number of students in the School was 271, made up of 124 full-timers (including 54 ex-servicemen) and 147 part-timers (of whom 84 were ex-servicemen). There were 23 women students and 15 from overseas.

Town-planning legislation caused the Scottish Office in 1947 to urge the College to provide an intensive course, for the planning departments in the towns and counties had statutory responsibilities but lacked trained staff. There was a general shortage of architects, and those in post were unlikely either to want full-time training or to be available for it. A continuous building boom, inspired by low interest rates, public policy and public expenditure, increased the demand for architects and planners. By November 1947 a Diploma in Town Planning achieved in four terms of full-time study or in two sessions of part-time day and evening courses was ready for implementation in Session 1948-9. These arrangements were given temporary approval by the Town Planning Institute, but a major constraint was the shortage of suitable staff. However, the course was operational in 1949-50.

The Visiting Board of the Royal Institute of British Architects inspected the whole School in June 1949 and confirmed their recognition of the courses for professional exemption. Student numbers continued to increase, and substantial numbers began to receive the Diploma from 1950 onwards. At the time of the School's Jubilee in 1953 there were 28 Diplomates, 8 successful

TABLE 7.2   Enrolments in the Department of Mathematics, 1944-50

Session	Day	Evening	Total Enrolments
1944-5	351	672	1,023
1945-6	373	603	976
1946-7	558	626	1,184
1947-8	671	735	1,406
1948-9	739	807	1,546
1949-50	744	876	1,620

Sources: JBC, Annual Reports, 1944-50.

postgraduates in Town Planning and 15 holders of the School's certificate, and the number of awards continued to rise in succeeding sessions. Professor Smith retired in 1959 and was the first Emeritus Professor of Architecture to be recognised by the University of Strathclyde. His successor, Frank Fielden (1959-68), came from King's College, Newcastle (University of Durham) where he had been Senior Lecturer in Architecture. The joint arrangements with the Glasgow School of Art continued till 1965, one year after the University of Strathclyde had received its Charter.[39]

Engineering's expansion clearly had implications for departments which provided service teaching. Enrolments for Mathematics, for instance, greatly increased after the war; by 1950, as Table 7.2 indicates, the expansion of degree and associateship courses had resulted in more full-time students studying within the Department of Mathematics, which did not itself offer a degree or associateship. Most Engineering students studied Mathematics for at least two years and, in some instances, in the third and final year also. Mathematics could be offered as a principal subject in Mechanical Engineering, and a significant minority with good records in the subject were encouraged to continue with it.

The increase in student numbers led to further appointments, two in September 1946 and three more in 1947. One of these was a senior lectureship replacement, filled very adequately by Reginald D. Lord, who became a very significant non-professorial influence in the discussions leading up to the University Charter many years later. Lord quite early in his Royal College career offered a special course on 'Operational Methods' which attracted a number of students. Problems occurred with first-year failure rates in degree courses among those with minimum entry qualifications, but generally, Diploma students performed competently. Advanced evening classes were in great demand from some of those enumerated in Table 7.2, but there was also a considerable amount of Ordinary and Higher National Certificate teaching which later fell into the ambit of the local education authorities.

John C. Eaton joined the staff at the beginning of Session 1949-50 and soon acquired an affection for the College's traditions which led him later to become an outstanding advocate for university status. An avid reader of UGC Returns and Government Reports, he applied his statistical skills not only to the teaching of the Department but also to the cause of the College. In 1951 Professor Reginald O. Street retired owing to ill-health. He had served the College for seventeen years and since 1948 also been an excellent chairman of the Board of Studies. Street's successor, Albert Thomas Price, had been Assistant Professor and University Reader in Applied Mathematics at Imperial College. With particular interest in Geomagnetism, he had published many research papers and done war work for the Admiralty including investigations into underwater explosions and the Mulberry Harbour. Price only stayed a short time, moving in 1953 to the University of Exeter.

Price had begun a review of undergraduate and other courses, and changes were gradually being introduced; greater attention was also being paid to research, which, because of teaching loads, had assumed a low priority except for staff researching for Ph.Ds. Walter Martyn joined the staff in Price's period of tenure (1952); Lord, Eaton and he gradually formed a formidable triumvirate concerned to advance the reputation and status of the College and the position of the non-professorial staff. Donald C. Pack, M.A., D.Sc., (1920-) a distinguished graduate of Oxford (1941 and 1944) and St Andrews (1951), combined excellent teaching experience with a fine war-work research record to add to his peacetime research field of investigation into compressible flow and shock waves. During the war he served with the Ordnance Board, working on ballistics and the trajectories of shells; later, he was engaged on research relating to gas dynamics, with particular reference to supersonic flow and the effect of shock waves, and problems involved in the penetration of armour plating. After the war Donald Pack was concerned for a time with work at the captured German supersonic station at Völkenrode. An author of numerous publications, he brought the depth in research which the Department needed. His department grew from strength to strength during his tenure, and he became a distinguished Vice-Principal in the University of Strathclyde.

An Associateship in Applied Mathematics was introduced in Session 1954-5. Designed to prepare students for industry or the Scientific Civil Service, this course lasted ten terms and included some vacation industrial experience. Although it attracted relatively small numbers in the early years, the course was economically managed, the first two years being pursued in common with the Associateship in Applied Physics. The first Associateships were awarded in 1957, since three candidates were eligible to enter directly into the second year in 1954-5. Although an attempt to establish an Honours degree course in Applied Mathematics under the Ordinance of Affiliation with the University of Glasgow was unsuccessful, all the preliminaries had been completed for the introduction of degrees in Mathematics, once the Charter of the new University of Strathclyde had received royal assent.

Much effort also went into providing courses for specialist groups within the College and beyond. In September 1955, for instance, a course of evening lectures on Statistical Quality Control in Industry was arranged in collaboration with Fibreglass Ltd. More good young staff such as Brian Helliwell and Ben Noble, both to take Chairs elsewhere, were recruited; international research colloquia were organised; research contracts were gained, including one from the United States Air Force. Apart from sponsoring Statistics, Donald Pack's department was one of the first to introduce computing into the curriculum. Thus, Mathematics, the bedrock of good Engineering courses, developed a wider significance within the College.[40]

The Department of Natural Philosophy shared some of the early post-war experience gained by Mathematics but remained something of a sleeping giant in this period. With 1,171 enrolments in 1945-6 and 1,506 in 1949-50, this department had a higher proportion of full-time day students than Mathematics. The expansion of the 'Engineering Group' had been a benevolent influence, but Natural Philosophy had more courses on offer to other client groups. A new course for the Final Certificate in Applied Physics was introduced in 1947, and new laboratories were commissioned in 1949-50, and an Electronic Microscope delivered by Metropolitan-Vickers. Yet the department suffered – as did others – from a shortage of appropriate space. Slowly, this problem was tackled as elementary work was moved out of the College. Meanwhile, as students developed greater practical experience in the specialist laboratories in the senior years, the market for them became more buoyant.

The Electron Microscope provided the facility for more research, some of it directly related to problems encountered by industry, and other departments, for instance Technical Chemistry,

32 Industrial Administration was taught at Chesters Management Centre, Bearsden in a converted mansion given to the Royal Technical College by Alexander Turnbull, Vice-Chairman of the Governors (left). Lord Strathclyde (second from right), Under-Secretary of State for Scotland, opened the Centre on 10 October 1955. Sir Andrew McCance, Chairman of the Board, is second from left, and on the right is Sir David S.Anderson, Director of the College.

provided collaborative assistance to John W. Sharp who took charge of this laboratory. It was also the subject of a summer course in 1955 which attracted wide interest. Further advanced work developed in X-Ray, Vacuum Physics, Molecular Physics, Acoustics and Applied Optics. A.S. McLaren and Tom Boag had been associated in the mid-1950s in research work in photo-elasticity for the Ministry of Supply. A significant number of publications began to appear as these projects matured.

Additional staff, appointed in 1958-9, enabled the department to cope with significant increases in student numbers, and additional undergraduate laboratories were being operated. About 500 first-year students required laboratory spaces and supervision in Session 1958-9. Apart from academic research, the Electron Microscope was being used for industrial testing especially relating to corrosion and metal fatigue. Clearly, expansion brought many opportunities and also a few problems, especially those arising from inadequate space and resources.[41]

Frank Spring's tenure of the Freeland Chair of Chemistry (1946-59) added an extra dynamism to a department which already had consistently displayed great effectiveness both in teaching and research. He was staunchly supported by Dr Andrew McCance (1889-1983) as Lay Convener of the Chemistry and Metallurgy Committee. McCance, a Fellow of the Royal Society (1943), educated at Morrison's Academy, Allan Glen's School, the Royal Technical College (1906) and the Royal School of Mines, was possibly the most distinguished businessman-metallurgist of the twentieth century. Knighted in 1947, he became the last Chairman (1950-64)

TABLE 7.3   Students Taking Chemistry, 1948-59

Session	Total	PG	Applied Chem.	Metallurgy	Engineers	Pharmacy	Bakers & Textiles	Chemical Engineers	Applied Physics	Architects
1948-9	565	22	193		134	91	37	18		70
1949-50	704	18	224		83	100	26	79		79
1950-1	655	19	211		187	107	12	26		93
1951-2	558	16	147		196	109	12	27		51
1952-3	576	19	161		199	105	18	21		53
1953-4	588	23	168		179	114	13	18	10	63
1954-5	634	21	160		217	120	-	17	13	86
1955-6	627	22	174		233	81	-	22	15	80
1956-7	637	21	174		226	73	-	41	22	80
1957-8	689	21	133	55	305	61	-	36	22	56
1958-9	835	22	167	74	355	78	-	35	26	78

1. PG - Postgraduate.
2. Engineers includes degree and associateship courses, naval architects and miscellaneous applied science / technology specialisms.

Source: JBC, Departmental Reports, 1948-59.

of the Board of Governors and College Council before the University of Strathclyde was inaugurated; he was also Chairman of Colvilles (from 1956) during an exceptional period of technical development.[42] Moreover, Spring was able to mobilise the support of Sir (in 1957) David Anderson whose tenure as Director of the College closely coincided with his own period of service. Spring's annual departmental reports are a model of clarity and make it possible to chart many indicators of progress. As Table 7.3 shows, the department had a diversity of teaching responsibilities in this period. Its classes were attended by engineers, pharmacists and others apart from students specialising in Chemistry. Evening-class students were gradually transferred to local authority Continuation Classes, the number attending the College declining from 690 enrolments in 1944-5 to 530 in 1948-9, representing 199 students; by 1958-9 there were only 41 evening students left.

The chemical industry after the war had an apparently insatiable demand for graduates and diplomates. It was growing by over 5 per cent per annum by the mid-1950s and was organised in very large firms in which chemists often made their way in management as well as in production and research. College alumni were to be found in many divisions of ICI but especially in Nobel at Ardeer. Since ICI employed about one-third of the total labour force in the industry in the 1950s, this entrée was very important. However, alumni found posts in all sorts and sizes of chemical firms at home and abroad.

Up to 1952-3 demand for places by ex-servicemen and women greatly influenced total student numbers in the department, but the major constraints on growth were accommodation and staff. To maintain and develop research, the Governors in 1944 had adopted a policy of providing demonstrators and research assistants so that teaching loads did not become a crippling burden. Some seasoned campaigners, such as Dr A.B. Crawford (associated with the College from 1914 to 1961) in Inorganic Chemistry, reorganised the courses for which they were responsible within a departmental framework to provide an intellectually demanding and work-related programme. Professor W.M. Cumming in 1945 had prepared a plan to reorganise the department, but his main interest appeared to be the expansion of his Technical Chemistry section. Urgent repairs and alterations to laboratories had begun before Spring's arrival, and he continued a steady programme of improvement in teaching and research facilities.

Such a policy was vital, for in 1948 the number of students entering Chemistry Honours had to be limited to 72 on account of available laboratory accommodation. When Professor Cumming retired in 1949, the title of 'Director of the School of Chemistry' was discontinued, and the Young Chair and staff of Technical Chemistry pursued a less cohesive policy. Undergraduate courses made a clear distinction between 'Pure' and 'Applied' Chemistry, but significantly, Spring believed it right to attempt to tailor classes to the specialised interests of students as far as this was reasonable. Gradually, staffing improved, and excellent teaching was provided not only in Organic and Inorganic Chemistry but also in Physical Chemistry which, however, remained something of a Cinderella. Dr. (later Professor) John McLean acquired a reputation for inspiring teaching which alumni recall with pleasure. Semi-micro methods of qualitative analysis were widely introduced into undergraduate classes in Session 1952-3; the first-year laboratory had been considerably improved by direct-fan fume cupboards; more advanced experimental techniques had been introduced into the senior physical and inorganic chemistry laboratory classes; and for those interested in research, a short intensive course in advanced techniques in Organic Chemistry. The completion of the Montrose Street Extension (phase 1) in Session 1954-5 improved the accommodation by making a large lecture theatre available, but space constraints remained until the completion and occupation of the Thomas Graham Building (1964).

In research, Spring and his colleagues (including John McLean) made the College an internationally recognised centre of excellence in Organic Chemistry. Research laboratories were rebuilt, a micro-chemical laboratory was established, and the chemistry library enhanced. During his tenure of the Chair Spring and his collaborators produced about 120 papers on natural product chemistry; his election to the fellowship of the Royal Society occurred in 1952. Peter Pauson followed Spring in 1959 as Freeland Professor, a post he was to hold till the current decade. The base was in existence for the successful strengthening of Inorganic and Physical Chemistry. After Dr A. B.Crawford's retirement in 1962, Dr David W.A. Sharp was appointed to a senior lectureship in Inorganic Chemistry and later promoted (1965) to the revived Chair. At the time when the Graham Building was commissioned, Dr. Manfred Gordon was appointed as the first Professor of Physical Chemistry (1964). Research on a wider front prospered, although Organic Chemistry remained a strength of the infant University.[43]

Patrick D. Ritchie was appointed to the Young Chair of Technical Chemistry in 1953, a position he held till 1973. The Department of Technical Chemistry also grew in the 1950s and early 1960s (becoming the Department of Chemical Technology in 1956). Its output of graduates and diplomates remained relatively steady till the early 1960s and these alumni are to be found in many industries where applied chemistry training is a prerequisite. Experts were recruited to the staff in several specialised areas, including the traditional interest in fuels. Ritchie, the author of *A Chemistry of Plastics and High Polymers*, introduced these subjects to the undergraduate curriculum and developed research in polymer chemistry. Existing researches – dyestuffs, fuels, spectroscopy, surface chemistry, distillation and gas absorption and chemical reactor design – continued to flourish, but the position of the separate department became less viable with the growth of the Department of Chemical Engineering. Unity of the two departments came again in 1964 with the creation of a large multi-professorial Department of Pure and Applied Chemistry.[44]

Metallurgy was a small department with strong industrial and financial support for research from the British Iron and Steel Federation and kindred Scottish bodies. The numbers of associateships and certificate-holders qualifying in any one year had been rarely more than a dozen, but student numbers rose after 1945. The staff complement was four or five and subject to worldwide competitive pressures; it included one woman, Dr Helen Towers, a ceramics expert, who became a research fellow at Massachussetts Institute of Technology in 1953, after a period of study leave there, partly supported by the Fulbright Commission (1951-2). Professor Hay in 1945 reviewed the courses with his senior staff and ordered new items for the laboratory, including a Philips geiger-counter, X-Ray spectrometer and high frequency induction heating equipment. The revised curriculum for the Associateship was arranged on the 'sandwich' system and extended over four years. The industrial experience gained by students over the years included periods in Europe, Rhodesia and Canada, because the department became expert in handling placements with leading multi-national firms. Phased expenditure over several years led to the acquisition of equipment for ore-dressing, refractories, powder metallurgy and electro-metallurgy.

Between 1944 and 1949 refresher cources for steel plant personnel attracted students from all parts of Britain, and a similar course for blast furnace personnel attracted 16 students from 13 firms in 1949, reflecting the fragmented nature of the industry, which did not survive for long. By 1949 the final-year students numbered 27, and the strain on staff and laboratory space was considerable, somewhat alleviated in 1950-1 by the provision of new laboratories and a library in the John Street Extension. Recognition by London University for B.Sc. degrees in Metallurgy meant that students from 1950 could graduate without reference to the University of Glasgow's Ordinance of Affiliation. Evening students were also being prepared for the examinations of the Institution of Metallurgists.

By the mid-1950s the provision of laboratories and related equipment had transformed the instruction offered to students. The research programme was well supported by the British Iron and Steel Research Association and by Colvilles. New impact testing machines had been installed and also a Vickers' hardness machine; a large oil-fired muffle furnace and carbon tube resistor furnace had been assembled in the high-temperature laboratory; research was also being conducted at Clyde Ironworks. In 1956-7 new courses in Ceramics were introduced which were incorporated within the senior years of the curriculum of Applied Chemistry. Advanced classes in Physical Metallurgy and Corrosion of Metals were offered to evening students that session, and HNC students were being transferred into the Associateship course. Although it was very difficult to retain staff because of alternative opportunities in industry and American and Canadian universities, staff replacements were gradually filling the gaps; significantly, most of them were alumni.

Professor Hay, a member of staff since 1919, had stayed on beyond normal retirement age at the Governors' request, but elected to leave on 31 March 1959. That same session, Dr P.T. Carter, Senior Lecturer in the department, who joined the staff in 1939, was tragically killed in a mountaineering accident. Both these individuals had assisted together with John Taylor in creating the department's reputation for research in the field of slag chemistry, and in the physical chemistry of iron and steel-making reactions. The department had much better laboratories than in 1945, and the number of students was increasing. Ten students were working for the Ph.D. degree, and interdisciplinary links had been established with Mechanical Engineering and Applied Physics, particularly valuable for the facilities for testing and the Electron Microscope, respectively. Hay's successor, Edwin C. Ellwood, took up post on 1 April 1959, but encountered no unpleasant surprises: the base was strongly laid, and further opportunities for adding to the department's reputation were taken. By 1964 more space had become available (25 acres at Townhead) and plans had been laid for expanding the department and its facilities in a new building.[45]

As Table 7.3 indicates, the Department of Pharmacy was well established by 1948-9, but up to

that date most students had taken the professional examinations rather than the degree awai
This situation changed in the 1950s, and exemption (arising from the award of a degree) from t
professional examinations became commonplace. Enrolments during the war had been limit
by agreement between the Ministry of Labour and the Pharmaceutical Society, and thus stude
numbers were low in 1944 and 1945. Professor J.P. Todd's valuable war work with the Blo
Transfusion Service led to his further research in bacterial pyrogens and made him a power
pharmaceutical education; external examinerships came his way, including acting for t
Pharmaceutical Society of Great Britain. He became Honorary Consultant Pharmacologist
the Glasgow Royal Infirmary (1950), and his formulation of a burn cream was extensively us
in the Burns Unit. Apart from his duties as head of department, he was responsible for the Scho
of Bakery and the developing area of the Bio-Sciences. Staff were still away on military serv
and essential war work, including Squadron Leader John Boyes, a mycologist, who was releas
from the Royal Air Force specially to work on the manufacture of penicillin by ICI.

Gradually, staff returned to find themselves dealing with considerable numbers of studer
including refresher courses for ex-service personnel. There was a shortage of retail chemists, I
no rapid solution to this problem was available. Most students attended College in the day and
there was no long-standing group of evening students able to take up employment. Special sh
evening courses in handling penicillin were, however, provided in 1946 at the request of the lo
branch of the Pharmaceutical Society to deal with the first of the new antibiotics. Great effo
were made to recruit students, the only permanent solution to the shortage of personnel, and
1946-7 there were signs that these were succeeding. Accommodation problems were
inevitable consequence of success, particularly as teaching and research in Microbiology w
also beginning to develop.

As the Pharmaceutical Society tightened its regulations relating to entry to the profession,
a degree became the most desirable qualification to obtain. By 1956 classes preparing for
professional qualification examinations were no longer viable, and a degree class of about
became commonplace. Difficulty in servicing the laboratories with young males led to
recruitment of young women as laboratory assistants, and thus a significant gender change pav
the way for greater participation by women in the profession because, apart from providin
nucleus of trained technical staff, this group included several with excellent educatio
qualifications well able to benefit from a degree course.

Although the pressure of heavy teaching loads adversely affected the department's resea
capacity, much good work was done, not only by staff but also a growing number of full-ti
and part-time researchers. Mary Dawson worked on the properties of pyrogens and
improvement of the pyrogen test; D.H.O. Gemmell on the absorption of medicaments throu
the skin; Frank Fish studied the active principles of *Digitalis purpurea* with the intention
improving methods of estimating the quality of cardiac drugs; James Chilton and Allan Com
investigated the factors which affect the biogenesis of the Ergot alkaloids, in the hope of devis
a method of producing them through fermentation. There was also a growing research outpu
Biology and Microbiology.

The number of full-time students approached 200 by 1954, and there were 20 resea
workers, the vast majority members of staff. Accommodation was in continuous use, and s
lecture rooms were too few; laboratory work was difficult to maintain at current levels beca
of the shortage of space; this compounded the difficulties encountered by research workers si
they were compelled to work in the teaching laboratories. Student quality, measured
qualifications at entry, was steadily rising, many completing a sixth year at school bef
entering the department. The curriculum had been diversified to take account of professio

requirements, Biochemistry, Physiology and Pharmacology, and Microbiology assuming greater importance and adding to the pressure for more accommodation. Pharmaceutical Chemistry, first taught in the Department of Pharmacy in 1945, had become a Final Honours subject in 1954 and in succeeding years acquired a momentum of its own. Only the opening of the Montrose Street Extension prevented an immediate crisis, as undergraduates and research workers increased in numbers.

Food Science emerged from the chrysalis in Session 1956-7. Initially very dependent on evening students, it prospered under Dr John Hawthorn (1921-93), a distinguished alumnus who was elevated to a Chair in 1958, the first in Europe. Intending to become an engineer, Hawthorn was apprenticed for two years to G. and J. Weir of Cathcart before enrolling in 1939 at the Royal Technical College and the University of Glasgow for the B.Sc. Engineering joint course. His aptitude for Chemistry was such that, on the advice of his lecturer, John McLean, he changed his course, graduating with First Class Honours in 1943. During the war John Hawthorn was directed to industry, working for Trent Yeast Extract Company, Burton-on-Trent, as assistant chemist, ultimately becoming chief chemist at Batchelors Peas Ltd., Sheffield. His dualistic training and experience in Engineering and Chemistry stood him in good stead in an industry where the mass processing of food required the creation of an appropriate technology. After the war he joined J.P. Todd's benevolently organised academic empire. Todd was impressed by the growing importance of 'Food Science' and Technology, and Hawthorn in 1950 became the first lecturer in this area, teaching Associateship courses. Thus, Glasgow's booming food industries were very early served by an outstanding individual who carefully built up a very effective staff. As far as the United Kingdom's industrial structure is concerned, it should be noted that, after the easing of food controls and the end of rationing in the 1950s, the food industries, building on pre-war growth, expanded very rapidly indeed.[46]

Microbiology first developed after the war to serve the needs of Pharmacy and then, also, Food Science. Biology and Biochemistry also emerged because their service teaching was essential to these other academic areas. The industrial applications of these 'service' disciplines expanded after 1950 and by 1961 a Chair of Applied Microbiology was being filled by Dr. Ernest O. Morris who had worked before the war as a laboratory technician in a hospital and in the Departments of Cancer Research, Pathology and Bacteriology in the University of Birmingham. After war service he had taken advantage of ex-service training schemes and graduated B.Sc. (1950) and Ph.D. (1952) in the same university. Thereafter, he worked under Sir Ian Heilbron as Head of the Microbiology Division of the Brewing Industry Research Foundation, working on a range of projects such as the physiology of yeast and the development of techniques for use in the fermentation industries. In 1956 he was appointed Lecturer in the Microbiology division of the Department of Pharmacy and was promoted to Principal Lecturer (1959).[47]

Thus, when Professor J.P. Todd came to retire in 1961, he left not only a strong department of Pharmacy but also two new infant departments in the Biosciences. His successor, Professor John B. Stenlake, an outstanding pharmaceutical chemist with a very strong research record, had joined the department in 1952. A substantial reallocation of accommodation had taken place from 1957-8, as sections of Engineering occupied the Montrose Street Extension. Drawing offices were transformed into Pharmaceutical Chemistry laboratories; Stenlake and his colleagues were to make excellent use of these. Industrial contacts flourished, and by 1964 the major pharmaceutical companies were sponsoring research on a significant scale.[48]

As the College concentrated its efforts on advanced courses and its research portfolio became more diversified, relationships with the University of Glasgow were likely to come under review. Full-time student numbers were increasing and new courses were being developed. Scale of operations raised the question of whether an institution recognised for funding purposes by the University Grants Committee since 1919 should be subordinated to the rules and regulations of another body. Associateship courses successfully completed by students provided an entry to postgraduate study in universities south of the Border, including Cambridge and Birmingham, but were not recognised by Glasgow. Inevitably, the University of Glasgow had its own interests to protect and its own plans for development; these occasionally clashed with the worthy aspirations of the College. It could provide new associateship courses, but the University reserved its right to judge whether new degrees could be awarded.

Membership of the Board of Governors was constantly retained by the Principal of the University, Sir Hector Hetherington, but his attendance was very irregular; this contrasted strongly with Principals' pre-war behaviour. It is true that Principals were – and are – busy people, and almost certainly, the other representative of the University kept Sir Hector informed. One suspects that he shared many common British prejudices about applied science and technology and was not convinced that these disciplines had a proper place in a university. Most of the other Governors were from industry and commerce and occupied senior positions in their firms; deference was not in their nature. Men like Sir Andrew McCance, Sir James French, Sir John Richmond and Tom Craig were entrepreneurs by nature, and if they felt that the University of Glasgow's ordinances obstructed what they regarded as reasonable objectives, then a strategic plan for the College might be framed in terms of independence. It is important to realise that Governors served on the University Advisory Joint Committee – together with the Director and some professors – and therefore formed their opinions first-hand. Undoubtedly, David Anderson shortly after his appointment as Director had come to the conclusion that a more equal relationship had to be forged. It was, in his view, a matter for the University of Glasgow to determine how this was to be achieved. If it proved impracticable, then the alternative was a carefully phased movement towards independence.

Practical issues proved to be the gadfly which tested relationships between the two institutions. In 1943 there had been discussions about where the study of 'Town and Country Planning' should be based. Dr Robert Robertson, the Chairman of the Governors, believed that its proper place should be with the School of Architecture, although there was talk of establishing a department in the University of Glasgow.[49] In 1946 the five-year course in Architecture could not be made to fit the rubric for degree courses which lasted for only four years. A preliminary year before entry to the degree course was adopted as an *ad hoc* way of dealing with this problem. The ambitious building programme which the Governors endorsed in 1947 was a clear indication of their intention to expand; such capital projects required UGC support, and the changing nature of the student body had the implication of a greater recurrent grant.[50] Thus, the status of the College was likely to become an issue of public policy.

In April 1950 the Advisory Council on Education in Scotland floated the idea of a Federal University of Technology; the proposed constituents were the five Central Institutions; this proposal did not find favour with the Chairman's Committee which, nonetheless, discussed it fully. Higher technological education was placed firmly on the national agenda, as concern about the technical performance of the British economy, especially the manufacturing sector, became more strident.[51] Lord Woolton, Lord President of the Council in Winston Churchill's government, proposed to the Cabinet in 1952 that a new group of three free-standing higher technological institutions of university rank should be created; he had in mind Imperial College, London, Manchester Institute of Technology and the Royal Technical College, Glasgow. All three, he thought, should be specially funded to allow their expansion to occur. Woolton specified his purpose clearly:

TABLE 7.4   Government Funding of the Royal College (£): Actual and Planned, 1945-64

Session	SED	UGC	Total G.F.	% UGC of Total G.F.	Total General Purposes Acct.
1945-6	61,887	27,750	89,637	31	124,274
1951-2	181,562	83,000	264,562	31.38	326,563
1952-3	137,671	169,000	306,671	56	370,162
1953-4	154,137	187,000	341,137	56	404,206
1954-5	161,765	230,941	392,706	59	459,955
1955-6	170,208	158,492	428,700	60.24	499,488
1956-7	226,199	286,749	512,947	55.86	584,779
1957-8	205,082	368,381	573,463	64	706,036
1958-9	157,314	404,208	661,522	61	778,504
1962-3*	108,000	758,000	893,000	88	-
1963-4*	103,000	920,000	1,023,000	91	-

Sources: Actual – Abstracts of Annual Accounts for the Sessions stated; Planned(*) – SUA, E1/1/39; RCST, Governors' Minutes, 1961-3, p.30.

I regard the ultimate object as nothing less than a technical revolution in British industry. To achieve this, I consider that we have to mobilise the technically-minded young people in the industrial districts ...

In Cabinet, Woolton was supported by the Secretary of State, James Stuart, who was naturally concerned to expand provision in Scotland, and the Lord Privy Seal, Lord Swinton, who had a particular interest in applying modern science and technology to defence. As a senior Tory with vast business experience – and a long-standing friendship with Churchill – Woolton was able to get a good hearing. However, the Cabinet decided to seek the advice of the UGC via the Treasury. The UGC then became the honest broker, supporting the expansion of Imperial College and accepting the desirability of extra funding for the Manchester and Glasgow colleges.[52]

A paramount and continuous concern for the UGC was how to avoid having two universities in the same city. One solution was to approach Manchester and Glasgow Universities with the notion that they should each incorporate a college within a new Faculty of Technology. Certainly, the substance of Woolton's memorandum had percolated both the Scottish Office and the Glasgow institutions. Indeed, well before the Cabinet discussion, on 31 December 1951 a letter from Sir Hector Hetherington had suggested that discussions should begin between the two institutions; the College Governors had thought it wisest to wait to discover the government's plans first. Discussions between the two institutions occupied the next five years, and there were also talks with Scottish Education Department officials.[53] The most significant change following the Woolton Memorandum was more generous funding from the Treasury via the UGC as Table 7.4 makes clear; from Session 1952-3 the University Grants Committee had become the majority stakeholder in the future of the Royal Technical College.

In February 1954 it was reported that the College had submitted three sets of proposals to the University, but none was acceptable. Both parties had agreed to report back to the Scottish Education Department and the UGC.[54] The University Grants Committee then sent a deputation to the College to discuss its future status; UGC then suggested by a later letter that the College should accept Faculty status within the University of Glasgow. Chairman's Committee on 21 October 1954 then 'reaffirmed its previous view that separate degree-granting powers was the only wholly satisfactory solution'.[55] Not surprisingly, the next meeting with

University representatives came to grief; the College delegation had insisted on its favoured option.

Discussions between the relevant staffs of the two institutions about new degrees in Technology were no more fruitful. By 1955 the UGC had become the sole arbiter in the inter-institutional discussions and was kept informed about them.[56]

Summarising the main points within these complex negotiations during the period 1952-7, one cannot help but draw the conclusion that entrenched positions on both sides had been formed in the early 1950s. The government through its agencies had a perfect right to ask the institutions to consider how their academic work could be effectively coordinated, since both were largely supported from public funds. As Woolton's memorandum indicates, the politicians also wanted a solution to the issue of degree-granting powers. Eden's government was equally concerned about the supply of technologists and scientists; hence the conferring of the title 'College of Advanced Technology' on a substantial number of technical colleges which were undertaking advanced work following the White Paper of 1956 on Technical Education. This was a timid solution, but it led to the creation of the Council of National Academic Awards and more rigorous validation processes.

In the case of the Royal Technical College degree-granting powers was the main issue around which the discussions with the University of Glasgow foundered. Four possible solutions of this issue were discussed. The preferred option was independent university status and a royal charter. For reasons already given, up to 1957 and afterwards, the UGC was advising the Government against this. The second possible answer was the incorporation of the College within the University. This was broadly acceptable to the University – although some 'cherry-picking', excluding some academic areas, was being mooted – 'but was wholly unacceptable to the College'. The third solution made the cherry-picking explicit: certain College departments would form a Faculty of Technology within the University. The University imposed the condition that the College Professors in these departments should be appointed and paid by the University Court. The logic of this condition is clear, but it would have reduced the standing of the College considerably and was, therefore, rejected. The fourth solution was, in fact, adopted: a modification of existing arrangements under the affiliation scheme.

The changes proposed seemed significant but were, in practice, cosmetic; they did not alter the balance of academic power which still rested firmly with the University. A major practical change was the freedom of the College Engineering departments to frame their own examination papers and to hold separate degree examinations from those held in the University. The degree awarded was the same for both groups of students. Existing Joint Boards of Studies – Applied Science and Architectural Science – would be joined by a new Joint Board in Engineering (previously under Applied Science). Proposals for new degrees and amendments to existing courses were to be discussed at the appropriate Joint Board which would then report to Senate. When the Senate considered these degree proposals, the College Professors would be invited as voting members.

One price the College paid for accepting this revised system of operating the ordinances was the University's retaining the right to introduce new degrees 'for some of the new technologies'. Disagreements arising from the implementation of these new arrangements were to be settled, if possible, by a Joint Committee of Court and Governors (four from each institution); if this Joint Committee failed to reconcile differences, both sides would report to the University Grants Committee. Finally, to prevent unnecessary duplication and unnecessary public funding, the two institutions agreed to exchange information about any proposals in Applied Science and Engineering 'likely to involve substantial capital expenditure'.[57] Thus, the matter rested till the arrival of a new College Principal.

A widening of the College curriculum was gradually espoused by the Board of Studies and the Governors after 1945, leading to the formation of the Department of Industrial Administration in 1947. Chesters House, Bearsden, a magnificent gift in 1953 by Alexander Turnbull, Vice-Chairman of the Governors, became the base for postgraduate study and residential short courses. The first Head of Department was James M.S. Risk (1947-9), B.Com., C.A., who had wide commercial experience. He was followed by Kenneth Shone (1949-56), formerly Assistant Professor of Industrial Engineering at McGill. While supporting this venture, the Scottish Education Department suggested that this Department should concentrate on courses for those who were qualified in Science and Technology, leaving other forms of management training to the Glasgow and West of Scotland Commercial College. Co-operation between the two institutions was encouraged by the SED, and a fruitful collaboration managed by a joint committee resulted. Thus, in one significant area, Management Studies, the two institutions which later were joined in the University of Strathclyde had over a decade of experience in working together. At the institutional level a short-term loan of £50,000 made by the Royal College to the Scottish College perhaps added a financial cement to their cooperation.[58]

The Department of Industrial Administration was given the responsibility in 1957 for developing General Studies in the College for all Associateship students. There was a general discussion in the 1950s about general education of graduates stimulated by C.P. Snow's portrayal of 'The Two Cultures', representatives of which found it difficult, according to Snow, to communicate across the divide between the Arts and Sciences. The University of Glasgow had, in the quinquennium 1952-7, been asked to provide teaching to bridge this gap but declined to do so. Thus the appointment was made in 1958 of a Senior Lecturer, I.F. Clarke (later Professor of English), who devised a very successful course running through all four years and organised the recruitment of a small team of four lecturers, J. Butt, D.R. Gordon, P. Green and C. Wiseman, who each played a significant part not only in the team teaching but also in reducing any potential opposition to a wider diversification of the discipline base of the Royal College. The University Grants Committee thought it desirable that any bid for university status should be strengthened by a clear commitment to expand in the Arts and Social Studies; to this the Governors responded positively.[59]

The non-professorial staff felt that they should be represented on the Board of Studies and also on the Board of Governors. Within the organisation provided by the local branch of the Association of University Teachers as early as 1955 they had begun the discussions which honed their views on the structure and governance of the university-to-be which Sir Samuel Curran recalled vividly. The Governors, having changed the name of the College to the Royal College of Science and Technology in 1956, were at first reluctant to accede to the views of the non-professorial staff, although the Board of Studies had six members from that group by 1956. The Chairman and Past Chairman of the Board of Studies were, however, co-opted to the Board of Governors in 1956; the following year five representatives of the Board of Studies, including two from the non-professorial staff, were admitted. When the Secretary of State directed that there should be a review of the 'Royal Technical College Scheme 1935', a public inquiry resulted (1958) to which Governors, staff and students submitted their views on representation. The Royal College of Science and Technology, Glasgow Scheme (1961) brought the governance of the College more into line with the Courts of the Scottish Universities and made provision for staff representation; the Board of Studies was replaced by the Academic Board. These changes were implemented in 1962-3.[60]

When Sir David Anderson decided to retire in 1959, issues of governance, the status of the

33 Prince Philip visited the Royal College of Science and Technology in May 1961. Here he is being shown a piece of equipment by Professor Adam S.T. Thomson, Professor of Mechanical Engineering, 1946-73, with the Royal College's last Director, Dr Samuel C. Curran F.R.S., and Professor Robert Kenedi looking on.

Royal College of Science and Technology and its further development were continuing business. Yet there had been massive changes since Sir David had taken up the position of Director in 1945: extensions to the main Royal College building, a new Students' Union (1959) and considerable growth in the full-time student body; academic diversification and plans for more new buildings. A solid base had been laid for a new era in the College's history.[61]

To this inheritance with its manifold and substantial problems came Dr. Samuel C. Curran, F.R.S. (1912-) at the age of forty-seven. An outstanding nuclear physicist, he went up to Glasgow University on a bursary at the age of seventeen, graduated first in the final honours examinations in 1933 and proceeded on a Metcalfe Scholarship to research in Physics on the diffraction of beta rays for which he was awarded his Ph.D. Essentially, his early ambition to go up to Cambridge for postgraduate study was fulfilled as a consequence of becoming a Carnegie Scholar, and he was accepted by Lord Rutherford in 1937 to start research in the Cavendish Laboratory. There he worked with P.I. Dee's group in the Austin Laboratory till war threatened in 1939. That summer Dee and several of his research team, including S.C. Curran and Miss Joan E. Strothers (later Curran), visited the Royal Aircraft Establishment at Farnborough. That was the beginning of a hectic and rapid period of challenging war work – research on proximity fuses, marriage (7 November 1940), centimetre radar work for the Ministry of Supply, positive refinement of devices via the application of magnetrons in Samuel's case and countering enemy radar by 'Window', strips of thin aluminium sheet to be dropped by plane, which Joan invented.

Samuel Curran was a natural recruit for the 'Manhattan Project' as one of the massive

34 Professor John B. Stenlake (left) with Dr Curran and Professor Emeritus James P. Todd, the first Professor of Pharmacy (right) on the occasion of Professor Stenlake's inaugural lecture, 28 November 1961. Professor Stenlake led the research team which discovered atracurium, a major relaxant drug.

international team which worked in the United States from 1943 to 1945 to ensure that the Allies constructed an atom bomb first. He went to California to work in the Radiation Laboratory at Berkeley in July 1944; the main objective in this laboratory was to improve the supply of pure U^{235}; there he invented the scintillation counter (1944), an instrument which detected the alpha particles of uranium and was, therefore, of major significance for Nuclear Physics and for post-war industrial applications. Professor Ernest O. Lawrence, the team leader at Berkeley and an outstanding theoretical physicist, then sent Samuel Curran to Oak Ridge to improve the performance of production electromagnetic separation. Their relationship was a major stimulus to Curran, which he freely acknowledges.

Although Lawrence and he remained in close personal contact after the war, leading to offers of posts in the University of California, P.I. Dee in 1943 had secured a promise from Curran to join him at Glasgow University. Thus it was back to *alma mater* in December 1945 and ten years of research and teaching, made more productive by the fortuitous expansion of knowledge and instrumentation which war research had ensured. Apart from his discussions and daily contacts with some of the brightest intellects in twentieth-century physics, Samuel Curran had enriched his experience in engineering, especially in electronics. Books and articles followed in profusion, and the election to the fellowship of the Royal Society (1953). Physics in Glasgow had revived.

From 1955 to 1959 Samuel Curran worked at the Atomic Weapons Research Establishment at Aldermaston as deputy chief scientist to Sir William Penney in charge of the Radiation Measurements Division (later Chief Scientist), one of the most successful periods in the history of that large organisation. There was much to be learned about large-scale research and its efficient administration, lessons transferable to the university world, and Curran later used this experience to good effect.

Changes in the location of fundamental research teams caused Samuel Curran to think of leaving the Atomic Energy Authority in 1959, and thus he became the outstanding candidate for the post of Principal of the Royal College of Science and Technology and took up office in December 1959. Sir David Anderson ensured that there was no interregnum, introducing Principal Curran to the Heads of the thirteen departments. Discussions at the interview and afterwards with Sir Andrew McCance had convinced the new Principal that the Governors were both intent on obtaining university status and ambitious about developing research, both objectives which he shared; otherwise, he would not have accepted the appointment, having first thought of the possibility as early as 1937. He had then been much impressed by the quality of postgraduates going to Cambridge from the Royal Technical College, including his friend (Sir) John Atwell, later Chairman of Court.

Principal Curran's reputation as a scientist and his determination to break down barriers erected against engineering led him inevitably to examine critically the College's relationship with the University of Glasgow, which several of the Professors – Donald Pack of Applied Mathematics and James Rankine (1894-1960) of Natural Philosophy, for example – found unsatisfactory and disadvantageous. It was as a result of the nature of the scheme of affiliation and its weaknesses – and not from a clash of personalities – that differences were bound to arise. There were a number of courses – Chemistry, Applied Mathematics, Applied Physics, Food Science – where difficulties arose about their recognition for degrees; Associateships recognised for higher degrees universally elsewhere were denied their proper place in Glasgow; the belief that school-leaving qualifications apparently mattered more than later academic achievement was constantly asserted and reasserted by the Principal of Glasgow, a position which would be regarded as nonsensical today in that university. Barriers to personal academic progress were the name of the game, not bridges! The ethos of the College clearly conflicted with that of the University in the early 1960s, and Principal Curran presented that forcefully and clearly to many influential external bodies including the University Grants Committee. He was particularly concerned that seven completely new universities had been founded since 1958, when the Royal College, an institution on the UGC's funding list since 1919, was being apparently kept back.

It was not simply operational principles that were important, although 'Access', especially for mature students (i.e. those over 23 in 1960) had been an important characteristic of the College throughout its history. What could not be gainsaid were the results in terms of output of qualified people in great demand throughout the economy. In discussions with Sir Keith Murray (Lord Murray) in early 1960, Principal Curran pointed out that the Royal College produced more than ten per cent of all those with university-level technology qualifications in Britain and more than all four of the Scottish Universities combined. Sir Samuel admits that some of these early discussions at the University Grants Committee with Sir Keith were occasionally argumentative and heated, but after being sceptical about this claim the Chairman of the UGC had to admit that it was true after consulting UGC Returns. By early 1961 Sir Keith Murray was personally convinced that the Royal College should be raised to university status, and in the Spring of 1962 had convinced his Committee.

'More means worse' was the clarion call of some traditionalist members of the Committee of Vice-Chancellors and Principals, but it was unable to contain the general demand for expansion which the Committee on Higher Education (the Robbins Committee) was to recognise. Sir Andrew McCance and Principal Curran had met Sir Keith Murray and the Secretary of the

35 Princess Margaret visits the Royal College of Science and Technology on 31 May 1962. Dr Samuel C. Curran introduces Professor Adam S.T. Thomson to the Princess. To Dr Curran's left is Sir Andrew McCance, the last Chairman of the Board of Governors.

UGC, Sir Cecil Syers, and heard that the UGC intended to recommend to the government that the Royal College should become a university and that a statement was under consideration by the Treasury. That statement was made on 29 May, 1962. Although the decision had been made before the Robbins Committee reported, its views were ascertained and were supportive.

Sir Keith Murray's advice was that the Royal College should establish an Academic Advisory Committee; this, headed by Sir Edmund Hirst, was operational by the summer of 1963. He also suggested that university constitutions of recent foundations, especially Sussex, should be studied before formulating a Charter. Much effort and many visits went into preparing the Charter. Its progress was regularly reported to the Academic Advisory Committee and was of burning interest to all members of the academic community. The non-professorial staff wanted substantial representation in decision-making at Senate, and the conflicting interest of the need for efficient executive action was met by the Academic Planning Committee of Senate upon

36 An Alumnus (1908) returns to Alma Mater. Lord Reith, the first Director-General of the BBC (centre) about to enter the Assembly Hall of the Royal College with Sir Andrew McCance and Dr Samuel Curran to present awards to the students. 7 December 1963.

which there were non-professorial members. It was not all sweetness and light, but there was unity over the objective of producing a Charter which would work in the interests of all members of the University. There was a refreshing approach to student representation and healthy discussion about future expansion. There was considerable debate about a name for the university-to-be; Sir Keith Murray advised selecting a territorial name. Hence 'Strathclyde', harking back to the ancient history of Scotland, was chosen, but Anderson's name was attached to the Library.

The planned development of a 'Faculty of Industrial and Social Studies', which became Arts and Social Studies, began with four departments – 'Industrial' Economics, Politics, Administration and 'Industrial' and Social History – to which a fifth, Psychology, was added slightly later. The first appointments were made with effect from 1 October, 1962. The Robbins Committee recommended that the Scottish College of Commerce should be amalgamated with the Royal College; this was agreed by the UGC and Governors and took place in May 1964, immediately strengthening the prospects of diversification in Modern Languages, Accountancy and Business Studies.

Sir Keith Murray, in a conversation with Principal Curran, defined the characteristics of an ideal first Chancellor for the new University: a distinguished scientist, maybe a Nobel Laureate; a person of influence in British Higher Education; a Scot, if possible from Glasgow. Quickly, Principal Curran replied that he thought Sir Keith was thinking of Lord Todd, and this was not denied. Lord Todd met all these criteria and, in addition, was a former pupil of Allan Glen's School, with which the Royal College had been closely associated for many years. Sir Andrew

McCance, that doughty campaigner for the College over a long period, might have been a reasonable choice also; the UGC might well have thought that he was too much associated with the difficult and unsatisfactory negotiations with Glasgow University in the 1950s to be a good choice as first Chancellor. Instead, his name is associated with the main administrative building of the University, begun in 1962 and topped out on 28 March 1963. Originally intended for the Library and Faculty of Arts and Social Studies, it was soon inadequate for both purposes.[62]

The Charter and Statutes were sent to the Privy Council in draft form and duly approved. The University of Strathclyde came into existence in June 1964; the Royal Charter was sealed at Balmoral by Queen Elizabeth II in August; Senate met for the first time in September, and Court in December. An old story had reached its conclusion; a new adventure had begun!

REFERENCES

1 Sidney Pollard, *The Development of the British Economy 1914-90* (4th edn. 1992), pp. 193 ff.

2 JBC, GWSTC, Governors' Minutes, 1895-6, pp. 2, 8, 9; RCST Board of Studies Minutes, 1953-63, *passim*.

3 It was still common after 1945 for Professors to do 'a search' for suitable personnel in disciplines which were difficult, because of competition from industry, to staff. Interviews, always used for Chairs, became more general.

4 JBC, RCST College Newsletters, especially the Jubilee Newsletter of September 1964.

5 Ibid., RTC Governors' Minutes, 1944-5, pp. 67-8, 72, 92. Cumming had been Director of Explosives Research in Scotland, using the College labs. during the war.

6 Ibid., Governors' Minutes, 1932-3, p.78; Governors' Minutes, 1944-5, pp. 82, 114, 116, 128; Governors' Minutes, 1948-9, p.68.

7 Ibid., Governors' Minutes, 1944-5, p.130.

8 Ibid., Governors' Minutes, 1946-7, pp. 5-6, 7.

9 Ibid., pp. 50, 127.

10 Ibid., pp. 79, 129.

11 Ibid., pp. 51, 72, 98.

12 Ibid., pp. 98-9, 148.

13 Ibid., pp. 16, 134, 136.

14 Ibid., pp. 112, 148.

15 Ibid., pp. 18, 54, 56, 64A, 97, 104, 137, 138, 144, 158, 163, 165 ff., 171 ff.

16 JBC, Annual Reports, 1945-64.

17 National Certificate and Higher National Certificate work was moved out on an *ad hoc* basis after consultation with the local authorities, and ultimately the Schools of Bakery and Navigation were taken over by Glasgow Corporation.

18 JBC, Annual Report, 1927-8, p.3; Calendar 1939-40; Governors' Minutes, 1946-7, pp. 36-39; Submissions to the University Grants Committee, December 1960.

19 JBC, A.S.T. Thomson, 'Notes on Developments in Technology in the Royal College of Science and Technology 1946-64 ... ', pp. 1-2; RTC Governors' Minutes, 1950-1, p.81.

20 Ibid., RTC Governors' Minutes, 1946-7, pp. 20, 21, 60, 76, 92, 116; Governors' Minutes, 1948-9, p.7; Governors' Minutes, 1950-1, p. 81.

21 Ibid., Governors' Minutes, 1946-7, pp. 154, 173.

22 Ibid., RCST Governors' Minutes, 1956-7, p.19.

23 Ibid., Accounts, 1950-5.

24 Ibid., RTC Governors' Minutes, 1946-7, p.128; RCST Governors' Minutes, 1956-7, p.34.

25 Ibid., RCST Governors' Minutes, 1956-7, pp. 34-5.

26 Ibid., p.35; Buchan, pp. 36-7.

27 JBC, RCST Governors' Minutes, 1956-7, p.35; Governors' Minutes, 1958-9, pp. 46, 129.

28 Thomson, 'Notes ... ', p.4; JBC, RCST Governors' Minutes, 1958-9, pp. 73 and 107.

29 Ibid., pp.4-5; there are many references in Departmental Reports to the Governors after 1955 to the difficulty of placing students in practical training with firms. Apparently, employers were torn between thinking of accepting overseas students for goodwill and future sales and refusing to have them because they represented a cost which would not be immediately recovered.

30 Thomson, 'Notes ... ', p.5; Departmental Reports to Governors in RCST Governors' Minutes, 1960-4.

31 Thomson, 'Notes ... ', pp.6-7; Departmental Reports to Governors, 1948-64; Buchan, p.37.

32 Thomson, 'Notes ... ', p.7; Departmental Report, 1963-4.

33 Thomson, 'Notes ... ', pp.7-8.

34 JBC, RTC Governors' Minutes, 1946-7, p.130; Governors' Minutes, 1948-9, pp. 17-18.

35 Ibid., Governors' Minutes, 1948-9, pp. 78-9, 149-54.

36 *Centenary*, p.8; Thomson, 'Notes ... ', p.9; JBC, RTC Governors' Minutes, 1950-1, pp. 42 ff; Governors' Minutes, 1952-3, pp. 41 ff, p.133; RCST Governors' Minutes, 1954-5, pp. 64 ff, 135 ff; Governors' Minutes, 1956-7, pp. 44 ff, 145 ff; Governors' Minutes, 1958-9, pp. 56 ff, 140 ff.

37 Thomson, 'Notes ... ', pp. 10-11; JBC, Departmental Reports, 1948-64.

38 JBC, RTC Governors' Minutes, 1946-7, p. 72; Thomson 'Notes ... ', p.12; Departmental Reports, 1954-63.

39 JBC, RTC Governors' Minutes, 1946-7, pp. 14-15, 134, 136, 171-2; Governors' Minutes, 1948-9, pp.25-6, 116; Governors' Minutes, 1950-1, pp.61, 101-2; Governors' Minutes, 1954-5, pp.24-5, 105-6; RCST Governors' Minutes, 1958-9, pp.25, 100-1, 163; Departmental Report, 1964-5.

40 Pack, pp.5-6; JBC, Departmental Reports, 1944-64; RTC Governors' Minutes, 1946-7, pp. 44, 119; Governors' Minutes, 1948-9, pp. 42, 43, 139; Governors' Minutes, 1950-1, pp. 27, 112, 157; Governors' Minutes, 1952-3, pp. 22-3, 95, 116-7; Governors' Minutes, 1954-5, pp. 42-4, 115-6; RCST Governors' Minutes, 1956-7, pp. 27-8, 120-1; Governors' Minutes, 1958-9, pp. 37-9.

41 JBC, Departmental Reports, 1944-64; RTC Governors' Minutes, 1946-7, pp.120-1; Governors' Minutes, 1950-1, pp.4-5, 112 ff; Governors' Minutes, 1952-3, pp.24-6, 118-20; Governors' Minutes, 1954-5, pp.46-7, 119-20; RCST Governors' Minutes, 1956-7, pp.29-30; Governors' Minutes, 1958-9, pp.34-6, 115-7.

42 Payne, *Colvilles ...* , pp. 141 ff. Sir Andrew McCance also had been Chairman of the DSIR Committee on the Supply

and Training of Metallurgists (1943-4), and Professor Hay was a member.

43 Pollard, pp. 245-6; JBC, RTC Governors' Minutes, 1944-5, pp. 52, 95, 117, 119; RCST Newsletter, Spring 1962; Governors' Minutes, 1946-7, pp. 21, 48, 60, 123-4, 157; Governors' Minutes, 1948-9, pp. 45-7, 142, 145; Governors' Minutes, 1950-1, pp. 29 ff, 115 ff, 118; Governors' Minutes, 1952-3, pp. 29-30, 121 ff; Governors' Minutes, 1954-5, pp. 50-3, 121-3; RCST Governors' Minutes, 1956-7, pp. 125-9; Governors' Minutes, 1958-9, pp. 40, 42, 118, 120, 163; Nuttall, pp. 12-14.

44 Nuttall, pp. 13 ff; JBC, Departmental Reports in Technical Chemistry, 1954-64.

45 JBC, RTC Governors' Minutes, 1944-5, pp. 4, 22, 71, 73, 100, 123; Governors' Minutes, 1946-7, pp. 46-50, 122-5; Governors' Minutes, 1948-9, pp. 44-7, 142-3, 147; Governors' Minutes, 1950-1, pp. 5-7, 33, 120-1; Governors' Minutes, 1952-3, pp. 27, 33-4, 127; Governors' Minutes, 1954-5, p. 126; RCST Governors' Minutes, 1956-7, pp. 75, 125, 132-3; Governors' Minutes, 1958-9, pp. 40, 45, 102, 124-6; SUA, E1/1/39 RCST Governors' Minutes, 1961-3, p. 90

46 JBC, RTC Governors' Minutes, 1944-5, pp. 30 ff, 109 ff, 136; Governors' Minutes, 1946-7, pp. 28-30, 74-5; Annual Report, 1945-6; Governors' Minutes, 1948-9, pp. 21-4, 57-9, 173-6; Governors' Minutes, 1950-1, pp. 12-13, 52-5, 137-41; Governors' Minutes, 1952-3, pp. 57-60, 142-7; College Reports on Research, 1953-64; Governors' Minutes, 1954-5, pp. 21-3, 145-9; RCST, Governors' Minutes, 1956-7, pp. 53-7, 155-60; *Royal Society of Edinburgh Year Book*, 1995, pp. 106-8, Obituary of John Hawthorn by Professor W.R. Morrison; T.L. Johnston, N.K. Buxton and D. Mair, *Structure and Growth of the Scottish Economy* (1971), pp. 74, 75, 76 (Table 4.1), 161-3, 271-2; J.N. Randall, 'New Towns and New Industries', in Richard Saville, ed., *The Economic Development of Modern Scotland 1950-1980*, (Edinburgh, 1985), pp. 249 ff and Tables 2 and 3; SUA, E1/1/37, RCST, Governors' Minutes, 1958-9, p. 72.

47 JBC, RCST Newsletter Vol.3, No.3 (1961); RCST Governors' Minutes, 1956-7, pp. 155, 156, 157; Governors' Minutes, 1958-9, pp. 104, 150, 151, 152, 153, 154, 155.

48 JBC, RTC, Governors' Minutes, 1952-3, p. 57; RCST Governors' Minutes, 1958-9, pp. 66, 152; SUA, E1/1/38, RCST, Governors' Minutes, 1960-1, p. 173.

49 JBC, RTC Governors' Minutes, 1944-5, pp. 8, 104.

50 Ibid., Governors' Minutes, 1946-7, pp. 15, 154.

51 Ibid., Governors' Minutes, 1950-1, pp. 64, 108.

52 Public Record Office, Cabinet Papers 1952, Higher Technological Education: Memo of the Lord President of the Council.

53 JBC, RTC Governors' Minutes, 1952-3, pp. 82, 88, 165. The Senate and Court in December 1951 had approved a memorandum reviewing the operations of existing ordinances and were prepared to make significant changes.

54 Ibid., RTC Governors' Minutes, 1954-5, p. 26.

55 Ibid., p. 91.

56 Ibid., p. 107.

57 Ibid., RCST Governors' Minutes, 1956-7, pp. 82, 83.

58 Ibid., RTC Governors' Minutes, 1946-7, pp. 98-9, 148, 174-5; Governors' Minutes, 1948-9, pp. 183, 185-7; Governors' Minutes, 1950-1, p. 67; Governors' Minutes, 1952-3, pp. 85, 164; Governors' Minutes, 1954-5, pp. 26, 76, 89, 101, 154, 163; RCST Governors' Minutes, 1956-7, pp. 63, 64, 65, 87, 88, 109, 165, 167.

59 Ibid., RCST, Governors' Minutes, 1958-9, pp. 25, 160, 161; Sir Samuel Curran, *Issues in Science and Education, Recollections and Reflections*, (1988), pp. 64-5; J. Butt, 'General Studies at Glasgow', *Technology* (February, 1961); JBC, RCST, Submissions to the University Grants Committee (December, 1960), Submission 1, pp. 2-3; Submission 2, pp. 2-4.

60 JBC, RCST, Governors' Minutes, 1956-7, pp. 19, 164; City of Glasgow, Royal College of Science and Technology, Glasgow Scheme, 1961, paras. 3-6.

61 JBC, RCST, Governors' Minutes, 1958-9, pp. 95-6, 103.

62 Ibid., pp. 162-3; Curran, *Issues in Science and Education* ... , pp. 5-72; University of Strathclyde *Gazette* (Autumn, 1980), pp. 10-19, transcript of a television interview of Sir Samuel Curran by Professor Esmond Wright; *Academic Who's Who* (1973-4 edn.), p. 110; SUA, E1/1/39, RCST, Governors' Minutes, 1961-3, pp. 87, 94-5, 132; AUT, *Jubilee Newsletter*, September 1964; L. McGougan, 'Arts, Social Studies and Library Building', Annual Conference of University Buildings Officers (Exeter, 1964), *passim*; Draft Charter, 1963 and Royal Charter, 1964; S. Curran, 'The Years of Change, 1960-1964', University of Strathclyde *Gazette* (January, 1974), pp. 4-9 and *idem* (April, 1974), pp. 21-8.

CHAPTER EIGHT

The Second Merger, The New Academic Agenda and Expansion

'There have been efforts, most misguided, to show that expenditure in science need not necessarily be directly related to economic success or industrial achievement. While a direct connection cannot be proved, the reverse has never been proved ... it is still entirely possible that investment in education and in science results in industrial and economic prosperity. The fact that we cannot prove there is a connection does not mean that the connection is non-existent ... I have still to see a prosperous, stable country in which education was neglected. Good education, not least in science, must be given greater priority in our schemes for the future ... '

Sir Samuel C. Curran, *Gazette* of the University of Strathclyde, Spring, 1979.

A VISION OF THE UNIVERSITY OF STRATHCLYDE as having great significance for the Scottish economy and for the wider world was central to the new Vice-Chancellor's thinking. The Royal Technical College's close involvement with industry and the need to apply better science and technology to the needs of society came logically together, and thus he was committed to a new academic agenda which was commonly called 'the technological university'.[1] Yet his experience at Aldermaston and in America had also convinced him of the absolute necessity for the proper management of businesses and for the dynamic and imaginative administration of the new university. Inhibition on these matters was not in his nature.

The deliberations of the Robbins Committee had delayed rather than altered the implementation of his ideas. Among the recommendations of the Robbins Committee was an apparent revival of the Woolton Memorandum of 1952: the creation of Special Institutions of Scientific and Technological Education and Research [SISTERS] and naming Imperial College, the Manchester Institute of Technology and the new Glasgow institution, which it also recommended should amalgamate with the Scottish College of Commerce. The SISTERS concept clearly ran into trouble probably because the special funding that it involved could not be found at a time of general university expansion with a number of new institutions being established on 'green-field' sites. In the counsels of the University Grants Committee the idea of specially funded institutions was not likely to find favour: to admit Technology and Applied Science to an equal share of the feast, some thought, was a concession. Principal Curran believed that the only solution might have been assigning responsibility for funding SISTERS to a department other than the Department of Education and Science.[2] Suffice to say, it was an opportunity lost not only for British Higher Education but also for the betterment of the economy.

However, the future of the Scottish College of Commerce was a different matter. Like the Royal College, it had a long and distinguished history. The Glasgow Educational Association which had stimulated advances in the 1830s, notably David Stow's Normal School, was reconstituted in the 1840s; its main leader was Robert Reid, a textile manufacturer, and in November 1845 the Association published a circular which he probably drafted urging the cause of 'further education'. A copy was handed to James Provan when leaving a chemistry lecture at the Andersonian, and he gave it to his brother, Moses. Moses Provan was the mainspring of the Glasgow Commercial College, and its secretary, Robert Rae, sought the use of the 'large hall' in the Andersonian for four months from 1 February 1846 from 6 am to 7.30 am for lectures on Logic, an application which the Andersonian's managers granted. After a successful first session, Rae wanted the use of the hall for the next two sessions, and this request was also successful.

Moses Provan was more ambitious and wanted to form an organisation like the Manchester Athenaeum with 'spacious apartments handsomely furnished ... a newsroom, a reading room, a library ... a comfortable coffee room, a gymnasium and baths'. Part of this vision was realised in 1847 when the Assembly Rooms in Ingram Street were rented, and an inaugural soirée held in the City Hall on 28 December, when the chair was occupied by Charles Dickens, at that time the well-known author of *Pickwick Papers* and *Oliver Twist*. Among the nine pictorial shields, 'ornamented with evergreens', was one inscribed with the name of John Anderson.[3] From its very beginning there were clearly links between commercial education and Anderson's institution.

The establishment of the Glasgow and West of Scotland Technical College resulted in co-operation with the Athenaeum. Its *Calendar* for session 1892-3, for instance, carried a list of classes with fee and timetable information. As two central institutions, they were guided by the Scotch Education Department from the early 1900s; in 1915 the Royal Technical College had a representative on the Board of Governors (Professor Mellanby later became Chairman), and when the Department of Industrial Administration was established in RTC in 1947, the Glasgow and West of Scotland Commercial College (as it was then) suggested the formation of a Joint Board 'to secure full correlation of courses, and co-operation of departments'. Thus, a Glasgow School of Management emerged in the 1950s, using the resources of both institutions.[4]

When it became clear in 1962 that university status would be conferred upon the Royal College of Science and Technology, the Governors of the Scottish College of Commerce sought a closer association and sent a memorandum to that effect to the Academic Advisory Committee before the findings of the Robbins Committee were known. After discussion at its second meeting on 25 February, 1963 the Academic Advisory Committee informed the Scottish College of Commerce that their proposals would be deferred for some months. Sir Keith Murray, Chairman of the University Grants Committee, visited the Royal College, the Scottish College and also spoke to Sir Andrew McCance about the prospect of a closer relationship between the two institutions.[5] On 21 August, 1963 he put his views to Principal Curran:

I am sure that the right answer is absorption, especially as it seems to be the College's wish. With the possible exception of the Secretarial course, all its courses and its entrance requirements for these courses seem to be of university level; and it is possible ... the secretarial course ... might well become a degree course. Academically then I see few if any obstacles to absorption ...

If the two Colleges are to join forces ... There are great advantages in doing this as quickly as possible. It might be argued that your College has sufficient of its own problems resulting from its transition ... and that this additional problem would be the last straw ... do not have fears on this score ... I believe that amalgamation with the Scottish College might well facilitate the developments of your faculties.

The first task is to get an academic blue print ... and I think we were agreed ... the production of the academic plan should not take too long.[6]

Indeed, Sir Keith anticipated that the academic plan for the new university would be complete by the end of 1963 and went on to indicate that 'the next phase would be discussion on the organisational changes ... required'. The Robbins Committee in its Report (23 October, 1963) endorsed in broad terms much of what the Chairman of the UGC had written to Principal Curran. It recognised that the Scottish College was ready for 'a close form of association with an appropriate university' or indeed for university status in its own right.[7]

Strong support from the UGC and a wink and a nod from the Robbins Committee led to the formation of a small working party; its members were Principal Eric Thompson and Sir David Anderson (who after retiring as the last Director of the Royal College of Science and Technology became Chairman of the Board of Governors of the Scottish College) and Principal Curran, Professor Todd and, from the fourth meeting, Professor S.G.E. Lythe, founding Professor of Economic History.

In fact, the working party met on five occasions between the beginning of September and early December 1963. The form and content of the courses were reviewed; a possible future departmental structure within the Faculty of Arts and Social Studies was considered; and a tentative distribution of staff of the Scottish College formulated. Work of non-university standard was reviewed and entry standards were evaluated. The Scottish College had 69 members of staff: 6 Heads of Department, 3 Principal Lecturers, 10 Senior Lecturers, 49 Lecturers and 1 other. They were distributed over six departments – Business Administration, Economic and Social Studies, Management Studies, Accountancy and Company Secretaryship, Secretarial Science and Modern Languages – and taught Associateship, Degree, Diploma and Certificate courses to 938 students.

The working party strongly favoured amalgamation. Certain departments would increase the range of subjects which could be offered, and the Department of Modern Languages would fill a major gap in course provision. Business Studies would be greatly strengthened, and the Department of Industrial Administration might become the core of an additional faculty.

Secretarial Science presented the working party with a problem for they had already concluded that this Department's staff, although technically excellent, could not be regarded as of university standard. They thought a three-year general degree should replace existing qualifications in Secretarial Science, and its curriculum should be broad. Those students intending to become either teachers of commercial subjects or well-qualified secretaries might well attend for additional shorthand and typing during the fourth term in the summer months of each year.[8]

Essentially, the existing School of Arts and Social Studies would be reorganised, and a new School of Business and Industrial Administration formed. Outside this framework remained the Hotel School, the School of Librarianship and the 'Secretarial Laboratory'. Transfer of staff into these two schools, it was thought, would present little difficulty, and so in the event it proved, although there was some discussion at the Academic Board.

At their November, 1963 meeting the working party sought ways of expediting the merger, following the general advice given earlier by Sir Keith Murray. It investigated the possibility of both Colleges signing a Declaration of Intent and Purpose defining the course of action to be followed. This had a number of merits including removing any feelings of uncertainty among the staff. Matters of complexity or difficulty could be handled in an orderly way without haste, and detail could be settled without the impedimenta imposed by bargaining positions which

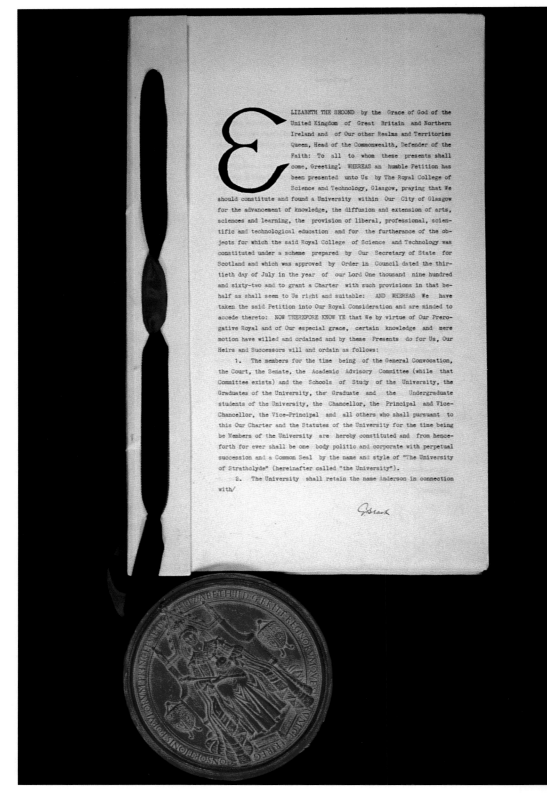

ELIZABETH THE SECOND by the Grace of God of the United Kingdom of Great Britain and Northern Ireland and of Our other Realms and Territories Queen, Head of the Commonwealth, Defender of the Faith: To all to whom these presents shall come, Greeting! WHEREAS an humble Petition has been presented unto Us by The Royal College of Science and Technology, Glasgow, praying that We should constitute and found a University within Our City of Glasgow for the advancement of knowledge, the diffusion and extension of arts, sciences and learning, the provision of liberal, professional, scientific and technological education and for the furtherance of the objects for which the said Royal College of Science and Technology was constituted under a scheme prepared by Our Secretary of State for Scotland and which was approved by Order in Council dated the thirtieth day of July in the year of our Lord One thousand nine hundred and sixty-two and to grant a Charter with such provisions in that behalf as shall seem to Us right and suitable: AND WHEREAS We have taken the said Petition into Our Royal Consideration and are minded to accede thereto: NOW THEREFORE KNOW YE that We by virtue of Our Prerogative Royal and of Our especial grace, certain knowledge and mere motion have willed and ordained and by these Presents do for Us, Our Heirs and Successors will and ordain as follows:

1. The members for the time being of the General Convocation, the Court, the Senate, the Academic Advisory Committee (while that Committee exists) and the Schools of Study of the University, the Graduates of the University, the Graduate and the Undergraduate students of the University, the Chancellor, the Principal and Vice-Chancellor, the Vice-Principal and all others who shall pursuant to this Our Charter and the Statutes of the University for the time being be Members of the University are hereby constituted and from henceforth for ever shall be one body politic and corporate with perpetual succession and a Common Seal by the name and style of "The University of Strathclyde" (hereinafter called "the University").

2. The University shall retain the name Anderson in connection with/

37 The Charter of the University of Strathclyde, 1964. After the merger of the Royal College of Science and Technology and the Scottish College of Commerce in May 1964, the Charter was sealed at Balmoral Castle by Queen Elizabeth II in August. This is the constitutional basis of the University.

could not be easily surrendered. Throughout the negotiations the Scottish Education Department was regularly kept informed as was the UGC; at every important stage the College lawyers were consulted. These interested parties approved the procedure being followed.

The draft Agreement provided for the transfer of all the assets and obligations of the Scottish College to the Royal College of Science and Technology, and, in particular, specified that no individual should suffer any financial loss or disadvantage as a result of the amalgamation. The Agreement provided for three representatives of the Board of Governors of the Scottish College to become co-opted members of the Council of the Royal College (thereby conferring upon them life membership of the General Convocation of the University of Strathclyde when the Charter came into effect). Thus, continuity of interest between one governing body and another was secured.[9]

The Academic Advisory Committee had also been kept informed and indicated its final approval of the plan on 10 January, 1964. The Academic Board of the Royal College was advised about the discussions in October 1963 and established an Advisory Committee in November to consider the academic details. A special meeting of Governors at the Scottish College on 27 December, 1963 accepted the Agreement in principle. Three days earlier on Christmas Eve, 1963 a special meeting of Council in the Royal College of Science and Technology accepted three resolutions. First, the Council accepted the Statement of Intent and favoured amalgamation of the Colleges in principle. Secondly, it asked the UGC to advise the Privy Council of the state of negotiations between the two Colleges. Thirdly, it invited the Academic Board to consider the Working Party's findings on the proposed academic structure and to report.[10]

In fact a 'Transition' Committee did much of the detailed work, arranging the transfer of departments and individuals to form two schools of study: the School of Arts and Social Studies was enlarged, and a new School of Business and Administration created. The Academic Board approved of these arrangements in March, 1964 and the final agreement was signed on 11 May.[11] A month later the Royal College was elevated to university status, and the Charter of the University of Strathclyde came into effect in August. The Senate and the Court, the main decision-making bodies of the University, were then established.

Much routine work for the new university had already been completed: draft Statutes and Ordinances had been framed and were approved; degree curricula and regulations had been evaluated and approved by the Academic Board.[12] There was speculation about moving to a 'green-field' site at East Kilbride which the Development Corporation of the new town was prepared to offer the University, but a conscious decision was taken to stay in the city centre. Town and Gown were not to be divided; the integration of the University of Strathclyde into the old heart of the city would lead to substantial redevelopment of Townhead, which could not have been accomplished without the co-operation and help of the City.

The academic agenda was determined by the Schools of Study, and the initial groupings of departments were already in place before the Charter received royal assent. Yet the Charter vested in the Senate the powers to determine what should be taught and by whom, what research should be undertaken and, in the case of undergraduates and postgraduates, what degrees they should receive.[13] It ratified much of the work already accomplished by the Academic Board and took within its ambit the courses and students of the two Colleges. Draft Ordinance 2 had to be amended to take account of the two new Schools of Study. The School of Arts and Social Studies included Economic History, Economics, English Studies, Geography, Modern Languages, Politics, Psychology and Sociology; the School of Business and Administration began with

38 The University of Strathclyde and the Royal College had long and happy relations with Norway and Norwegian students. In November 1966 an honorary degree was conferred on King Olav V to symbolise that relationship. (Left to right:) William Francis Robertson, first Chairman of the University Court (1964-8); Lord Todd of Trumpington, first Chancellor of the University (1964-91); Dr Samuel C.Curran, first Principal and Vice-Chancellor (1964-80); George P. Richardson, Registrar (1964-73).

Accountancy, Administration, Commerce, Industrial Administration and Law. In 1963-4 there were 2,307 Royal College students and 1,147 Scottish College students, a total of 3,454. In the first session of the University of Strathclyde, 1964-5, the student population was 4,107.[14]

In April, 1965 the first congregation of the University was held in the Kelvin Hall, when Lord Todd of Trumpington was installed as the Chancellor. Senate in a generous retrospective gesture decided that year to grant degrees to holders of the Associateship of the Royal College and those of the Scottish College and to diplomates of the Glasgow School of Architecture. This cleared the decks of past prejudice and discrimination against clear instances of 'useful learning'.

The UGC, taking account of demographic trends, had forecast that the 1960s would be the beginning of a wave of expansion, and building plans up to 1968 were submitted by April, 1960. The quinquennial plan had initially forecast a Royal College total student population of 3,600 by 1970, but clearly this was too pessimistic. Both projections of recurrent grant and also capital grant proved inadequate and had to be revised upwards. From April, 1965 no further funds were received from the Scottish Education Department, and the University had naturally become a child of the UGC.[15] It was an open question whether this change was a total blessing, for sometimes expansion is better funded by two paymasters rather than one. However, the University of Strathclyde was well served by its Buildings Officer, Louis McGougan (d. 1994) (later Bursar), in the years before and after the granting of the Charter. A man who was committed to fostering academic development rather than auditing it (although he ensured that happened), he greatly impressed Sir Keith Murray and the permanent staff of the UGC.[16]

Long-established disciplines and departments started their university life with many advantages, although expansion brought them problems too. Three Schools were created to cover Engineering: Mechanical Engineering, Chemical Engineering and Naval Architecture; Civil and Mining Engineering and Applied Geology; and Electrical Engineering. Much of their accommodation was in James Weir Building which, by the standards of the time, was excellently equipped. Electrical Engineering and Naval Architecture remained in the Royal College and, particularly the former, required more support.

In 1964 the various sections of Mechanical Engineering were as large as most large university departments. Additional Chairs were created over the next few years: in 1966 in Production Engineering, and Thermodynamics and Mechanics of Fluids; in 1969 in Dynamics and Control, and Mechanics of Materials; in 1971 in Engineering Design, and Bioengineering. A Group structure replaced the single department in 1970. The Mechanical Engineering Group consisted of six departments: the Department of Engineering Design and Drawing with Professor Thomas Allan as Head; the Department of Dynamics and Control with Professor William B. McHutchison as Head; the Department of Mechanics of Materials with Professor James Harvey as Head; the Department of Thermodynamics and Mechanics of Fluids with Professor Hugh C. Simpson as Head and Professor J. (Jack) F. MacLaren as a Personal Professor; the Department of Production Engineering with Professor Donald S. Ross as Head; and the Bioengineering Unit with Professor Robert M. Kenedi as Head and Professor John P. Paul as a Personal Professor. Professor Adam Thomson had become the first Vice-Principal of the University and later Deputy Principal, thus compounding the need for additional professorial appointments; however, he remained Chairman of the Mechanical Engineering Group and Professor of Mechanical Engineering till his retirement in 1973.

The Bioengineering Unit from December 1972 was housed in the Wolfson Centre, accommodation purpose-built for its research activities. The other five departments were housed in the Weir Building and taught the full range of undergraduate and postgraduate classes as well as supervising and conducting research. There were seventeen main laboratories and five specialist teaching and research laboratories in the Weir Building, and the quality of provision was for many years exceptional. The four-year Honours degree course bore a strong family resemblance to the Associateship which it replaced. The first two years provided an introduction to Mechanics, Thermodynamics and Electrical Engineering as well as the fundamentals of Applied Science and Engineering. The final two years allowed students to specialise in the various fields of Mechanical Engineering, and some fourth-year students elected to undertake projects in Bioengineering, otherwise entirely devoted to postgraduate studies. Facilities for research in Mechanical Engineering were excellent, and there were also a number of postgraduate instructional courses.

Subjects in Production Engineering had, for many years, formed an important part of the degree course, but in Session 1969-70 two new degrees were introduced, one a specialist Honours degree in Production Engineering and the other a Joint Honours programme in Production Engineering and Management. Both degree courses attracted students of high calibre and were successful. Further innovation occurred in the late 1970s. In Session 1977-8 a new B.Sc. B.Eng. degree with Honours in Manufacturing Sciences and Engineering was introduced and was intended to attract highly qualified school-leavers to a career in industry. Organised industrial training (a partial return to the 'sandwich' system), a particular interest of Professor William Scott, was also reintroduced.

The origins of Bioengineering have been discussed in the previous chapter, but in this period the Unit acquired an international reputation for the quality of its research and grew substantially. The Biomechanics Research Group, supported with a grant of £50,000 from the Medical Research Council, began with a full-time staff of three academics and two technicians; by 1970 there was a Research Professor with a full-time staff of twenty-eight academics, backed by the necessary technical and administrative staff. In addition, there were thirty-seven postgraduates and Senior Research Fellows. In its first decade the Unit attracted nineteen clinicians, bioengineers and medical scientists from Europe, Australia, India and North America, and postgraduates came from eleven countries and fifteen different British universities. This success was partly explained in terms of dynamic leadership by Robert Kenedi and John Paul who made the necessary contacts with Glasgow-based clinicians and tackled problems of direct interest to them. The research undertaken by this wider group assumed major clinical and scientific significance and attracted substantial financial support totalling £1.2 million from a range of benefactors during the period 1962-72.

An Advisory Committee on Bioengineering, consisting of clinicians, engineers and scientists, assisted the Unit in a number of ways. It screened research projects on the basis of their importance to medicine, – and their suitability and practicability – and discussed their relative priority in relation to ongoing programmes. Research related to plastic and orthopaedic surgery, obstetrics, artificial organs, locomotion and lower limb prosthetics and orthotics, and biocompatability of artificial materials. The research was carried forward into development work in technology relevant to these fields, new instruments and devices, and innovative techniques. Five divisions – Biomechanics, Tissue Mechanics, Biochemical Engineering, Clinical Measurement and Data Analysis – thematically separate the work, and all are backed by central facilities such as workshops, election microscopy, histology and data processing and computing.

To the existing activities was added in 1972 the National Centre for Prosthetics and Orthotics with [Professor] John Hughes as Director. The Centre arose from the recommendations of the Denny Report on the *Future of the Artificial Limb Service in Scotland* (1970) which included an educational programme for prosthetists designed to raise their professional standard and to keep them in touch with the most up-to-date methods and research. Postgraduate courses were introduced for medically qualified personnel and for prosthetists already in service. Short courses were provided for paramedical personnel including a number from overseas.

In other divisions of the Mechanical Engineering Group research activity also blossomed. Computer-aided design took root in the Department of Engineering Design and Drawing; other research interests included gear design, lubrication and the application of lasers to problems involving stress, deformation and vibration. The obvious integration of this research with manufacturing and production was typical of so much of the work of the Mechanical Engineering Group. In the Department of Dynamics and Control research was undertaken on compressor valve dynamics, holographic techniques, plate vibration and general dynamic measurement problems.

In the Department of Mechanics and Materials there was also a wide range of research activity in these years – the inelastic behaviour of piping systems; shell and pressure vessel design; thin-walled structures. Many of these activities were of major importance to significant national industries – petrochemicals; oil and gas production, supply and storage; nuclear engineering. The Department of Thermodynamics and Mechanics of Fluids had an extensive programme of contract and academic research on such matters as desalination, safety studies associated with pressurised water nuclear reactors, gas compressors, rocket propulsion, industrial aerodynamics, the design of oxygen lances for steel converters and roto-dynamic machinery. In the Department of Production Engineering one of the main research interests was electro-chemical machining; others included the application of microcomputers to shopfloor production control and the design of production systems.[17]

Professor Alexander W. Scott (1904-93), the first occupant of the Chair of Chemical Engineering (1956-71), encouraged the broadening of the undergraduate degree, a process greatly accelerated by his successor and former student, Gordon S. G. Beveridge (later Vice-Chancellor of Queen's University, Belfast) in 1972-3. Subjects such as pollution, systems analysis and biochemical engineering entered the undergraduate curriculum. A new instructional M.Sc. course in Plant and Process Design replaced the existing general course. Alex Scott had always maintained good links with industry and the first six graduates of a part-time (3-year) M.Sc. in Chemical Engineering, made available to industry in Ayrshire, received their degrees in 1972. Commitment to industry was reflected in consultancy work designed to aid firms and the Scottish economy. This often had spin-offs into research: designs of evaporators, powder technology, spray drying, fermentation, reaction kinetics and computer-aided plant design. Energy conservation and dust emission control reflected growing staff interest in environmental issues.[18]

Naval Architecture, something of a Cinderella department before 1964, benefited from the flexibility which the Charter allowed. Internationally, shipbuilding was growing, but the local industry encountered major difficulties. The Department aimed to improve British competitiveness against strong overseas competition, but an emphasis on shipbuilding was not sufficient; there were major problems arising from inadequate capital investment and poor industrial relations. An M.Sc. course in Ship Production Technology was introduced in 1968, the first of three specialist postgraduate courses, which attracted a satisfactory response especially from overseas students. A Chair of Shipbuilding and Naval Architecture was created in 1970 and occupied by Ian Bridge, and accommodation in Livingstone Tower (from 1967) was a great improvement on the old quarters in the Royal College. In the 1970s research and teaching which was computer-based became more significant, as did oil-related activity. A substantial grant from the Science Research Council supported Project MASS [Maintenance Activities Subsea Surface] which also involved five other departments. The contribution from the Department was in the area of support systems – the problems of launching and retrieving submersibles and the mooring and stationing of support vessels near to offshore rigs – where Professor Chengi Kuo rapidly acquired an international reputation.[19]

The School of Civil and Mining Engineering and Applied Geology had at its core in 1964 a strong Department of Civil Engineering with some 300 undergraduate students and a staff complement of fifteen, including Professor William Fraser. In Session 1965-6 instructional M.Sc. courses were started in a number of specialist areas – structural engineering, soil mechanics, hydraulics, public health engineering, traffic and highway engineering, and environmental control and resource utilisation. Each of these supplied personnel to expanding sectors of the British and international economies. A Chair of Structural Engineering was established in Session 1966-7 and occupied by Professor Alexander Coull, and the first Visiting Professor, R.C.H. Russell, Director of the Hydraulics Research Station at Wallingford, was appointed. Staff numbers increased rapidly in these early years after the Charter.

The Department occupied about 10,000 sq. ft. of laboratory space in the James Weir Building, but this soon proved to be inadequate. New laboratories were provided in the Colville Building from 1966-7 for Hydraulics, Public Health, Traffic and Surveying, and a converted minesweeper, RV *Strathclyde* (1967-70), was purchased to aid research. The untimely death of Professor William Fraser (1968) led to re-examination of the academic leadership of the Department. Dr. Ian H. Barr was appointed to a Chair of Hydraulics, and Laing Barden to a Chair of Mechanics of Soils in Session 1968-9, replacing the single Chair of Civil Engineering. Thus, by 1969 the Department encompassed three main areas of responsibility – Structural Engineering under Professor Coull, Hydraulics, including Public Health Engineering, under Professor Barr and Soil Mechanics, with Traffic and Highway Engineering, under Professor Barden – and the Headship was held in rotation.

Although the Department in the early 1970s had about 42,000 sq. ft. of laboratory space in the Weir, Colville and John Anderson Buildings, its staff moved to John Anderson Building at the end of Session 1970-1. Major modifications were made in the undergraduate programme in Session 1972-3, with the Department undertaking nearly all teaching in the second, third and fourth years, and a new B.Sc. (Building Structures) was instituted in collaboration with the Department of Architecture and Building Science. Ten years after the Charter the Department, with a staff of about 30, was producing over 90 graduates per year and had a full-time graduate school of over 50.

Professor Laing Barden resigned in Session 1973-4, ultimately to become Director of Newcastle Polytechnic, and his successor was Professor David G. McKinlay. Other changes included the election of Professor Coull to the Regius Chair at the University of Glasgow and the appointment of Professor Iain A. MacLeod, a great piper and structural engineer, as his successor. The period of rapid growth was over by 1974, and the rest of the 1970s was relatively stable, a period of consolidation.

The Department's industrial and academic research programme was very extensive, growing with every member of staff appointed. The Clyde Port Authority commissioned a hydraulic model of the estuary and tidal river which was used to improve and alter the Clyde; expenditure on this consultancy approached £250,000 over five years; investigations were carried out for the South of Scotland Electricity Board on power station cooling-water problems; much work was undertaken to assist the establishment of fish farming in Scotland; near-shore Oceanography and the computer control of Glasgow traffic were other directly applicable instances of contract research. The links between industrially-sponsored research and the main lines of academic research were often close but not exclusive. The Department became involved in Project MASS (already discussed in terms of Shipbuilding and Naval Architecture), successfully testing a surveying and navigation system for divers and submersibles in Session 1978-9. Much research work was undertaken in the field of Construction Materials, so vital to the whole gamut of the construction industries.[20]

In Mining Engineering, specialist expertise in the fields of ventilation, occupational health and underground working conditions made a move into a new degree course in Environmental Engineering in 1965 a sensible diversification, particularly as the National Coal Board ran down many of the older collieries in the Scottish coalfields and directed part of their workforces to Yorkshire and the East Midlands. This new course had considerable potential which it soon began to demonstrate; by 1972 a separate Department (the first in any British University) of Environmental Engineering had been created with Alex W.K. Stewart as Reader (later Professor) and Head; by 1974 this new department had been relocated in the School of Mechanical and Chemical Engineering and Naval Architecture.

George Hibberd, Professor of Mining Engineering, retired in 1968, and his successor was Professor D. Jenkins. Much of the responsibility for academic leadership and administration, however, fell on the shoulders of Dr (later Professor) George Maxwell, for Professor Jenkins suffered from long bouts of serious illness in the years before his death in 1979. Another alumnus, J.R. Cowan, Member of the National Coal Board and Director of its Scottish Area, became a Visiting Professor. The Department inevitably took a considerable interest in petroleum engineering in the 1970s but was always too pressed for resources – especially staffing – to exploit this considerable opportunity. Research was also inhibited for the same reason, but this small department investigated a number of significant issues – roadway collapses in deep mines, for instance – which had immediate relevance for mining operations.[21]

Another small but significant development was the creation of a separate Department of Applied Geology in 1967 with well equipped laboratories, two years after a B.Sc. in the subject had been instituted. The first Head of Department was Professor A.K. Pringle, and he was responsible for extending postgraduate instructional courses, providing support for civil engineers, forensic scientists, and urban and regional planners as well as mining engineers. Field visits to major civil engineering projects were a feature of the later years of the undergraduate course. Research into sources of metals, gas and petroleum and water were main planks in the postgraduate portfolio which extended well beyond the British Isles.[22]

The School of Electrical Engineering began with a single department within which Electronics also had a place. Growth was both rapid and highly significant after 1964, largely reflecting external demand for graduates but also inhibited by the 'stops' and 'gos' of Government policy which, from time to time, caused the University to insist on tight undergraduate quotas. As with so many undergraduate courses, there was extensive revision on the eve of the granting of the Charter, but this was simply the beginning of a continuous process as the staff not only took account of what was happening in industry but also anticipated the future pattern of education required in specific areas. Evident success in this objective increased industry's demand for the Department's graduates, a circumstance which ceased to be reassuring and, for the Dean, Professor Aeneas M. Rosie, in 1978 became 'alarming' because of excessive pressure on resources. A new B.Sc. course in Electronic and Microprocessor Engineering was introduced in 1979 designed to meet demand for those with a university education in Electronic Systems with a particular bias towards the digital processing of data, signals and information. This was the beginning of major development in the 1980s.

Dennis Taylor, a distinguished scientist and engineer, was appointed to take charge of a new Department of Electronic Science and Telecommunications in 1967; his Chair was endowed by the Hoover Foundation in 1968. The two departments remained apart until 1982 when they were reunited as the Department of Electronic and Electrical Engineering. Before joining Strathclyde, Taylor had been involved with development work on radar during the war and afterwards became Chief Scientist for Plessey and later UNESCO Professor in the University College of Nairobi. He introduced Telecommunications as an option for first-year students and soon established a research group in the field of electronic instrumentation. His death in 1972 was a sad blow to the new department, but his successor, Aeneas Rosie, continued his research group, giving it new impetus and direction. In the Age of Aerospace, the spin-offs to industry were numerous, but the veritable explosion of information technology in the 1980s found Rosie and his colleagues well placed. These developments readily won the support of Sir Samuel Curran, who, partly through his wartime experience, had a sense of the potentiality of electronics ever afterwards.

In research the Department of Electrical Engineering after 1964 greatly extended its programmes in Power Systems and Electrical Machines. Component Technology was an area which developed in the 1970s, as did work on semi-conductors and insulators, and insulating liquids. Compared with the situation of the 1950s which Professor Bruce put to rights by developing exciting research in High Voltage Engineering, it was the wide range of research issues which impressed experts such as Visiting Professor J.S. Forrest F.R.S. in the 1970s. However, the Department never lost its research commitment to Power Engineering, and this remained throughout the 1970s and 1980s a major division. Bruce's mantle fell upon David J. Tedford who took the Foundation Chair and greatly extended the Department's influence in the University and further afield.

Research in Electronics and Telecommunications also was wide-ranging, but the three most significant general areas were communications, control, and signal processing. Work was undertaken in teletraffic theory and optical communication, in ultrasonic underwater inspection of offshore installations and underwater navigation, and in image processing (associated principally with Dr [Professor] Tariq Durrani. Short postgraduate courses for engineers from industry and government establishments became a feature of the Department's work and had obvious benefits in garnering industrial support and government contracts.[23]

The School of Mathematics and Physics was also highly dynamic in its response to research and teaching opportunities and to the wider world of industry and commerce. Much of its work involved service teaching for all students of science and engineering, and as other related departments expanded, so these two departments grew correspondingly. However, both gained from the freedom which the Charter brought, specialist associateships being phased out as degree courses became operational from 1964.

A second Chair of Mathematics (in Solid Mechanics/Applicable Mathematics) was created in 1964 to which Professor Collins was appointed and a third Chair of Mathematics (Numerical Analysis/Fluid Dynamics) was filled in 1966 by David Butler. The Royal Society's Committee on Postgraduate Education in Applied Mathematics recognised the Department in 1968 as a Major School for research in Fluid Dynamics, one of eight in the United Kingdom and also as a Minor School for research in Solid Mechanics. Both these areas continued to flourish throughout the 1970s and were joined by new research areas in applied statistics, the numerical solution of differential equations and functional analysis.

New undergraduate programmes were launched for Joint Honours degrees with Economics, Psychology and other social sciences. Teaching included Computer Science; the Department had taken responsibility for the University's first computer, a Ferranti Sirius machine donated in 1963 by Colvilles, and promoted courses in programming for staff to stimulate their use. From the Department of Mathematics emerged a new and separate Department of Computer Science in 1967. Teaching by television was one method of dealing with very large classes, and the Department pioneered this development, with the first-year class of 600 anticipating the Open University by several years. The staff time saved was applied to more tutorial teaching. More specialist tuition for more senior years was also the subject of experimentation with television. The growth of audio-visual services was an inevitable consequence of this type of activity.

A new B.Sc. degree in Mathematical Sciences was introduced in Session 1976-7 and soon established itself. Increasingly computers replaced television as a form of instruction; the last session for the large first year of TV instruction was 1978-9. By then there was extensive and growing use of computers for both service and specialist classes. The improvement of degrees for in-service teachers of mathematics (for which Reginald Lord deserves great credit) was undertaken by a two-year part-time course which the Department provided from 1962 to 1967 and again from 1971 to 1975, thus improving the supply and quality of Mathematics teachers in the region; the recipients of these awards welcomed not only the pure mathematics but also the applications – statistics, numerical analysis and computing – which became so important to the secondary schools from the 1970s.

Two additional Chairs were created to take account of these developments in Applied

39 Baird Hall of Residence, Sauchiehall Street. This Art Deco building, acquired in 1964, was originally the Beresford Hotel (architects Weddell and Inglis), built to provide accommodation for visitors to the Empire Exhibition of 1938. Possibly the best of Glasgow's architecture from the 1930s, the conversion provided residential places and public rooms for nearly 350 students. The foyer contains an excellent collection of John Logie Baird memorabilia.

Mathematics: George Eason in Mathematics for Applied Scientists (1971), and Rupert Leslie in Statistics (1971). Further professorial appointments were made with the promotions of Dr Gary F. Roach (1978) and of Dr Frank Leslie (1979). By the mid-1970s there were 40 staff, more than 200 undergraduates specialising in Mathematics and about a dozen research students. Service work was bound to remain very important in a university with such a strong commitment to Engineering and Science, but the Department of Mathematics, under the leadership of Professor Donald C. Pack (also Vice-Principal 1968-72), had come of age.[24]

At first the Department of Computer Science was essentially providing a service: about one-fifth of all undergraduates received some instruction in programming by the early 1970s. A Chair was established in 1970, and Andrew Colin was appointed. A specialist degree was initiated and facilities were provided for postgraduate studies. With the increasing availability of microcomputers in the late 1970s, programming was taught interactively using Commodore PET personal computers, and Dr (later Professor) Andrew McGettrick and Professor Colin produced texts dealing with the programming language ALGOL 68. Commercial organisations gradually became interested in the Department's expertise and research, especially in machine languages. More significantly, the student client group enjoyed this new experience and, in terms of pass rates, this innovative Department was successful.[25]

The discipline with the oldest pedigree in the University, Natural Philosophy, began to flourish once again. In 1971 the John Anderson Building (home also to Civil Engineering) was opened, providing purpose-built accommodation for the Department of Natural Philosophy and Applied Physics. Undergraduate programmes in Natural Philosophy had some problems with recruitment in what for most disciplines was a period of considerable expansion; Applied Physics with a new Chair, filled by Edward Eisner (1968), was more popular, since its new degree, after a common course with Natural Philosophy for the first two years, seemed to deal with major issues facing the world outside the University. Yet the division between the two was more artificial than most between departments, and to outsiders seemed to revolve around personalities rather than fundamental intellectual differences.

By the late 1970s growth in the student population in Natural Philosophy was growing, running contrary to national trends. Staff teaching quality was high; dedicated and highly motivated individuals managed to push pass rates in service classes up to levels never reached before. Graduates with the specialist degree were snapped up, and this was also the case in Applied Physics where the Honours project, generally involving industrial placement, proved popular with students and employers alike. This form of assessment was introduced for Pass degree students but mainly conducted in-house.

Both Departments were very active in research. In Natural Philosophy the main fields were laser and plasma physics. In Applied Physics work was more varied: theoretical population dynamics, experimental biophysics, fluid mechanics, photophysics, appropriate technology for the underdeveloped world, environmental physics and solid state physics. Advanced instrumentation, coupled with entrepreneurial activity, marked out the group led by Dr (later Professor) David Birch and Dr (later Professor) Robert Imhof. Postgraduate numbers began to increase in the late 1970s in both departments, a very satisfactory basis for the considerable expansion of research activity in the 1980s.[26]

The School of Chemical and Materials Sciences comprised three departments – the newly unified Pure and Applied Chemistry (1964), Metallurgy and Fibre Science (from 1978 Fibre Science and Textile Technology). Considerable expansion in Chemistry had been planned for the quinquennium 1962-7: the Thomas Graham Building was ready for use in 1964 and Manfred Gordon was appointed the first Professor of Physical Chemistry, making three Chairs in the

Department; David W.A. Sharp was promoted to take the revived Chair in Inorganic Chemistry in 1965; and by 1974 with Professor Peter Perkins of Inorganic Chemistry (1968) there were five professorships and many additional staff appointed to cope with the expansion of student numbers. In Technical Chemistry the expansion of instruction and research in polymer chemistry and technology begun by Professor Patrick Ritchie in the 1950s continued apace. Facilities for teaching were much improved in the new building, and research continued to prosper. The long-term interest in fuels and dyestuffs remained but fresh areas included spectroscopy, surface chemistry, distillation and gas absorption, and chemical reactor design.

However, the greatest growth occurred in other sections of the Department, partly because of their extended commitments to service teaching. Revised undergraduate curricula for the three chemistry degrees had much in common. There was an Honours degree in Applied Chemistry and Pass and Honours Degrees in Chemistry, with teaching only becoming specialist in the Final year, students then taking separate pure and applied courses. All students conducted projects, and inevitably in all years practical work was of great significance, much of direct industrial relevance being part of the instruction in the senior years. Following a nineteenth-century tradition, the Department remained strong in Analytical Chemistry and offered an instructional M.Sc. with an emphasis on instrumental methods appropriate to metallurgy and to trace element analysis. An M.Sc. in Applied Colloid and Interface Science was also provided, which, apart from dealing with fundamentals, considered industrial applications – aerosols, paints, soaps and pharmacy.

In 1980 Pure and Applied Chemistry had 38 members of staff, 28 post-doctoral fellows and over 70 postgraduate students. By the late 1970s the recurrent research budget at any moment was of the order of £1 million scattered over the four sections of the Department, and most of it derived from external funding. Connections with industry remained close and produced many significant research issues, going beyond normal consultancy and yet having industrial consequences.

Organic Chemistry had two professors. Peter Pauson, holder of the Freeland Chair, was elected to the *Deutsche Akademie der Naturforscher*, Leopoldina in 1976 and by 1980 was the author of over 160 publications, mainly in organometallic chemistry; his research in the late 1970s was concerned with the use of organometallic systems as catalysts and synthetic intermediates. Hamish Wood was engaged in research into pteridine, flavin and co-enzyme chemistry at the interface between chemistry and biochemistry. Members of staff in this section had a range of research interests: terpenoid, heterocyclic, and alkaloid chemistry; the application of biochemical principles to organic synthesis; matrix isolation of reactive intermediates; and free radical substitution including halogenation reactions.

Inorganic Chemistry had Peter Perkins as head. Author of *Elementary Molecular Bonding Theory*, his research interests in theoretical inorganic chemistry included the study of the optical, magnetic and electronic properties of materials. Research was also being undertaken in silicon and boron compounds and their possible therapeutic effects, the development of inorganic pigments and the investigation of trace metals, in particular copper and gold, in relation to the treatment of rheumatoid arthritis.

Alistair North, the Burmah Professor of Physical Chemistry (1968) and later Vice-Principal, was the author of two books on kinetics and reactions in liquids, and his research investigated the relationship of the physical and chemical behaviour of polymer systems to their chemical structure through understanding their molecular behaviour. The study of crystallisation processes, solid state reactivity and the structure of molecular crystals, principally associated with the work of Professor John Sherwood, was a research area for which the Department had acquired an international reputation and substantial research funds. Other research groups were undertaking work on the surface structure of alloys and on the surface properties important in adhesion using photoelectron spectroscopy, the chemistry of polymerisation processes and the theory of quantum and statistical mechanics.

After the retirement of Patrick D. Ritchie, the new Young Professor was Neil Graham, appointed in 1973. His principal research interest was in developing the use of polymers for the controlled release of drugs, which potentially had many medical applications; Neil Graham's particular ambition, derived from family experience, was to attempt to provide a means of reducing the need for caesarian sections in childbirth, a dangerous and costly medical procedure. He was also investigating the use of polymers for the industrial concentration of dispersions. Much fundamental work on polymers was also being conducted in the Department; at least two sections were interested in this research by the late 1970s.

The Department by 1980 was very well equipped with sophisticated instrumentation and equipment, often backed, where appropriate, by computers, and a number of specialised research laboratories were described by visitors as 'state of the art'. There were some space shortages, and these were to grow in the 1980s, but in general, large numbers of staff and students used the Department's facilities and were impressed by them. The specialist library, named after Sir Alexander Fleck (Chairman of ICI and an alumnus), provided ready access to the periodical literature and research texts.[27]

Textile technology and manufacture, as subject disciplines, had a long history in the Institution but the textile industries had been in structural decline for most of the twentieth century. International appeal and scientific and technical transfer became the *leitmotif* of this Department's activities after 1964. Professor Reginald Meredith (1917-93) joined the Royal College in 1957 with a substantial research reputation. A first-class Honours graduate in Physics from Manchester University (1938), he worked in the Shirley Institute during the Second World War, carrying out pioneering work on the physics of fibres, particularly in the area of mechanical properties and X-ray diffraction. Taking the M.Sc. (1945) and being awarded D.Sc. (1955), he was a world authority at the time of his election to the Chair on account of his contributions to Fibre Physics.

Because of their increasing interest in man-made fibres, in 1964 Professor Meredith and his staff decided to seek Court's approval for a change of departmental name to the Department of Fibre Science. The research approach which also affected undergraduate and postgraduate instruction was unashamedly utilitarian; there was a strong emphasis on social and economic relevance. Glass and carbon fibres as well as synthetic elastic materials were the subject of investigation, and reinforced plastics for use in supersonic aircraft such as Concorde were the subject of research. Work was also done on artificial sinovial fluid for lubrication of human joints.

Postgraduate places were taken up, and the staff were professionally very active. However, in the 1970s there was a decline in the number of British students applying for places on the undergraduate programme, and Senate decided that the University should withdraw from this form of teaching; the final intake of students took place in October 1978. Thus, the resources of the Department were devoted increasingly to postgraduate instruction and research. Staff also assisted as requested on M.Sc. courses in Forensic Science and Applied Colloid and Interface Science. Professor Meredith retired in 1977, and thereafter the Department, with approval of Court, added Textile Technology to its title. Renewed contacts with the textile industry were made with the assistance of two members of Court, Mr (later Dr.) Harry R. Crone, an alumnus, and Dr. W. D. Coats. In August 1980 the Department ceased to exist; a newly created Fibre and

40 Ross Priory: a hand-coloured engraving c.1820 taken from John Preston Neale's *Views of the Seats of Noble Men in England, Wales, Scotland and Ireland*, published by W.H. Reid in six volumes (1818-23). The Priory was purchased in 1971 for use as a University staff house and centre; after extensive restoration it came into use in 1973.

Textile Research Unit was established within the Department of Pure and Applied Chemistry with responsibility for Diploma and M.Sc. courses in Textile Evaluation, for the supervision of postgraduate students, and for staff commitment to research.[28] Thus, a distinguished history waned with the fortunes of the British textile industry.

Another department of high quality which suffered from fluctuations in student demand was Metallurgy. Yet the opportunities for graduates were far more than Scotland's single department could meet. Facilities for teaching and research were much improved in Session 1967-8 when the Colville Building came into use. Professor Edwin C. Ellwood led a very effective group of staff, and much high-quality research in chemical and physical metallurgy, industrial metallurgy and metal physics was undertaken. John Taylor (1906-92) had joined the staff in 1945 after an academic and industrial career in Newcastle and County Durham; in 1965 he became Professor of Extraction Metallurgy, a just reward for a man who was one of the world's experts on blast furnaces and an academic practitioner who did much to improve Britain's iron and steel industry after 1945.

After Edwin Ellwood's untimely death in 1973, the Department was singularly fortunate in his successor, Professor Norman Petch F.R.S. (1917-93), the first person to be elected a Fellow of the Royal Society while on the staff of the University. A graduate of Glasgow, Petch went to the Cavendish Laboratory in Cambridge where he undertook highly original work in the physical metallurgy of iron and steel and began research on the strength of materials which was to occupy most of the rest of his working life. His work was of tremendous value to the steel industry, and he impressed both staff and students with his modesty and intellect.

After Professor Taylor retired in 1971, Paul Grieveson became Professor of Extraction Metallurgy and faced the nadir of the Department's popularity with applications reaching only 59 in 1976. However, in the late 1970s there was a revival of demand. A new undergraduate

41 After a congregation in the City Hall a graduate is congratulated by a proud relative. In the background is the Ramshorn church, now the University's theatre.

syllabus was written, overseas students continued to apply in numbers, and the main areas of research continued to prosper. When Professor Grieveson left to take the Chair of Applied Metallurgy at Imperial College in 1978, Henry B. Bell, an alumnus, became Professor of Extraction Metallurgy, and the resurgence of undergraduate applications continued. Despite tribulations this high-quality department managed to maintain its independence and its reputation.[29]

The School of Pharmacy prospered after 1964. It continued to teach undergraduates and to supply well-qualified pharmacists to meet the demand from the retail sector, the hospitals and industry. A new Chair in Pharmacology was established in 1966 to which Professor William Bowman (later Vice-Principal) was appointed. The Medical Research Council set up the Drug Metabolism Research Unit in 1967 with the Professor of Pharmaceutical Chemistry, John Stenlake, as Director. Postgraduate activity was flourishing with nearly sixty graduates preparing for higher degrees by the early 1970s, and research was thriving in the fields of drug absorption, drug modification of enzyme systems, tissue culture and the bio-availability of drugs from formulated medicines.

Undergraduate applications were running at ten for every place in the School in the mid-1970s. Curricula were subject to scrutiny from the professional body, but there was little support from the conventional research councils until the Science Research Council instituted a Pharmacy Advisory Panel upon which Professor Bowman served. Harmonious relationships with hospitals, particularly the Royal Infirmary, were cultivated. Professor Frank Fish built up the Forensic Science Unit from 1966, offering a unique M.Sc. course and a laboratory service to police forces in the West of Scotland before they developed their own facilities. Dr (later Professor) Brian Caddy was an admirable supporter of Professor Fish who left in Session 1977-8 to become Dean of the School of Pharmacy in the University of London. The University continued this Unit under Professor W. J. Tilstone and it continued to do excellent work. Other M.Sc. courses were developed – in Pharmaceutical Analysis and Clinical Pharmacy, the latter being of particular importance to the Health Boards.

Staff research was highly varied and extensive. Professors Bowman and Stenlake were working independently on muscle relaxants, a long task which bore financial fruit in the 1980s and 1990s. Professor (1975) J. R. Parratt was involved with work on cardiology; research was being conducted on toxins as tools in neurobiology, on phyto-chemistry, on anti-cancer agents. Some work was the subject of patents, but most found its way into the learned periodical literature. However, by Session 1978-9 the muscle relaxant developed by Professor Stenlake and his team was on clinical trials, a quite exceptional development for a University department. Atracurium (BW 33A) was shown to be a clinically acceptable muscle relaxant free of most of the principal disadvantages of existing agents and therefore highly suitable for major operations. Via the Wellcome Foundation Ltd. the University was about to benefit from a bonanza, as were the research team and the School.[30]

From the care of Pharmacy had emerged the School of Biological Sciences – the Departments of Food Science, Applied Microbiology, Biology, and Biochemistry. In this period they were scattered over several buildings, and Food Science spent some time in Horselethill Road until the James P. Todd Building was opened in Session 1970-1. New Chairs were created in Biochemistry (1966) and Biology (1966) and departments emerged. Undergraduate recruitment to the School was of the order of 100 students in the 1970s undertaking a variety of degree courses which were developed and refined – Biology and Genetics, Microbiology and Genetics, Biochemistry and Pharmacology, Food Science, Applied Microbiology – usually having a common core curriculum and specialist options. In 1979 a biotechnology option was introduced into the B.Sc. Technology and Business Studies programme in which all four departments were involved. Accommodation, especially bench space in laboratories, was a problem constraining recruitment but by the end of the 1970s that restraint was being overcome as a consequence of refurbishment and upgrading in the Royal College.

This School was very active in research, much of it with industrial support. In Food Science Professor John Hawthorn and his colleagues conducted research on animal fats, the technology of special diets, fundamental aspects of dehydration, freezing and food bacteriology, all work of immediate importance to the convenience food industries. In the second half of the 1970s, new staff brought fresh research interests: the chemistry of cereal lipids, flavour aspects of food and whisky, and unusual sources of edible carbohydrate, for example. Professor Ernest Morris and colleagues in Applied Microbiology also developed an international reputation for the study of yeasts and fermentation technology; Dr (later Professor) John Smith conducted highly regarded investigations of fungi, and work was begun in collaboration with the Scottish Marine Biological Laboratories on primary production in sea lochs. Food and medical microbiology (in collaboration with local hospitals) also developed as research interests.

In Biology, there was also a wide range of research interests: pests and pesticides, marine biology, genetics and parasitology. Professor William Fletcher stimulated relevant research but also encouraged colleagues to undertake fundamental work. Dr (later Professor) William Hutchison won the Koch medal for his pioneering work in parasitology and also fascinated generations of undergraduates with his dedication to effective teaching. Professor Peter Heald and colleagues in Biochemistry developed research in three main areas after 1966: the biochemistry of reproduction; biochemical pharmacology; and biochemical technology. In the first, a Medical Research Council Group worked on problems associated with implementation mechanisms in early pregnancy, ovary function, hormones and post-coital antifertility agents. Later, studies in immunology became important, and the medical orientation remained strong, although in Session 1977-8 Heald left to become Dean of the Faculty of Science in the Memorial University of Newfoundland. His successor, Robin D. Marshall, arrived in 1979 from the Department of Chemical Pathology of St Mary's Hospital, London which may help to explain the continuity. One very significant development was the creation of the Biotechnology Unit (1978-9) which was greatly assisted by the quiet diplomacy of Dr John Blain, Dean of the School.[31]

The Glasgow School of Architecture was dissolved after the granting of the Charter. A broadening of architectural education followed. The first Professor of Architecture in the University of Strathclyde was Frank Fielden who was also the last Director of Studies in the Glasgow School. Fielden's tenure (1959-68) was notable for the creation of the new degree of Bachelor of Architecture and for his design of the Architecture Building which was completed in 1966. Fielden and his colleagues were committed to introducing the Fine Arts to their undergraduates and through Art Fellowships attracted a number of creative workers to the Strathclyde School.

In Session 1966-7 two new Chairs were established. The first in Urban and Regional Planning, to which Professor Ronald E. Nicoll, formerly Chief Planning Officer in the Scottish Development Department, was appointed, continued the discipline's association (since 1949) with the School of Architecture and indeed contributed to undergraduate teaching. The second, in Building Science, to which Professor Thomas A. Markus, formerly Reader in the Welsh School of Architecture, was appointed, emphasised that it was important to associate design with the practical virtues of social awareness and technical expertise. After Fielden's resignation – to become Secretary of the Royal Fine Art Commission – the Chair of Architecture was taken in

1970 by Professor F. N. Morcos-Asaad, formerly Director of Structural Studies in the School of Architecture in the University of Liverpool.

Undergraduate numbers were between 180 and 190 students in the 1970s, and in the programme there was a strong emphasis on project and design work which increasingly concentrated on urban rehabilitation (in reaction to the local planning blights resulting from area demolition), housing, energy efficiency in buildings and conversions. One interesting student team project examined the possibility of alternative uses for workshops at New Lanark, an indication of the growing concern with the heritage.

Staff research and consultancy (through units such as ASSIST and ABACUS) concentrated on environmental improvement, energy-efficient buildings and tenement rehabilitation. Close industrial liaison was established, and the local authorities and Scottish Development Department also sponsored major projects such as the Ferguslie Park study (completed 1978-9). Other areas of research interest included nineteenth- and twentieth-century architectural history, especially of Glasgow, associated with Frank Walker and Peter Reed, timber structures (with the support of the Science Research Council) undertaken by Edwin N. Morris, and soil stabilisation techniques for low-cost housing in developing countries in which Professor Markus and colleagues from three other departments were involved.

The Department of Urban and Regional Planning was essentially a postgraduate enterprise with full-time and part-time instructional courses dominant, although it was also possible to take the degree of Ph.D. by research. Projects overseas especially in countries bordering the Mediterranean were undertaken in the 1970s: the Athens city region, Montpellier, the Languedoc-Roussilon area, and Barcelona were closely examined. There was much emphasis on environmental impact analysis and the processes and procedures of planning.[32]

About two-fifths of the University's undergraduates in this period were in the School of Arts and Social Studies and the School of Business and Administration. A proposal to establish a Faculty of Industrial and Social Studies, made to the UGC in the late 1950s, had emerged with substantial changes arising from the circumstances of the amalgamation with the Scottish College of Commerce. Ventures in Industrial Administration and General Studies had paved the way, and by 1962 the first appointments at professorial level had been made, and the schedule for the completion of the McCance Building approved.

The founding Professors were S.G.E. Lythe (Economic History), K.J.W. Alexander (Economics), Allan Potter (Politics), T.T. Patterson (Administration) and Gustav Jahoda (Psychology). Edgar Lythe (1910-) soon emerged as the most influential figure in this group (Vice-Principal 1972-6) and was invited in 1963-4 to assist in the negotiations which led to the assimilation of the Scottish College. The first students were admitted to the School of Arts and Social Studies in October 1963 and they embarked upon a five-subject curriculum, from which they were to select two principal subjects in Session 1964-5. This, like the degree of BA, broke with Scottish traditions in one sense, but its major merit was the flexibility of choice which enabled students to change their preferred specialisation and yet remain on course. The lecture programmes were heavily reinforced by a tutorial system, not then common in the Scottish system; this made tutors familiar with groups of students and reduced the danger of alienation arising from the anonymity of large classes.

This structure was created with the agreement of the founding professors, but Edgar Lythe was its principal architect. He believed that students should appreciate that subject boundaries were artificial; that the inter-relationship of disciplines and their usefulness to one another was best assessed by undergraduates pursuing a broad course; that single honours should be a late rather than an early option. These characteristics attracted many able students whose initial commitment to a single discipline was unsure. Significant proportions of undergraduates did change their intended courses after the first year: as many as 45 per cent changed at least one of their principal subjects in one cohort of the 1970s.

Another merit of the structure was the ease with which additional disciplines and departments could be accommodated within it. Slotting in new principal subjects as departments were added to the initial five posed no difficulty, and indeed, Modern History [with J.T. Ward as Professor (1974)], Modern Languages, English Studies, Sociology, Geography, Law and Librarianship were soon part of the School. The student body welcomed the additional subject choices given to them, and well-qualified school-leavers found the new School very attractive.

Within the University new staff felt they had to demonstrate their teaching abilities and research credentials, possibly more so than in a traditional university. In large measure, they pioneered the progress of the new school: a steady stream of books and articles appeared, and the relatively low non-completion rates of students was one crude indicator of highly competent teaching. Teaching programmes were regularly reviewed, and new staff brought fresh expertise and new options. They were also very active in their professional bodies and within a short time made many academic connections abroad.

The culture of the Andersonian somehow made its impression on this new School. Its graduates proved to be highly employable, and most made their way into industry, public service, and commerce. The Scottish Education Department recognised many of the degree subject combinations as qualifying for teacher training, and indeed, new subjects were entering the secondary school curriculum which Strathclyde graduates were uniquely qualified to teach. Yet a relatively low proportion of graduates entered teaching. However, from 1971 the University validated the B.Ed. degrees of Craigie and Hamilton Colleges.

Perhaps one illustration of the commitment to useful learning will suffice. An early decision was to create a federal Department of Modern Languages (French, German, Spanish, Italian and Russian) rather than separate departments; another was to insist that graduates in Modern Languages had to take three languages in their degree rather than the traditional two. More significantly, there was great emphasis on competence in the spoken and written language. It was not that literature was neglected; indeed, a dichotomy would be false, for reading the modern literature of a country assists the development of linguistic competence. A constant supply of native speakers was central to the teaching strategy; usually young and recruited for one or two sessions, their empathy with undergraduates was marked. A few native speakers were recruited to the permanent staff. Amongst the most eminent was Dr (later Professor) Medardo Fraile (1925-), already one of Spain's most prolific short-story writers by the early 1970s; wherever Modern Spanish literature is taught, his work is likely to be found in the curriculum – or in private reading.

The usual diagnostic tests of academic quality were applied to the new School. The Social Science Research Council (later Economic and Social Research Council) made grants to support research in all the appropriate departments – Economic History, Politics, Psychology and Sociology; Economics, which operated in the School but was placed for administrative purposes in the School of Business and Administration, gained the Fraser of Allander Institute (1975), the cardinal forecasting organisation for the Scottish economy. A range of other bodies supported staff research and the growth of graduate study.[33]

The main features of the BA structure also applied to the School of Business and Administration, and a substantial amount of teaching – and therefore, undergraduate learning experience – crossed the School boundaries. Joint Honours degrees could be taken which crossed these frontiers also: one particularly successful combination was Marketing and Modern

Languages, perhaps another manifestation of the Andersonian spirit. Originally based in the Scottish College building in Pitt Street, the New School of Business comprised seven departments and also included the Scottish Hotel School, then based at Ross Hall. The opening of the Stenhouse Building in 1972 allowed a greater integration of the School within the University, and it expanded substantially in terms of student numbers and staff thereafter.

However, by the late 1970s consolidation was the order of the day, mainly because of external financial pressures which affected all universities. Some departments suffered from excessive popularity which the flexible degree structure allowed but could not limit. Thus in the Department of Accountancy and Finance it became necessary to impose quotas to reduce a massive teaching load. A first-year class was also introduced in 1977-8 to cater for non-specialists. Service teaching developed between the School and the B.Sc. B.Eng. course and a Joint Honours programme was developed in Technology and Business Studies. The Law School continued to develop options throughout the 1970s including European Community Law and Welfare Law. The principal development here, however, was the introduction of the Diploma in Legal Practice which was an essential qualification for all graduates intending to become practising lawyers from 1980.

Postgraduate instructional diploma and masters' courses were provided by several departments. The Department of Marketing, led by Professor Michael Baker, grew to be the largest in Europe, largely because of its extensive postgraduate commitment which coincided with very large undergraduate numbers. The MBA programme involved several departments and expanded considerably in this period. The long-standing Diploma in Secretarial Studies remained popular with graduates intending to enter industry and commerce; this course had an outstanding record in placing diplomates in well-paid employment.

Generally, the School had a fine record in placing its graduates and postgraduates. About 70 per cent in the late 1970s were making their way directly into industry and commerce. This record was soon common property among school-leavers and guidance teachers, and thus there was great pressure on places. Since the School of Business and the School of Arts and Social Studies followed co-operative policies, pressure on places was of mutual concern and was partly alleviated by joint action, including the provision of more joint undergraduate programmes.

Despite its extensive teaching commitments the School's research activities became more diverse. Aspects of manufacturing technology, advertising, employer/employee labour relations strategies, industrial innovation, tourism, central and local government relations, Health Service operations and, as already mentioned, the comparative performance and direction of the Scottish economy were some of the subjects of research in the latter half of the 1970s. Publications and conference papers multiplied as the School assumed a leading role in the United Kingdom.

The Chesters Management Centre had, in the 1950s, pioneered high-powered management courses which developed into MBA programmes. These were merged in the Strathclyde Graduate Business School programme, based in the Sir William Duncan Building (completed in Session 1976-7) which also provided residential accommodation for students. This programme, mainly aimed at intending or actual senior managers, could draw upon the staff resources of the whole University. In 1970 the Scottish Business School, consisting of Divisions representing the Universities of Glasgow, Edinburgh and Strathclyde, was established, in the forlorn hope that joint action would stimulate a favourable response from the UGC. Instead the UGC proposed a tripartite structure which in the long term had no future. The largest component was the Strathclyde Graduate Business School with more residential courses than the other two Divisions.[34]

The central administration and the essential services of the University naturally responded to the growth which has been delineated. George P. Richardson was Registrar during the critical early days of the University till his retirement in 1973, and he and Louis McGougan (Bursar from 1966) made a fine team in assisting the Principal, Court and Senate to achieve agreed objectives. David W. J. Morrell succeeded Richardson and created an administrative team including Ronald L. Crawford, Secretary to Court, Martin J. B. Lowe, Secretary to Senate, and Michael G.E. Paulson-Ellis, Secretary (Academic Administration). This group was sensitive to the objectives of the Principal and the Court and the key committees of Senate responsible for Academic Planning and fully conversant with the external constraints which from time to time restricted expansion.[35]

One of the main services, the Andersonian Library, endured two relocations in this period. The Librarian, Charles G. Wood, held one of the offices of the University to which the Charter specifically referred. Appointed in June 1953, his domain was a relatively small area of the first floor of the Royal College. From the beginning he was fascinated by the history of the institution which he had joined and was the moving spirit behind the 96 Group, members of which held annual meetings to hear papers concerned with Anderson and the heritage of the College. In February 1964 he supervised the transfer of the Library to the McCance Building and reopened after a week of strenuous activity and reorganisation. To assist the growing number of student readers, Mr Wood and his staff provided short courses of reader instruction and reference desks with specialist staff.

The main problems were an inadequate book and periodical stock and insufficient reader spaces. In the transition to university status, Strathclyde was not given the financial support by the UGC which the 'green-field' universities enjoyed, possibly because it was mistakenly believed that its history ensured adequate provision. Some alleviation of overcrowding took place with the opening of the John C. Eaton Reading Room (opened in 1973), but major improvement was dependent upon the transfer of the main library to the Collins factory building (the Curran Building) in Cathedral Street. This exceedingly large property, acquired in 1973 at a cost exceeding £1 million, only became available for use in 1979-80 because of cuts in public expenditure in the intervening years.[36]

Another service in increasing use was the Audio-Visual Unit. Established in 1964 it was intended to examine ways of exploiting television for teaching purposes. One of its early experiments was the pre-recorded lectures in Mathematics already mentioned. It was also used in staff training, an area where the University of Strathclyde's Centre for Education Practice became a pioneer.[37]

The demand for computer services by departments led to the foundation of the Computer Centre with its own director. It was first extensively used by staff and postgraduates for research purposes but increasingly computers invaded other spheres. Student and financial records were computerised by the mid-1970s, and this enabled rapid calculation and assessment of a range of activities, especially market analysis of the student population.[38]

The building up of Welfare and Advisory Services for students was a steady process predating the Charter. The Student Medical Service was established in 1961, and excellent care and advice was provided by Dr William G. Manderson, Physician-Consultant at the Royal Infirmary, and his assistants who attended the University for a period every day in term. A Student Accommodation Office provided information about accommodation available through the University and lists of suitable lodgings. In 1964 the University acquired the Beresford Hotel (built in Sauchiehall Street, for the Empire Exhibition of 1938) which had gone through several changes of use. This was rehabilitated to provide over 340 student residence places and was called Baird Hall. In 1968 Balmanno Residence on campus was opened, and the first 'new-build' campus residence was Birkbeck Court (1972). Plans were ineffectually laid for the building of residences on Corporation land which was in fact used for Glasgow Polytechnic (now Caledonian University). However, the intention was clear: the University had a clear interest in providing more residential places for its student body.

Welfare services also included staff volunteers who agreed to counsel first-year students in their own School of Study. This was a patchy system which worked well in some areas of the University and not so well in others. A University chaplaincy emerged from initial efforts made by the Students' Association. A disused church, St Paul's, was converted to become an interdenominational centre and was in use from Session 1978-9. Chaplains were appointed to individual religious communities, and this service was extended according to student demand.[39]

An evening-class programme was traditional in the University and its antecedents, the main contact with the intelligent laity of the region. The range of endeavour was wide, from professional refresher training to cultural classes. Some mature people wanted more structured learning, occasionally seeking to join day classes on a part-time basis. By the late 1970s there were Continuing Education Certificates in Arts awarded for attendance at and examinations in three classes.[40]

Another feature of town/gown relations was the Collins Gallery with its exhibitions and shows. Usually, there were about a dozen of these events in any year, and they generally attracted media attention because of their interest and quality. Music and Theatre also flourished in this period. There was close liaison between the University and the Royal Scottish Academy of Music and Drama, and lunch-hour concerts, the annual March Entertainment, the University Chorus, the Jazz Club and the Big Band all made their mark in this period. The Strathclyde Theatre Group, formed in 1970, encouraged dramatic performances not only in the University but also at the Edinburgh Festival. Drama was poorly housed at first, but it made its way under Hugo Gifford's excellent leadership. By the late 1970s the Students' Association and the Court's Advisory Committee on Cultural Activities were able with external sponsorship to mount an Arts Festival.[41]

Student life beyond the classroom also flourished. In Sports and Athletics there were many achievements, personal and institutional: Bobby McGregor (Architecture), managed to dominate British swimming for about five years, representing the United Kingdom twice at the Olympic Games, and yet graduated to time. Alan Lawson (Hotel School), who captained the University Rugby Club in 1968-9, went on to grace the international scene. In Athletics, Frank Clement took the University's name to the heights of achievement. Whether in individual or team events, the University had acquired through the efforts of its students and the coaching staff an international reputation. Much sporting activity was for fun and companionship, but there was also the pleasure of winning![42]

Mooting and debating started from a low base at Strathclyde, but like student journalism and entertainment, their participants gained a considerable reputation well beyond the campus. The Students' Union extension was completed in 1976 and further added to the opportunities available for recreational activity. Relations between the student body and the University were remarkably good in this period, particularly when one considers what was happening during the late 1960s and early 1970s in other universities. The tone was set by Principal Curran and the Senior Officers, but they inherited a non-professorial staff attitude of support for student representation on the governing body of the Royal College. Most Strathclyde students lived at home, and this may have assisted the process of harmonious relations; the composition of the student body with a heavy preponderance of engineers and applied scientists, including a mature group, may also have been influential. However, it should be clearly stated that students never

TABLE 8.1   Physical and Economic Changes at Strathclyde University, 1960-1980

	1960	1980
Land area owned	45 acres	400 acres
Floor area of buildings	0.5 m sq. ft.	2 m sq. ft.
Annual revenue	£1 m	£20 m
Capital assets	£2.6 m	£34 m
Research contracts	£24,000 p.a.	£3 m
Student residential places	40	1,220
Full-time students	2,000	6,491
Staff	700	2,600

Source: JBC, University of Strathclyde *Gazette*, Autumn 1980; figures supplied by Louis McGougan.

felt excluded from staff advice and help (at all levels) during these years; indeed, there was generally an open-door policy at departmental level.[43]

Any conclusions about these years of growth for the University of Strathclyde must begin from the standpoint that a city-centre campus had been created in an unpromising environment. In the first ten years one of the oldest and most decayed parts of the city had been virtually transformed, and more was planned than could be achieved. At a capital cost of about £11 million, thirteen major buildings had been erected, and the clear outline of a university precinct could be detected. The hillside from George Street to Cathedral Street had lost its derelict and decaying properties. Not all were pleased with the architecture which replaced them, but money was not in abundance, and occupants were urgently moving from poorer accommodation. Landscaping and Gerald Laing's sculpture based on the standing stones of Callanish followed.

Apart from its impact on the City of Glasgow and the region, Strathclyde continued to stretch its influence overseas, as its antecedents had done since the 1850s. Members of staff attended international seminars, accepted secondment to help universities in the Commonwealth and elsewhere, and assisted the process of international recognition by the quality of their published research. Principal Curran favoured a two-way system of visiting professorships; he also selected a special association with Politechnika Lodzka during a visit to Poland which has endured since 1967 and broke the 'Iron Curtain' long before its frailty was exposed. Links were forged with universities in Europe, North America, and other parts of the world.[44]

By other measures it is easy to demonstrate that in the years of Sir Samuel Curran's Principalship, major advances had been made. Table 8.1 summarises many of them. Although many people make a University successful, including staff and students, the principal strategist in academic and other important matters was Sir Samuel Curran. Single-minded in his desire to advance the interests of the University, he could be sharp with critics or questioners who appeared, often unintentionally, in the early days to doubt the wisdom of a particular direction or policy. Once he was convinced that all were aiming for the same objective – as for instance, when Strathclyde in 1964 had to pursue the Carnegie Trust at law – his attitude was very different. The University developed a corporate spirit which enabled him to practise a more mellow style of leadership. He had become in these years the architect of Scotland's fifth university, 350 years after the foundation of the fourth.[45]

REFERENCES

1 Curran, *Issues in Science and Education*, pp. 198-246.

2 JBC, University of Strathclyde, *Gazette*, Autumn 1980, p.15. Interview of Principal Curran by Professor Esmond Wright; University *Gazette*, January 1974, pp.5-9; April 1974, pp. 16-19.

3 John Graham, *One Hundred and Twenty Five Years* (1964), pp. 4-11.

4 SUA, B1/4 Minute Book of the Andersonian, 1830-64, 17 November 1845; 29 April 1846; JBC, GWSTC, Calendar 1892 ff; RTC, Governors' Minutes, 1946-7, pp. 175-6; Graham, pp. 47-8.

5 Curran, *Issues in Science and Education*, pp. 62-3; JBC, Confidential Memorandum on the Proposed Merger of the Scottish College of Commerce with the Royal College of Science and Technology, 6 February, 1964, p.1.

6 JBC, Copy letter, Sir Keith Murray to S.C. Curran, 21 August, 1963.

7 Confidential Memorandum ... 6 February, 1964, p.2.

8 JBC, Minutes of Joint Working Party of the Colleges, September-December 1963.

9 JBC, Copy Draft Agreement between the Colleges, 1964.

10 JBC, Minutes of Academic Board, November 1963, p.25; Scottish College of Commerce, Governors' Minutes, 27 December 1963; RCST, Council Minutes, 24 December, 1963.

11 Ibid., Academic Board Minutes, March 1964; Final Agreement between the Colleges, 11 May 1964.

12 Ibid., Academic Board Minutes, 1963-4, *passim*.

13 Charter of the University of Strathclyde.

14 JBC, 'Transition' Committee Minutes, presented to Academic Board, 17 March, 1964.

15 SUA, E1/1/38 RCST, College Governors' Council Minutes, 1960-1, pp. 24, 26; E1/1/39, RCST, College Council Minutes, 1961-3, pp. 21, 30, 89-90; E1/1/40 RCST College Council Minutes, p.34.

16 JBC, *Prism*, March 1994, Tribute to Louis McGougan by Sir Samuel Curran.

17 G.P. Richardson, *A Decade of Progress 1964-74* (University of Strathclyde, 1974), pp. 33-4; JBC, A.S.T. Thomson, Notes on Development of Technology in ... the University of Strathclyde, 1964-74, pp. 13-19; JBC, Annual Reports, 1964-80, *passim*; University *Gazette*, Spring 1978, pp. 18-20.

18 Richardson, p. 34; Thomson, p.20; Annual Reports, 1964-80, *passim*; *Prism*, August 1993, Obituary of Emeritus Professor Alexander Scott; JBC, Notes on Chemical Engineering, 1964-74.

19 Richardson, p.34; Thomson, pp.21-2; JBC, Naval Architecture at Strathclyde, 1964-74; Annual Reports, 1964-80, *passim*; University *Gazette*, Spring 1979, pp. 6-8.

20 Richardson, p.34; Buchan, *A Godly Heritage* ... , pp. 37-40; Thomson, pp.23-5; Annual Reports, 1964-80, *passim*.

21 Thomson, p.26; Annual Reports, 1964-80, *passim*; Richardson, p.35.

22 Richardson, p.35; Thomson, pp. 27-29; Annual Reports, 1967-80, *passim*.

23 JBC, Notes on Electrical and Electronic Engineering, 1964-74; Richardson, p.35; Thomson, pp.30-1; *Centenary Brochure*, pp.8-9; Annual Reports, 1964-80, *passim*.

24 Richardson, p.27; Annual Reports, 1964-80, *passim*; Pack, pp. 6-8.

25 Annual Reports, 1970-80, *passim*; Richardson, p.29.

26 Annual Reports, 1964-80, *passim*; Richardson, p.27.

27 Annual Reports, 1964-80, *passim*; Nuttall, pp.12-16; Richardson, p.28.

28 RCST, Governors' Minutes, 1957-8, p.154; Annual Reports, 1964-80, *passim*; *Prism*, June 1993, Obituary of Emeritus Professor Reginald Meredith; Richardson, p.31; University *Gazette*, Winter 1977, p.27; Spring 1978, p.32.

29 Richardson, p.31; Annual Reports, 1964-80, *passim*; *Prism*, December 1992, Obituary of Professor John Taylor; Ibid., January, 1993, Obituary of Professor Norman Petch.

30 Annual Reports, 1964-80, *passim*; Richardson, p.29; University *Gazette*, Summer 1978, pp. 5-7.

31 Annual Reports, 1964-80, *passim*; Richardson, pp. 29-30; Curran, *Issues in Science and Education*, p.102.

32 Annual Reports, 1964-80, *passim*; Richardson, p.37; H.C.S. Ferguson to J. Butt, 25 January 1982, History of Architecture Department; University *Gazette*, Summer 1980, pp.6-8.

33 Annual Reports, 1964-80, *passim*; Richardson, pp. 39-40; J. Butt and J.T. Ward, eds., *Scottish Themes: Essays in Honour of Professor S.G.E. Lythe* (Edinburgh, 1976), pp. vii-ix and xi-xiv; Curran, *Issues in Science and Education*, pp. 65 and 81; Correspondence between Professor M.M. Fraile and J. Butt, 1972-present; University *Gazette*, Spring 1979, pp. 14-15.

34 Curran, *Issues in Science and Education*, pp. 62-9; Richardson, pp. 41-4; Annual Reports, 1964-80, *passim*; University *Gazette*, Winter 1978-9, p.20.

35 University *Gazette*, January 1974, pp. 14-15 and 23; Curran, *Issues in Science and Education.*, pp. 116-19; *Prism*, March 1994.

36 JBC, RTC, Governors' Minutes, 1952-3, p.155; SUA, E1/1/40, RCST, Council Minutes, p.34; Annual Reports, 1964-80, *passim*; Richardson, p.45; Curran, *Issues in Science and Education*, pp. 130-1; University *Gazette*, June 1974, pp. 27-32.

37 Annual Reports, 1964-80, *passim*; Richardson, p.34; University *Gazette*, Spring 1975, p.32; Winter 1976, pp.2-4.

38 Richardson, pp. 45-6; Annual Reports, 1975-80, *passim*.

39 SUA, E1/1/38, RCST, Governors' Minutes, 1960-1, p.131; Richardson, p.46; Curran, *Issues in Science and Education.*, pp. 131ff; University *Gazette*, Spring 1976, pp.5-6; Winter 1978-9, p.4.

40 Peter Nelson was the first Director appointed in 1976. Annual Reports, 1972-80, *passim*; University *Gazette*, Spring 1978, pp. 27-9; Spring 1979, pp.4-5.

41 University *Gazette*, January 1974, pp. 30-3; April 1974, pp. 35-8; Summer 1976, pp. 15-17, 20; Summer 1977, pp. 27-8; Autumn 1977, pp. 19-20 and 32-3; Winter 1977, pp.21-2; Summer 1979, pp. 24-9.

42 *The Student Telegraph* and University *Gazette* in this period carry regular reports of sporting and recreational activities, in the latter case usually a report by Duncan Matheson, Director of Physical Education; *Handbook and Directory of the Scottish Hotel School* (compiled by David Gee, 1994), p.9.

43 Curran, *Issues in Science and Education*, pp. 136-7, 105-113; Richardson, p.46; Annual Reports, 1964-80, *passim*.

44 Curran, *Issues in Science and Education*, pp. 82-5, 105-113; University *Gazette*, Autumn 1977, pp.3-8.

45 Curran, *Issues in Science and Education*, pp. 69-71.

CHAPTER NINE

The University in the 1980s

'Certainly Strathclyde is on an independent course seeking ... to manage its own affairs for the benefit of its students, its staff and, not least, of Glasgow, Scotland and the U.K. Such a path of sturdy independence would be in keeping with our Founder's view of higher education ...'

Sir Graham J. Hills, *Annual Report*, February, 1988

AFTER AN UNTYPICAL PERIOD OF ILLNESS, Sir Samuel Curran retired as Principal in 1980, having served the Royal College and the University for over twenty years. His successor was Graham John Hills (1925-), appointed by the Court after consultation with the Senate (in accordance with Statute IV). In several respects Graham Hills might be regarded as in the Andersonian tradition despite his lack of previous connection with Scotland. After leaving school early, he began his career as a chemical research assistant with May and Baker Ltd. in 1941, combining this with part-time study at Birkbeck College and graduating B.Sc. in Physical Chemistry in 1946. Thereafter he completed his Ph.D. (1950) and D.Sc. (1962) at Birkbeck, having moved into academic life in 1949 as a lecturer in Physical Chemistry at Imperial College. In 1962 Dr Hills was appointed to the Chair in Physical Chemistry at Southampton University where he spent eighteen years. During this period he held several senior administrative posts: Chairman of the University's Board of Extra-Mural Studies (1964-74), Dean of Science (1974-6) and Public Orator (1975-8). From 1976 Professor Hills was Deputy Vice-Chancellor of the University and encouraged the development of four-year and five-year degree courses in science and engineering similar to those at Strathclyde and post-experience short courses. His experience also included visiting professorships at Western Ontario, Cleveland and Buenos Aires and important offices on professional and academic committees – the Faraday Society, Chemical Society, Royal Institute of Chemistry, Science Research Council Data Advisory Panel and the British Association for the Advancement of Science.[1] Shortly before joining Strathclyde Graham Hills married Mary, his second wife, a tremendous support during his tenure who took up a number of good causes which he might justifiably have missed.

It was not the best of times to be joining the University as Principal. For a number of years the economic philosophy of monetarism had been gaining ground in government and among public servants. The Bank of England had created money supply targets from 1973 in the forlorn hope that government would accept them, without any need for external pressure, as a means of reducing the rising tide of inflation. Pressure from the balance of payments and then from the International Monetary Fund forced the Labour Chancellor, Denis Healey, in 1976 to accept monetary targets, to cut projected public expenditure and through Shirley Williams at the Department of Education to impose full-cost tuition fees on overseas students. Thus, changes in university funding were initiated, although with no deeply held commitment to Milton Friedman's ideas about cutting social expenditure.

For the Labour Government's monetarism did not involve an ideological commitment to the free market. Inflation had, in fact, peaked in August 1975 at 16.9 per cent and by June 1978 the rate had fallen to 7.4 per cent, and yet the average growth rate for the economy between 1976 and 1979 was 2.7 per cent. It was the attempt to restrain the growth of wages and the response of the unions to that aspect of monetarism which was largely responsible for Mrs. Thatcher's first electoral success in 1979. Essentially a product of self-help, Margaret Thatcher produced a novel brand of conservatism which largely destroyed the influence of the Tory grandees and introduced a sea-change in economic ideas. Individualism, an end to state bureaucracy known as 'rolling back the state', and a self-conscious populist radicalism were central to her notions of 'Victorian values'. Beneath these pillars of Thatcherism stood a commitment to supply-side Friedmanite economics – 'privatisation', tight monetary controls via interest rate management, lower taxes and lower public expenditure, and freer markets. These were the instruments for arresting Britain's relative economic decline, or so it was believed.[2]

'Stop-go' economic policies had afflicted British universities before the Thatcher era, but what was new arose from supply-side economics. A university had to behave like an efficient business, providing value for money in the market place, satisfying client groups such as students and employers and demonstrating a research capacity which could be assessed. It followed that greater public accountability would become a central tenet of the 1980s. Individualism involved a notion of social responsibility as well as economic freedom. If universities provided education of merit, students should be prepared, it was thought, to obtain it at less cost to the state and more cost to them or to their parents. Mass higher education could not be an objective of government at the old prices: value for money meant a reduction in the unit of resource provided by the state. Operational efficiency in universities needed to be checked: quality audit and assessment were certain to emerge as instruments of educational policy.

Many of these ideas were totally foreign to the managers and staffs of universities, and many vice-chancellors did not detect the full implications for their institutions of the sea-change in social and economic ideology. Graham Hills was not one of them. He was committed to extending access to American or Japanese levels but did not believe government of any party would pay the traditional price for such a policy. Moreover, he was among the first to see where Thatcherism would lead the universities and, therefore, recognised the need for drastic change in style and governance. An early interview given to *The Times* indicated his agenda, which was percipient to a high degree: a commitment to debate and discussion about the objectives of higher education; the need for reform of what he clearly regarded as a slow-changing, conservative, defensive world; an elevation of student choice and broader education; commitment to access and innovative approaches to the teaching and learning experience; a review of the academic year which implied a move to semesters and modular courses. His liberal ideas also included his belief that markets work better than governments in producing beneficent changes, and at the domestic level this meant that academics in their departments knew better than administrators how best to deploy the resources available to universities.

Some of these ideas struck a responsive chord at Strathclyde; others did not. However, Graham Hills enjoyed challenges, and the tradition of Strathclyde ensured that radical thinking and innovation, if not always joyously accepted, would somehow triumph.[3] Discussion had already begun in Sir Samuel Curran's period on how to deal with the financial difficulties facing the University (1977 onwards), which inevitably centred on reducing staff costs. Louis McGougan, the Bursar, invented the idea of early retirement with part-time re-engagement

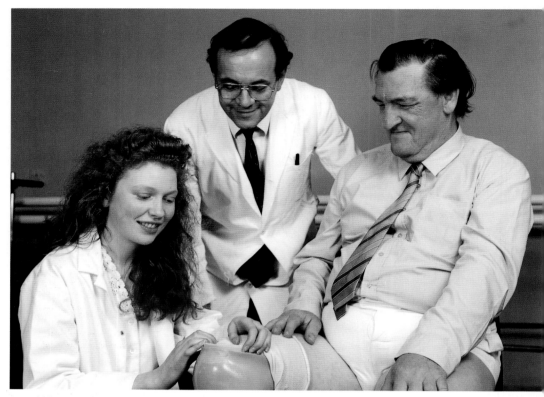

42 Useful learning is central to the ethos of the University of Strathclyde and so is service to the community. An amputee is being fitted with a new limb by a student in training at the Centre for Prosthetics and Orthotics.

before the UGC devised a similar scheme framed in the context of English universities. The University Court had seen reserves wiped out after two years of deficits (1977-9) arising from public expenditure cuts and decided not to expect any largesse from government in 1979-80 but to reduce expenditure by five per cent (£800,000 in a full year). By the time of Graham Hills' appointment, the University had embarked on the self-help route to solvency as a consequence of the decisions of Sir (1976) John W. Atwell (1911-), the Chairman of Court (1975-80), and his colleagues.[4]

Budget Day 1981 brought further news of public expenditure cuts which up to 1984 were projected to amount to 14 per cent in real terms. Graham Hills took the view that universities could not expect to escape the privations endured by British society during the depression of the early 1980s. He felt that the continued evolution of the University pointed to larger units of organisation, and in 1982 four faculties were formed from the nine schools – Science, Engineering, Arts and Social Studies, Business Studies. The allocation and re-allocation of resources changed in line with the transformation of the schools into faculties; devolution of resources, at first limited, to the new units allowed academic staff to make their spending and savings priorities within the framework of a university financial plan, which provided for the retention of a strategic fund at the centre. Two things were regarded as essential: flexibility in responding to opportunities and dangers, and recognition of the University's total interest.[5] Generally, this devolved system with a resource allocation formula has stood the test of time. Deans of faculties have assumed greater responsibilities and powers but they depend on the goodwill of their constituents, the academic staff.

43 and 44 Stalwarts from the laity! In the difficult financial years of the 1980s (left) Dr Stephen Newall, Chairman of Finance Committee and University Treasurer (1984-8) and Chairman of Court (1988-93), and (right) Dr Tom Johnston, alumnus and University Treasurer (1988-93), provided expert advice to their academic and administrative colleagues.

By Session 1982-3 the University's recurrent financial position was satisfactory. The Premature Retirement Compensation Scheme, approved by the UGC to the point of meeting some of its costs, produced major economies in staff costs. Reductions in expenditure in other areas were made but were less important because staffing was the major cost within the University's accounts. Attempts to increase income from sources other than the UGC were also made: fees from overseas students (11 per cent of the student body) rose significantly to the point where about 40 per cent of all fee income derived from this source. Sponsored research and contract work were substantial and increasing. A positive response to government restrictions on funding, these activities required a better administrative base, and in 1982-3 a full-scale reorganisation took place leading to the formation of the Research and Development Office with a mandate to promote industrial research and development, the transfer of science and technology to the economy on a profitable basis and the protection of the University's intellectual property rights.[6]

The surplus in 1982-3, £260,000, was the basis of the Academic Development Fund which was used to underwrite and pump-prime new initiatives. Yet the University still faced major problems, especially in the area of replacing scientific equipment, so necessary if it was to keep pace with modern developments. The objective of becoming less dependent on direct government funding could only be achieved progressively over a number of years; this policy was both a cause and a consequence of Strathclyde's becoming even more of an entrepreneurial University. To use the UGC's own metaphor, the University climbed aboard the financial up-escalator through its own efforts.[7]

Whereas in 1982-3 the UGC provided 64.9 per cent of income, by 1985-6 it provided 58.2 per cent. In the latter session tuition fee income rose by 10 per cent, and overseas fee income accounted for just over 10 per cent of total revenue. Sponsored research income represented 17.8

TABLE 9.1   Revenue Account: Sources of Income (£m) (1985-90)

Year	UGC / UFC	Fees	Research Grants and Contracts	Other Income	Total
1985	25	9	6	1	41.9
1986	27	10	8	1	46.5
1987	29	10.5	9.7	1.8	51.8
1988	30.6	11.3	10	2.3	55.2
1989	34	11.8	12.3	3.5	63
1990	38.3	12.6	13.7	12.8	79.6

Source: Annual Reports, 1985-90.

per cent of total revenue compared with 14.2 per cent in 1982-3, indicating still further the ability of the University to develop commercial and industrial relationships. Thus, the University of Strathclyde became firmly committed to that independent course which Principal Hills commented upon in his foreword to the Annual Report of 1986-7. Difficult financial circumstances, essentially produced by reductions in real terms of the resources made available by government, had been effectively handled. In the late 1980s, there was some concern about a possible shortfall in overseas fee income, and budgets were set generally assuming lower revenue from this source than happened in practice. It was a sensible precaution, but more significant was the greater rise in income from other sources, especially from research contracts and services rendered.[8]

Despite an accumulated surplus, after sensible provisions for staff restructuring costs and other items, in 1986-7 cuts in expenditure with savings targets for the faculties were in place because of what appeared to be a hostile financial environment. The main feature of prudent financial planning was accurate forecasting and ensuring that faculties had the maximum notice of the need for savings and for additional income generation. In this regard the University was greatly assisted in the late 1980s and early 1990s by the business experience of lay members of Court, particularly Stephen Newall and Tom Johnston who were in the key positions of Chairman and Treasurer.

The end of an era came in 1988-9 with the demise of the UGC and its replacement by the Universities Funding Council. This new body was empowered to achieve economy and effectiveness in the of public money and efficiency in university management. Principal Hills disliked the prospect of blind bidding by institutions one against the other for government subsidy, instead favouring a system where the universities received nothing from the government directly, and vouchers for the real cost of higher education were issued to students. Thus the market could operate relatively freely, and universities gain their financial and academic independence. He anticipated great improvement in the general standard of teaching and pastoral care once students became customers of universities; the government dallied with the idea but did not implement it.[9]

As Table 9.1 indicates, the main sources of income between 1985 and 1990 had changed in terms of their relative significance. In volume terms all sources had grown but the sharpest rate of increase had occurred under 'Other Income' and 'Research Grants and Contracts'. Strathclyde had done better than most universities from UGC/UFC grants but their relative importance to total income progressively declined from 64.9 per cent in 1982-3, to 58.2 per cent in 1985-6 and down to 48.11 per cent in 1990-1. Fee income had accounted for 18.7 per cent in 1982-3 and had declined marginally to 15.83 per cent in 1990-1. Research grants and contracts commonly are a balancing item on both sides of the account but provide vital financial support for additional staff; they accounted for 14.2 per cent of total income in 1982-3 and 17.21 per cent in 1990-1. 'Other Income' represented 1.6 per cent of total income in 1982-3 and 16.08 per cent in 1990-1, a ten-fold increase. The decade had begun with the wiping out of accumulated reserves arising from cuts in public expenditure and ended with an accumulated surplus of over half a million pounds, an insubstantial amount considering the general size of the business which the University represented, but clearly on the right side of the balance.

Principal Hills perceived the management structure of the University to be too diffuse through the committee system typical of most universities. He therefore devoted considerable energy to making Strathclyde a better managed university, in particular attempting to reduce the number of committees and the time taken to make decisions. The appointment of the Jarratt Committee (on Efficiency in Universities) confirmed his opinion that decision-making procedures had to be improved, and with Court's agreement in session 1987-8 a joint committee with Senate was established, the University Management Group [UMG], responsible to both but, in effect, the principal day-to-day operational manager of the University. It comprised the Principal, Vice-Principal, Deputy Principals, Deans, Chairman of Court, Treasurer and other appropriate Court Officers, the Registrar and Bursar. This structure was reinforced by the University Management Secretariat which was responsible for ensuring that papers were properly prepared for UMG, and where appropriate new options papers were produced. The unification of the administration – finance, property, and academic services and administration – under the University Secretary later completed the transition to a form of business management. Senior Officers – Vice-Principal and Deputy Principals and Secretary – became major budget-holders alongside the Deans, responsible to Court and Senate via UMG.[10]

A clear system for dealing with the wide range of University business soon emerged from UMG aided by the activities of the University Management Secretariat [UMS]. The main areas were UGC and other external matters, academic and strategic planning, finance, estates and buildings and important staff questions. UMG, although making recommendations to Court and Senate on new matters of policy, was given freedom to implement already agreed courses of action.[11] For instance, UMG reviewed the position of Spanish Studies in September 1987 in preparation for a visit by representatives of UGC. The UGC Report on Hispanic Studies had favoured discontinuation of the subject at Strathclyde, a recommendation inconsistent with the University's own academic plan; UMG, therefore, decided to continue support for Spanish and emphasised the special features of language teaching at Strathclyde to the visiting group.[12] Rationalisation and change were, however, built into plans prepared for the UGC up to 1990, especially the submission of a 'balance sheet' of early retirements, cases of voluntary severance and new staff appointments, some involving retraining costs. As part of the University's Academic Plan, this 'balance sheet' was, in effect, a bid for UGC financial support.[13]

From 1985 external environmental pressures were such that a 'Rolling Academic Plan' revised annually had become essential, for it was not possible to stick to a fixed quinquennial plan, for so long favoured by UGC. The four Faculties submitted their revised academic plans; the University Management Secretariat from 1987 reviewed them to ensure their consistency and to draw to the attention of UMG any implications for the University's overall planning; such matters as home student numbers, overseas student numbers, and resource allocation might well arise from Faculties' plans. After UMG had discussed the latest version of the draft 'Rolling Plan' which incorporated the individual plans of the Faculties, it was transmitted to Court and Senate where it was extensively scrutinised, revised in detail, and hopefully approved.[14]

Major issues were dealt with by UMG 'Green Papers'. These were discussion papers which might, with Court and Senate approval, have a relatively wide circulation within the University. The objectives were transparency of procedures and consultation. In 1987 there was a Green Paper on Resource Allocation and the formula in use and another on the Rolling Academic Plan. In 1988 Green Papers were devoted to the reorganisation of the University's teaching year (with the first proposals for semesterisation), staff appraisal, and the recruitment strategy regarding overseas students. A major issue properly decided by Court alone was the clear commitment that the University should be an 'Equal Opportunities Employer'; other details for implementation of this policy, including advertising, were left to UMG.[15]

The outcome from Green Papers can perhaps be illustrated by one important example. Resource allocation was a process with a certain historical inertia incorporated within it. Existing Faculty budgets at first had been built up by aggregating departmental budgets and then adjusted annually to take account of inflation or savings targets which had to be met. The main objection to this approach was its preservation of previous allocations of resources. Thus some departments, historically well-funded, continued to be so rather than reaching that position by a rational planning decision based upon agreed University priorities. Rapid changes in student load needed to be matched by some redistribution of resources. UGC was using formula funding, but total funds available to the University were below an aggregation based upon national average unit costs. Thus, a resource allocation formula had to be created which would distribute the available funds equitably. Correction of anomalies could not be achieved instantly, and therefore, the formula had to produce manageable budgets for the Faculties and for Central Services and yet phase in change. Thus the agreed formula provided for a basic level of funding and a 'steering' element of 15 per cent designed to reward prowess and to provide incentives. The Green Paper did make the resource allocation process intelligible to the University community and also indicated, clearly, the agreed priorities.[16]

Preparation for UGC and Research Council inquiries on such matters as special initiatives in Engineering, research selectivity exercises, and interdisciplinary research centres was initiated by UMG with Senior Officers carrying direct responsibility. For instance, Professor John Sherwood had special responsibility as Deputy Principal for research (including the Research and Development Office) and therefore was heavily involved in co-ordinating departmental and faculty responses to the Research Selectivity Exercises and in promoting research centres. Overseas student recruitment (and the International Office) became the remit of Vice-Principal (and Deputy Principal) David Tedford. Reports on progress were made by particular services direct to UMG at frequencies determined by it. For instance, the Estates and Buildings Division tended to report more frequently than the Librarian or the Careers Service. Some reports were timed for specific meetings because of their importance at particular times in the academic session. Admissions were monitored by Deans in the summer and early autumn, for example, and UMG received frequent reports via the Secretary's office on how recruitment was proceeding during this period against the quotas which had been previously set. Reviews of departments, and services and structural changes which the Faculties wished to implement, were also discussed at UMG. Perhaps most important of all in terms of the future progress of the University, UMG was empowered by Court and Senate to consider bids from Faculties against the Development Fund and to make allocations from it.[17]

The gradual erosion of the binary line between the public sector colleges and the universities was welcomed at Strathclyde because it was felt that positive gains could result from collaboration with institutions in the West of Scotland. A joint working party with Glasgow College (now Glasgow Caledonian University) was established by UMG and a number of worthwhile initiatives emerged from its discussions. These included a joint course in Industrial

45 Scottish Hotel Students prepare a feast for the world's top gourmet club, the Confrèrie de la Chaine des Rôtisseurs in February 1991. Courtesy of Caledonian Newspapers Ltd.

Mathematics and the flotation of the Scottish School of Journalism, both postgraduate instructional enterprises.[18]

It should be clear that UMG was designed to improve and expedite decision-making by the University's sovereign bodies, Senate and Court, and in no way infringed upon their powers and responsibilities. Court had, in fact, made some major decisions before the establishment of UMG which were to have a significant and positive impact upon the University's development. For instance, the relocation of the Scottish Hotel School (1982) to new accommodation in Cathedral Street (officially opened by Reo Stakis in 1983) was preceded by the decision to sell Ross Hall (1981), its premises since Session 1948-9. Morrin Square and Collins Street were purchased in 1982 for use as student residences; the idea of a student village was revived, but it was to be part of the campus. The decision was made to sell the outlying residences, including Chesters Residential Management Centre, in order to fund campus development; this policy was implemented over the next three years. An anonymous benefaction of £500,000 had been received by the University in 1981 for the building of a new student residence, and this became the catalyst for imaginative developments over the next dozen years. Murray Hall, built in a native Scottish style and clearly influenced by Charles Rennie Mackintosh, was substantially funded by the anonymous benefaction and was the first (1984) of the new residences. A week earlier, the Lord Todd (1984) was opened, sited close to Murray Hall, the social centre of the Campus Village and Townhead which provided restaurant, bar, lounge, recreational and laundry facilities and linked with Birkbeck Court (1972). Garnett Hall (1986), Forbes Hall (1987) and the 'solar residences' were to follow.[19]

The gradual acquisition of land in Townhead including the Barony Church made the realisation of the Student Village concept feasible, and the way was cleared for expansion to the line of the planned ring road. Stretching from George Street to the Cathedral, the Campus had acquired a unity and cohesion which was bound to breathe new life into an old area of the city. Provand's Lordship and the Cathedral and the High Street represented the old heart of Glasgow, and landscaping (completed in 1984) improved amenity and environment for staff and students in a substantial adjacent area.[20]

Lay members of Court and Estates and Property Services staff combined with academics in other physical developments. The purchase of Marland House, the old British Telecommunications building, was completed in 1987; work soon began on what is now the Sir Graham Hills Building to make parts of it useable but it was to be a long haul, a gradual process dependent on resources becoming available. Glasgow Corporation, an old partner in the University's history, participated in a number of ventures. Part of Castlemilk housing estate was refurbished by the Corporation and provided student housing. The leased Exchange House, on the corner of George Street and Montrose Street opposite the Royal College, came into use (1987-8) for the Centre for Computer Integrated Manufacture, the Transputer Centre, the Information Technology Associate Company Scheme and the British Telecom Software Centre. The major task of refurbishing the Royal College began.[21]

Undoubtedly, for many members of the University the major achievement, in terms of physical development, was the magnificent restoration of the Barony Church. A ceremonial hall especially to take the large congregations at graduations, had been a serious deficiency in the University's estate. Sir Graham Hills saw the possibilities which the Barony presented. A fine Gothic building (1886-90) by one of Scotland's most distinguished architectural firms, Burnet, Son and Campbell, it is usually attributed to Sir John J. Burnet, although it is not clear which partner of the firm was responsible for the design. The eastern chapel was the Allan Glen's Chapel of Remembrance, a sombre connection with the Royal Technical College since so many Allan Glen pupils made their way there before joining the forces. After purchase from the Church of Scotland for a nominal sum in 1984, essential repair work was carried out in 1987 and the building brought into limited use. In 1990 the restoration programme began in earnest with Maurice Hickey watching the University's interest and funding being provided by the University, Historic Buildings and Monuments Council, Glasgow District Council and the Scottish Development Agency. Other donors assisted the completion of restoration, and Barony Hall was first used for the installation of the second Chancellor, the Right Honourable the Lord Tombs of Brailes in April 1991.[22]

In summary, sixteen major projects authorised by the Court were completed from 1980 to 1990 — a new computer centre and library in the Curran Building opened by the Right Honourable George Younger, MP, Secretary of State for Scotland, the Engineering Applications Centre, and eight new halls of residence. Three important purchases were made: the Ramshorn Church which became the home of Strathclyde Theatre Group; Marland House; and the Barony Church. Additional land was bought south of George Street where the possibilities for locating new research centres and providing further residences will be explored. In 1989 the Court adopted a new Campus plan which very rapidly required additions when the merger with Jordanhill College became a possibility in 1991. Ambitious plans for Ross Priory on Loch Lomond (purchased in 1971), for the sports ground at Stepps, and for a new Business School were also in place.[23]

Such an expansion of property assets in a period of marked financial stringency for universities and generally high interest rates placed obvious pressures on the University's capital account. Without anatomising debate or discussion at varying levels within the University, the full extent of concern cannot be properly assessed. However, it is sufficient to say that great

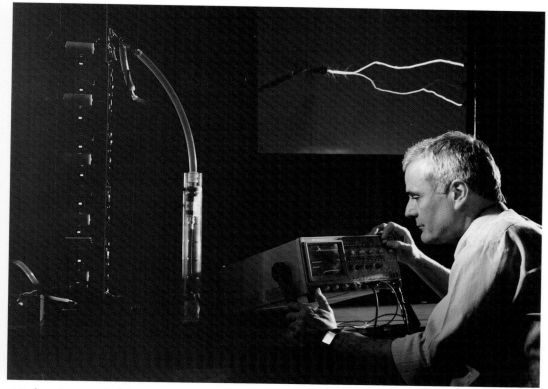

46 Professor Owen Farish of the Centre for Electrical Power Engineering investigating electrical discharges on insulator surfaces using a high-voltage lightning surge generator.

business skills were deployed by Court and its officers as well as by the Bursar and Finance Office staff to secure the necessary long-term funding. As Tom Johnston, Treasurer of the University, reported in 1989, delay in completing these negotiations had the effect of reducing the University's working capital, and the temptation to seek short-term funding had to be avoided 'if possible because of the less advantageous interest rate'. Adequate long-term facilities were provided by the University's bankers, and by 1991 the net book value of land and buildings was over £85 million, of which nearly £21 million was in the form of freehold student residences.[24]

Senate tenaciously guarded what it believed to be the University's academic interests in these difficult years. UGC was intent on rationalisation by which was meant the closing of some departments in universities and the merging of others. Mining, Geology and Philosophy were three examples of academic areas with which, UGC believed, the country was over-supplied. After much resistance Mining at Strathclyde was closed, Geology transferred to the University of Glasgow and Philosophy phased out. The restructuring of Social Sciences brought a threat to Sociology but this discipline, after the retirement and death of Professor Andrew Sykes, became part of a very effective Department of Government. The commitment to a federal Department of Modern Languages probably saved those sections with relatively small staff numbers, but the vitality of the language teaching and the degree in Modern Languages and its growing importance to an international University, intent on forging more links with Europe, were equally significant to the Faculty of Arts and Social Studies and ultimately to Senate.[25]

The senior officers chosen by Senate during this period to represent its interests and concerns

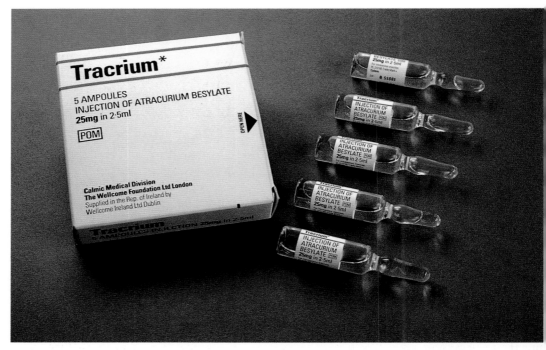

47 Behind the University's academic development in the later 1980s lay the growing income from Professor B.Stenlake's atracurium, the new muscle relaxant marketed by the Wellcome Foundation. Royalties from sales had risen to over £1,000,000 by 1990-1.

had already acquired reputations for high-quality teaching and research – Professor Hamish C. S. Wood of Organic Chemistry, Professor David John Tedford of Electrical Engineering and Professor William Bowman of Physiology and Pharmacology. While taking a University-wide view that allowed no favourites, they promoted ideas for improving teaching and research facilities and aided the Deans when fundamental academic values were threatened. Principal Hills was concerned to avoid academic stagnation in the face of difficult economic circumstances to the point of occasionally provoking Senate. He felt the need to improve the Faculties of Science and Engineering in the early 1980s was more urgent than amelioration elsewhere, and hindsight confirms his opinion.[26]

Despite the temptation to freeze staff appointments when expenditure had to be cut, Principal Hills believed that would produce fatal hypothermia for the University's progress. Additional appointments were made in strategic areas: a second Chair in Electrical Engineering in 1980, and Chairs in Electronics and Physics (Photonics) in 1982. Academic rebuilding took place elsewhere: in 1982-3 personal chairs were given to Professor Allen in the Centre for the Study of Public Policy, to Professor Durrani in Electronics, to Professor McGettrick in Computer Science, to Professor Ottaway in Chemistry and to Professor Smith in Geography. Significant replacements were appointed at professorial level in Statistics (Professor Ripley), in the Hotel School (Professor Jeffries), and in Pharmacy (Professor Midgley). The 'anti-freeze' in 1982-3 was clearly effective![27]

Undoubtedly, the financial saviour of the University's academic development in the later 1980s was the growing income from Professor John B. Stenlake's atracurium, the new muscle relaxant marketed by the Wellcome Foundation and the consummation of twelve years of research. Largely because of its sales in America, by 1984-5 royalties topped £338,000, well over half a million by 1988-9, and over a million by 1990-1.[28] It is not that new academic

TABLE 9.2 Full-time Student Numbers, 1979-91

Session	Undergraduate	Postgraduate	Total
1979-80	5497	994	6491
1980-1	5630	1038	6668
1981-2	5756	1038	6794
1982-3	5778	1104	6882
1983-4	5842	1257	7099
1984-5	6119	1282	7401
1985-6	6113	1367	7480
1986-7	6111	1435	7546
1987-8	6171	1459	7630
1988-9	6320	1443	7763
1989-90	6577	1484	8061
1990-1	6771	1488	8259

Sources: JBC, Annual Reports, 1979-1991.

developments would not have occurred but, rather, changes were made with less discomfort than might otherwise have been the case. As it was, significant numbers of staff took advantage of the premature retirement scheme, and savings thereby made for increased manoeuvrability.

A refusal to be diverted from the strategic objectives of the University – the growth of the Campus Village, reorganisation of departments into four large faculties, devolved budgeting, an improved estate, and flexible academic planning – also included a clear decision to increase student numbers which is detailed in Table 9.2 Between Session 1979-80 and Session 1990-1, undergraduate numbers had increased by over 23 per cent, postgraduate numbers by slightly less than 50 per cent and the total student population by over 27 per cent. The balance within that population had also changed as indicated in Table 9.3. There was a steady growth in the postgraduate proportion of a larger total student population, coming close to the SISTER concept of the Robbins Committee.

Examining the student population by Faculty and taking account of the flexibility of movement between departments and faculties, especially at the end of the first undergraduate year, an interesting story emerges from comparing Table 9.4 (Full-time Student Numbers by Faculty, 1981-2) with the same data for Session 1990-1 given in Table 9.5. Total applications rose by about 8 per cent over this period, and intake by only 6 per cent. Well qualified applicants able to benefit from a university education were either being turned away to Further Education and particularly to centrally funded colleges, or were being compelled to return to school with a view to meeting higher competitive entry standards or were temporarily abandoning the idea of undergraduate study. Applications for Science places were at best stable (taking account of entry

TABLE 9.3 Percentage Composition of Student Population, 1979-91

Session	Undergraduate	Postgraduate
1979-80	84.69	15.31
1984-5	82.68	17.32
1990-1	81.98	18.02

Source: Derived from Table 9.2.

TABLE 9.4   Full-time Student Numbers by Faculty, 1981-2

	Science	Engineering	Arts and Social Studies	Business	Total
Applications	4934	5278	2747	3330	16289
Intake	521	706	306	401	1934
Undergraduate	1614	1850	1000	1292	5756
PG Research	209	111	25	41	386
PG Instruction	66	159	68	359	652
Total	1889	2120	1093	1692	6794
First Degrees	334	410	236	355	1335
Higher Degrees	123	160	34	125	442
Diplomas	1	12	42	207	262

Source: JBC, Annual Report, 1981-2.

into joint Science/Engineering courses in 1990-1) and those for Engineering declining while demand was buoyant for places in the Business School and in the Faculty of Arts and Social Studies. Staff/student ratios in these last two Faculties were allowed to drift upwards but consistent with reasonable pastoral care; balancing the University budget was partly achieved by this method. Postgraduate instructional courses were most significant in the Business School at the beginning and end of this period, but in all Faculties greater numbers were graduating in 1990-1 than in 1981-2. The social composition of the student body became more international as the period proceeded, although the impact of European exchanges was yet to be fully felt. In terms of occupational classification of parents, the Strathclyde undergraduate population was probably the most egalitarian of any Scottish university, but the lowest economic groups were not sending their offspring to universities in numbers consistent with their general significance in society. Local recruitment of the bulk of students was still most important to the University, but its effects were much modified by wider recruitment both in Scotland and the United Kingdom and overseas.[29]

Table 9.6 giving details of staffing in this period reveals a fall in total staffing from 1982-3 to 1985-6 and then an increase especially in academic staff up to 1990-1. More research contracts leading to many short-term research posts, generally externally funded, broke this general trend, since an increase under this head was both marked and consistent. Administrative posts resisted the general trend also, but the cost of central and administrative services as a proportion of total

TABLE 9.5   Full-time Student Numbers by Faculty, 1990-1

	Science	Engineering	Jt. Science / Engineering	Arts and Social Studies	Business	Total
Applications	4059	4145	213	3476	5628	17521
Intake	449	664	41	433	464	2051
Undergraduate	1527	2090	183	1209	1762	6771
PG Research	269	188	-	56	68	581
PG Instruction	80	155	40	41	591	907
Total	1876	2433	223	1306	2421	8259
First Degrees	353	534	55	303	482	1727
Higher Degrees	165	211	30	45	549	1000
Diplomas	15	29	15	32	345	436

Source: JBC, Annual Report, 1990-1.

TABLE 9.6   Staff Statistics, 1982-91

Academic Staff	1982/3	Years 1985/6	1990/1
Professors	82	87	125
Readers and Senior Lecturers	188	162	198
Lecturers	396	381	379
Total	666	630	702
* Academic Research Staff	252	310	359
Senior Library Staff	28	21	25
Administrative Staff	87	86	118
Other Academically Related Staff	59	66	104
+ Clerical, Secretarial Staff	393	366	413
+ Manual Staff	578	546	511
+ Technician and Related Staff	413	351	321
Total	2476	2376	2553

* Virtually all short-term externally funded
+ University-funded staff only

Source: JBC, Annual Reports 1982-91.

expenditure varied little. New investment in areas such as Alumni Relations, Research and Development Office and the International Office produced a greater return in financial support for the University, more research contracts and a larger overseas tuition fee income. The *caveats* indicated in the Notes to Table 9.6 are important. That referring to manual and technical staff is particularly significant. For example, many contracts covered the cost of technicians; this had the effect of taking them off the normal budget and helps to explain why research income and expenditure were balancing items in the accounts.

Table 9.7 derived from the reports of the Careers Advisory Service shows the first destinations of graduates as recorded six or nine months after graduation. Clearly industry and commerce were the main employers, especially in prosperous years; the downturn in 1990 and 1991 reflects the reality of the developing depression, as does the rise in those seeking

TABLE 9.7   First Destinations of Graduates (Percentages), 1985-91

	1985[+]	1986[+]	1987[+]	1988[+]	1989*	1990*	1991*
Industry and Commerce	43.5	42.8	41.7	44.3	45.9	36	31.3
Government Service	11.8	11.8	10.8	12.8	11.9	12.7	10.2
Further Study	14.7	14.9	15.8	16.8	16.5	15.8	20.5
Teacher Training / Teaching	4.4	3.7	3.1	2.4	1.4	2.0	3.4
Overseas Students Returning	8.9	12.2	15.2	11.1	8.9	9.4	10
Employment Overseas	2.4	1.9	2.6	1.8	2.2	2.4	2.9
Temporary Employment	1.6	1.2	1.3	2.1	1.5	3.4	4.9
Seeking Employment	7.8	5.9	5.3	4.3	6.5	6.3	7.5
Not Available for Employment	0.6	0.6	0.6	0.5	1.8	2.7	2.9
Unknown	4.3	5.4	3.5	3.8	3.4	9.2	4.6

+ Date of Census was 31 March
* Date of Census was 31 December

Sources: JBC, Careers Advisory Service Reports.

48 Postgraduates at work in the Strathclyde Graduate Business School. The MBA programme is a major success in the University's armoury of Business Studies courses.

employment or in temporary employment. Further study was a growing trend, probably accentuated by the depression of the early 1990s, since acquiring postgraduate qualifications, especially in Business subjects, was perceived as enhancing employment prospects. Teacher training or direct entry to teaching was less significant as an outlet for Strathclyde graduates than for most others. The strongest employment areas in the 1980s for Strathclyders were in electronics, computing, pharmacy, accountancy, retail management, sales and marketing, and the service sector. The University was visited by about 200 organisations seeking to recruit graduates in Session 1986-7, and approximately 5,000 interviews took place on campus. Companies with household names – Unilever, Shell, ICI, Glaxo, KPMG Peat Marwick, GEC and Marks and Spencer – took part in this activity. The rising number of those going overseas for their first appointment after 1988 reflects the Careers Advisory Service's responsiveness to the requirements of multinational business and the flexibility of Strathclyde graduates. Many were also attractive to small and medium-sized companies and organisations, an increasingly important element in the labour market of the 1990s.[30]

Reviewing the Faculties in this period is fraught with difficulty because there were so many developments in teaching and research. All four reviewed their curricula regularly and by the late 1980s had modularised their courses, and a modified approach to semesterisation had taken place which with later minor reform made the new system more rational. Reluctance to abandon good practice for novelty was totally explicable, but it was not possible to retain every characteristic of old methods if the advantages of the new system were to be realised.

In Engineering education this decade saw dramatic change. The implementation of the new extended degree, B.Sc.B.Eng. in Manufacturing Sciences and Engineering (1978) – which retained a 'sandwich' element of industrial experience – led to the first cohort of graduates in

1983 and widening success for the course later. As already indicated, a growing problem of the 1970s had been the difficulty of providing students with appropriate industrial placements during vacations. A review of all courses apart from the new degree was begun in 1979 under the chairmanship of Deputy Principal Professor James Harvey. Then appeared the Finniston Report to the Engineering Council in 1980 favouring some of the policies already discussed by the Harvey Review Group including practical training. Soon after his appointment, Principal Hills came to the conclusion that the universities could not expect government funding to meet the cost of the Finniston proposals. Senate and Court supported a decision of the Engineering Departments to introduce an in-house system of practical training, and from this emerged the Engineering Applications Centre (1983) at a cost of £1 million; valuable help came also from the UGC and local industry.[31]

Teaching Company partnerships with industry were pioneered by the Department of Production Management and Manufacturing Technology from 1977, and more ventures of this sort developed in the 1980s, for instance with IBM (Greenock) in 1983. Financed by the Science and Engineering Research Council and the Department of Industry, with significant contributions from the firms, these schemes were designed to bring academic knowledge and expertise into the workplace, thereby improving industrial efficiency and competitiveness. A number of other departments followed this initiative, including the Departments of Mechanics of Materials and of Pure and Applied Chemistry. The Business School, especially the Department of Marketing, began to extend this concept outside Engineering and Applied Science. The benefits to companies included receiving very able graduates on secondment for two years or more by agreement and an objective review of operations. Graduates benefited from the specific industrial experience, and this percolated often into teaching practice. Undoubtedly the main source of recent industrial and commercial experience to the Faculty of Engineering and others was the contribution of Visiting Professors.[32]

In the early 1980s the Faculty of Engineering's research efforts were mainly directed to industrial and social needs, some present and some future.[33] More than eighty main areas of investigation were being examined. The Department of Thermodynamics and Mechanics of Fluids acted as consultants to HM Nuclear Installations Inspectorate and was involved *inter alia* in experimental studies of methods of injecting emergency cooling water together with computational studies in relation to postulated accidents in pressurised water reactors. Research in image processing in the Department of Electronic and Electrical Engineering was supported under the European Strategic Programme of Research and Development in Information Technology (ESPRIT), one of the few awards made to British universities at that time. Pioneer work in the application of plastic sheets and grids in soil reinforcement in dams and other earthworks was being conducted by the Department of Civil Engineering. A research team in the Department of Dynamics and Control was engaged with industry in designing a new continuously variable transmission (CVT) for automobiles. Much work was being undertaken by the Department of Ship and Marine Technology on motion-controlled work bases offshore.

Most departments in the Faculty were active in the general fields of Computer Aided Design, Manufacture and Engineering (CAD/CAM/CAE), combining research, industrial collaboration and undergraduate and postgraduate teaching programmes. One of the longest established CAD groups in Britain was ABACUS (1970) within the Department of Architecture, which pioneered the effective use of computers in architecture and building. In Session 1985-6 the CAD Centre was established under the direction of Dr (later Professor) K. J. MacCallum with the remit of promoting CAD ventures in Engineering including the application of artificial intelligence techniques developed in the University-associated Tring Institute.

49 One of the longest- established Computer Aided Design groups in Britain has been ABACUS (1970) within the Department of Architecture, which pioneered the effective use of computers in architecture and building.

Another significant development was the Energy Studies Unit, with Dr John W. Twidell as Director. Dr Twidell had a special research interest in alternative and efficient energy sources and was a strong advocate of the 'solar' student residences later built in the Campus Village. Largely self-financing through contracts with outside agencies, the Unit by 1985-6 had twelve projects into wind, solar and biofuel energy sources. Co-operation with other departments within the University was an essential feature of much of this work, but other collaborators outside the University, for example the North of Scotland Hydro-Electric Board and the Rutherford Appleton Laboratory, were also sought.[34]

In Session 1987-8 the Bioengineering Unit celebrated its twenty-fifth anniversary. During the 1980s it added to its original research interests significantly. Studies on the mechanics of body tissues led to the use of lasers in plastic and cardiac surgery. Work on the application of the pulsed Ruby laser to remove certain tattoos without damage to the skin was completely successful; this was followed by work to remove disfiguring birth marks. Using lasers to assist in joining vessels in cardiac surgery was also at the development stage. Using bovine tissue in replacement heart valves was a collaborative venture with the Department of Cardiac Surgery at Glasgow Royal Infirmary and an industrial company. Much work was also in progress to mitigate the effects of spinal cord injuries and to develop membrane technology.[35]

The National Centre for Training and Education in Prosthetics and Orthotics under Professor John Hughes also went from strength to strength. Much better facilities were made available in the Curran Building from 1983, including the most advanced clinical, manufacturing and teaching equipment. Aiding the disabled attracted many able undergraduates into the first

Honours course in Europe, B.Sc. in Prosthetics and Orthotics, which produced its first graduates in 1987. CAD/CAM became a feature of the research of this centre with the possibility of cheapening the costs of production of devices and their customised design for the individual patient.[36]

Silt cleared from the River Clyde was used successfully as topsoil for the Glasgow Garden Festival site as a consequence of the activities of Professor George Fleming and his colleagues in Civil Engineering. Their feasibility study received a commendation from the Prince of Wales at the Royal Society of Arts in 1988 and clearly had environmental implications for other areas of Britain. The University as a whole became involved in the Garden Festival which was visited by over four million people; thirty departments devised over 180 demonstrations and events covering a five-month period and providing a layman's guide to some of the teaching and research of the University.[37]

Strathclyde was one of eight universities to receive further special support from UFC in Session 1989-90 for developments in biotechnology involving collaboration with industry. The Department of Bioscience and Biotechnology and the Division of Chemical Engineering had earlier received pump-priming support from UGC, and in Chemical Engineering the principal interest was in the field of fermentation technology covering a wide range of environmental and manufacturing processes.[38]

Support from industry for Strathclyde's engineers was constant in the 1980s. One of the largest contracts – for about £1 million over five years – was awarded by British Telecom in 1990, beginning with the Network Management Centre with Professor Geoffrey Smith of Electronic and Electrical Engineering as director. University teams were to assist British Telecom and other interested companies to develop advanced services for customers. The West of Scotland Science Park, a joint venture with the University of Glasgow (1983), became the home for the Engineering Design Research Centre in 1990; this was Britain's national centre for research into engineering design and was to be an agency for work on industrial and consumer products.[39]

It is clear that in some areas of research interdisciplinary activity crossed faculty boundaries. However, in Science, as in Engineering, industrial partners were often equally important. The development of optical communications systems stimulated demand for new materials in the early 1980s and the Physical Chemistry section became a partner in a consortium of British electronic and chemical firms to develop methods of creating materials with the appropriate properties. Work was also being undertaken in the Chemistry Department in collaboration with Rank Xerox to develop a new method of production for 'toner'. In Applied Chemistry/ Chemical Technology the preparation of thin films for microelectronic applications using chemical vapour deposition was one of several industry-related projects. Inorganic Chemistry staff were investigating *inter alia* the uses of novel forms of computer-controlled instrumentation for automatic ion-exchange separation of detergent mixtures and for trace element analysis by atomic absorption. In Organic Chemistry staff were studying the design of enzyme inhibitors as potential new chemotherapeutic agents amongst other topics. Many new patents were filed in consequence of the work of Professor Neil Graham and colleagues, whose research activities over two decades were beginning to show promise of commercial exploitation.[40]

Laser studies, as already noted, were being pursued in a number of departments. However, the Department of Physics had by the end of the 1980s outstanding facilities and staff for tunable laser studies. In the early 1980s the Department's researchers had played an important role in the development of highly reliable carbon-dioxide lasers, a joint project with Barr and Stroud. Two staff, Dr David Birch and Dr Robert Imhof, had designed a unique opto-electronic instrument, a coaxial flashlamp which was the key component in a Time Domain Spectrometer, manufactured by Edinburgh Instruments Ltd, a company based in Heriot-Watt University's Science Park. This instrument had a wide range of possible applications in dealing with analytical problems in physics, chemistry, pharmaceutics, medicine and food science. The emergence of a highly talented Superconducting Devices Group led to remarkable progress in the creation and application of Superconducting Quantum Interference Devices [SQUIDS]. These micron-scale magnetic sensors had great potential for a wide range of medical and industrial uses.[41]

Research studies into the behaviour and properties of liquid crystals and optical display devices were undertaken in the Departments of Mathematics and Pure and Applied Chemistry, both separately and as collaborative ventures. BDH Chemicals Ltd. and the Science and Engineering Research Council had funded this theoretical and experimental work. In Mathematics numerical analysis, applied analysis, statistical research and mathematical aspects of systems and control theory were other major fields of investigation.[42]

The advance of Information Technology made the work of the Computer Science Department of special importance in the 1980s. With Electronic and Electrical Engineering, this Department developed new undergraduate programmes to suit the age. The main research areas were man-machine interaction, software technology, advanced database systems and automated systems. Substantial research funding was obtained from external sources to support this work — in excess of £2 million by the middle of the 1980s.[43]

The Department of Bioscience and Biotechnology, formed in 1982 from the smaller departments discussed in Chapter 8, conducted both fundamental and applied research, the latter leading to the formation of several companies. In Applied Microbiology much research was devoted to fungi and yeast; much effort in Biology was expended on the environmental 'stress' response of cells. Control of bracken and its destruction was obviously important in many parts of Scotland; a search for a more effective means of restricting this fern was a feature of the department in the 1980s. A healthy range of activity was also present in Immunology, Biochemistry and Food Science.[44]

The Department of Pharmacy comprised two divisions: Pharmaceutics with Professor A. T. Florence as academic leader and Pharmaceutical Chemistry with Professor J. M. Midgley as Head. The main research in the former division was directed at drug formulation and delivery with a number of other related interests. In Pharmaceutical Chemistry research interests were diffused over a wider spectrum: phytochemistry, pharmaceutical analysis, molecular pharmacology and medicinal chemistry. New sterile laboratories were opened in 1983 designed for undergraduate teaching and research. Development work in sterile products, including the preparation of materials for use in clinical trials, was thereby made possible. These facilities and the staff's expertise provided a sound basis for collaborative research with the Department of Clinical Oncology at the University of Glasgow which led to the establishment of the Formulation Research Unit (aided by the Cancer Research Campaign) for testing anti-cancer drugs.[45] There was a deliberate attempt to reinforce the staff of the Department in the late 1980s after a UMG review. Moreover, the establishment of the interdisciplinary Strathclyde Institute for Drug Research in 1988 also added an extra impetus.[46]

Physiology and Pharmacology, closely related to Pharmacy, through joint teaching for the B.Sc. (Pharmacy), was a strong research department also. For instance, collaboration with Organon Laboratories led to the testing of a number of new neuromuscular blocking drugs of which one, tested by Dr (later Professor) Ian Marshall and Dr. N.N. Durant, and later called vercuronium, proved to be highly effective and free from unwanted effects. Thus, from one university two major muscle relaxants — atracurium being the other — had entered production.

Sudden Infant Death Syndrome (Cot Death) was extensively investigated, and one approach (by Dr. John Jackson and his team) was an alerting device/alarm which indicated when a baby was having breathing difficulties; sudden stimulation is generally sufficient to cause the baby to restart breathing normally. Asthma, ischaemic heart disease, myasthenia gravis, and retinitis pigmentosa are all serious medical conditions which researchers in this Department were investigating.[47]

There were a number of significant developments in the Business School in the 1980s to add to those already described in Chapter 8. The Fraser of Allander Institute established its reputation through its *Quarterly Economic Commentary* which was widely regarded as the most accurate forecast of short-term trends in Scottish economic performance. The David Livingstone Institute of Development Studies provided appropriate consultancy advice as well as a substantial interdisciplinary research programme relating to developing economies. The Department of Marketing created an Advertising Research Unit which applied private sector practices to public sector organisations, advising the Scottish Health Education Group *inter alia* about its campaign against smoking and alcohol abuse. A Centre for Police Studies, established within the Department of Administration in 1982, rapidly acquired a sound research reputation and attracted a number of distinguished academic visitors.[48]

A joint company was set up in Session 1985-6 by the Scottish Development Agency and the University (Department of Marketing) called Scottish Marketing Products, designed to assist industry to market more effectively in an increasingly competitive world. Marketing theory and best practice were to be spread more widely through this initiative, and participating firms of whatever size were expected to gain. A self-funding Centre for Professional Legal Studies, with Professor J. Ross Harper as Director, was created within the Law School; it had four principal objectives: the professional training of law graduates; provision of post-qualification legal education for practitioners; legal training for other professions; and the development of international links between practising lawyers.[49]

In Session 1988-9 the most important development was the creation of the Strathclyde Graduate Business School. An autonomous, financial and managerial unit within the Business School, it employed its own management team and planned to have a core staff of eighteen academics who would liaise with departments to seek additional help as and when required. Its income was derived from student fees, and this was expected to meet all expenditure including mortgage repayments on the new building planned for Cathedral Street. Its main product was the MBA, and the Graduate Business School had to stand on its ability to market this programme throughout the world.[50]

Another initiative was the Centre for Europe attached to the Dean's Office. This was a Faculty centre and not simply the product of one or two departments, and it was expected to take advantage of the possibilities presented by the expansion of the European Community. One objective was greater collaboration with universities in Europe. International business perspectives were built into a new undergraduate programme launched in 1988-9, the degree in International Business and Modern Languages. This course was aimed at students intending to take up careers in business and administration with an international dimension. Wherever European languages held linguistic sway, this course might have applicability.[51]

The core disciplines of the Business School – Economics, Accountancy, Administration, Industrial Relations, Management Science, and Marketing – produced a mixture of basic and applied research as well as teaching courses to undergraduates and postgraduates. The Department of Accountancy and Finance was involved in developing multi-media packages for teaching the principles of the discipline, and researched a wide range of accountancy practices,

50 and 51 The cultural activities of the University have greatly expanded since 1964. Music – choirs and music-making groups – has flourished and (top) an ensemble plays before a town and gown audience and (foot) an exhibition, 'Submarines', by Tom McKendrick (1990) in the Collins Gallery, another contribution to the cultural life of the city and the university.

52 At the highest natural point on the John Anderson campus stands Gerald Laing's steel sculpture commonly known as 'Steelhenge'. This is a popular meeting place in the summer for students and their friends and relatives, especially after graduation ceremonies. The sculpture marked the completion of the 'greening' of Townhead and is based on the standing stones of Callanish.

the behaviour of stock markets, takeovers and bankruptcies. A new Chair of Human Resource Management, supported by the Institute of Personnel Management, was created in 1988-9, and nine other companies added their sponsorship. This complemented the activities of the existing Chair in Industrial Relations held by Professor John Gennard. Research themes included the impact of information technology on industrial relations processes and institutions, management and labour strategies in a range of industries, private and public, and the industrial relations behaviour of multinational companies.[52]

The Faculty of Arts and Social Studies in the 1980s remained, despite a high competitive entry standard, one of the most popular student choices in the University, as Table 9.5 indicates. This was representative of the British university scene; applications and admissions figures for 1987-8, for example, showed substantial increases. The merits of a flexible degree structure in which it was possible to include subjects from the Business School curriculum were amply demonstrated. Savings targets for this Faculty were partially offset by growth in the student population, and the belt was tightened as staff/student ratios drifted upwards. The University's determination to retain Spanish was successful when the UGC withdrew its recommendation that it should cease to be offered. Thus five languages, French, German, Spanish, Italian and Russian, remained on offer at Strathclyde, not only to the Faculty's own students but also to undergraduates in Science, Engineering and Business.

New developments included the establishment within the Department of English Studies of the John Logie Baird Centre for Research in Television and Film (1983) in collaboration with the University of Glasgow. Relevance to the modern world was also a feature of the Addiction Research Group based in the Department of Psychology. Active in hospitals, clinics, treatment centres and prisons, the Group was self-funding and had contacts with a number of commercial organisations. In Session 1988-9 the Centre for Occupational and Health Psychology was established, bringing together workers in the fields of addiction and stress. The Industrial Archaeology Survey Unit within the Department of History, sponsored by the Royal Commission on the Ancient and Historical Monuments of Scotland, made inroads into the recording of Scotland's industrial heritage and advised local groups on such matters as restoration. Several grants were received by departments to aid research into current problems. For instance, in Session 1982-3 the Department of Politics obtained support from the Leverhulme Trust for a comparative study of unemployment policies and new technology in the United Kingdom.

Urban life in nineteenth-century Glasgow with particular reference to housing was the subject in the History Department's project on Glasgow which attracted major support from the Economic and Social Research Council from 1987 onwards. There was also support for interdisciplinary research in Scottish Studies and the Scottish/Irish Conference on Economic and Social History: a book emerged from the proceedings of each meeting. A range of topics from early-modern to twentieth-century history were under examination; a steady flow of publications emanated from these investigations.

The Department of English Studies combined the study of literature, literary linguistics, philosophy, drama, film and television. The role of language and other media in contemporary culture looms large. The Department of Geography suffered a loss through the transfer of three physical geographers to the University of Stirling in 1986 but developed its focus upon applied regional and human geography. Work on the social geography of cities, the quality of life, rural housing and urban regeneration was undertaken with diminished resources but to good effect.

In the Department of Modern Languages there were four principal areas of strength in the 1980s: the study of European literature in the last two centuries; linguistic, syntactic and

53 Dr Magnus Magnusson (an honorary graduate of the University) opens the Senior Studies Institute in November 1993. This marked the end of the evolutionary phase in the 'Learning in Later Life' programme, directed by Lesley A.Hart.

54 The last degree congregation of Sir Graham John Hills, second Vice-Chancellor (1980-91).

semantic problems in the five languages studied; area studies, including the history of ideas; and the methodology of teaching modern languages. Great variety was an inevitable feature of the published work. This was also the case in the Department of Politics (later Government). Industrial, employment and training policies, policy analysis and policy process in Britain and the United States, elections and electoral behaviour, federalism and regionalism, and nationalism are simply examples of major areas of research interest.

Although the Faculty was relatively small in terms of others in the University, it consistently demonstrated a high research profile and provided its undergraduates with a stimulating learning experience, according to their representatives. In the world of public accountability it did well in an early research assessment exercise and certainly provided value for money. Internationally, it built links with American and Canadian universities and with many of Europe's leading centres of learning.[53]

Hard times demanded hard choices. More decisions were taken at Faculty and University level and less at the departmental stratum. Yet faculties tended to become more cohesive rather than less. Philistinism did not triumph. Even in straitened times, Music, Drama and the Visual Arts did better than simply survive. Access to the University was a concern of Senate and resulted in one of the celebrated 'Green' papers. The Learning in Later Life Programme, with Mrs. Lesley Hart in charge, became a feature of the University's offerings in 1987 and rapidly flourished. Environmental Studies became important, and its champions arose to place the main issues firmly on the academic agenda in the late 1980s. The Programme of Opportunities for Women developed in 1989 and became an important University initiative. There was much discussion of collaboration with other institutions – with Glasgow Polytechnic, the University of

Glasgow, and Craigie College of Education, for instance. Merger, except in the latter case, was never really on the agenda but the more efficient use of mutual resources certainly was.[54]

The advent of a new era was signalled by the retirement of the first Chancellor, Lord Todd, and the installation in April 1991 of Francis, Lord Tombs of Brailes, 'one of the most successful engineer-managers of the post-war era', as second Chancellor.[55] Sir (1988) Graham J. Hills had already intimated his retirement, and a successful search for his successor had been concluded. The old era entered history as an age of financial difficulties and problems overcome by tenacity and style, of challenges met, of opportunities grasped and of fundamental changes to the University made necessary by a harsh environment.

REFERENCES

1   JBC, *Bulletin of the University of Strathclyde* (*BUS*), January 1981, p.1.
2   Pollard, pp. 376-432; Kent Matthews and Patrick Minford, 'Mrs Thatcher's Economic Policies, 1979-1987', *Economic Policy*, 5 (1987), pp. 65 ff; Peter Riddell, *The Thatcher Decade* (Oxford, 1989), *passim*; Keith Robbins, *The Eclipse of a Great Power: Modern Britain 1870-1992* (1994 edn.), pp. 345-396.
3   JBC, J. Butt, 'Energy, Commitment, Tenacity, Style: Professor Sir Graham Hills, Vice-Chancellor and Principal of the University of Strathclyde 1980-1991 ... ', *Prism Extra*, October 1991.
4   JBC, Court Minutes, 1978-81, *passim*.
5   JBC, Annual Report, 1981-2.
6   JBC, Annual Report, 1982-3.
7   JBC, Annual Reports, 1982-4; University Accounts, 1982-4.
8   JBC, Abstracts of Accounts, 1985-91.
9   JBC, Annual Report, 1988-9.
10 These features were consequences of the Report of the Court Committee on the Organisation and Efficiency of Decision-Making (COED) following the Jarratt Report of 1985. COED consisted mainly of distinguished external authorities on management, and its Report was approved by Senate and Court in March 1987. UMG Minutes, 15 December 1987; Court Minutes, 27 October 1987; 5 and 6 December 1987.
11 JBC, UMG Minutes, 1987-91.
12 JBC, UMG Minutes, 8 September 1987; 8 March 1988.
13 JBC, UMG Minutes, 22 September 1987; 18 April 1989; 16 May 1989,
14 Much discussion on strategic planning and the 'Rolling' Academic Plan took place at UMS, UMG, Senate and Court between 1986 and 1991.
15 JBC, Green Papers 1987-8; UMG Minutes, 6 October 1987.
16 JBC, Green Paper on Resource Allocation, 1987; UMG Minutes, 6 October 1987; 3 November 1987; 8 March 1988; Senate Minutes, 16 December 1987; 16 March 1988.
17 JBC, UMG Minutes, 1987-91, *passim*.
18 These academic ventures were managed by the committee mentioned and chaired by the Vice-Principals in rotation. Students were later registered in alternate years by what became a consortium of two universities. UMG Minutes, 20 June 1989 and 4 July 1989; *Prism*, August 1989.
19 JBC, Annual Reports, 1981-91, *passim*; *BUS*, February 1983, pp. 8-9.
20 JBC, Court Reports to Senate, 1981-4, *passim*. The Campus Plan: Court Minutes, 3-4 December 1988; Senate Minutes, 8 February 1989.
21 JBC, Annual Reports, 1985-8, *passim*; UMG Minutes, 28 June and 12 July 1988, Report from Estates and Buildings Division.

22 Andor Gomme and David Walker, *The Architecture of Glasgow* (1968) gives the best account of the Barony Church; JBC, Court Minutes, 30 May 1989. The Barony is listed A category in the List of Buildings of Architectural or Historic Interest, kept by the Scottish Office.
23 JBC, Annual Reports, 1980-91, *passim*.
24 JBC, Financial Statements by the Treasurer in Annual Reports, 1988-91; UMG Minutes, 1989-91, *passim*; Court Minutes, 1988-91, *passim*.
25 JBC, Senate Minutes, 1984-90, *passim*; UMG Minutes, 6 June 1989.
26 JBC, Annual Report, 1982-3, Principal's Statement; much of the rest of this paragraph is based on the author's personal experience and conversations with Deans at various times.
27 JBC, Annual Reports, 1981-3, *passim*.
28 JBC, *BUS*, February 1983, pp.1-2; Annual Accounts, 1988-91.
29 Access to universities is a major topic, but data available on the University of Strathclyde suggest that 15-19 per cent of students came from the lowest income/occupational groups in the period 1985-90.
30 JBC, Careers Advisory Service Reports, 1981-91.
31 JBC, Annual Report, 1982-3; *BUS*, December 1983, pp. 7-10.
32 JBC, Annual Reports, 1977-91.
33 Much of what follows is drawn from Annual *Research Registers* from 1979 onwards; Annual Reports, 1981-91, *passim*.
34 JBC, Annual Report, 1985-6.
35 JBC, Annual Report, 1987-8; *Prism*, June 1990; J.P. Paul's 96 Group Lecture, 1995, *passim*.
36 JBC, Annual Reports, 1982-3 and 1986-7; *BUS*, June 1983, pp.1-2; University of Strathclyde *Gazette*, 1981, pp. 17-20.
37 JBC, Annual Report, 1987-8, pp. 18-20.
38 *Prism*, November 1989; February 1990.
39 JBC, Annual Report, 1990-1; *BUS*, June 1983, p.8.
40 JBC, University of Strathclyde *Gazette*, 1981, pp. 14-15; Annual Report, 1982-3; Registers of Research, 1979-86; Documents for Research Selectivity Exercises.
41 JBC, *BUS*, December 1983, pp. 2-3; Registers of Research, 1979-86; Annual Reports, 1981-91.
42 JBC, Registers of Research, 1979-86; Annual Reports, 1981-91; Documents for Research Selectivity Exercises.
43 JBC, Annual Reports, 1981-91; Registers of Research, 1979-86; Documents for Research Selectivity Exercises.
44 JBC, Registers of Research, 1979-86; University of Strathclyde *Gazette*, 1981, pp. 26-7; 1981-2, p.3; Documents for Research Selectivity Exercises.
45 JBC, Registers of Research, 1979-86; University of Strathclyde *Gazette*, 1981, p.23; *BUS*, June 1983, pp.2-3;

Prism, September 1990; Documents for Research Selectivity Exercises.

46 JBC, UMG Review of the Department of Pharmacy chaired by the author; Court Minutes, 19 January 1988.

47 JBC, Annual Reports, 1979-91; Registers of Research, 1979-86; Documents for Research Selectivity Exercises.

48 JBC, Annual Reports, 1981-91; Registers of Research, 1979-86; University of Strathclyde *Gazette*, 1981-2, pp. 6-8.

49 JBC, Annual Reports, 1985-90.

50 JBC, Annual Report, 1988-9; UMG Minutes, 7, 21 March and 4 April 1989; Court Minutes, 17 January 1989.

51 JBC, Annual Report, 1988-9.

52 JBC, Annual Reports, 1980-91; Registers of Research, 1979-86.

53 JBC, Annual Reports, 1979-91; Registers of Research, 1979-86; *BUS*, June 1983, p.8; *SASS* Newsletter of the Faculty of Arts and Social Studies, No.6, March 1988; Documents for Research Selectivity Exercises.

54 JBC, Senate Minutes, 17 May 1989; 16 October 1989; 14 March 1990; *Prism*, October 1987, February 1988; UMG Minutes, 13 January 1989; *Prism*, February and March 1989.

55 JBC, *Prism*, October 1990; Installation Brochure, April 1991.

55 The installation of a new Chancellor in April 1991. The academic procession leaves the Barony Hall led by the first Chancellor, Lord Todd, and the second Chancellor, Lord Tombs of Braites, followed by Principal John Arbuthnott, Sir Graham Hills and Sir Samuel Curran.

CHAPTER TEN

The Third Merger and Into the Next Millennium, 1991–

'The merger of Jordanhill College with the University of Strathclyde comes at a time of great change within higher education, with the removal of the binary line and the creation of a new, unified higher education system in Scotland funded by an independent Scottish funding council. It is no coincidence that the formation of the new and enlarged University of Strathclyde occurs on the same day as the Scottish Higher Education Funding Council is born ... The merger represents an historic step forward for the University within the tradition of "useful learning" advocated by its founder, John Anderson ... '

Professor John P. Arbuthnott, Principal and Vice-Chancellor,
Prism (Commemorative Issue), 1 April 1993

SITTING COMFORTABLY ON A WARM SUMMER'S DAY in 1991 in the Queen's Hospital, Nottingham where the Principal-designate was still leading his Microbiology research team, Peter West, Secretary to the University, and the author, then Vice-Principal, raised the question of whether he would favour a merger with Jordanhill College of Education. We had been asked to do so by the outgoing Vice-Chancellor, Sir Graham Hills, who was himself very positive in his support of the proposal.[1] Professor Arbuthnott was equally supportive and soon became personally involved in the preliminary discussions between the senior officers of the College, Dr. T.R. Bone and Dr. J.McCall, and the University during June and July. The objectives were overwhelmingly academic: to widen access for those living and studying in the West of Scotland at a time when government was expanding provision; to enhance teaching and research through unity; to respond to the changing educational needs of society. Proposals – subject to the approval of Senate and Court and the College's Governors and Academic Board – were framed, and a thorough examination of conditions and consequences then began in both institutions.[2]

In constitutional terms, what was at stake was clear: the Academic Board had to agree to give up its independence in exchange for appropriate representation of staff on Senate; the College's Governors had to be willing to give up their powers; the Senate had to approve the establishment of a Faculty of Education with a large staff and student body, ensuring that these new members of the University were treated equally; the Court of the University had to accept responsibility for the Jordanhill campus and about 700 staff; the Funding Council's Scottish Committee had to be satisfied that the merger met its criteria; and the Minister for Education had to give approval.[3] All these stages were completed successfully, and thus, the third major merger in the history of the University was accomplished.

56 Lord Goold (Chairman of Court 1993-) assists Sir Graham Hills on the occasion of the University conferring his Fellowship upon the former Vice Chancellor. Courtesy of Caledonian Newspapers Ltd.

The scrutiny by interested parties was thorough and involved many people. As far as the University was concerned, its evidence to the Scottish Tertiary Education Advisory Council [STEAC] in 1985 had favoured the abolition of the binary line in Higher Education and the incorporation of Teacher Education within the university system. There was little or no academic overlap between the two institutions and therefore no jobs were at risk, and there were possibilities of growth because of merger which might provide more career openings. Teaching and research might benefit considerably, and the wider world might gain by the existence of a larger and more flexible University able to respond rapidly to the changing needs of society.

Between October 1991 and March 1992 a Joint Working Party, established by the Court and the College Governors, worked rapidly and to good effect, assessing the feasibility of the merger in all its aspects and exposing potential problems through smaller specialist groups. As had been expected, the Secretary of State referred the merger to UFC's Scottish Committee. The joint submission made to that body dealt with all the relevant issues, and by 1 September 1992, political approval had been conferred on the proposal for merger, although Strathclyde's advice to STEAC had not been taken earlier.[4]

A merger implementation group [MIG] then took charge which included students, staff and lay members. The students had always been positive: those at Jordanhill were attracted by improved social amenities and better student services, and the attractions of Jordanhill's sporting facilities and the prospects of adding about 2,500 additional members were material advantages as far as their Strathclyde counterparts were concerned. Their representatives clearly believed that what problems existed could be overcome. This optimism proved to be realistic with the

57 The David Stow Building (1922) on the Jordanhill Campus. Like the Royal College, it was designed by the firm of H. and D. Barclay. The merger of Jordanhill College with the University of Strathclyde was a major event in the history of Higher Education in Scotland.

formation of a single students' union.[5] Staff members were equally concerned to make the merger practicable; legal and operational arrangements were in place for 'Day Zero' (the day of merger, 1 April, 1993).

One important recommendation of the Joint Working Party was the sensible idea of 'ring-fencing' the new Faculty of Education for two years from 'Day Zero'. Thus, where differences existed between the two institutions before merger, rapid changes need not necessarily be enforced. Inevitably, there were problems. Staff being represented by different unions; conditions of service such as lecturing hours undertaken by staff; holiday entitlement; expectations about research are examples where there were well established disparities, but a great deal of goodwill prevailed, and these matters are in the process of being settled. Fears that Jordanhill staff had about joining the University were generally dissipated quickly. Some Strathclyde staff had warned of inheriting a financial deficit; 'ring-fencing' provided a ruthless answer to that, although any Faculty would be assisted to balance its books, a common practice in difficult financial years. The non-academic trade unions had reasonable apprehensions about job losses; yet it was intended to maintain services on both campuses even if they were unified, and a guarantee of no redundancy was given. Time to work out changes, which 'ring-fencing' allowed, was particularly important in this area.[6]

Craigie College of Education in Ayr had had its degree courses validated by the University for about twenty years and had just become the University's Institute of Education before talks began with Jordanhill. Craigie was immediately informed when they started and kept up-to-date. Discussions took place with Craigie when it was clear that Jordanhill was likely to join the

University, and between September 1991 and February 1992 these centred around the idea of a Faculty of Education with two campuses. The Governors and staff at Craigie were naturally apprehensive that in the event of any future attempt at rationalisation on one site, that would be at Jordanhill; therefore in February 1992 they decided to merge with the University of Paisley and with Strathclyde's blessing (and regrets) parted company.[7]

Thus the third major merger in the history of the University was completed but, of course, its consequences are a matter for the future. The history of both institutions forming the enlarged University of Strathclyde is auspicious. As we noticed in Chapter 3, the President, Trustees and Professors of Anderson's University had processed on the founding day of David Stow's Normal School, the ancestor of Jordanhill College. Established in 1837 at Dundas Vale, the Normal School was the first institution built in Britain specifically for teacher training. As a condition of receiving a government grant, in 1841 the management of Dundas Vale was transferred to the Church of Scotland, and after the Disruption, Stow established a second teacher training institution, the Free Church Seminary, in 1845.

Growth of demand for teachers grew rapidly after the Scottish Education Act of 1872 and Dundas Vale and the Free Church Seminary prospered. At the beginning of the twentieth century the Scottish Office reorganised teacher training, establishing four provincial committees mainly to serve the needs of the four cities but also to act as regional controllers of teacher supply more widely.[8] In this connection Allan Glen's School was recognised by the Scotch Education Department in 1906 as a training centre for junior students in science and technical subjects, and for a number of years the Glasgow Provincial Teachers' Training Committee, its administration and inspectors, were housed in the Technical College.[9] This body assumed responsibility for the two Glasgow Colleges, now known as Dundas Vale College and Stow College.

Teacher training classes were taught in several places in Glasgow apart from Allan Glen's School, and the need for a large new college was easily demonstrated, but the wheels of government, although lubricated by voluntaryist endeavours, moved exceedingly slowly. In due course the 67 broad acres of Jordanhill – the estate which had belonged to James Smith, the President of Anderson's University – were purchased from Parker Smith for £425 an acre. Work began on the new Jordanhill College in 1912 but the war delayed completion. When the campus was declared open in 1921, the David Stow building was still incomplete.[10] Meanwhile, the Provincial Teachers' Training Committee had vacated its accommodation in the Royal Technical College and took up residence at Jordanhill.[11] Despite the vicissitudes of depression and war, Glasgow Provincial Training Teachers' Training College (1907-59) and Jordanhill College of Education (1959-93) flourished and by dint of great effort by its staff became the premier training college in Scotland and the largest teacher training institution in the United Kingdom.[12]

The Royal Technical College and its successor, the Royal College of Science and Technology, continued to participate in teacher refresher courses and training, beginning with Dr David Ellis in the 1920s.[13] In the 1950s the Department of Mechanical Engineering provided summer courses for technical teachers, part of its general effort to raise awareness in schools of opportunities in engineering. Thus, the alliance with Jordanhill College in 1993 presented no assault on the existing method of the University despite two different traditions, particularly as two members of staff, Professor George Gordon and the author, had acted as Chairmen of the Board of Governors of Jordanhill and Craigie respectively, and Sir (1967) Henry Wood, the revered Principal (1949-72), had given good service in retirement to the University as its Assessor in Education.

The two estates, John Anderson Campus and Jordanhill Campus, had a common architectural root in the firm of H. and D. Barclay which designed the Royal College building and the David Stow building (1922). Each of these buildings became the core of its campus.[14] In the 1990s further growth will require astute estate management so that the best return can be achieved from existing buildings, since SHEFC capital funding is likely to be in short supply.

The enlarged University of Strathclyde represents a considerable challenge in terms of day-to-day management. Viewed as an ordinary business, its annual turnover approaches £120 million (1993) and it employs in 1995 nearly 5,000 people. The Secretary to the University, Peter West, exercises the responsibility of ensuring that a unified administration serves staff and students working in the two campuses efficiently and well. When the merger was agreed in principle by the two institutions in October 1992 the administrative sections in each began to work together – Finance, Personnel, External Relations, Estates Management and Management Information. The result was the development of mutual respect for the expertise and management skills which each section found in its counterpart. The two Print Units were merged under the leadership of staff on the Jordanhill Campus and became more productive and much more profitable than previously.

The general objective of serving the needs of staff and students on both campuses has led Peter West to express caution about the eventual structure of management; he is intent on a management style which responds to need:

> There may well be a continuing need for a separate section of the Personnel Office to deal with particular issues affecting ... employees on the Jordanhill Campus. Likewise, sections of the Finance Office may be operated in tandem on both campuses.
>
> Whether or not these are separate sections, however, all parts of the Administration will be guided by the same principles of quality and customer care and will be continually looking to improve the quality of the management which they provide.[15]

This is a message which all can understand, and most will accept. By 1994 harmonisation of central services was virtually complete.

The student population reached about 13,000 as a consequence of the merger. The Students' Association of the enlarged University expects to see considerable benefits from the merger in several areas of vital moment to students. Commercial services, such as catering, bars, shops and entertainment, are likely to expand. The John Anderson Campus already possesses the largest students' union in Scotland: its ten floors house the country's biggest, and possibly best, student welfare service, an excellent student newspaper, over two hundred clubs and societies and a sports union which provides for about forty different activities. At Jordanhill Campus a serious attempt is being made to improve student welfare and other services, to generate more events and to improve the use of existing facilities, which are being refurbished where necessary. The range of academic opportunities is gradually being increased as a consequence of the joint teaching facilities available in the larger University. Courses which might not have been possible before the merger are likely to grow in number, as departmental contacts are made, and student demand and career opportunities are assessed.[16]

Of the central services, the one with most magnetic appeal – to students especially just before examinations – is the Library. The University Library is now located on two campuses but managed by one married couple, Albert and Margaret Harrison. In the 1990s the Library has become an even more heavily used resource than ever before because of the growth of student-centred learning practices. The Andersonian Library possesses about 675,000 volumes – books, periodicals and other materials – in the Arts, Social Sciences, Engineering, Science and Business Studies. There is a range of services enabling staff and students to access not only this repository

TABLE 10.1   Main Sources of University Income (£m), 1989-1993

Academic Session	1989-90	1990-1	1991-2	1992-3
UFC and SHEFC Grants	38.3	32.7	29.77	35.67
Fees and Support Grants	12.64	20.7	28.36	32.8
Residence and Catering	4.7	5.57	5.88	7.25
Other General Income	2	3.8	5.2	8.72
Research Grants & Contracts	13.7	14.8	16.4	18.53
Other services rendered	4.2	5.1	8.1	9.93
Total Income	79.59	85	96.78	116.33

Total income includes minor items not separately listed here.

Sources: Annual Accounts for the years stated.

but also via vast databases to ascertain what is held in libraries elsewhere. Jordanhill Library is well known for its collections in the field of Education; it possesses over 200,000 books, periodicals and audio-visual materials. Together, the two collections represent a major resource for learning and scholarship in good surroundings.[17]

The enlarged University naturally faces challenges and will no doubt make from them opportunities as it tended to do ever since the Charter was granted in 1964. An essential prerequisite for success is the ability to raise funding from diverse sources. Despite the world-wide depression of the early 1990s progress in finance has been remarkable, as may be judged from Table 10.1 which provides a statistical skeleton of main heads of income before merger with Jordanhill up to 1991-2. In the figures for 1992-3 total income for four months (April-June) for Jordanhill was £6.643 million and was matched by equivalent expenditure. The merger has been assessed by the Funding Council's Visitation Committee and judged a success.

The attempt to reduce dependence on direct government funding, apparent from the 1980s, continued, partly because the reduced unit of resource available via the Funding Council made this inevitable. The growth in the value of services rendered and of research grants and contracts more accurately reflects, the praiseworthy and successful efforts to diversify sources of income. However, more research grants and contracts naturally result in more expenditure under these heads, illustrating the simple fact that a narrow annual balance on the accounts is generally as much as can be expected. The University has been singularly fortunate that its Strategic Fund for academic development has been largely financed from royalty income (from Atracurium, mainly). Reserves can only be accumulated over a period of years, and in this regard, the evidence suggests that the University is better placed in 1994-5 than it has been for many years. One potential source of danger was the effect of the world depression on international recruitment, but overseas fee income has remained remarkably stable, tending to increase marginally. This is explained by the perceived added value of Strathclyde qualifications by overseas students and governments, but in a highly competitive market place, the efforts of the International Office staff and their academic colleagues have been outstandingly successful.[18]

Despite the growth of a free market ideology, intervention in the internal affairs of universities by government agencies was a fact of life in the early 1990s. Concern that society received value for money was one avowed motive; another was the belief that universities did not respond adequately to the needs of their client groups – students and employers. The principal monitoring methods were the research assessment exercise, teaching quality audit, and teaching quality assessment. Emphasis, after investigation and discussion by peer groups, was on public availability of information through Funding Council reports placed in the public domain and therefore not only available to interested individuals and groups but also the subject of comment in the press.

In all these exercises the University of Strathclyde did very well. The preliminary visit by the Teaching Quality Audit Group (December, 1991) was intended to ascertain whether the University had proper mechanisms in place to monitor effectively the teaching activities of departments. Broadly, this group were very satisfied with what they found and made only minor suggestions for improvement. The University agreed (1991-2) to allow SHEFC to run pilot studies in Electronic and Electrical Engineering and Economics so that the proposed methodology for Teaching Quality Assessment could be tested and refined. In the Research Assessment Exercise [RAE] report of January 1993 eight departments received the highest rating, a number of others were close, and the generality more than satisfactory; every department was eligible to receive at least core funding for research.

In order to generate more SHEFC income for research it will be necessary to improve on the RAE performance of 1993. A feature of University management is concern for the long term. It is, therefore, a clearly stated objective in the University's Strategic Plan that performance should improve, and to encourage this a Strategic Fund designed to provide support for new research developments has been established. Departmental programmes were first considered by a Research Task Force in December, 1992, and this led to a Research Monitoring Exercise to prepare for future external reviews of research. Crude indicators, such as improved staff participation in research, more publications and more research grants and contracts, show that performance is definitely improving.[19]

SHEFC soon created a rota of visits to major departments to assess Teaching Quality. Up to 1995 the University of Strathclyde has assumed top place among the Scottish universities in the league tables inevitably created by educational correspondents. The first 'Excellent' came in Electronic and Electrical Engineering in August 1993, and the number of departments/cognate areas so assessed has grown significantly.[20] Table 10.2 summarises the situation at the end of Session 1994-5.

Greater accountability is a feature of other parts of university life. The Funding Councils have established a Committee with specialist sub-committees to provide, after consultation with the universities, agreed performance indicators for a range of important aspects of university management: financial management, management of estates, buildings and equipment, for example. Sound strategic planning should result from proper internal procedures, but is externally audited by the Funding Councils.[21]

Proper scrutiny has to be preceded by considerable work by staff within the universities. Accountability imposes internal discipline but it also creates bureaucracy and results in the consumption of scarce staff time on matters other than teaching and research. SHEFC has been concerned to recognise the diversity of missions within the Scottish university sector and is aware of the need to avoid undue bureaucracy in order to maintain worthwhile institutional flexibility and freedom. The University of Strathclyde has reason to be proud of its domestic management at all levels but with other universities it has expressed these natural concerns to SHEFC.[22]

Modularisation had provided more flexibility for curriculum design and student choice of classes; semesterisation had not simply brought the University into line with North American and many European universities. These developments made it possible for engineers and scientists, for example, to select a foreign language or languages so that they could survive during a study year abroad as part of the Erasmus initiative. Large numbers of students avail themselves of this opportunity and just as many European students come to Strathclyde.[23]

TABLE 10.2   Departments / Cognate Areas Assessed by SHEFC Teaching Quality Teams

Department	Date	Grading	Comment
Electronic & Electrical	1993	Excellent	Largest dept. in University
Economics	1993	Satisfactory	3 point scale
Mechanical Engineering	1994	Excellent	Counted as one cognate area
DMEM	1994	Excellent	
Chemistry	1994	Excellent	
Physics	1994	Excellent	
Civil Engineering	1994	Highly satisfactory	
Geography	1994	Excellent	
Mathematics & Statistics	1994	Highly satisfactory	
Computer Studies	1994	Highly satisfactory	
Business Studies	1995	Excellent	Counted as one cognate area
Architecture	1995	Excellent	
Education	1995	Highly satisfactory	
Scottish Hotel School	1995	Highly satisfactory	

The faculties represent the real core of the University. Although they naturally conform to the agreed objectives of the institutional plan, which they help to frame and through Senate and Court to approve, they exercise delegated powers and enjoy considerable authority. Resources are allocated to them by an agreed formula, which changes little within a planning period, and each is accountable whenever Senate meets for academic matters; UMG monitors as a matter of course their academic and financial progress with a full-scale mid-year budget review. Each faculty has a review procedure, involving an independent chair person and external assessors usually, and departments are reviewed in terms of their academic performance and potential development once every five years.

As Table 10.2 indicates, the main departments in the Faculty of Science have emerged very creditably from the Teaching Quality Assessment of SHEFC. Chemistry and Physics were graded as excellent, Mathematics and Statistics, and Computer Science as highly satisfactory. The School of Pharmacy has yet to be assessed, but an internal review, during which the opinions of representative students were sought, gave it a very clean bill of health. In consequence of that review, the School, which consists of two departments – Pharmaceutical Science and Physiology and Pharmacology – and the Strathclyde Institute for Drug Research was reorganised in 1991 with Dr Gordon Smail as Head of School. A new department of Immunology emerged from Biosciences in 1991, headed by Professor William Stimson with a large research portfolio of projects and £2 million of funding, much of it derived from industry.[24]

A new building for Health Sciences is at an advanced planning stage, and by early 1994 £7 million of the estimated £11 million required had been raised, starting with a particularly generous donation from the Robertson Trust. A new Neuropharmacology laboratory in the Department of Physiology and Pharmacology was in commission by 1993 where research on drug dependence and Alzheimer's disease is proceeding. Researches on anti-malarial drugs, asthma, cot-death, fatty acids, and combating tropical parasites are simply a few examples of work being undertaken by the group of Health Science departments.[25]

Chemistry has so much research in progress and completed since 1991 that it is impossible to

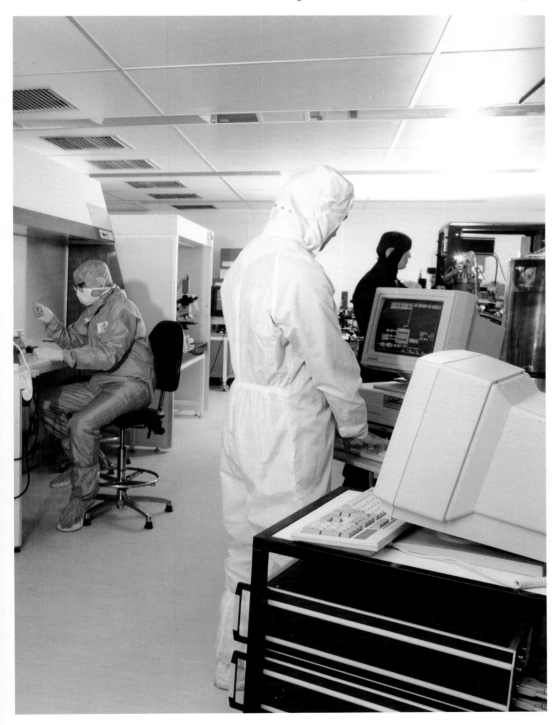

58 A clean room established by the Superconducting Devices Research Group in the Department of Physics and Applied Physics. Some of the most sensitive magnetic field sensors in the world are made here, using thin film superconducting technology including new superconducting materials. One example is the making of SQUIDS (Superconducting Quantum Interference Devices) to monitor the electrical activity of the foetal heart in unborn babies.

do justice to it. The main areas include organometallic chemistry where Professor Peter Pauson was leader until his recent retirement. He was honoured by Merck Ltd. in 1994 which endowed the Pauson Chair for work in Preparative Chemistry – synthetic organic and organometallic research. Much work is proceeding on the ultrapurification, growth and perfection of crystals in which Vice-Principal Professor John Sherwood has been a notable leader. Polymers and polymerisation processes have engaged the attention of a substantial group which has involved *inter alia* Professor Neil Graham and, more recently, Professor David Sherrington as team leaders. Work on carbon fibre composite materials and resins to bind them, much lighter than conventional substances, inspired by ICI's subsidiary Fiberite, has supported that firm's successful bid to supply Boeing with the main structural material for the tail of the new 777 jet.

The range of research in Physics is also colossal, varying from the immediately applicable to wealth creation to the highly theoretical 'blue skies' category. Much good work on instrumentation has been undertaken by David Birch and Robert Imhof, both recently elevated to personal Chairs. Laser physics, atomic/plasma physics and opto-electronics engage others. One of the most significant developments in human and economic terms is the use of SQUIDS [Superconducting Quantum Interference Devices] which operate at only four degrees Celsius above absolute zero. The Superconducting Devices Group in Physics hopes to create in collaboration with clinical colleagues at the Southern General Hospital an effective system of health-monitoring of unborn babies using SQUIDS to record the electrical activity of the foetal heart. These complex microelectronic circuits are made in the Department in the 'high-tech' clean room. Their applications are apparently very numerous wherever detection devices are important elements in activity: oil exploration or astronomical observatories.

Mathematics has recently received the ultimate accolade in that Professor Frank Leslie has been recently (1995) elected to the fellowship of the Royal Society. He joins distinguished predecessors in the old 'Tech' and Andersonian. His significant contributions to the mathematical modelling of liquid crystals have been made over twenty-five years and have practical implications for their industrial uses. Leslie's theory of twisted nematic alignment in magnetic fields led to the first liquid crystal display, now so common in electronic goods, gadgets and toys, and was the beginning of continuous work which ensured his pre-eminence in the field. In Mathematics and Statistics and Computer Science, to add to good teaching quality assessments, much practical research is being undertaken in spatial statistics, mathematical biology, continuum mechanics, numerical analysis, industrial mathematics, and novel methods for information accessing and retrieval.[26]

The Faculty of Engineering had, in June 1993, 2,200 undergraduates, 500 graduate students and research assistants and more than 200 academic staff working in nine departments. Annual expenditure was about £17 million, of which about 50 per cent was spent on research covering almost every area of engineering and technology. By far the largest concentration of engineering expertise in Scotland, the Faculty has performed particularly well in this period of growing public accountability. In the RAE of 1992-3 two departments were assessed in the top band and others came close. Since then, as Table 10.2 indicates, the Faculty has been highly regarded by visiting TQA teams of SHEFC. The Departments of Electronic and Electrical Engineering (1993), Mechanical Engineering, and Design, Manufacture and Engineering Management (1994) were awarded 'excellent' ratings, and Civil Engineering (1994) came close with 'highly satisfactory'. The assessors commented in their report on Mechanical Engineering and DMEM on 'the very imaginative elements in course design including a strong commitment to a European dimension' and particularly commended the leadership provided by Professor John Spence. Many undergraduates take European languages with the intention of studying in Europe

59 Crystals grown at the Optical Materials Research Centre, Department of Physics and Applied Physics, for laser and non-linear optical applications.

for part of their course; several staff have contacts in Europe, and Professor Tom Gray and Dr Colin Walker have been particularly prominent in stimulating student exchanges.

The Faculty in 1995 has eight departments as a consequence of Metallurgy and Materials Science merging with Mechanical Engineering. Since the last RAE an ambitious programme of Faculty Scholarships and Bicentennial Scholarships has been mounted; this brings about forty highly qualified young researchers into the Faculty and is designed to extend the base of research excellence. Collaborative relationships with industry are long established but can never be taken for granted. Much effort has been expended to create effective partnerships with industrial firms, a necessary element in improving funding from the Engineering and Physical Sciences Research Council.

Many of the staff have international reputations in their disciplines: there are concentrations of expertise in Bioengineering, the Built Environment, Control Engineering, Optoelectronics, Engineering Materials, Information Technology and Power Systems. An unusually high proportion of research funding is derived from industry or for projects which involve government and EC programmes which specify partnership with industry. Although much fundamental research is being undertaken, the importance of applicable research as an essential tool in wealth creation is at last being recognised. Here the Faculty is exceptionally strong. A number of specialist centres exist for the express purpose of linking *academe* with industry, commonly described as 'windows for industry', for example the Centre for Electrical Power Engineering [CEPE], the Centre for Advanced Structural Materials [CASM] and the Architecture and Building Aids Computer Unit [ABACUS].

As with the other Faculties it is only possible to illustrate a small section of the research activity; immediate industrial or human significance has been used as a crude indicator. What has been colloquially called 'using bugs like factories' is one example. In the Department of Chemical and Process Engineering research by Dr Carl Schaschke and others is concerned with producing naturally occurring proteins using genetically modified micro-organisms. The possibilities are limitless even if one only considers medical requirements for insulin, interferon and human growth hormone. Yeast is the most commonly used micro-organism but the problem is in recovering and purifying the protein in an economic and safe fashion. One method of recovery being investigated is putting high pressure carbon dioxide into the yeast and controlling its release through using the energy in the bubbles created by the gas which may transcend the problem of damaging the molecular structure of the protein.

In Bioengineering much effort is going into creating an artificial knee 'with brains'. A microprocessor-controlled artificial knee which will adjust itself as the person walks will clearly make walking easier for patients recovering from amputations. Improving the quality and performance of artificial limbs is also a research concern of the National Centre for Prosthetics and Orthotics. Staff of the centre have developed a computer-based system with good quality graphics which will allow skilled prosthetists to quantify their methods and to transfer their skills and personal knowledge. Thus patient measurement, limb design and manufacture may become easier and hopefully cheaper and more beneficial.

The University has an international reputation for computer-aided design research. The field is interdisciplinary, and thus researchers require access to a wide range of expertise. The Intelligent Design Systems Forum acts to link faculty members broadly interested in 'artificial intelligence' and its applications. Thus research resources are more economically used and, hopefully, practical results expedited.

CASM uniquely has its own autoclave, a type of high-pressure moulding oven which can be used for a number of purposes, and therefore there is a well-organised queue of researchers

60 Principal Arbuthnott stands beside the sculpture 'Prometheus' with its creator Jack Sloan.
In the background is the Wolfson Centre.

61 The Intelligent Design Systems Forum links faculty members broadly interested in artificial intelligence and its applications. Here a robotic head demonstrates the fruits of collaboration between DMEM (Design Manufacture and Engineering Management) and Computer Science.

wanting to use it. It can make or test components from modern composite materials like carbon fibre reinforced plastics. Materials research and development is therefore greatly aided by this facility, as the Director, Professor W. Banks, rightly asserts. Dr James McKelvie is leading a project investigating the safe remaining operational life of components that have been damaged. This clearly has many practical implications for aircraft structures, for example. The consortium involved in this project includes Yard (UK), the University of Stuttgart, the German Aerospace Laboratory, and the Italian firm, D'Appolonia.

Lighter, stiffer alloys are essential for the improvement of airframes and aerospace performance. Professor T. Neville Baker and colleagues are testing powdered metal and ceramic mixtures with the intention of improving composites. Special properties are often needed in specific places; for example, the surface of a component may be required to perform differently from its main body – 'the functionally graded component'. Professor Baker's group has used lasers to treat the surface to achieve this. The use of ceramics in engines presents many problems for researchers to solve. The fragility of ceramic materials dictates that they have to be reinforced and joined to metal components. The Ceramics Research Group led by Professor Alan Hendry is working with industry to test new ceramic-based composites.

Electronic and Electrical Engineering has so many practical applications in industry, in public places and in the home that research is vital to improve the human condition. New ways of disposing of hazardous waste are the product of research in CEPE. Leslie Campbell and Martin Stewart are developing systems that use plasma – gas stripped of its electrons by passing it through a very strong magnetic field – to decontaminate waste. Temperatures up to 6,000 degrees Celsius can be achieved by this method as compared with a normal incinerator

62 An ROV (remotely operated vehicle) being launched from a rig into the sea for subsea work. Strathclyde University's Department of Ship and Marine Technology has done work on problems relating to launches into frequently stormy waters. Courtesy Subsea Offshore Limited, Aberdeen.

temperature of about 1,000 degrees. Considerable developments have occurred in signal processing resulting from the research of Professor Tariq Durrani and colleagues. Noise control using sound waves is the interest of Dr Robert Stewart; this research has many potential customers including the automobile and aeronautical industries. Many research projects in the field of Optoelectronics – with Professor Brian Culshaw as group leader – are underway.

Unmanned underwater vehicles that perform tasks at ocean depths have an obvious application for oil exploration and exploitation. Three projects relating to these vehicles funded by the Research Council [EPSRC] and industry have come to the Department of Ship and Marine Technology led by Professor Chengi Kuo, and a fourth – the creation of an efficient underwater vision system – is within the ambit of the Signal Processing Division of the Department of Electronic and Electrical Engineering.

In Civil Engineering and in Architecture and Building Science much research effort is expended on improving design of major structures, and in the case of the Construction Management Division of the Department of Civil Engineering examining the industry from a management perspective to improve performance in overseas markets. The London Underground's Jubilee Line extension and other major construction projects outside Britain recruit postgraduate students in order to improve their economic efficiency. Computer modelling of urban environments, housing conservation and urban design are major areas of research for the Department of Architecture and Building Science, and each of them has an implication for how societies live and work.[27]

The Business School does not fit conveniently – department by department – into the categories established for RAE or Teaching Quality Assessment visitation; it is, therefore, considered almost in its entirety as a cognate area. Despite this, it has performed exceedingly well, most of its staff achieving the highest rating in the RAE of 1993 and the SHEFC TQA of 1995. In addition, the Strathclyde Graduate Business School has flourished: by 1992-3 it had 1,800 students proceeding by various modes of study – full-time, part-time, and distance learning. Its new building has proved to be a great asset. Built on Cathedral Street and connected with the Sir William Duncan Building on Rotten Row, it cost £11.6 million and appears to be worth every penny! The new facilities, opened in 1992, include two 75-seater lecture theatres, 18 seminar rooms, 21 offices, 34 excellent bedrooms and a Business Information Centre. Concerned with postgraduate and post-experience management education, its product leader has been the MBA programme which has proved very attractive to home and overseas students. Foreign earnings, especially from the MBA distance learning courses, led to the Queen's Award for Export Achievement in 1993, the Graduate Business School being the only educational institution to win the award up to that time.

Reviews of undergraduate programmes are regularly undertaken by departments, but nowhere is it more important than in the Business School. In October 1992, 95 students enrolled for a part-time Law degree, Ll.B., recruited from 900 applicants. The flexibility of the degree structure encourages students from other faculties to seek a Business Studies option to add to such established degrees as Marketing and Modern Languages.

As one of the largest business schools in Europe, the Strathclyde Business School has a number of research strengths: international business and inward investment; modelling the United Kingdom economy; Social Marketing and the study of the consequences of types of advertisement; methods of making the British food industry more competitive (sponsored by 13 major British food companies); employee participation in business and trade union strategies; the impact of telecommunications and technological innovation on organisations; tourism and hotel management.

There is much involvement in public sector research and consultancy issues as well as work sponsored by private firms. The Scottish Local Authorities Management Centre is based in the Business School and apart from undertaking research for local authorities also provides for the training needs of their staff. The Fraser of Allander Institute has become a recognised authority on the Scottish economy, and its bulletins and forecasts are closely perused by public servants at all levels and also by business economists more widely. The media inevitably have taken a keen interest in both these research centres: in the former case Professor Alan Alexander investigated the effect of the collapse of BCCI on the finances of the Western Isles and has been newsworthy ever since; in the latter the Fraser Institute contains experts on most sectors of the Scottish economy and therefore they are constantly in the news. The European Policies Research Centre has, as its name suggests, a wider remit. Professors Allen and Yuill lead teams which undertake research for public and private-sector organisations across a variety of policy areas in both western and eastern Europe.[28]

The Faculty of Arts and Social Studies (Social Sciences in 1995) is smaller than the other faculties but is of demonstrably high quality. Three of its professorial members have been elected fellows of the British Academy; FBA is the highest accolade open to practitioners in the Arts and Social Sciences, the equivalent of F.R.S.. Emeritus Professor Gustav Jahoda (1988) of Psychology was the first; Professor Richard Rose (1992) of the Centre for the Study of Public Policy, the second; and Professor Thomas M. Devine of History, most recently (1994), the third. In the RAE (1993), the Department of Government and the Centre for the Study of Public Policy were given the highest rating, and others came close, with most staff being classified as conducting research of national or international excellence. The History Department was granted Mode A recognition for doctoral training by the Economic and Social Research Council in 1992, only one of five departments in Britain given full three-year recognition. Only one department has so far been assessed for teaching quality, Geography (1994) which was graded 'excellent'. Generally, the Faculty has a reputation with students for providing stimulating teaching and solid pastoral care.

In research, the Faculty in the last RAE had the highest proportion of 'research-active' staff of any in the University and the highest of any Arts Faculty in Scotland. All members of the staff are conducting research, and they perceive that commitment to be vital to their role as effective teachers. The Faculty has researchers of international distinction in electoral behaviour, public policy, Scottish Historical and Literary Studies, German Political History in the twentieth century, interactive learning, European languages and literature, linguistics, addiction studies and media culture.

There has been a clear attempt to prepare for the next Research Assessment Exercise and a comprehensive strategy has been developed. One component of that is the use of graduate assistants so that staff can complete research and publication by 1996. Another element is the creation of research centres in Scottish History, in Literature, Culture and Communication and in Occupational and Health Psychology to add to the existing Centre for the Study of Public Policy. On behalf of the Faculty a Research Task Group monitors, advises and evaluates research initiatives. Thus within limited resources, an enriched research environment has been created.

Special projects of interest include a projected three-volume history of Glasgow. The first volume appeared in 1995 and its writers were given a civic reception. Who were the working-class Nazis and why did they support the National Socialists are two significant questions being addressed in an international project headed by Dr Conan Fischer. Professor Terry Wade is researching 1,500 Russian words for the first etymological dictionary of the Russian language to be written in English. Pioneering work in teaching Spanish language, bringing together new technologies and language acquisition theory, is being undertaken by Dr Miranda Stewart and Ms Custina Ros of Modern Languages as part of the UK-wide Technology Enhanced Language Learning consortium. Investigating alcohol and aggression has been one of the activities of the Centre for Occupational and Health Psychology. The findings of this research, funded by the Alcohol Education and Research Council, are important in a country where alcohol abuse is a much more significant problem than drug abuse.

How young people form their aspirations about their future life and what influences this important process are two significant questions being examined by sociologists in the Department of Government. Notable work in the Department of Government includes an analysis of voluntary organisations in Scotland which employ 30,000 people, have an income of £2 billion, and organise about one million volunteers. John Curtice with colleagues in London and Oxford has recently (1994) completed *Labour's Last Chance*. This is based on the 1992 British Election Study, the third to be directed by Curtice and his colleagues. The Economic and Social Research Council have agreed to fund a Centre for Research into Elections and Social Trends, a recognition of the importance of the work of Curtice and his colleagues. The Centre for the Study of Public Policy is engaged on a survey-based research programme on mass behaviour in post-Communist societies in co-operation with research institutes in Eastern Europe and the United States.[29]

An extensive range of teaching is provided at the undergraduate and postgraduate diploma/ certificate levels in Education, as might be expected, in the newest Faculty formed from Jordanhill College of Education in 1993. It has been assessed by SHEFC in 1995 and rated as 'highly satisfactory'. However, the Faculty has a wider remit than teacher training, providing courses in Community Education, Social Work, Sports Science and Speech and Language Therapy. In the RAE (1992-3) it proved to be the best of the public sector institutions, with many staff conducting research of national excellence.

Assimilation into the University meant that new staff appointed from April 1993 would be offered University contracts, with no disturbance to employment conditions of those already in post. Dr T.R. Bone retired as Principal in September 1992 and was later appointed a Professor in the University and Deputy Principal with special responsibility for assisting the Principal in assessing developments in Scottish Higher Education. After due process, five staff of the Faculty became Professors: James McCall, Tony Mangan, Douglas Weir, Tom Bryce and John MacBeath. Subsequently, at the next annual review in 1994, Myra Nimmo joined them. James McCall became Dean of the Faculty and immediately was faced with dealing with a substantial accumulated deficit which had to be set against the Capital Account. A budget had to be set for 1993-4 which would create a surplus in order to begin reducing the deficit. This was successfully accomplished, although the actual surplus was smaller than that projected. Reductions in in-service provision for teachers and in the intake to teacher training (which is determined by the Secretary of State) meant that the Dean and his colleagues did not have much flexibility.

Yet the Faculty reorganised its structure in 1994, creating 14 departments and three Vice-Deans, and conducted a full academic review. An extensive range of research activities is being undertaken (1995) and some substantial research contracts have been won. For instance, Professor John MacBeath secured a £330,000 contract with colleagues in the University of London to examine and improve the quality of Scottish schools. A major collaborative venture, the Scottish Institute for Sports Medicine and Sports Science, with the support of the Scottish Sports Council and the University of Aberdeen, has been established, the Patron being HRH the Princess Royal. Partners in the Centre for Training in Residential Care include the Save the Children Fund and Who Cares (Scotland) and Langside College, clearly an important activity for the community. Work is also proceeding on the provision of social work services to ethnic

63 Professor John MacBeath of Strathclyde's Quality in Education Centre leads a team of researchers intent on providing policy-makers with better guidance when they discuss how to improve education. A number of research initiatives are being sponsored by external agencies, including an inquiry into attendance and absence in schools supported by the Scottish Office. This Centre is Scotland's leading research facility for understanding and improving the quality of primary and secondary education.

minorities; on information technology awareness in students (already revealing that much practical help is necessary); on practical assessment in science education; on speech difficulties and the effectiveness of therapy. Professor Mangan, an internationally recognised expert in Sports History and the History of Education, continued work in this field. The possibility of extending the research base has been improved as a consequence of the creation in the Library of a CD-Rom Database called *Scottish Education Bibliography 1970-1990*, itself a research exercise of considerable merit.[30]

Students and staff in all faculties rely on the central services of the university for the effective management of important functions: finance, academic administration, medical, counselling and welfare services, estates, catering and residence services. Two are particularly important to undergraduates. The first is the Schools and Colleges Liaison Service which may have influenced the choice of university in the first place or supplied with the help of academic colleagues information about particular courses. The annual Entrance Information sessions held in September regularly attract between 6,000 and 7,000 visitors. In addition, staff of this service, led by Jennifer Foulds, regularly visit schools and colleges throughout the United Kingdom and attend fairs and conventions wherever information about university entrance is required. The second is the Careers Service which works in partnership with the departments to improve the employability of students and to assist them when seeking employment. Keith Dugdale and Barbara Graham, the two directors of the service in the 1990s, have pioneered a number of important initiatives such as Jobline, a computer and telephone listing of vacancies which students and employers have commended. By 1994 the worst of the international depression was deemed to be over when the percentage of Strathclyde graduates unemployed six months after graduation was 6.7 per cent, but the University has always been in the top ten as far as employers are concerned.

Undergraduates receive help when they require it from the Centre for Academic Practice, from the medical services which a dedicated team of doctors supply and from the counselling and welfare services. The University, like others, has been particularly concerned about the growing evidence of significant student poverty, which is a matter for much greater anxiety than the statistics relating to academic failure. For more has not meant worse! Access to University and awareness of what it can offer has been a particular mission of the Science and Technology Forum, led by Dr Robert H. Nuttall. The Forum has provided, with the aid of industrial sponsors, aid to primary schools with the intention of making Science and Technology attractive to the young.[31] Our undergraduates have also volunteered to play their part in a BP-sponsored scheme of tutoring in schools which was initially organised by Visiting Professor Peter McNaught, formerly Principal of Craigie College. Summer schools have been organised to introduce students from Access courses in Further Education Colleges to the University, a venture to which staff devote considerable time in the non-existent long vacation.

The quality of university life is much enhanced for all its members by the music, drama and arts programmes which are also accessible to a wider community. The combination of city centre facilities such as the Collins Gallery with those at Jordanhill has been used to good effect: for classical music, music-making, art exhibitions, drama by the Strathclyde Theatre Group, folk, rock and *pots pourri* cultural events. Although the University provides core funding for these activities, there is much very welcome grant support from public bodies as well as income from ticket sales.[32]

The University has been singularly well served by its lay members of Court throughout its history. In the 1990s the adjustment to greater public accountability was to some extent discounted by earlier successful attempts to restructure university management and administration which Court had initiated. Dr Stephen Newall, Chairman of Court (1988-93), Dr Tom Johnstone, alumnus and Treasurer till 1994, and Dr James Drury, chairman of Staff Committee, with their colleagues set a very high level of devoted service because apart from the time they gave willingly, they brought considerable business experience which their academic colleagues respected. James, Lord Goold, Chairman of Court (1993-), joined the Court in 1988 and gave the University the benefit of his many years of experience in the construction industry by becoming chairman of Estates Committee. Roy Johnson, the recently appointed Treasurer, will no doubt use his considerable accountancy skills and experience to plumb the mysteries of university finances. A university is not any old business, and these and other Court members respect that. Yet they have a responsibility to see that the University of Strathclyde is managed in a business-like way, that the academic members use the University's resources wisely and that there is proper regard for the future.[33]

Principal John P. Arbuthnott (1991-) is deemed, for the purposes of public finance, to be the University's Chief Accounting Officer. He is admirably equipped for the task of leading the University of Strathclyde into the next millennium. Born and educated in Glasgow, his academic career in the University of Glasgow, as Professor of Microbiology in Trinity College, Dublin (1976-88) and at the University of Nottingham (1988-91) marks him as a formidable academic leader. At Trinity College he became University Bursar (1983-6) with day-to-day responsibility for its property and financial management; in 1992 along with Mary Robinson, President of Ireland and a former professorial colleague, John Arbuthnott became an Honorary Fellow of the College.[34]

64 From the 1960s Strathclyde acquired a considerable reputation in international debating circles. Lively inter-varsity debates became commonplace, as did the winning of trophies!

65 Professor John P. Arbuthnott, Third Principal and Vice Chancellor of the University (1991-),
shares a rooftop view with SRC President Vicki Jones.

His first six months at Strathclyde were spent *inter alia* visiting every department in the University on a fact-finding and assessment mission. He greatly impressed staff both by his equable temperament and by his perspicacity. During his early years in the University, much personal effort was expended on successfully completing projects which had been underway when Sir Graham Hills retired.

Among these were the launching of the Graduate School of Environmental Studies, led by Jean Forbes of the Department of Planning and Ralph Kirkwood of Bioscience and Biotechnology (1991), and a collaborative agreement with Bell College of Technology (1992). The former led to further collaboration with the University of Glasgow, and the latter increased access opportunities for the people of North Lanarkshire. The first phase of the George Street East project was completed in May 1992, and two further phases of residence blocks, Chancellor's Hall and James Young Hall, were finished that year, providing in total another 300 places. Thus, the student village, essentially Sir Graham's vision, was virtually completed. The solar residences, James Blyth Court and Thomas Campbell Court, won the top prize of the Energy Efficiency Award in 1993, and the transformed Ramshorn Theatre, the restored Barony Hall and the new Strathclyde Graduate Business School were recognised as buildings of extraordinary merit and received a number of British design awards in 1992-3. The renovation of the Barony was also recognised by an award from Europa Nostra, the premier association concerned with the European heritage. Expansion of the Library, so badly needed with greater student numbers, proceeded apace in 1992, and the Royal Scottish Geographical Society (which took offices in the Sir Graham Hills Building) transferred its specialist library to the Andersonian.

Much support is given to the University by volunteers and donors, possibly a reflection of its integration into the local, national and international communities which it serves. More than one hundred visiting professors and honorary lecturers assist departments, and many former students bring their practical experience to their *alma mater*, and a substantial number assist in fund-raising. *Campaign 2000*, the University's fund-raising campaign, launched in 1990, has King Harald of Norway as Royal Patron, aims to raise £42 million by 2000, within three years had raised £10 million, and goes from strength to strength at a time when SHEFC funding is very tight.

As Table 10.2 indicates, the University staff is committed to excellence in teaching so that students have a stimulating experience in the lecture theatre, the laboratory and the tutorial and seminar. The *Daily Telegraph* (20 August, 1994) recognised Strathclyde as a 'Centre of Teaching Excellence'. The mission is also to be recognised generally as a centre of excellence in research. The University is distinctive in its outward orientation: both staff and students are involved in community activities, and much research is devoted to improving the regional, national and international economies.[35]

In terms of recurrent grants for teaching and research in the bicentenary session of 1995-6 the University of Strathclyde is third in the ranking of Scottish Universities with a total SHEFC grant of over £53 million, unfortunately a cut in real terms compared with session 1994-5.[36] The auguries for future SHEFC funding appear relatively gloomy, but the challenge can be turned into an opportunity if the supporters of the University rally round as they have throughout its history. Mass higher education cannot be funded on the same basis as the elitist system of the past. The University of Strathclyde and its ancestors have provided bridges of access and opportunity for generations of students from Scotland, the United Kingdom and every continent. It will continue to do so; fulfilling the vision of its founder, John Anderson, the University will remain committed to useful learning and ' ... the good of Mankind and the Improvement of Science' – a sufficient and appropriate motto for an international university.

66 A degree congregation in the restored Barony Hall. Converted from the Barony Church (architects Sir J.J. Burnet and John A. Campbell,1886-90), this magnificent ceremonial hall came into the University's possession largely as a consequence of the vision of Sir Graham Hills. In 1993 Europa Nostra, the principal organisation concerned with the European Heritage, made an award to the Barony Hall.

REFERENCES

1   JBC, author's own record. UMG and Senate August/ September 1991; UMG 4 and 18 February, 1992; Senate 5 February, 1992.

2   Ibid., Minutes of the Joint Working Party of Strathclyde University and Jordanhill College, 1991-2, *passim*.

3   These matters are fully discussed by J.P. Arbuthnott and T.R. Bone, 'Anatomy of a Merger', *Higher Education Quarterly*, Vol.47, No.2 (Spring 1993), pp. 103-19.

4   Scottish Office Education Department, press release in which Lord James Douglas Hamilton approved the merger, September 1992; UFC, Scottish Committee, *Criteria for Assessing Merger Proposals from Institutions of Higher Education* (Edinburgh, 1991), *passim*; Scottish Office Education Department, *Future Strategy for Higher Education in Scotland* (Cmd. 9676, STEAC Report, 1985), *passim*.

5   These attitudes were apparent to the author who chaired many of the Joint Working Party meetings; JBC, MIG, 6 December, 1993.

6   JBC, Minutes of Joint Working Party and Sub-Groups, 1991-2; MIG Reports, 19 October 1992, 14 December, 1992; *Prism*, Commemorative Issue, 1 April 1993.

7   JBC, Author's own record.

8   Anon. [Irene Hynd and Amanda McKenzie], *70 Years of Excellence in Education: Jordanhill College 1921-91* (Glasgow, 1991), pp. 3-4; Wood, *David Stow*, *passim*; Saunders, pp. 296 ff.

9   JBC, GWSTC, Governors' Minutes, 1905-6, pp. 66, 141, 152, 156-7. Professor George Gibson was a member of the Provincial Committee.

10   *70 Years of Excellence* ... , p.4.

11   JBC, RTC, Governors' Minutes, 1920-1, pp. 7, 58-9.

12   *70 Years of Excellence* ... , pp. 5 ff. It was the largest college in terms of the number of teachers trained.

13   JBC, RTC, Governors' Minutes, 1920-1, p.49.

14   Professor P. Reed, in Commemorative Issue of *Prism*, 1 April, 1993, p.6.

15   Peter West in *Prism*, 1 April, 1993, p.7.

16   Stuart Millar, President of the Students' Association, 1992-3, in *Prism*, 1 April 1993.

17   *Prism*, 1 April, 1993, p.8.

18   JBC, Annual Accounts, 1989-94; UMG and Court discussions of current financial state, 1989-92, *passim*.

19   JBC, University of Strathclyde, Institutional Planning, 1991-5 (February, 1992); SHEFC Reports, 1993-4; RAE Report ,1993.

20   JBC, SHEFC Teaching Quality Assessment Reports, 1993-5.

21   The Funding Councils have consulted the Universities and are preparing a final report (June 1995).

22   These issues commonly occur at Faculty meetings as well as being raised by senior management at inter-university meetings, especially at Committee of Scottish Higher Education Principals [COSHEP].

67 A party of academic and administrative staff about to depart for South-East Asia to conduct graduation ceremonies in Singapore and Kuala Lumpur. From left to right: Professor Owen Farish, Professor Tom Devine, Charles Turner (holding mace) and Ursula Laver. Courtesy Caledonian Newspapers Ltd.

23 Cf. Deputy Principal Professor T.M. Devine, Letter to *The Herald*, 13 May, 1995. Professor Devine wrote that 1,061 Strathclyde students had spent a period of study in Europe between 1992 and 1995.

24 JBC, SHEFC, Reports on TQA, 1994; *Prism*, Nos. 72 and 73, October 1991; author's private record of Pharmacy Review which he chaired.

25 Senate Minutes, 2 February, 1994.

26 Faculty of Science, *Research Prisms*, October 1994 and March 1995; Annual Reports, 1991-4; Draft Submissions for RAE, 1991-2; *Prism*, No.116, March 1995.

27 Faculty of Engineering, *Research Prisms*, June 1994 and February 1995; Court Visits to Departments – personal record; SHEFC *TQA Reports* for Civil Engineering, Electronic and Electrical Engineering, Mechanical Engineering and DMEM, 1993-4.

28 SHEFC, *TQA Reports* for Economics (1993) and Business Studies (1995); JBC, personal record made as Vice-Principal.

29 JBC, personal record made on RAE as Vice-Principal; *Prism*, No.83, June 1992; *Research Prisms*, April and December 1994; SHEFC, *TQA Report* on Geography, 1994;

30 University Management Group, Minutes, January-March 1994; MIG, 28 February 1994; *Research Prism*, January 1995; SHEFC, *TQA Report* on Education, 1995.

31 By June 1993 the Science and Technology Forum had been visited by 5,000 pupils.

32 JBC, Annual Reports, 1991-4.

33 JBC, Court Minutes, 1988-92; *Prism* Court Reports, 1992-5.

34 The Irish President visited the University on 1 July 1992 and much admired the Strathclyde Graduate Business School.

35 Professor Ian McNicoll of the Department of Economics has estimated that for 1991/2 the University created an estimated output of £230 million in the Scottish economy, and established the equivalent of 5,380 full-time jobs and £94.5 million in labour income.

36 JBC, *Prism*, April 1995; SHEFC, Information for Institutions, March 1995. The University by 1992-3 received only 54 per cent of its recurrent income from government funding and continues to reduce that proportion as a matter of policy. Annual Report, 1992-3, pp.2-3.

T.M. Devine and G.Jackson, eds., *History of Glasgow* Vol.I (Manchester, 1995).

campaign 2000

UNIVERSITY OF STRATHCLYDE

68 Campaign 2000, the University's fund-raising campaign, was launched in 1990 with King Harald of Norway as its Royal Patron. It aims to raise £42 million pounds by the year 2000 and within three years had raised £10 million.

APPENDIX I

Anderson's University and Anderson's College
Medical Professors and Lecturers, 1800-1886

Name	Appointed	Resigned	Academic Area
John Burns	1800	1818	Midwifery and Surgery
William Cummin	1816	1818	Botany
Granville Sharp Pattison	1818	1819	Anatomy and Surgery
William Mackenzie	1819	1828	Anatomy and Surgery
James Armour	1828	died 1831	Midwifery and Medical Jurisprudence
James Brown	1831	1841	Midwifery
George Watt	1831	1842	Medical Jurisprudence
Forbes	1831		Medical Latin
Robert Hunter*	1828	1841	Anatomy
A. Hannay	1828	died 1846	Theory and Practice of Medicine
Andrew Buchanan	1828	1838	Materia Medica and Pharmacy
James Smith Candlish	1829	died 1829	Surgery
James Adair Lawrie	1829	1850	Surgery
J.P.Cheetham	1830	1831	Veterinary Surgery
John Stewart	1833		Veterinary Surgery
John Scouller	1829	1861	Mineralogy, Geology, Natural History
W.D.Hooker	1838	1839	Materia Medica
Andrew Anderson*	1840	transferred 1846	Institutes and Theory of Medicine
J.A.Easton	1840	1855	Materia Medica
Moses S. Buchanan	1841	died 1860	Anatomy
James Paterson	1841	1863	Midwifery
George Gardner	1842	1843	Botany and Natural History
John Crawford	1842	1856	Medical Jurisprudence
Thomas Edmonston	1845	1845	Botany and Natural History
Andrew Anderson*	1846	1863	Practice of Medicine
A.M.Adams	1846	1849	Institutes of Medicine
Joseph Bell	1848	died 1862	Botany and Natural History
Robert Hunter*	1849	1850	Institutes of Medicine
Robert Hunter*	1850	1860	Surgery
Ebenezer Watson	1850	1876	Institutes of Medicine
James Morton	1855		Materia Medica
John B. Cowan*	1856	transfer	Medical Jurisprudence
George Buchanan*	1857		Assistant in Anatomy
George H. B. Macleod	1857	1859	Lecturer in Military Surgery
George Buchanan*	1860		Anatomy
George H.B.Macleod*	1860	1869	Surgery
John B. Cowan*	1863	1865	Practice of Medicine
William Leishman	1863	1868	Medical Jurisprudence
James G. Wilson	1863	died 1881	Midwifery
Roger Hennedy	1863	died 1876	Botany
T. McCall Anderson	1866		Practice of Medicine

Name	Appointed	Resigned	Academic Area
P.A.Simpson	1868		Medical Jurisprudence
John R. Wolfe	1869		Ophthalmic Medicine and Surgery
D.C.McVail	1876	1880	Institutes of Medicine
R.H.Patterson	1877	1879	Botany
James Christie	1878		Public Health
Alexander S. Wilson	1879		Botany
J. Cowan Woodburn	1879		Dental Surgery and Pathology
James R. Brownlie	1879		Dental Mechanics and Metallurgy
James Crooks Morrison	1879	died 1881	Dental Anatomy and Physiology
Thomas Barr	1879		Aural Surgery
John Barlow	1880	1883	Institutes of Medicine
Samson Gemmill	1880		Practice of Medicine
David Taylor	1881		Dental Anatomy and Physiology
Abraham Wallace	1881		Midwifery

*   Transfers

Source: Minute Books of the Andersonian, 1796-1886.

APPENDIX II

The Andersonian, 1796-1886
Professors, Lecturers and Teachers Outside the Medical Faculty

Name	Appointed	Resigned	Academic Area
Thomas Garnett	1796	1799	Natural Philosophy
Robert Lothian	1798		Mathematics and Geography
George Birkbeck	1799	1804	Natural Philosophy
Andrew Ure	1804	1830	Natural Philosophy and Materia Medica
John Cross	1810	1812	Mathematics and Geography
Thomas Longstaff	1816		Astronomy
James Galloway	1817		Law
John Crosbie	1817		Elocution
Robert Wallace	1824	1827	Mathematics and Geography
Thomas Atkinson	1824		'Craniology'
Peter Wilson	1828	transfer 1833	Mathematics and Geography
Alexander Watt	1828	1830	Astronomy and Geography
William Ross	1829		Theory and Principles of Painting and Sculpture
B. Jourdain	1829	1833	French and Italian
Mr. Revira	1829		Spanish and Portuguese
William Hunter	1830	1833	Logic, English Composition
John A. Gilfillan	1830	1841	Drawing and Painting
William Heron	1830	1833	Natural Philosophy
Thomas Graham	1830	1837	Chemistry
François Foucart	1832		Gymnasium
Rev. Robert Hardie	1833	1837	Logie, Rhetoric and Ethics
Peter Wilson	1833	1845	Natural Philosophy
Rev. John Moncrieff	1833		Oriental Languages
Theodor Weber	1836		German
James French	1837	1842	Logie and Ethics
William Gregory	1837	1839	Chemistry
Dr. Murray	1838		Geology
Frederick William Penny	1839	1869	Chemistry
Mr. Craig	1839		Geology
Dr. Dubeac	1839		French Literature
Mr. Young	1840		Writing and Bookkeeping
Andrew Donaldson	1841	1843	Drawing and Painting
Mr. Wolski	1841		Modern Languages
Herman Jonas	1842		German
Lithgow	1842		Music
Thomson	1842/3		Classics
Simeon	1842/3		French
Robertson	1843	1845	Drawing and Painting

Name	Appointed	Resigned	Academic Area
Koerner	1843/6	transfer to Chair	German
Evans	1843		English
Ordon	1843		French
Woodward and Walker	1844		Phonography
George Greig	1845	transfer	Rhetoric and Belle lettres
Alexander Bain	1845	1846	Natural Philosophy
John Crawford	1845	transfer to Chair	Drawing and Painting
William Weir	1845/7		Phrenology
Flint	1845		Arithmetic
George Greig	1846		Geography
Alexander Laing	1846	1881	Mathematics
Dr. John Taylor	1846	1861	Natural Philosophy
W.H.Long	1847	1848	Writing
Koerner	1847		German
William Anderson	1847	1853	French
James Robertson	1847	1852	English Language and Literature
John Crawford	1848	1853	Drawing and Painting
Rev. Robert Gill	1848		Psychology
Hugh Macfarlane	1849	1853	Writing
Henry Lesingham	1852	1853	English
N. Meyer	1853		French
John Mitchell	1853	1854	English
Thomas Dudgeon	1853		Drawing and Painting
D.C.McLean	1853		Writing and Bookkeeping
James Brown	1854		English
Colin Brown	1860		Music
James Galbraith	1861	1864	Commercial Law
George Carey-Foster	1862	1865	Natural Philosophy
Macklin	1862		Latin, Greek and Hebrew
Henderson	1862		Spanish
Moffat	1863		Elocution
J.A.Dixon	1864		Commercial Law
Macklin	1865		Latin, Greek and Hebrew
Moffat	1865		Elocution
William Stewart	1865		Drawing
Edouard Quillet	1865	1866	French
Clément F.F.Masse	1866		French
Alexander S. Herschel	1866	1871	Natural Philosophy
William Henry Perkin	1869	never took up post	Young Technical Chemistry
T.E.Thorpe	1870	1874	Chemistry
Gustav Bischof	1871	1875	Young Technical Chemistry
George Forbes	1872	1880	Natural Philosophy
Laurence Hill	1872		Marine Engineering
William Dittmar	1874		Chemistry
Edmund J. Mills	1875		Young Technical Chemistry
W.T.Rowden	1876		Applied Mechanics
James Blyth	1880		Natural Philosophy and Mathematics
John Young	1882		Lecturer, Geology; Curator of Hunterian
Walter Bergius	1883		Lecturer, Astronomy

Source: SUA, Minute Books of the Andersonian, 1796-1886.

APPENDIX III

Presidents of Anderson's Institution
and University, 1796-1887

Date	Name	Occupation
1796	Hugh Cross	Merchant
1797	Alexander Oswald	Merchant, property speculator, cotton spinner
1798	William McNeil	Cotton merchant and manufacturer
1802	James Monteath	Doctor and surgeon
1803	John Geddes	Owner of Verreville Glassworks
1805	Alexander Oswald	
1806	John Semple	Bleacher and dyer, Finnieston
1807	William Anderson	Surgeon
1809	Robert Austin	Gardener and seed merchant
1810	Johua Heywood and William Anderson	Heywood, a cotton merchant
1811	James Cleland	Superintendent of Public Works, statistician and author
1812	John Hamilton	Merchant
1814	John More	Royal Bank cashier
1816	James Euing	Merchant and banker
1819	John Geddes	
1820	Walter Ferguson	Cotton merchant and manufacturer
1824	James Andrew Anderson	Merchant and banker, Union Bank
1830	James Smith, FRS, of Jordanhill	Merchant and rentier
1839	James Andrew Anderson	
1844	William Murray	Iron and steel magnate
1858	Walter Crum, FRS	Calico printer
1865	William Euing	Insurance broker
1868	James Young, FRS	Oil magnate
1877	Richard Stedman Cunliff	Engineer and shipbuilder
1879	John Lennox Kincaid Jamieson	Shipbuilder
1883	Andrew Fergus, MD	Doctor

Source: Minute Books of the Andersonian, 1796-1887.

APPENDIX IV

Professors of the Glasgow and West of Scotland College, Royal Technical College and Royal College of Science and Technology, 1887-1964

Name (in alphabetical order)	Appointed	Resigned or Retired	Died	Discipline
Alexander, Kenneth	1962			Economics
Andrew, John	1920	1932		Metallurgy
Blyth, James	1881		1906	Natural Philosophy
Bourdon, Eugène	1904		1916	Architecture
Bruce, Frederick M.	1948			Electrical Engineering
Bryan, Andrew Meikle	1932	1940		Mining Engineering
Burns, Daniel	1902/1909	1932	1939	Mining Engineering
Campion, Alfred	1909/11	1918		Metallurgy
Caven, Robert	1920		1934	Inorganic and Analytical Chemistry
Cumming, William Murdoch	1932	1949		Technical Chemistry
Desch, Cecil H.	1918	1920		Metallurgy
Dittmar, William, F.R.S.	1874		1892	Chemistry
Ellis, David	1904/1924		1937	Bacteriology
Ellwood, Edwin C.	1959		1973	Metallurgy
Fielden, Frank	1959	1968		Architecture
Frazer, William	1956		1968	Civil Engineering
Fulton, James B.	1920		1922	Architecture
Gibson, George	1895	1909	1930	Mathematics
Gourlay, Charles	1888/95		1926	Architecture & Building
Gray, Thomas	1889/1903		1932	Technical Chemistry
Hawthorn, John	1950/1958		1993	Food Science
Hay, Robert	1918/1932	1959		Metallurgy
Heilbron, Isidor [Ian] M.	1909/1919	1920		Chemistry
Henderson, George Gerald, F.R.S.	1892	1919		Chemistry
Hibberd, George	1946			Mining Engineering
Hughes, T. Harold	1922	1942		Architecture
Jahoda, Gustav, FBA	1963			Psychology
Jamieson, Andrew 1881 1899	1912			Electrical Engineering
Kenedi, Robert	1963			Bioengineering
Irving, John	1961			Natural Philosophy
Kerr, William	1936	1946	1959	Civil and Mechanical Engineering
Longbottom, John Gordon	1895/1904		1924	Mechanics
Lythe, Samuel George Edgar	1962			Economic History
Maclay, Alexander	1880	1903		Machine Design
Maclean, Magnus	1899	1923	1937	Electrical Engineering
McCrae, Christopher	1956	1963		Industrial Administration
McQuistan, Dougald B.	1938	1942		Natural Philosophy
Mellanby, Alexander L.	1905	1936		Civil and Mechanical Engineering

Name (in alphabetical order)	Appointed	Resigned or Retired	Died	Discipline
Miller, John	1899/1909	1934		Mathematics
Mills, Edmund James F.R.S.	1875	1901	1921	Technical Chemistry
Moncur, George	1905/1910	1933		Civil Engineering
Morris, Ernest O.	1961			Applied Microbiology
Muir, James	1900/1906	1938		Natural Philosophy
Pack, Donald C.	1953			Mathematics
Patterson, Thomas T.	1963			Administration
Pauson, Peter	1959			Organic Chemistry
Potter, Allen	1962			Politics
Price, Albert Thomas	1951	1953		Mathematics
Raitt, William	1881		1895	Mathematics
Rankin, James S.	1942	1960		Natural Philosophy
Ritchie, Patrick D.	1953			Technical Chemistry
Rowden, William Thomas	1876	1904	1924	Applied Mathematics
Scott, Alexander W.	1956			Chemical Engineering
Sexton, Alexander Humboldt	1884	1909	1932	Metallurgy
Shone, Kenneth	1947	1956		Industrial Administration
Smith, Stanley Parker	1924	1948		Electrical Engineering
Smith, William J.	1946	1959		Architecture
Spring, Frank Stuart, F.R.S.	1946	1959		Organic Chemistry
Stenlake, John B.	1961			Pharmacy
Street, Reginald O.	1934	1951		Mathematics
Thomson, Adam S.T.	1946	1973		Engineering Group
Todd, James P.	1921/1937	1961		Pharmacy
Watkinson, William H.	1893	1905	1932	Prime Movers
Wilson, James Forsyth	1906/1919		1944	Organic Chemistry

1   Where two dates are given, the first indicates a specific lectureship and the second elevation to a chair.
2   Where no end date is given, this indicates membership of University of Strathclyde.

Sources: JBC, Minute Books of the institutions named (1887-1959); SUA, Minute Books, 1960-4.

Bibliography

Place of publication is only given where books are published outside London.

PRIMARY SOURCES

ANDERSONIAN LIBRARY RARE
BOOKS DEPARTMENT

THE PAPERS OF JOHN ANDERSON

MS/1	John Anderson's Commonplace Book, 1748-56
MS/2	Essay on the Inducements to study Natural Philosophy
MS/3	John Anderson's Commonplace Book, 1754-5
MS/7	John Anderson's Correspondence with Duke of Richmond
MS/8	John Anderson's Cheap and Speedy Plan for Increasing the Power of Artillery
MS/12	John Anderson's Remarks on the Poetical Remains of James VI and I
MS/15	Book with rain gauge records, 1784-92
MS/15/2	John Anderson's Essay on Rain Gauges, 1780
MS/16	John Anderson's Essay on Artillery
MS/17	John Anderson's Military Sketches
MS/19/2	Dispute in the University of Glasgow
MS/20	Fossils
MS/22	John Anderson's Papers on the Roman Wall
MS/23	John Anderson's Military Essays
MS/24	Physics
MS/25	On the Erection of a Statue to George Buchanan
MS/26	John Anderson on Barometers
MS/27	Catalogue of Fossils, 1767
MS/30	Directions to Operators
MS/31	John Anderson at Dumbarton Rock
MS/33	John Anderson's Journey to the Western Isles
MS/34	Contents of Cloak Bag, 1764
MS/36	Fossils
MS/41	Enquiry into the Conduct of Certain Students, 1782
MS/41/1	John Anderson's Case against Hugh Macleod
MS/41/2	Further Notes against Hugh Macleod
MS/41/3	Declarator, Anderson v. Traill and Others, 1775
MS/48	Alphabetical Collection of Books
	Almanacks 1772, 1775, 1778
	Dr Peter Wright's copy of John Anderson's *Institutes of Physics*

JOHN BUTT COLLECTION

GLASGOW AND WEST OF SCOTLAND
TECHNICAL COLLEGE

Annual Reports, 1888-1913.
Calendars, 1887-1912.
Governors' Minutes, 1887-1912.

ROYAL TECHNICAL COLLEGE

Annual Accounts, 1913-53.
Annual Reports, 1914-55.
Calendars, 1913-39.
Chairman's Committee Minutes, 1913-55.
Governors' Minutes, 1913-55.

ROYAL COLLEGE OF SCIENCE
AND TECHNOLOGY

Academic Board Minutes, 1963-4.
Annual Reports, 1955-64.
Board of Studies Minutes, 1953-63.
City of Glasgow RCST Scheme, 1961.
College Newsletters.
Departmental Reports, 1954-65.
Governors' Minutes, 1956-61.
Merger Papers, 1963-4.
Newsletters, 1960-64.
Reports on Research, 1953-64.
'Transition' Committee Minutes, 1964.

SCOTTISH COLLEGE OF COMMERCE

Copy Draft Agreement, 1964.
Governors' Minutes, 1963-64.

MISCELLANEOUS

Copy letter from Sir Keith Murray to S.C. Curran, 21 August, 1963.

UNIVERSITY OF STRATHCLYDE

Annual Reports, 1964-94.
Careers Advisory Service Reports, 1981-94.
Copy Charter of University of Strathclyde, 1964.
Court Minutes, 1965-92.

Installation of New Chancellor – Brochure, April 1991.

Senate Minutes, 1964-92.

Abstracts of Annual Accounts, 1964-92.

Correspondence with Professor M. M. Fraile, 1972-95.

Documents *re* Research Selectivity Exercises, 1983, 1989, 1992.

Memorandum *re* Architecture from H.C.S. Ferguson to J. Butt, 25 January, 1982.

Memorandum: Dr Mary Dawson to John Butt, 11 April, 1974.

Merger with Jordanhill Papers, 1991-3.

Minutes of University Management Group, 1987-92.

Minutes of University Management Secretariat, 1987-92.

Private Record of Pharmacy Review, 1990.

Professor Adam S.T. Thomson's 'Notes on Engineering...'

Registers of Research, 1965-86.

Reminiscences of Archie M. Pennie, Ottawa, Canada, 1973.

Research Assessment Report, 1993.

Scottish Higher Education Funding Council Teaching Quality Reports and Circulars.

Scottish Office Education Department, Press Release, September 1992.

University Rolling Plans and Institutional Plans, 1987-95.

STRATHCLYDE UNIVERSITY ARCHIVES

A2/1	John Anderson to Gilbert Lang, 1750.
AX/2/2	John Anderson to Gilbert Lang, 1755.
A/5	Benjamin Franklin to John Anderson, 1788.
A/8	John Anderson to Fund for Provision of Widows and Children of Ministers, 1755.
A/10	Account of Instruments, 1756.
A/13	Memorial to Visitors.
B1/1	Anderson's Institution Minute Book, 1796-9.
B1/2	Anderson's Institution Minute Book, 1799-1811.
B1/3	Minute Book of the Andersonian, 1811-30.
B1/4	Minute Book of the Andersonian, 1830-64.
B1/5	Minute Book of the Andersonian, 1865-81.
B1/6	Minute Book of Anderson's University, 1881-7.
B10/1	Anderson's University Report, 1832.
B11/3	Financial Statement, 1844.
B11/4	Financial Statement, 1845.
B13/2	Draft Contract, 1798.
C1/1	Glasgow Mechanics' Institution Minute Book, 1823-34.
C7/1	Mechanics' Institution Letterbook, 1824-42.
C7/2	Mechanics' Institution Letterbook, 1855-61.
C7/3	Mechanics' Institution Letterbook, 1861-75.
C11/8	43rd Annual Report of Mechanics' Institution, 1866.
C11/9	Annual Reports of Mechanics' Institution, 1876-81.
C11/10	Annual Reports of Mechanics' Institution, 1881-7.
DB/3/4	The Atkinson Institution Act, 1861.
E1/1/3	GWSTC Governors' Minutes, 1889-90.
El/1/4	GWSTC Governors' Minutes, 1891-2.
E1/1/7	GWSTC Governors' Minutes, 1897-8.
E1/1/9	GWSTC Governors' Minutes, 1901-2.
E1/1/37	RCST Governors' Minutes, 1957-9.
E1/1/38	RCST Governors' Minutes, 1960-1.
E1/1/39	RCST Governors' Minutes, 1961-3.
E1/1/40	RCST Governors' Minutes, 1963-4.
K10/5	C.G. Wood, 'John Anderson: Some Fresh Aspects', *96 Group Paper*, 1959. C.G. Wood, I.F. Clarke *et al*, 'John Anderson', *96 Group Paper*, 1966. C.G. Wood, 'John Anderson's *Vis Matrix* – his "Actuating Spirit" throughout the years of conflict and dissidence', *96 Group Paper*, 1994.
K10/3/3	D.A.R. Forrester, 'John Anderson's Views on Accounting', *96 Group Paper*, 1974.

Pocket Diary of James Young.

General Notes/68. List of Japanese Students prepared by Sami Kita, 1980.

BIRMINGHAM REFERENCE LIBRARY

JWP 3/37 No.16 James Watt Papers.

BRITISH LIBRARY

Add MSS 37845 Windham Papers.

EDINBURGH UNIVERSITY LIBRARY

Laing MSS lv 17.

Laing MSS II, 99/60.

Laing MSS, 352/1.

GUILDHALL LIBRARY, LONDON

GH 11937/38 Sun Fire Insurance Company Policy Register.

MITCHELL LIBRARY, GLASGOW

MS C311730 View of the Constitution and History of Anderson's Institution, 1825.

PUBLIC RECORD OFFICE

Cabinet Papers 1952, Higher Technological Education.

NATIONAL REGISTER OF ARCHIVES (SCOTLAND)

0217 Moray Muniments John Anderson to the Earl of Moray, 21 March, 1752.

SCOTTISH RECORD OFFICE

Acts and Decreets DAL 23 November, 1787.

Newhailes MSS, 476/1, John Anderson to Lord Hailes, 8 July, 1782.

YALE UNIVERSITY LIBRARY

Essais sur l'artillerie de campagne (Paris, 1791).

BRITISH PARLIAMENTARY PAPERS

21/22 Vict. c.83 Medical Officers Act, 1858.

39 and 40 Vic. x/v Allan Glen's Institution Act, 1876.

40 Vic. c.12 Anderson's College Act, 1877.

Educational Endowments Commission, Minutes of Evidence, 1883.

Educational Endowments Commission, 1880-90, Reports of the Committee of Governing Bodies Giving Technical and Science Teaching in Glasgow, 30 June, 1883.

Royal Commission on Scientific Instruction and the Advancement of Science, 1872.

Scottish Office Education Department, *Future Strategy for Higher Education in Scotland* (STEAC Report).

Submissions to the University Grants Committee, December, 1960.

UFC, Scottish Committee, *Criteria for Assessing Merger Proposals from Institutions of Higher Education* (Edinburgh, 1991).

University Grants Committee Returns, 1921-2, 1934-5, 1937-8.

SECONDARY SOURCES

THESES

Butt, J., 'James Young, Industrialist and Philanthropist', unpublished Ph.D. thesis, University of Glasgow, 1964.

Forrester, Leslie L., 'Technical Education and the Economy of the West of Scotland, 1870-1914', unpublished Ph.D. thesis, University of Strathclyde, 1991.

Logan, John C., 'The Dumbarton Glass Work Company, c. 1777-c.1850', unpublished M.Litt. thesis, University of Strathclyde, 1970.

Logan, J.C., 'An Economic History of the Scottish Electricity Supply Industry, 1878-1930', unpublished Ph.D. thesis, University of Strathclyde, 1983.

BOOKS

Academic Who's Who (1973-4 edn.).

Adams, James, *Biographical Sketch of the late Frederick Penny* (Glasgow, 1870).

Anderson, John, *The Institutes of Physics* (Glasgow, 1795).

Anon., *Biographical Sketches of the Lord Provosts of Glasgow, 1833-1883* (Glasgow, 1883).

Anon., *Memoirs and Portraits of One Hundred Glasgow Men* (Glasgow, 1886).

Anon. [Irene Hynd and Amanda McKenzie], *70 Years of Excellence in Education: Jordanhill College, 1921-91* (Glasgow, 1991).

Armytage, W.H.G., *Civic Universities* (1955).

Arnold, M., *Schools and Universities on the Continent* (1868).

Browning, H.H., *The Andersonian Professors of Chemistry* (Glasgow, 1894).

Buchan, A.R. (ed.), *A Goodly Heritage: A Hundred Years of Civil Engineering at Strathclyde University, 1887-1987* (Glasgow, 1987).

Burke's Peerage (1884 edition).

Butt, J., and Ward, J.T. (eds.), *Scottish Themes: Essays in Honour of Professor S.G.E. Lythe* (Edinburgh, 1976).

Campbell, R.H., *Carron Company* (1961).

Campbell, R.H., *The Rise and Fall of Scottish Industry, 1707-1939* (Edinburgh, 1980).

Cardwell, D.S.L., *The Organisation of Science in England* (1957).

Carvel, J.L., *Stephen of Linthouse* (Glasgow, 1950).

Chalmers, A.K. (ed.), *Public Health Administration in Glasgow* (Glasgow, 1905).

Chalmers, Thomas, *On the Christian and Economic Polity of a Nation* (Glasgow, 1839).

Checkland, Olive, *Philanthropy in Victorian Scotland* (Edinburgh, 1980).

Checkland, S.G., *Scottish Banking* (1975).

Cockburn, H., *An Examination of the Trials for Sedition in Scotland* (1888).

Cotgrove, S.F., *Technical Education and Social Change* (1958).

Coutts, James, *A History of the University of Glasgow* (Glasgow, 1909).

Curran, Sir Samuel, *Issues in Science and Education, Recollections and Reflection* (Carnforth and New Jersey, 1988).

Devine, T.M., *The Tobacco Lords* (Edinburgh, 1975).

Donaldson, Robert (ed.), *Bicentenary of the James Watt Patent* (Glasgow, 1970).

Dupin, Baron C., *The Commercial Power of Great Britain, Exhibiting a Complete View of the Public Works of the Country* (1825).

Dyer, Henry, *Technical Education in Glasgow and the West of Scotland* (Glasgow, 1893).

Electronic and Electrical Engineering, Department of, *Centenary* (Glasgow, 1992).

Ensor, R.C.K., *England, 1870-1914* (1964).

Farley, J.J., *Making Arms in the Machine Age* (Philadelphia, 1994).

Fleming, J. Arnold, *Scottish Pottery* (Glasgow, 1923).

Fox, Grace, *Britain and Japan, 1858-83* (Oxford, 1969).

Gee, David (compiled by), *Handbook and Directory of the Scottish Hotel School* (1994).

Gomme, Andor and Walker, David, *The Architecture of Glasgow* (1968).

Graham, John, *One Hundred and Twenty-Five Years* (1964).

Gray, John, *Biographical Notice of the Rev. David Ure* (Glasgow, 1965).

Hannah, L., *Electricity before Nationalisation* (1979).

Harper, J. Wilson, *The Social Ideal and Dr Chalmers' Contribution to Christian Economics* (Edinburgh, 1910).

Henderson, T.B., *The History of the Glasgow Dental Hospital and School, 1879-1959* (Glasgow, 1960).

Hole, James, *History and Management of Literary, Scientific and Mechanics' Institutes* (1853).

Hume, J.R. and Moss, M.G., *Beardmore: The History of a Scottish Industrial Giant* (1979).

Huxley, T.H., *Science and Education: Essays* (1893).

Johnston, T.L., Buxton, N.K. and Mair, D., *Structure and Growth of the Scottish Economy* (1971).

Kelly, Thomas, *George Birkbeck, Pioneer of Adult Education* (Liverpool, 1959).

Kirkwood, D., *My Life of Revolt* (1935).

Lloyd, J.A., *Proposals for Establishing Colleges of Arts and Manufactures* (1851).

Lythe, S.G.E. and Butt, J., *An Economic History of Scotland, 1100-1939* (1975).

Lythe, S.G.E., *Thomas Garnett (1766-1802)* (Glasgow, 1984).

McArthur, Tom and Waddell, Peter, *The Secret Life of John Logie Baird* (1986).

Mackenzie, T.B., *Life of James Beaumont Neilson F.R.S.* (Glasgow, 1929).

Mackintosh, G., *A Memoir of Charles Macintosh F.R.S.* (Glasgow, 1847).

McLaren, D.J., *David Dale of New Lanark* (Glasgow, 1985).

McNair, Peter and Mort, Frederick (eds.), *History of the Geological Society of Glasgow, 1858-1908* (Glasgow, 1908).

Middlemass, R.K., *The Clydesiders* (1965).

Mowat, C.L., *Britain Between the Wars, 1918-40* (1955).

Muir, James, *John Anderson, Pioneer of Technical Education and the College He Founded* (ed. J. M. Macaulay) (Glasgow, 1950).

Muirhead, James Patrick, *The Life of James Watt* (1859).

Murray, David, *Memories of the Old College of Glasgow* (Glasgow, 1927).

Murray, David, *Sir John Craig: Sixty-seven Years with Colvilles* (n.d., *c.*1956).

Musson, A.E. and Robinson, E., *Science and Technology in the Industrial Revolution* (Manchester, 1969).

Nuttall, R.H., *The Department of Pure and Applied Chemistry: A History, 1830-1980* (Glasgow, 1980).

Olson, R., *Scottish Philosophy and British Physics, 1750-1850* (Princeton, 1975).

Pack, D.C., *A Short History of the Department of Mathematics*, (n.d. *c.* 1975).

Pattison, F.L.M., *Granville Sharp Pattison, Anatomist and Antagonist, 1791-1851* (Edinburgh, 1987).

Payne, P.L., *Colvilles and the Scottish Steel Industry* (Oxford, 1979).

Pollard, Sidney, *The Development of the British Economy, 1914-90* (1992 edn.).

Post Office Directories of the City of Glasgow, 1887-1914.

Rae, J.A., *The History of Allan Glen's School, 1853-1953* (Glasgow, 1953).

Rait, R.S., *The History of the Union Bank of Scotland* (Glasgow, 1930).

Reid, Robert [Senex], *Glasgow Past and Present* (Glasgow, 1884).

Reid, Wemyss T. (ed.), *Memoirs and Correspondence of Lyon Playfair* (1899).

Reith, J.C.W., *Wearing the Spurs* (1937).

Reith, J.C.W., *Into the Wind* (1950).

Richardson, G.P., *A Decade of Progress, 1964-74* (University of Strathclyde, 1974).

Richardson, H.W., and Aldcroft, D.H., *Building in the British Economy Between the Wars* (1968).

Riddell, Peter, *The Thatcher Decade* (Oxford, 1989).

Robbins, Keith, *The Eclipse of a Great Power: Modern Britain, 1870-1992* (1994 edn.).

Roughead William (ed.), *The Trial of Dr Pritchard* (Glasgow, 1906).

Royal Society, Obituary Notices, Vol. ii (1936).

Royal Society of Edinburgh Year Book (1995).

Russell, J.S., *Systematic Technical Education for the English People* (1869).

Saunders, L.J., *Scottish Democracy, 1815-40* (Edinburgh, 1950).

Sexton, A.H., *The First Technical College* (Glasgow, 1894).

Shields, John, *Clyde Built* (Glasgow, 1947).

Stewart, G., *Curiosities of Glasgow Citizenship* (Glasgow, 1881).

Stuart, Charles (ed.), *Reith Diaries* (1971).

Tamaki, Norio, *The Union Bank of Scotland* (Aberdeen, 1983).

Taylor, J.R., *Reform Your City Guilds* (1872).

Thom, William, *Works* (Glasgow, 1799).

Thomson, A.M.W., *The Life and Times of Dr William Mackenzie, Founder of Glasgow Eye Infirmary* (Glasgow, 1973).

Thorpe, T.E., *Essays in Historical Chemistry* (1894).

Tilden, Sir William A., *Sir William Ramsay: Memorials of his Life and Work* (1918).

Travers, M.W., *A Life of Sir William Ramsay* (1956).

Waddell, P., *Man of Vision: A Jubilee Tribute to John Logie Baird...* (University of Strathclyde, 1975).

Walsh, J.J., *Dictionary of American Biography* (1948 edition).

Williamson, George, *Memorials...of James Watt* (Edinburgh, 1856).

Wood, Sir Henry P., *David Stow and the Glasgow Normal Seminary* (Glasgow, 1987).

PAPERS AND CONTRIBUTIONS TO BOOKS

Allan, J. Malcolm, 'John Anderson and his books', *96 Group Paper*, 1993.

Anderson, John, 'Of a new Rain Gage, of a weather register and of rainy climates', *Letters and Papers of Royal Society*, 1792.

Arbuthnott, J.P. and Bone, T.R., 'Anatomy of a Merger', *Higher Education Quarterly*, Vol.47, No.2 (Spring, 1993).

Brock, W.H., 'The Japanese Connexion: Engineering in Tokyo, London and Glasgow at the end of the nineteenth century', *British Journal for the History of Science*, Vol.14, No.48 (1981).

Butt, J., 'General Studies at Glasgow', *Technology* (February, 1961).

Butt, J., 'Working-Class Housing in Glasgow, 1900-39', in *Essays in Scottish Labour History*, edited by Ian MacDougall (Edinburgh, 1979).

Butt, J., 'Energy, Commitment, Tenacity, Style: Professor Sir Graham Hills, Vice-Chancellor and Principal of the University of Strathclyde, 1980-1991...', *Prism Extra*, October 1991.

Butt, J., 'The Industries of Glasgow, *c.*1830-1912', in *History of Glasgow*, Vol.2, ed. by W.H. Fraser and I. Maver (forthcoming).

Cable, J., 'Early Scottish Science: The Vocational Provision', *Annals of Science* (1973).

Catterall, R.E., 'Electrical Engineering', in N.K. Buxton and D.H. Aldcroft (eds.), *British Industry Between the Wars: Instability and Economic Development, 1919-39* (1979).

Copeman, W.S.C., 'Andrew Ure', *Proceedings of the Royal Society of Medicine* (1951).

Curran, Sir Samuel, 'The Years of Change, 1960-64', University of Strathclyde *Gazette*, January, 1974.

Forrester, D.A.R., 'Universities and Auditing', Typescript, 1963.

Forrester, D.A.R., 'John Anderson's Views on Accounting', *96 Group Paper*, 1974.

Forrester, D.A.R., 'John Anderson's Views on Accounting', *Philosophical Journal*, 1975.

Hardie, D.W.F., 'The Macintoshes and the Origins of the Chemical Industry', *Chemistry and Industry*, June, 1952.

Hurtwitz, S.J., *State Intervention in Great Britain: A Study of Economic Control and Response* (New York, 1949).

Logan, J.C., 'Electricity Supply: Electrical Engineering and the Scottish Economy in the Inter-War Years', in A.J.G. Cummings and T.M. Devine (eds.), *Industry, Business and Society in Scotland Since 1700* (Edinburgh, 1994).

McGougan, L., 'Arts, Social Studies and Library Building', Annual Conference of University Buildings Officers, Exeter, 1964.

Matthews, Kent and Minford, Patrick, 'Mrs Thatcher's Economic Policies, 1979-1987', *Economic Policy*, 5 (1987), pp. 65 ff.

Miller, W.S., 'Granville Sharp Pattison', *Johns Hopkins Hospital Bulletin* (1919).

Parsell, John, 'Memoir of Professor Anderson', *Glasgow Mechanics' Magazine* (1825).

Playfair, Lyon, 'The Chemical Principles involved in the Manufactures of the Exhibition as indicating the Necessity of Industrial Instruction', in *Lectures on the Results of the Great Exhibition of 1851* (1852).

Randall, J.N., 'New Towns and New Industries', in Richard Saville (ed.), *The Economic Development of Modern Scotland, 1950-1980* (Edinburgh, 1985).

Sher, R.B., 'Commerce, Religion and the Enlightenment in Eighteenth Century Glasgow', in *History of Glasgow*, Vol.1 (ed. T. M. Devine and G. Jackson) (Manchester, 1995).

Thomas, Mark, 'Rearmament and Economic Recovery in the late 1930's', *Economic History Review*, Vol.36, No.3 (1983).

Trebilcock, Clive, 'War and the Failure of Industrial Mobilisation: 1899 and 1914', in J.M. Winter (ed.), *War and Economic Development* (Cambridge, 1975).

Weber, B. and Lewis, J. Parry, 'Industrial Building in Great Britain, 1923-28', *Scottish Journal of Political Economy*, Vol.8, No.1 (1961).

Withrington, D.J., 'Education and Society in the Eighteenth Century', in *Scotland in the Age of Improvement* (ed. N.T. Phillipson and Rosalind Mitchison) (Edinburgh, 1970).

Wood, C.G., 'The Anderson six pounder field piece', *Philosophical Journal*, 10 (1973).

Wood, C.G., 'John Anderson's Rain Gauge', *Philosophical Journal*, Vol. 5, No.2 (1968).

CONTEMPORARY NEWSPAPERS, JOURNALS AND MAGAZINES

AUT, *Jubilee Newsletter*, September, 1964.

Bulletin of the University of Strathclyde *(BUS)*, January, 1981

Bulletin of the University of Strathclyde *(BUS)*, February, 1983.

Bulletin of the University of Strathclyde (*BUS*), June, 1983.

Bulletin of the University of Strathclyde (*BUS*), December, 1983.

Caledonian Mercury, 18 May, 1789.

Glasgow Journal, 29 March, 1756.

Glasgow Journal, 15 October, 1756.

Glasgow Mechanics' Magazine, 1825.

Glasgow Mechanics' Magazine, 1826.

Scots Mechanics' Magazine, 1825.

The Lancet, 1829-30 and 1830-1.

London Gazette, 6 December, 1803.

SASS, Newsletter of the Faculty of Arts and Social Studies, No.6, 1988.

University of Strathclyde *Gazette*, 1974-82

University of Strathclyde, *Prism*, 1987-95.

TELEVISION INTERVIEW TRANSCRIPT

Interview of Sir Samuel Curran by Professor Esmond Wright.

Index